AF594830

THINKING THROUGH

Aquinas

THINKING THROUGH

Aquinas

Essays on God, Humanity, and Christ

FREDERICK
CHRISTIAN BAUERSCHMIDT

Published by Word on Fire Academic, an imprint of
Word on Fire, Elk Grove Village, IL 60007

Printed in the United States of America

Interior art direction by Nicolas Fredrickson, typesetting by Clark Kenyon, cover design by Cassie Bielak, Rozann Lee, and Michael Stevens.

ISBN: 978-1-68578-107-1

Library of Congress Control Number: 2023917514

For Boyd and Holly Taylor Coolman

Contents

Preface

I had been teaching theology for almost a decade—and had written and published enough to be awarded tenure—before I dared to publish something on Thomas Aquinas. My hesitation had multiple causes.

The first was the immense scope both of writings by Thomas and of writings about Thomas: How could one master such a vast corpus? After all, I had chosen to write my dissertation on Julian of Norwich in part because she had written only one book (albeit in two versions) and, particularly when I was writing on her (the early 1990s), the body of serious secondary literature on her was not very large. With Thomas, the case was quite otherwise, and there was always the fear of having missed something, either something Thomas himself had written or something crucially important that had been written about him. And we all know that the greatest fear of every academic is that of having overlooked the key primary text or the epoch-making essay on a topic.

The second was my fear that I did not have a "proper" Thomistic pedigree, by which I mean that the people from whom I had learned Thomas Aquinas (James Clayton at the University of the South, George Lindbeck at Yale Divinity School, and David Steinmetz and Stanley Hauerwas at Duke University) were not known primarily as experts on Thomas and—a fact even more damning in the eyes of some—were not even Roman Catholics. I had a nagging suspicion that my reading of Thomas was somehow dangerously homegrown and might be deficient in its grasp of Thomist fundamentals.

The third was that Thomas himself seemed tame and, dare I say it, just a tad boring. He represented Scholastic officialdom, and one point of studying writers like Julian of Norwich had been to crack open the narrow canon of what counted as theology in the Middle Ages. Even Bonaventure, though a Scholastic, seemed preferable, with his weird numerology and proximity to Francis of Assisi (surely one of the most untamed figures in Christian history). While there were things to be learned from reading him, Thomas hardly seemed like a suitable thought partner if one wanted to engage in cutting-edge theology. He was undeniably important, but was he really all that interesting?

But I did eventually write something on Thomas, mainly because a good friend prevailed upon me to do so for a volume he was co-editing. Then, after a few more essays, I published a selection of texts from the *Summa theologiae* with accompanying commentary, much of which had been originally written to help the students to whom I assigned these texts as readings.[1] Working through these texts, rendering them in what I hoped was readable English, teasing out Thomas's distinctions and trying to explain his terminology—all of this helped me begin to think that maybe I did understand Thomas and that one didn't need to read everything in order to understand something. Requests for essays on Thomas from people who were not close friends, some of whom I had never even met, further suggested to me that perhaps I had something to say about Aquinas that was worth reading and that Thomas was himself perhaps not simply important but also interesting. Over time, the body of essays I have written on Thomas has grown to the point where it seemed appropriate to collect some of them into a book. I have lightly revised them, occasionally adding references to helpful scholarly work that has appeared since their original publication.

1. *Holy Teaching: Introducing the "Summa Theologiae" of St. Thomas Aquinas* (Grand Rapids, MI: Brazos, 2005). A second, revised and expanded edition has since appeared as *The Essential "Summa Theologiae": A Reader and Commentary* (Grand Rapids, MI: Baker Academic, 2021).

***

The first essay, "Shouting in the Land of the Hard of Hearing," serves as an overture to the collection as a whole, both as a kind of summary statement of how I approach Thomas Aquinas and as an *apologia* for my dubiously pedigreed, homegrown form of Thomism. The writer Flannery O'Connor and her self-description as a "hillbilly Thomist" serve in the essay as a way of developing a version of Thomas that might be called broadly Augustinian.[2] Looking back at this essay, I find a number of themes and emphases that recur throughout my writing on Thomas. There is the attempt, without sacrificing the principle that grace perfects nature, to highlight the way in which grace might also violently disturb nature. There is an embrace of a strongly apophatic reading of Thomas that takes him at his word when he says that we know better what God is not than what God is. There is an emphasis on Thomas's use of *argumenta ex convenientia*, a form of argument whose importance and fundamentally "aesthetic" character was first suggested to me by George Lindbeck in his seminar at Yale on Aquinas. There is a conviction that, while Thomas's theology is not "Christocentric" in the sense that, say, Karl Barth's is, Jesus Christ truly is central to Thomas's thought. There is also the strong sense that what Thomas attempted theologically in his day must necessarily be carried out in a quite different way in our own. The remainder of the essays in this volume, in various ways, unpack what is said in this first essay.

The first section of essays covers topics roughly corresponding to the First Part of the *Summa*—namely, the task of theology and God's nature and activity. Essay 2, "Aquinas, Contemplation, and Theology," engages the philosopher Jonathan Lear's reading

2. The name "The Hillbilly Thomists" has since been adopted by a group of Dominican friars who play a combination of old-time string band music and original compositions (e.g., "Bourbon, Bluegrass, and the Bible") that I believe show a similar Augustinian sensibility. See the Hillbilly Thomists, *Living for the Other Side*, CD baby, 2021, compact disc.

of Aristotle in order to explore the kind of knowledge Thomas thinks theology is. Lear's interpretation of Aristotle helped show me that the one whom Thomas called "the Philosopher" was actually, despite his seeming abstractness, asking fairly fundamental questions about what we are doing when we inquire and answered those questions in ways that remain helpful today. This helped me see that Thomas is similarly asking fundamental questions, and his thought is not wedded to an outdated metaphysical system but to a dynamic tradition of inquiry.

Essay 3, "*Praeambula Fidei*," began as a talk given to seminarians at St. Mary's Seminary in Baltimore and is a fairly basic presentation of what Thomas says about how what we know about God through natural reason (e.g., his "five ways" of demonstrating God's existence) relates to what we know about God through revelation. Of course, even a "basic presentation" of this topic leads one into a minefield of controversy since it raises issues of nature and grace, the foundations or lack thereof of Christian truth claims, and the very possibility of demonstrating God's existence. I find that, over time, I have grown friendlier to the claim that one can demonstrate the existence of what people call "God," though I have also grown more convinced that what one has accomplished in such a demonstration is something more modest than some people—both theists and atheists—think it is.

The fourth essay, "God as Author: Thinking Through a Metaphor," might at first glance seem only tangentially related to Thomas Aquinas, who comes up for discussion mainly in the section discussing the history of the metaphor of God as an author. Other thinkers, such as Roland Barthes and Michel Foucault, seem to feature as or more prominently. But in fact, the entire project of the essay arose from my attempt to explain to students how Thomas understood the nature of the God-world relationship. As one does when teaching, I was casting about for a metaphor or analogy that might shed some light on the topic when I landed on the way in which the action of a novel is—or ought to be—accounted for by the agents within the novel, but the novel as a whole must be accounted for by an author who is (typically) not an agent within the novel. This seemed to be a helpful metaphor to my students, and the more I played with it, the more interesting I found it. As Thomas himself shows, it is often when we are trying to figure out how to teach something we think we know that we come to understand it better ourselves. I would add that I am no longer as confident as I was in that essay that world-building fictional narratives are exclusively modern phenomena that are found only in the novel.

The fifth essay, "Imagination and Theology," was originally given as a paper at a conference titled Imagination and the Mediation of Religious Truth organized by Marianne Servaas at the Katholieke Universiteit Leuven and gives an account both of Thomas's understanding of human knowing and of the capacity and limits of that knowing when it comes to God. As sometimes happens, I had committed to presenting a paper on Thomas on a particular topic, only to discover that what he had to say on that topic did not seem particularly interesting. As also sometimes happens, further inquiry revealed that even though what he had to say might not fit with our modern expectations (in this case, the expectation that "imagination" is a key faculty of human creativity), it was pretty interesting on its own terms (in this case, as a way of understanding how human beings inhabit the world). One of the joys of reading Thomas (or really any thinker of the past) is having our sense of what is and is not "interesting" challenged.

The second section of essays covers topics found in the Second Part of Thomas's *Summa*—namely, human action as virtuous and vicious. Essay 6, "The Unity of the Virtues and the Journeying Self," was originally written for a *Festschrift* for my teacher Stanley Hauerwas and deals with the vexing question of whether one can have one virtue without having all the other virtues as well. This question received an almost universal answer of "no" in the ancient and medieval worlds and has in the modern era received an almost universal answer of "yes," since it seems overly perfectionist to demand, say, that one be temperate in order to be just (to say nothing of whether the virtue of justice requires supernatural charity). What Hauerwas helped me see was that behind the question of the quality of our actions is the question of the quality of our selves (what he calls "character"). The language of "virtue" is concerned first not with doing good or bad actions but with becoming good or bad people, and the ancient and medieval impulse to say that the virtues must be connected reflects the conviction that a virtuous self must be a unified self.

Essay 7, "Conversion, Coercion, and Persuasion: Thomas Aquinas on the Will," has never been published, originating as a lecture given at the Catholic Theological Society of America and then, in significantly revised form, at Yale Divinity School. In it, I look at Thomas's account of the will and how this relates to issues of consent, coercion, and persuasion, suggesting that modern concerns about consent face difficulties in distinguishing coercion from persuasion because they lack an account of the good toward which the will is properly ordered. I hint at the end that such a distinction may require a robust and even normative account of the good.

Essay 8, "Sin: A Reading of *Summa theologiae* 1-2.71.6," was written as an introduction to Thomas on the topic of sin and the importance of intention in his account, but it also sought to show that Thomas's account of intention means that sin can only be discerned within the context of a life that is extended in time. In this way, it is something of a companion piece to the fourth and sixth essays, both of which try to think of the self "narratively" in order to make sense of Thomas's views on the relation of divine and human action. "Narrative" is not a category that

Thomas makes much explicit use of, and certainly not in his account of the human person. But one of the things I have learned over the years is that in trying to understand Thomas and to use his thought for theological purposes, one is not obliged simply to repeat his categories.

The ninth essay, "Wine, Women, Kings, and Truth," was the first piece I ever published on Thomas, written for a volume on political theology. I agreed to write it not simply because of the importuning of William Cavanaugh but because I thought that by focusing neither on Aquinas's account of law nor on his treatise on kingship, but rather on his discussion in his *Commentary on John* of Jesus's exchange with Pilate and his odd little quodlibetal question on the relative strength of wine, women, kings, and truth, I might actually come up with a different angle on Thomas on politics. Working on this essay helped me see that though the *Summa theologiae* is Thomas's masterwork, there is much to be gained by reading around in his other works. It also forced me at the outset of writing on Thomas to face up to some of his limitations—limitations that we all have due to our situatedness in time and space.

The third section of essays covers topics found in the Third Part of the *Summa*—namely, Christology and the sacraments. Essay 10, "Incarnation, Redemption, and the Character of God," shows the importance of *convenientia* or "fittingness" in approaching the controverted topic of the motive of the Incarnation—the question of whether, if Adam had not sinned, God would have become incarnate. I tried to show in this essay that Thomas's position is not exactly what is often taken to be the "Thomist" one, and that perhaps Thomas and John Duns Scotus are not so clearly opposed to one another as is sometimes claimed.

The eleventh essay, "Taking Up and Taking Down: Ellacuría, Aquinas, and the Crucified People," brings Thomas into conversation with Latin American liberation theology. Once again, his notion of *convenientia* is placed in the foreground. This essay, which began life as a lecture at the Society of Christian Ethics and has not been published previously, seems to displease people on both the Thomist side (who are suspicious that I grant too much to Ellacuría) and the liberationist side (who feel that I am too critical of Ellacuría and insufficiently critical of Thomas). Having two different and in some ways opposed groups think you're wrong is not an indication that you're right—you may just be comprehensively wrong—but in this case, I do think that I have brought Thomas and Ellacuría into a mutually correcting and enriching dialogue on the important topic of how we think about the necessity of Christ's Crucifixion for our salvation.

Essay 12, "'That the Faithful Become the Temple of God': The Church Militant in Thomas's *Commentary on John*," is another fairly early essay on Thomas, which largely consists of combing through a single work by Thomas to see what it has to say about the Church. The potential tedium of reading such an exercise is, I hope, somewhat alleviated by my attempt to enlist Thomas in helping us reflect on what, alas, remains a pressing issue in the Church: how to maintain the creedal affirmation that the Church is "holy" in the face of the manifest failures of the Church, both in her individual members and in her institutional structures.

The thirteenth essay, "'The Body of Christ is Made from Bread': Transubstantiation and the Grammar of Creation," is, like essay 8, a close reading of a single article of the *Summa*, which is in turn a grammatical exegesis of a piece of Christian speech. Of course, every article of the *Summa* presumes many other articles (in this case, Thomas's discussions of creation and natural change), and Thomas's grammatical inquiries are simultaneously metaphysical inquiries, so this essay in some ways ends up touching on everything Thomas has to say about everything. And it is fitting that it is an article on the mystery of the Eucharist that is the occasion for displaying the interconnectedness of Thomas's thought, since it is this mystery of which Thomas is purported to have said at the very end of his life, "I receive you, price of my soul's redemption; I receive you, food for my journey. For love of you I have studied, watched, and labored. You have I preached; you have I taught."[3]

Essay 14, "Augustine and Thomas in Modern Catholic Rhetoric," forms a coda to this collection. Implicit throughout all the essays is the question of how one goes about using Thomas for contemporary purposes. This essay looks at one way of doing this that I judge to be particularly unhelpful: the rhetorical use of Thomas as a trope for optimism (with Augustine forming the opposite, pessimistic pole). In the course of writing this essay, I discovered that this was not only a false presentation of Thomas (and Augustine) but was also one of very recent vintage. In a sense, this essay returns to the project sketched in the first essay in the collection: the reconciliation of Thomas and Augustine that I call (with tongue only slightly in cheek) hillbilly Thomism.

A homily that I had the honor of preaching at St. Thomas Aquinas parish in Baltimore on their patronal festival forms a coda to the entire collection, an acknowledgment that though Thomas was a theologian, he was so for the sake of being a preacher, and the content of his preaching was the wisdom of the cross.

***

I have titled this collection *Thinking Through Aquinas* because this is what I have tried to do in these essays, and this in two senses.

First, I have tried to think through Aquinas in the sense of trying to figure out what he is saying and why he says it. In each of these essays, I have tried to follow Thomas's arguments, to

3. Guillaume de Tocco, *Ystoria sancti Thome de Aquino*, ed. Claire le Brun-Gouanvic (Toronto: Pontifical Institute of Mediaeval Studies, 1996), ch. 58.

grasp his distinctions, and to see the point in what he is arguing. Though Thomas is, in my estimation, an extremely clear thinker and writer, he is also an extremely subtle and sophisticated one, and one must sometimes wrestle with the text in order to understand it. Moreover, his terminology is sometimes unfamiliar, and his thought world is even less familiar. He presumes a Scholastic culture that is quite alien to modern readers: a set of disputational practices and a body of authoritative texts that every participant in that culture would know but that are *terra incognita* to us. Thinking Thomas through requires the labor of thinking ourselves, to the degree that we can, back into that world. These essays are in a sense the residue of my own struggle to understand Thomas.

Second, I have tried to think through Thomas Aquinas in the sense of viewing a range of theological questions with Thomas as my "lens." I think this, more than adherence to a particular set of positions, is what makes one a "Thomist," though I suspect some Thomists would disagree with me on this.[4] Thomas is not the only or even the best[5] thinker that the Catholic tradition has produced, but he is certainly a first-rate thinker, and in trying to grasp what Thomas thinks on a particular issue and why he thinks it, one simultaneously finds oneself understanding the issue better, spotting potential dead ends, grappling with the tradition up to and including Thomas, confronting difficulties, and engaging in a host of other things one must do to do theology well. So, I think through theological questions by thinking through Thomas, even when I do not end up thinking what Thomas thinks. Because I have found this so worthwhile an endeavor, I offer these essays as an encouragement to others to think through Thomas.

One of my initial hesitations about ever writing on Thomas was my sense of him as a "safe" and even boring thinker, and

4. Of course, Thomas himself was supremely unconcerned with whether he or anyone else was a "Thomist."

5. Upon being named "America's Best Theologian" by *Time* magazine, Stanley Hauerwas responded, "'Best' is not a theological category."

that doing focused work on him was never going to lead me to do exciting, creative theology. Over twenty years of thinking through Aquinas has shown me how ill-founded this fear was. It was ill-founded because there is probably no better recipe for theology that boringly repeats the common wisdom of the day than to set out to be exciting and creative. Thomas's theology is, in fact, immensely exciting and creative, not because it sets out to be such, but because it seeks to be faithful to a tradition that is vast and varied in its attempt to speak of the mystery of divine love, and in being faithful it joins its own voice to that vast variety. In thinking through Aquinas, we join him in the adventure of *sacra doctrina*—holy teaching—as we seek to hand on to others the fruits of our own contemplation of the divine mystery.

***

I have spent a couple of decades thinking with Thomas as my companion, but he has hardly been the only one. Colleagues at Loyola University Maryland and elsewhere—too many to mention by name—have been my companions as well. But two in particular stand out and must be named: Boyd Taylor Coolman of Boston College and Holly Taylor Coolman of Providence College. Boyd is one of the founders of the Boston Colloquy in Historical Theology and remains one of its prime movers. This annual gathering is an exquisitely curated conference of superb papers in late ancient and medieval theology, with generous amounts of time for discussions that are somehow—shockingly—free of academic grandstanding. I have had my horizons expanded by my annual participation in this colloquy. Holly, along with Gilles Mongeau, SJ, founded the Aquinas Studium, which meets each summer for a week of prayer, fellowship, and close reading of selected texts of Aquinas on a particular theme. The time spent with fellow lovers of St. Thomas is intellectually stimulating, informative, and incredibly fun (my family refers to it as "Aquinas Summer Camp"). Both Boyd and Holly have become not only co-laborers and colleagues, but friends who have welcomed me into their home and into the life of their sometimes chaotic and always interesting family. They exemplify that virtue that Thomas called *amicitia*, by which wise persons share their pleasure with those among whom they dwell. In gratitude for the *amicitia* they have shown to me, I dedicate this book to them.

Prologue

On Being a Hillbilly Thomist

1

Shouting in the Land of the Hard of Hearing

THE PICTURE OF A PERFECT THOMIST GENTLEMAN

There are certain things one expects of a good Thomist. He or she will highly prize reason, believing that human nature, though somewhat damaged by sin, on the whole functions quite well, and that assiduous application of human reason forms the basis on which it is possible to enter into dialogue with those who do not accept the Catholic faith. In contrast to the Augustinian/Protestant pessimism about human nature, the Thomist affirms the fundamental goodness of human nature and reason. Therefore, when confronted by some variety of unbelief—whether it be atheist, Buddhist, Muslim, or Protestant—the good Thomist will wield the weapon of logical rigor deftly but also serenely, knowing that the doubter's greatest enemy is his or her own natural reason. As the early-twentieth-century Thomist Walter Farrell said concerning Thomas's five ways, "The philosopher who, for reasons best known to himself, decides to challenge these proofs has entered a war of cosmic proportions; fortunately for himself, he cannot win."[1]

The commitment of good Thomists to reasoned argument means that they will be rhetorically austere and not prone to

* Originally published as "Shouting in the Land of the Hard of Hearing: On Being a Hillbilly Thomist," in *Aquinas in Dialogue: Thomas for the 21st Century*, ed. Jim Fodor and Frederick Bauerschmidt (Oxford: Basil Blackwell, 2004), 163–83.

1. Walter Farrell, *A Companion to the Summa*, vol. 1, *The Architect of the Universe* (New York: Sheed & Ward, 1941), 44.

passionate exhortation. With human nature and reason on their side, they have no need to inflame the emotions in order to bend the will. Indeed, the more dispassionate the discussion, the more the truth will be made manifest. Good Thomists can afford to be gentlemen. The climate of their discussions will be, as John Courtney Murray put it in a different context, "cool and dry, with the coolness and dryness that characterize good argument among informed and responsible men."[2]

Murray's phrase is so vivid that it can be too easily forgotten that Murray himself expressed doubts about the effectiveness of such arguments in what he, in the 1950s, already called the "post-modern" context.[3] Perhaps we live in a world in which informed and responsible men are in short supply, since cool and dry argumentation does not seem to be leading us to any sort of consensus about the "Ultimate Questions," and Murray frankly acknowledges that "the tradition of reason, which is known as the ethic of natural law, is dead."[4] Integral to modern pluralism "is the skeptic or agnostic view that it is useless or illegitimate even to ask 'Ultimate Questions.'"[5] And yet Murray, himself a good Thomist gentleman, in the end echoes Farrell's optimism that the "tradition of reason" will ultimately triumph, perhaps by a kind of resurrection from the dead, albeit one foreordained by nature. This is particularly the case with regard to knowing the truth, but it is also the case in the realm of practical reason; people are "by nature . . . natural law jurists" because "they reach the essential imperatives of their own nature and know them to be

2. John Courtney Murray, *We Hold These Truths: Catholic Reflections on the American Proposition* (New York: Sheed & Ward, 1960), 7. Speaking of the description of Aquinas's style as "dry," A.-D. Sertillanges compares it to Egyptian art or the metopes of the Parthenon and says, "A writer must be dry in that sense, if he is to say much in few words, and not put an obstacle between the mind and the truth" (*St. Thomas Aquinas and His Work*, trans. Godfrey Anstruther [London: Burns, Oates and Washbourne (no publication date, but *Imprimatur* 1932)], 111).

3. For Murray's clearest analysis of "post-modernism," see *The Problem of God: Yesterday and Today* (New Haven, CT: Yale University Press, 1964), 101–21. Murray's description is roughly equivalent to what Flannery O'Connor calls "nihilism."

4. Murray, *We Hold These Truths*, 293.

5. Murray, 128.

unthwartably imperative—however much they may subsequently deform them, and destroy their proper bases, by uninformed or prejudiced reflective thought."[6]

Such serene, unpolemical, gentlemanly convictions seem to accord with the tone of Thomas's own writings. The disputational form taken by the *Summa theologiae*, as well as other of Thomas's works, seems to be a bit of dialectical window dressing; though the form is that of an argument, the tone is "cool and dry." Thomas rarely evinces anger or resorts to sarcasm or employs any rhetorical technique to defeat his enemies. Indeed, it is sometimes hard to conceive of Thomas as *having* any enemies. Standing on the common ground of reason, intellectual opponents are in fact partners in the common search for truth. As Thomas O'Meara has put it, "His writings reveal a sense of tranquility: an appreciative contemplation of the structure of the cosmos is joined to a calm openness to all that exists."[7] Even if one is unwilling fully to endorse A.-D. Sertillanges's statement that Thomas "is hardly an 'author,' or even a 'man' but rather a channel connecting us directly with intelligible truth,"[8] it does seem that Thomas, too, is a perfect Thomist gentleman.

But without denying the serenity of Thomas's writing, I want to challenge the assumption that the substance of his writing consists in his cool, dry tone and that he really does write as if he were a "direct channel to intelligible truth." Put more concisely, does Thomas's theological conviction that "grace perfects nature" necessarily manifest itself in the pragmatic conviction that even nonbelievers are always at root open to reasoned argument? Is gentlemanliness the "substantial form" of Thomism? Or is it rather an accident of the particular context in which he wrote?

6. Murray, 317.

7. Thomas Franklin O'Meara, *Thomas Aquinas: Theologian* (Notre Dame, IN: Notre Dame University Press, 1997), 36.

8. Sertillanges, *St. Thomas Aquinas and His Work*, 109.

And if the latter is the case, might "Thomism" look and sound quite different in our quite different context?

In attempting to address these questions, I will invoke the aid of the American novelist and short story writer Flannery O'Connor (1925–1964),[9] who once wrote to a friend that everyone who had read her novel *Wise Blood* "thinks I'm a hillbilly nihilist, whereas I would like to create the impression . . . that I am a hillbilly Thomist."[10] Anyone familiar with O'Connor's work knows that it is quite ungentlemanly, not to mention unladylike, and that nothing could be further in tone from the writings of Thomas than O'Connor's stories, in which atheist prophets blind themselves, sweet old grandmothers get shot, and clever girls get their artificial legs stolen by itinerant Bible salesmen. But perhaps a modern follower of Thomas Aquinas, taking as her audience "the people who think God is dead,"[11] would write not with the serenely ordered cadences of the *Summa theologiae* but something more akin to the shocking, grotesque syncopations that one finds in O'Connor's novels and short stories.

HILLBILLY THOMISM: MYSTERY AND MANNERS

Mary Flannery O'Connor was born and lived most of her life in the American South, including the last thirteen years when

9. The secondary literature on O'Connor, like that on Aquinas, is voluminous. For an account of her life, which is particularly interesting for the way it interweaves it with accounts of the lives of three other American Catholic writers (Dorothy Day, Thomas Merton, and Walker Percy), see Paul Elie, *The Life You Save May Be Your Own: An American Pilgrimage* (New York: Farrar, Straus and Giroux, 2003).

10. Flannery O'Connor to Robie Macauley, May 18, 1955, in *Flannery O'Connor: Collected Works*, ed. Sally Fitzgerald (New York: Library of America, 1988), 934. The remark is typical O'Connor—a humorously self-deprecating recognition that, in an upcoming television interview, she wants to come across as erudite and intelligent but "will probably not be able to think of anything to say . . . but 'Huh?' and 'Ah dunno.'" At the same time, O'Connor is an author for whom the comic often serves as a delivery device for truth.

11. O'Connor to "A.," August 2, 1955, in *O'Connor: Collected Works*, 943. The woman identified in the published version of O'Connor's letters as "A." was Elizabeth Hester, to whom O'Connor addressed some of her most theologically searching letters. Hester, who briefly converted to Catholicism under O'Connor's influence, was also a longtime correspondent with Iris Murdoch. Her identity was finally revealed upon her death by suicide in 1998.

her health was ravaged by lupus, which killed her at the age of thirty-nine. Her status as a "regional writer" was established at the outset: she stood in the line of William Faulkner and Eudora Welty and excelled in the subgenre of "Southern-grotesque" or "Southern-gothic." Indeed, so grotesque were her characters that many of her early readers took her for a misanthropic atheist and missed the profound influence that O'Connor's Roman Catholicism had on her writing, an influence that was made abundantly clear with the publication of her letters in 1979. In many of these letters, she responds to misreadings of her stories that see them as fundamentally nihilistic. To one correspondent she wrote, "My stories have been watered and fed by Dogma,"[12] and to another, who had claimed to see affinities between her writing and existentialist authors, she wrote, "My philosophical notions don't derive from Kierkegard (I can't even spell it) but from St. Thomas Aquinas."[13]

But in what sense did Flannery O'Connor consider herself a Thomist? While she once described herself as "a Thomist three times removed," by which she meant "one who doesn't read Latin or St. Thomas but gets it by osmosis,"[14] she clearly *did* read Aquinas, as well as having him mediated through secondary sources, particularly through Maritain's *Art and Scholasticism*, which she mentions on numerous occasions in her letters.[15] Yet hers is not

12. O'Connor to Thomas Mabry, March 1, 1955, in *O'Connor: Collected Works*, 929.

13. O'Connor to Helen Greene, May 23, 1952, in *O'Connor: Collected Works*, 897. O'Connor also saw connections between her identity as a southerner and her identity as a Catholic. She writes in an essay, "There are certain conditions necessary for the emergence of Catholic literature which are found nowhere else in this country in such abundance as in the South" ("The Catholic Novelist in the South," in *O'Connor: Collected Works*, 854).

14. O'Connor to John Hawkes, April 20, 1961, in *O'Connor: Collected Works*, 1149.

15. Her claim that she read the *Summa theologiae* for twenty minutes each night before bed is quite possibly a joke (see her Letter to "A.," August 9, 1955, in *O'Connor: Collected Works*, 945), but she did go to the trouble to obtain a copy of *De veritate* in order to read what Aquinas had to say about prophecy (see her Letter to "A.," December 25, 1959, in *The Habit of Being: Letters of Flannery O'Connor*, ed. Sally Fitzgerald [New York: Vintage Books, 1980], 367). And while the mere presence of books in a personal library is no sure indicator of their influence, O'Connor did own several Aquinas anthologies, including Pegis's *Introduction to St. Thomas Aquinas* and Gilby's *Thomas Aquinas: Philosophical Texts*. See Lorine M. Getz, *Flannery O'Connor: Her Life, Library and Book Reviews* (Lewiston, NY: Edwin Mellen, 1980).

the Cajetan-tinged philosophical Thomism of Maritain, nor the Thomism of the Twenty-Four Thomistic Theses, nor is it the strict-observance Thomism of Réginald Garrigou-Lagrange. Above all, it is not the "rabbinic Thomism" that argues by way of citations from the *Summa*. Rather, it is the broad Thomistic humanism that was the shared inheritance of the Church from the *doctor communis*. In a letter to a college student troubled by religious doubts, O'Connor summed up her own beliefs:

> I believe what the Church teaches—that God has given us reason to use and that it can lead us toward a knowledge of him, through analogy; that he has revealed himself in history and continues to do so through the Church, and that he is present (not just symbolically) in the Eucharist on our altars. To believe all this I don't take any leap into the absurd. I find it reasonable to believe, even though those beliefs are beyond reason.[16]

This summary of "what the Church teaches" certainly has a broadly Thomistic cast to it: natural knowledge of God, analogy, revealed knowledge of God, and even transubstantiation. And the "three times removed" character of it—Thomas mediated through the common tradition of the Church rather than Thomas as the object of intensive study by specialists—might seem sufficiently unsophisticated to warrant the "hillbilly" epithet.[17]

Yet I would propose that there is something still more distinctively Thomist in O'Connor's work. This is the conjunction of what she calls "mystery" and "manners." She writes in an essay, "The mystery . . . is the mystery of our position on earth, and

16. O'Connor to Alfred Corn, June 16, 1962, in *O'Connor: Collected Works*, 1166.

17. My own experience is that one only writes of Thomas with fear and trembling because there is always some Thomist lurking around the corner, ready to leap out and demonstrate that you have focused too much on the *Summa theologiae* and ignored the Aristotelian commentaries or, even worse, your Latin is so poor that you have failed to appreciate Thomas's use of the ablative absolute in a particular passage. Of course, one might respond that Thomas himself dared to interpret Aristotle without knowing Greek, making him perhaps a "hillbilly Aristotelian."

the manners are those conventions which, in the hands of the artist, reveal that central mystery."[18] O'Connor names as "mystery" the irreducibly ungraspable reality that is at the heart of our existence: "Our life is and will remain essentially mysterious."[19] Despite our attempts to capture the essential in concepts, "it is not answerable to any of our formulas. It doesn't rest finally in a statable kind of solution. It ought to throw you back on the living God."[20] At the same time, we never encounter mystery in itself but always in conjunction with "manners"—not only the stylistic manner of the artist but also those highly particular traditions that accumulate like sediment over time and that structure our lives and make them livable in the face of mystery. As she notes in one of her essays, "Somewhere is better than anywhere. And traditional manners, however unbalanced, are better than no manners at all."[21] But manners are not simply a hedge against the annihilating presence of mystery. Indeed, without the backdrop of manners—culture, tradition, custom, dogma—mystery cannot appear. As O'Connor writes to a friend, "For me a dogma is only a gateway to contemplation and is an instrument of freedom and not of restriction. It preserves mystery for the human mind."[22]

O'Connor believes that this conjunction of mystery and manners is something alien to modern people. We like our mystery neat, without dilution by manners. We prefer "spirituality" to "religion," with its overlay of dead customs. We are fascinated by the exotic customs of other cultures while at the same time thinking that we are somehow beyond all that sort of thing. As O'Connor puts it, the modern writer is asked "to separate

18. Flannery O'Connor, "The Teaching of Literature," in *Mystery and Manners*, ed. Sally and Robert Fitzgerald (New York: Farrar, Straus and Giroux, 1969), 124.

19. O'Connor, "Some Aspects of the Grotesque in Southern Fiction," in *O'Connor: Collected Works*, 816.

20. O'Connor to Sister Mariella Gable, May 4, 1963, in *O'Connor: Collected Works*, 1182–83.

21. O'Connor, "The Catholic Novelist in the South," in *O'Connor: Collected Works*, 856.

22. O'Connor to "A.," August 2, 1955, in *O'Connor: Collected Works*, 943.

mystery from manners . . . in order to produce something a little more palatable to the modern temper."[23] Yet in separating them, we lose both, and thus we have the modern world, bereft of both mystery and manners, transcendence and tradition.[24] Those who still cleave to manners as the door into mystery inevitably appear to be "hillbillies" in the eyes of the modern world, no different from O'Connor's backwoods prophets. They lack the sophistication (or sophistry) needed to strip themselves of manners in order to be cosmopolitan global citizens.

Aquinas does not make much use of the term "mystery" apart from formulae such as "the mystery of the Incarnation" or "the mystery of the Trinity."[25] Nor does he speak often of "manners" (*mores)*, though he speaks frequently of "custom" (*consuetudo)*. Yet in Thomas, we find the same constellation of convictions that O'Connor indicates with her language of mystery and manners. Creation's rootedness in incomprehensible divine mystery is at the heart of Thomas's thinking. Our natural reason knows God best when it knows God as unknown: "The highest human knowledge of God is that which knows that it does not know God, inasmuch as it knows that what God is transcends whatsoever we conceive of him."[26] At the same time, Thomas devotes meticulous attention to human "manners." The Second Part of the *Summa theologiae* is devoted to the virtues and vices that give structure to human cultural life, and in the Third Part of the *Summa*, Thomas pays

23. O'Connor, "The Fiction Writer and His Country," in *O'Connor: Collected Works*, 803.

24. See her Letter to "A.," August 2, 1955, in *O'Connor: Collected Works*, 943–44: "Henry James said that the young woman of the future would know nothing of mystery or manners. He had no business to limit it to one sex."

25. Thomas offers little sustained reflection on the term "mystery." Apart from the formulaic use (as in speaking of "the mystery of the Incarnation" or "the mystery of the Trinity"), he seems to use the term, following the Greek usage, as a synonym for "sacrament."

26. *De potentia* 7.5 ad 14. As Karl Rahner comments on this passage: "It affirms that even in the beatific vision that which is known of God is known as the incomprehensible. The ultimate human knowledge of God is attained only when its character of mysteriousness is most forcibly displayed: supreme knowledge is knowledge of the supreme mystery as such" ("The Concept of Mystery in Catholic Theology," in Karl Rahner, *Theological Investigations*, vol. 4, *More Recent Writings*, trans. Kevin Smyth [New York: Crossroad, 1982], 59).

equally careful attention to the customary speech of the Church regarding the mystery of the Incarnation. These are the things that form the backdrop against which mystery appears.

It is Thomas's conviction that it is only in the conjunction of transcendent mystery and human tradition and teaching that justice can be done to either. God's transcendence must be articulated in teaching and embodied in tradition in order for us to know the divine mystery as an abyss of light (to use Josef Pieper's phrase) that gives us life rather than an annihilating abyss of darkness. Yet those teachings and traditions, because they are instances of human language, must always be understood as articulations of a truth that transcends them and to which they are ultimately not adequate. As Thomas says, the human language with which we attempt to say something about God "leaves the thing signified as uncomprehended, and as exceeding the signification of the term."[27] In O'Connor's terms, dogma is not an end in itself but a gateway to the contemplation of the divine mystery. Or, as Gregory the Great put it—in a passage quoted by both Aquinas and O'Connor—"Holy Scripture, in its manner of speaking, transcends all knowledge, because in one and the same utterance, while recounting an action, it discloses a mystery."[28]

To conceive of the conjunction of mystery and manners as being at the heart of Thomas's thought runs against the grain of what was, at least in years past, a prevalent image of Thomas. Thomas has been associated with a kind of apologetic

27. *Summa theologiae* 1.13.5. To put it in Thomas's typical language, our speech about God is true according to the *res significata* (i.e., we know that we can say true things about God) but not according to the *modus significandi* (i.e., we cannot know the *way* in which these things are true).

It is worth underlining here that Thomas holds this radical inadequacy of language to be the case not only in what later thinkers would call "natural" or "philosophical" theology but in "revealed" theology as well. A good example of this is the discomfort he feels (shared by Augustine before him and Barth and Rahner after him) with the dogmatic language of "persons" used in reference to the Father, Son, and Spirit. Though firmly embedded in the tradition of the Church, the language of divine "persons" can be misleading if taken in the ordinary sense of "person." See *Summa theologiae* 1.29.4.

28. Gregory the Great, *Moralia in Job* 20.1. Cf. O'Connor, "The Catholic Novelist in the Protestant South," in *O'Connor: Collected Works*, 863, and Aquinas, *Summa theologiae* 1.1.10.

rationalism—someone who thought that one could, by the exercise of reason, come to know quite a lot about God. In this view, what Thomas is primarily interested in are the things that reason can tell us about God and the world; the economy of salvation is given a peripheral place, which accounts for the way in which Christology is "tacked-on" to the end of the *Summa theologiae*.[29] According to this view, his chief *intellectual* (as opposed to devotional or homiletical) interest in Scripture and doctrine is in applying the tools of reason to them in order to forge a system that can draw conclusions with scientific certainty.[30] Not surprisingly, such a view of Thomas finds him far more interesting as a speculative metaphysician than as a theologian.[31]

This view of Thomas is increasingly rejected. On the one hand, numerous interpreters of Aquinas, while still approaching him primarily as a philosopher, stress the profoundly apophatic character of his thought, taking with absolute seriousness what he

29. The charge can be found in various places. See Karl Rahner, *The Trinity* [1967], trans. Joseph Donceel (New York: Crossroad Herder, 1997), 15–21. With regard to the structure of the *Summa theologiae*, and particularly the place of Christ, the debate in the past fifty years has been a busy one. For a discussion of these debates, as well as yet another constructive solution, see Jean-Marc Laporte, "Christ in Aquinas' *Summa Theologiae*: Peripheral or Pervasive?" *The Thomist* 67, no. 2 (April 2003): 221–48.

30. For one example of this image of Thomas, see Adolf von Harnack:

> Thus the theological science of the thirteenth century can be described as the submitting to dialectical-systematic revision of ecclesiastical dogma and ecclesiastical practice, with the view of unfolding them in a system having unity and comprehending all that in the highest sense is worthy of being known, with the view of proving them, and so of reducing to the service of the Church all the forces of the understanding and the whole product of science. (*History of Dogma*, vol. 6 [3rd ed., 1900], trans. Neil Buchanan [New York: Dover, 1961], 154.)

This characterization of Harnack's is not materially different from that of the neo-Scholastic Ludwig Ott: "According to the teaching of St. Thomas, theology is a true science, because it uses as principles the securely founded basic truths of Divine Revelation and draws from these new knowledge (theological conclusions) by a strict scientific method and unites the whole in a closed system" (*Fundamentals of Catholic Dogma*, ed. James Canon Bastible, trans. Patrick Lynch [Cork: Mercier, 1958], 1).

31. On the other hand, there are also philosophers who greatly admire Thomas on questions of philosophical psychology but reject his metaphysics. Anthony Kenny, for example, says of such venerable elements of "Thomist metaphysics" as the real distinction between essence and existence and the account of God as *esse ipsum subsistens* that "even the most sympathetic treatment of these doctrines cannot wholly succeed in acquitting them of the charges of sophistry and illusion" (*Aquinas* [Oxford: Oxford University Press, 1980], 60).

says about the fundamentally mysterious nature of God.[32] On the other hand, there has been a significant reassessment of both the depth and originality of Thomas's engagement with Scripture and doctrine.[33] In other words, central to Thomas's work is reflection on the mystery of God and the scriptural manner of speaking of that mystery.[34] Thomas is not interested simply in the scientific ordering of discrete bits of revealed "data"; rather, he seeks to discern the way in which the mystery of God is revealed in the *modo conversationis* or manner of life of Jesus of Nazareth, a manner of life that is not subject to *a priori* judgments of necessity precisely because it is the historical revelation of the divine mystery. There is a kind of dovetailing between the historical contingency of Jesus's life and the mystery of God because neither is subject to rational deduction.

While we do not find in Thomas the kind of appeal to "narrative" that became popular among theologians in the last part of the twentieth century, we ought not to underestimate the importance to Thomas of the concrete events narrated in Scripture, not simply as data upon which reason operates, but as in its totality

32. An early classic in this regard is Josef Pieper's *The Silence of St. Thomas: Three Essays* [1957], trans. John Murray and Daniel O'Connor (South Bend, IN: St. Augustine's, 1999). Another example would be Brian Davies's *The Thought of Thomas Aquinas* (Oxford: Clarendon, 1992), which is deeply influenced by Herbert McCabe's view that "when we speak of God, although we know how to use our words, there is an important sense in which we do not know what they mean" (Herbert McCabe, "Appendix 3: 'Signifying Imperfectly,'" in St. Thomas Aquinas, *Summa theologiae*, ed. and trans. Herbert McCabe [New York: McGraw-Hill, 1964], 3:104).

33. The significance of Thomas's official title at Paris—*magister in sacra pagina*—began to be recovered by scholars in the middle of the twentieth century. As Marie-Dominique Chenu wrote in 1950, "The *Summa* is embedded in an evangelical soil. By no means is this the result of some sort of devotion aiming to retain piousness within its rational systematization, but because therein is provided the law itself of its genesis" (*Toward Understanding St. Thomas*, trans. A.M. Landry and D. Hughes [Chicago: Henry Regnery, 1964], 233). For two more recent works in English that seek to undermine the view of Thomas as primarily a philosopher with a peripheral intellectual interest in Scripture and doctrine, see Fergus Kerr, *After Aquinas: Versions of Thomism* (Malden, MA: Blackwell, 2002), and Nicholas M. Healy, *Thomas Aquinas: Theologian of the Christian Life* (Aldershot, UK: Ashgate, 2003).

34. These two emphases on Aquinas as an apophatic theologian and on Thomas as a scriptural theologian converge in the work of the scholars associated with the Thomas Instituut te Utrecht. An introductory survey of "Utrecht-Thomism" can be found in Jozef Wissink, *Thomas van Aquino: De actuele betekenis van zijn theologie* (Zoetermeer, NL: Meinema, 1998).

a figure or image of the divine mystery.[35] As Thomas says in his commentary on John's Gospel, "The teaching of the Father is the Son himself."[36] What is offered for belief is not "data" but the figure of Christ rendered in the Gospels—a figure that, by the beauty of its "fittingness (*convenientia*)," draws one's will to assent to its truth even though that truth is beyond the grasp of reason. As Thomas himself says of theology, "The manner of proceeding of this discipline must be a narrative of signs, which serve to confirm faith."[37] Thus Thomas's theology serves as a kind of commentary on the narrative figure of Christ, pointing us to the mystery revealed in Scripture's manner of speaking and Christ's manner of life.

ARGUING IN THE CULTURE OF NIHILISM: SHOUTING TO THE HARD OF HEARING

Of course, whatever the agreement they may have regarding mystery and manners, the works of O'Connor and Aquinas are inflected quite differently. And this is not simply because Aquinas is a theologian and O'Connor a fiction writer; the difference is deeper and has to do with audience or, more precisely, the context in which they are writing.

O'Connor was a self-consciously modern—indeed, even "modernist"—writer, with Henry James, Joseph Conrad, and, later in life, Marcel Proust as literary heroes. More importantly, she was conscious that she was writing for an audience that did

35. Nicholas Healy makes the point that Thomas's emphasis on the literal sense of the biblical text can be seen as a commitment to the primacy of the narrative sequence of events over all conceptual explication of those events. "Spiritual interpretations make connections between events and things that often break up the narrative structure of revelation. This is certainly permissible, even necessary, but the diachronic structure of God's actions in the world from Genesis to the Book of Revelation must take precedence over the synchronic explication of those actions" (*Thomas Aquinas*, 43).

36. *Super Io.* 7.2.1037.

37. *Super Sent.* 1, prologue, 1.5.

not share her perspective on mystery and manners. She wrote to a friend,

> One of the awful things about writing when you are a Christian is that for you the ultimate reality is the Incarnation, the present reality is the Incarnation, the whole reality is the Incarnation, and nobody believes in the Incarnation; that is, nobody in your audience. My audience are the people who think God is dead. At least these are the people I am conscious of writing for.[38]

One might ask, however, if a professed Thomist shouldn't be able to surmount this difficulty by seeking a common basis in the truths of natural reason. After all, Thomas could enter into dialogue and disputation with Jews and Muslims who rejected the Incarnation. But as O'Connor sees the matter, she is in a fundamentally different situation from someone in the thirteenth century. It is not simply that modern people don't share her convictions regarding Christ. Rather, the modern world lacks even the sense that there is some choice to be made between existence and nothingness, good and evil. As O'Connor puts it, "If you live today, you breathe in nihilism."[39] We live in an age in which "the moral sense has been bred out of certain sections of the population, like the wings have been bred off certain chickens to produce more white meat on them." O'Connor goes on to add, "This is a generation of wingless chickens, which I suppose is what Nietzsche meant when he said God was dead."[40] By contrast, even when he writes *contra gentiles*, Thomas is not writing for those who think God is dead.

Thus, O'Connor's writing must inevitably be inflected differently than that of an author writing in the thirteenth century, and

38. O'Connor to "A.," August 2, 1955, in *O'Connor: Collected Works*, 943.

39. O'Connor to "A.," August 28, 1955, in *O'Connor: Collected Works*, 949.

40. O'Connor to "A.," July 20, 1955, in *O'Connor: Collected Works*, 942.

this inflection is one that gives her writing an extremely unstable or off-balance feel. Writing of Dante she says,

> I am often told that the model of balance for the novelist should be Dante, who divided his territory up pretty evenly between hell, purgatory and paradise. There can be no objection to this, but also there can be no reason to assume that the result of doing it in these times will give us the balanced picture that it gave in Dante's. Dante lived in the 13th century when the balance was achieved in the faith of his age. We live now in an age which doubts both fact and value, which is swept this way and that by momentary convictions. Instead of reflecting a balance from the world around him, the novelist now has to achieve one from the felt balance inside himself. There are ages when it is possible to woo the reader; there are others when something more drastic is necessary.[41]

While O'Connor shares the theological worldview of Dante and Aquinas, her relationship to that worldview is somewhat different. Religious faith is no longer woven into the fabric of a shared culture; rather, it has been interiorized. Whatever "felt balance" the writer achieves interiorly will not externalize itself in "balanced" writing precisely because there is no language shared between author and audience in which such a balance can be expressed.

As is well known, Thomas held that all arguments, including theological arguments, proceed on the basis of commonly accepted premises.[42] In some cases, where the premises of a valid argument are either self-evident or have been made evident by prior arguments, truth is clearly manifested to reason in such a way that reason cannot withhold assent: reason cannot deny the Pythagorean theorem without ceasing to be reason. However,

41. O'Connor, "The Grotesque in Southern Fiction," in *O'Connor: Collected Works*, 820.
42. See *Summa theologiae* 1.1.8.

there are cases where reason does not incline to either side of an argument, because the premises are not evident, and such is the case with those arguments that have to do with the nature of God. In those cases, the "wooing" of belief depends on our ability to recognize goodness where we cannot recognize truth. Thomas writes,

> Hence our understanding is determined by the will, which chooses to assent to one side definitively and precisely on account of something that is enough to move the will, though not enough to move the understanding, namely, because it seems good or fitting [*bonum vel conveniens*] to assent to this side. And this is the disposition of one who believes, as when someone believes the utterance of a person because it seems to him appropriate [*decens*] or useful.[43]

In the case of belief, what draws the will to move reason to assent is the perception of the good or fitting—*bonum vel conveniens.* This category of "fitting" is woven through the Third Part of the *Summa theologiae*; confronted with the mystery of God incarnate, we discern a goodness or fittingness that attracts the will no less inexorably than truth attracts reason.

Yet even in this case, there must be some shared sense of what constitutes goodness or fittingness in order for an argument *ex convenientia* to persuade. The perception of *convenientia* requires a sense of harmonious balance, an ability to see the way in which various contingent factors come together (*con-venire*) to form an object of compelling beauty. Thomas recognizes the analogy between aesthetic and theological persuasion in his commentary on Lombard's *Sentences* when he writes,

43. *De veritate* 14.1.

> Poetic knowledge is of things that, on account of a lack [*defectum*] of truth, cannot be grasped by reason, and therefore reason must be seduced by certain likenesses. Theology, however, is about things that are above reason. Therefore the symbolic mode is common to both, because neither is proportioned to reason.[44]

Both poetry and theology exert a symbolic appeal that compensates for the disproportion or imbalance between reason and what is aesthetically represented.

But according to O'Connor, this sense of balance, this ability to see goodness, much less to perceive truths of reason, is precisely what the modern world has lost, or rather, this is what has come to lodge within the interior space of personal artistic vision. But this is a forced confinement, which O'Connor refuses and meets with counterforce: "Instead of reflecting a balance from the world around him, the novelist now has to *achieve* one by being a counterweight to the prevailing heresy."[45] Lacking a shared language of goodness or balance with which she can "woo" her readers, she sets out to shock.

> When you can assume that your audience holds the same beliefs you do, you can relax a little and use more normal ways of talking to it; when you have to assume that it does not, then you have to make your vision apparent by shock—to the hard of hearing you shout, and for the almost blind you draw large and startling figures.[46]

The imbalance in O'Connor's writing is everywhere evident

44. *Super Sent.* 1, prologue, 1.5 ad 3.

45. O'Connor, "The Catholic Novelist in the Protestant South," in *O'Connor: Collected Works*, 862.

46. O'Connor, "The Fiction Writer and His Country," in *O'Connor: Collected Works*, 805–6.

and is usually identified by the description "grotesque." At times, O'Connor seems annoyed with this description of her work, thinking it superficial and misapplied.[47] At other times, she acknowledges her use of "freaks" as a way of addressing the modern reader, in whom the sense of evil—and consequently the sense of good—has become "diluted" or is completely absent. Her stories are peopled by large and startling figures of both good and evil: child molesters, thieves and murderers, backwoods prophets, vacuous liberals, and pseudo-sophisticates. Her stories often end with a violent death or with a violent realization that one must endure the rest of life with crushing guilt or chronic illness. In Hazel Motes, the protagonist of her novel *Wise Blood*, we find a figure who is grotesque in the strict sense of the term: a fantastic combination of nihilistic atheism and evangelical fervor in a single figure.

O'Connor's characters are also "grotesque" in the etymological sense of the term: they emerge from the grottoes of her interiorized "felt balance." This felt balance is the concurrence of mystery and manners, transcendence and tradition, that she shares with Aquinas but not with the contemporary culture of nihilism. Indeed, for the modern world, the convergence of mystery and manners is itself a grotesque figure. In a world that lacks a language of truth or goodness or beauty, the mystery of God incarnate appears not as "balanced" or "fitting" but as ugly and horrific. In contrast to the fitting contingencies that Aquinas reads in Christ's manner of life, O'Connor's stories offer seemingly random violence that accompanies unexpected revelations. Perhaps she hopes that if goodness and beauty cannot themselves be perceived, then they might be glimpsed in their shadows—the evil and ugliness of which the modern world seems so enamored.

O'Connor herself was still able to believe, to be drawn by

47. O'Connor wrote, "I have found that anything that comes out of the South is going to be called grotesque by the Northern reader, unless it is grotesque, in which case it is going to be called realistic" ("The Grotesque in Southern Fiction," in *O'Connor: Collected Works*, 815).

beauty and goodness to the truth. She was still able to say, in a letter to a friend, that "you can't have a peacock anywhere without having a map of the universe."[48] But she thinks that the ability to read this map is lost to the modern world. In her story "The Displaced Person," an unnamed priest comes to visit the Polish refugees working on Mrs. McIntyre's farm. When he sees a peacock spread his tail, he stands "transfixed, his jaw slack" and says in a loud voice, "Christ will come like that!"[49] But Mrs. McIntyre, hard-headed modern businesswoman that she is, for whom the peacock is just "another mouth to feed,"[50] thinks him "an idiotic old man," and at the mention of Christ, her "face assumed a set puritanical expression and she reddened. Christ in the conversation embarrassed her the way sex had her mother."[51] A woman like Mrs. McIntyre cannot see a map of the universe in either the peacock's tail or in Christ; she is, as Walker Percy would put it, "Lost in the Cosmos," and even more lost for not recognizing her lostness.

It is only when she is confronted by the death of her Polish worker in a random tractor accident—which she could have prevented but chose not to—that she begins to sense that she may not know where she is or where she is going. The priest returns to the farm to give the last rites to the dying worker. Seeing the priest leaning with the man's family over his crushed body,

> She only stared at him for she was too shocked by her experience to be quite herself. Her mind was not taking hold of all that was happening. She felt she was in some foreign country where the people bent over the body were natives, and she

48. O'Connor to "A.," November 25, 1955, in *O'Connor: Collected Works*, 971.

49. O'Connor, "The Displaced Person," in *O'Connor: Collected Works*, 317.

50. O'Connor, 289.

51. O'Connor, 317.

> watched like a stranger while the dead man was carried away in the ambulance.[52]

The story ends with Mrs. McIntyre abandoned by the rest of the workers on the farm, suffering a nervous breakdown and living her last days alone with no visitors except the priest, who comes weekly to feed the peacocks and to "sit by the side of her bed and explain the doctrines of the Church."[53]

For O'Connor, this is a story of the way in which grace works in a world that can no longer be wooed by beauty. The thriving farm that Mrs. McIntyre seeks to build comes crashing down like the Tower of Babel, and in the end, "nothing survived but [the priest] and the peacock and Mrs. McIntyre suffering."[54] Beauty is still present, in both the peacock and the teaching of the priest, but O'Connor does not seem to expect her audience to recognize that beauty or open themselves to its grace. Rather, she hopes that the grotesque fate of Mrs. McIntyre will act upon her readers as a disturbing grace, leaving them frightened, like the women at Jesus's empty tomb. But, in retrospect, O'Connor felt the story was unsuccessful precisely because her audience was unable to see the collapse of Mrs. McIntyre's world into suffering as the possibility of her redemption. "I missed making this clear but how are you going to make such things clear to people who don't believe in God, much less in Purgatory?"[55]

One always risks misunderstanding when shouting to the hard of hearing. O'Connor once wrote that "unless the novelist has gone utterly out of his mind, his aim is still communication and communication suggests talking inside a community."[56] But what community can O'Connor find with her audience?

52. O'Connor, 326.

53. O'Connor, 326.

54. O'Connor to "A.," November 25, 1955, in *O'Connor: Collected Works*, 971.

55. O'Connor, 971.

56. O'Connor, "The Regional Writer," in *O'Connor: Collected Works*, 844.

Certainly not the Christian community, but also not even the human community, since modern people have lost "even the sense of the human itself."[57] O'Connor seeks to communicate mystery in a world without manners, without the habitual ways of speaking and acting that make it possible for mystery to appear in a balanced and harmonious way. Yet she will not be deterred, for as a follower of Thomas, she seeks to "take every thought captive to obey Christ" (2 Cor. 10:5).[58] Though she once wrote that "the Church can't be identified with Western culture and I suppose the wreck of it doesn't cause her much of a sense of crisis,"[59] in practice she recognizes that a retreat from engagement with that culture would amount to a retreat into a dualism of mystery and manners. While the Church is not identical with Western culture, neither does it exist in isolation from it. The mission of the Church is not simply to speak *contra gentes* but to share in the apostolic movement *ad gentes*, a movement that was at the heart of Thomas's own vocation as a Dominican friar.

As O'Connor said, a hillbilly Thomist is likely to be mistaken for a hillbilly nihilist precisely because she seeks a way of proclaiming the Gospel through the guileful use of the nihilist's own idiom of distortion. But in robbing the modern world of its smug certainties, one might be seen as offering the abyss of nothingness rather than the abyss of faith. It is a risk O'Connor judges worth taking. She seeks to show that the human will cannot master the void, or even play safely within it, in order to open up the possibility that the void has already been mastered. She induces an awareness of lostness so that we may recognize ourselves as found.

57. O'Connor to Dr. T.R. Spivey, October 19, 1958, in *O'Connor: Collected Works*, 1077.

58. When Thomas first introduces the phrase *gratia perficit naturam* in the *Summa theologiae* in 1.1.8, he glosses it with Paul's phrase from 2 Corinthians 10:5: "Take every thought captive in obedience to Christ."

59. O'Connor to Dr. T.R. Spivey, October 19, 1958, in *O'Connor: Collected Works*, 1076.

GRATIA TURBIT NATURAM

If a hillbilly Thomist is likely to be mistaken for a nihilist, she is also likely to be mistaken, particularly by her fellow Catholics, for a Protestant. O'Connor mentions a review of her stories by "a priest who said that while my convictions may be Catholic, my sensibilities appeared to be Lutheran."[60] Presumably, what this reviewer meant was that she was overly pessimistic about human nature, thereby denigrating the goodness of creation, a sensibility Catholics often identify with Protestantism. As one pair of authors put the matter, at the heart of Protestant theology is a conviction about "the utter corruption of the human person as a result of the sin of Adam," with the result that "the individual, radically turned in on himself or herself and closed to any possibility of agapeic community, is locked into selfishness."[61] This is contrasted with Catholicism, which "has insisted in opposition to the darker views of the reformers that the human being, made in the image of God who is agape, remains in that image even after the fall and so is capable, even with great difficulty, of genuine other-directedness."[62] According to this view, we find in the case of Aquinas, with his belief that "grace perfects nature" (*gratia perficit naturam*), a particularly ringing endorsement of human life and culture and a deep sense that grace, while distinct from nature, is at the same time in continuity with nature. In Thomas O'Meara's words, for Aquinas, "grace is not a source of miraculous powers for curing cancer or handling poisonous snakes. Aquinas was little interested in the miraculous . . . but returned

60. O'Connor to "A." September 30, 1955, in *O'Connor: Collected Works*, 960.

61. Michael J. Himes and Kenneth R. Himes, *Fullness of Faith: The Public Significance of Theology* (New York: Paulist, 1993), 30.

62. Himes and Himes, 31. A similar characterization (from a different spot on the spectrum of Catholic theology) is made by John M. Haas: "One of the errors that arose in much Protestant thought, and persists to our own day even in secular culture, is that the natural and the supernatural orders are opposed to one another. Because of the doctrine of the total depravity of man, classical Protestantism tends to look at fallen man as radically over against God" ("The Relationship of Nature and Grace in Saint Thomas," in *The Ever-Illuminating Wisdom of St. Thomas Aquinas: Papers Presented at a Conference Sponsored by the Wethersfield Institute* [San Francisco: Ignatius, 1999], 63).

again and again to the invisible Spirit of Jesus working in people powerfully but respectfully."[63] Here, the claim that "grace perfects nature" seems to become the claim that grace *respects* nature.

Things seem otherwise in the world of O'Connor. There is nothing respectful about a grandmother shot by a serial killer or a child drowned in a river while seeking the kingdom of God. In O'Connor's fiction, grace appears to be a profoundly disrespectful and disruptive force that might very well appear in the form of snake handling and cancer cures or, even more likely, in the form of snakes that bite and tumors that kill.[64] Rather than perfecting nature and bringing it to fulfillment, the grace in O'Connor's stories seems to *disturb* nature: *gratia turbit naturam*. Whereas Thomas says that "grace does not take away nature but perfects it, therefore natural reason should assist faith,"[65] O'Connor seems to be saying that natural reason hinders faith and, correlatively, faith overturns natural reason. Regarding the legal notion of "the reasonable man," O'Connor wrote to a friend, "Mine is certainly something else—God's reasonable man, the prototype of whom must be Abraham, willing to sacrifice his son and thereby show that he is in the image of God Who sacrifices His Son."[66]

63. O'Meara, *Thomas Aquinas: Theologian*, 115. O'Meara also writes, "The entire [*Summa theologiae*] unfolds Aquinas' axiom, '*gratia perficit naturam*,' 'grace brings nature to its full destiny.' Cosmos and church, being and life, art and ecstasy do not point to death but to life; the Catholic mind . . . delights in the ways in which the Incarnation continues" (126).

64. For some insight on the workings of grace manifested in incurable cancer, see O'Connor's "Introduction to *A Memoir of Mary Ann*," in *O'Connor: Collected Works*, 822–31.

65. *Summa theologiae* 1.1.8.

66. O'Connor to "A.," November 10, 1955, in *O'Connor: Collected Works*, 968. While O'Meara claims that Thomas's theology is "the polar opposite of any fundamentalism" (*Thomas Aquinas: Theologian*, 116), fundamentalists are among O'Connor's favorite subjects, precisely because they offer us a Gospel that has no respect for our idea of what is reasonable, a Gospel that is, in fact, fanatical. Writing to Sister Mariella Gable, O'Connor said,

> About the fanatics. People make a judgement of fanaticism by what they are themselves. To a lot of Protestants I know, monks and nuns are fanatics, none greater. And to a lot of monks and nuns I know, my Protestant prophets are fanatics. For my part, I think the only difference between them is that if you are a Catholic and have this intensity of belief you join the convent and are heard from no more; whereas if you are a Protestant and have it, there is no convent for you to join, and you go about in the world getting into all sorts of trouble and drawing the wrath of

The example of Abraham evokes Kierkegaard far more than it does Thomas.

Does this mean that O'Connor's "hillbilly Thomism" is in fact an ersatz Thomism? Is it Protestant fideism in Thomist drag? There are two possible ways to address these questions. The first is to see if, in Thomas's account, grace is quite so "respectful" of nature as some have claimed; the second is to see if O'Connor really does pit grace against nature.[67] Is it possible to see grace taking the radically disruptive form that it does in O'Connor's fiction and still affirm the view that *gratia perficit naturam*?

The difference between Thomas and Calvin or Luther is sometimes said to be that, whereas the Reformers taught that human nature is "totally depraved" by sin, Thomas holds that it is merely "wounded" and retains its essential integrity. And it is certainly true that Thomas holds that the goodness of human nature is diminished by sin but not entirely destroyed,[68] and it is also true that he uses the language of the "wounding of nature" (*vulneratio naturae*) to describe this diminishment.[69] Yet he makes clear that this wounding is not on the order of a paper cut; rather, it constitutes the *destitutio* of nature.[70] In the order of being, the goodness of human nature retains its fundamental integrity, inasmuch as the fallen human person remains a rational animal (otherwise, sin would be impossible), but in the moral order, the diminishment of the natural inclination to good can proceed, as

> people who don't believe anything much at all down on your head. (May 4, 1963, in *Collected Works*, 1183)

O'Connor concludes her letter saying, "I am more and more impressed with the amount of Catholicism that fundamentalist Protestants have been able to retain. Theologically our differences with them are on the nature of the Church, not on the nature of God and our obligation to him" (*Collected Works*, 1184).

67. A third approach would be to see if Catholic accounts of Protestant theological anthropology are accurate, or rather cartoonish caricatures.

68. See, e.g., *Summa theologiae* 1-2.85.2. One might adapt Aquinas's adage about grace and nature to state his position on the effect of sin on nature: *peccatum non tollit naturam, sed deficit.*

69. *Summa theologiae* 1-2.85.3.

70. *Summa theologiae* 1-2.85.3.

Aquinas says, to infinity.[71] The integrity of human nature imposes no limits on human depravity.

But even if we grant, in theory, that the human inclination toward virtue can asymptotically approach zero, is this in fact our situation? Thomas certainly says that human beings, even in the state of corrupted nature, can do particular good acts, such as building houses or (what is a far more significant moral achievement) having friends,[72] and we ought not to underplay Thomas's insistence on these things as genuine goods. At the same time, we should not overlook Thomas's statement that these are *particular* good acts; our doing of them is contingent and circumstantial and they do not move us toward our ultimate end. And whereas prior to sin human beings could fulfill God's commands in such a way as to be pleasing to God, after sin and without grace, this is simply impossible.[73]

Thomas does say something that is akin to the claim that grace is "respectful" of nature in *Summa theologiae* 1.62.5, where he writes, "Grace perfects nature according to the mode of that nature, just as every perfection is received in what it perfects according to its mode." Thomas says this in reference to the angels, whom God rewards with grace according to their natural

71. *Contra Gentiles* 3.12.7: "The natural tendency toward good can therefore be diminished infinitely through evil habits. Nevertheless it is never taken away totally, but always accompanies the nature that remains."

72. Thomas mentions building houses, along with planting vineyards, in *Summa theologiae* 1-2.109.2. The mention of friendship, usually overlooked by those commenting on this question, is in *Summa theologiae* 1-2.109.5.

73. *Summa theologiae* 1-2.109.8 ad 1: "Human beings can avoid each but not every sinful act, except by grace." In *Summa theologiae* 1-2.63.2 ad 2, Thomas says that sin, even mortal sin, is compatible with individual acquired virtues, since sin is an act and not a *habitus*. But in 1-2.65.1, he makes clear that acquired virtues must be guided by *prudentia* in order to be connected in what we might call a virtuous life. He further argues, in 1-2.65.2, that in order for prudence to operate correctly, a person must be properly disposed toward his or her ultimate end, and that this disposition can only be brought about by grace, through the infused virtue of *caritas*. Thus, it would seem that while all of the actions of a person in the state of corrupted nature are not themselves evil, such actions are in no way salvific. See also *Summa theologiae* 1-2.109.5, as well as Thomas's discussion in *Super Rom.* 14.3.1140 regarding Romans 14:23: "Whatever is not from faith is sin."

perfections, something that is not true of humans.[74] But with regard to human beings, he also says that "divine providence provides for everything in accordance with its mode."[75] We might say that, while grace is never a reward for the good that is in human nature, in observing the "way of being" (*modus*) of a nature, the grace bestowed by divine providence does show a certain "respect" for that nature. Grace cannot operate by external coercion (*coactio*) upon human nature precisely because to do so would be to destroy human nature, to which it belongs to act voluntarily. Put in the simplest terms, human beings do not have to become something other than human, whether angel or beast, in order to attain the vision of God.

But we should be clear about what this does and does not entail. We ought never to forget that the respectful *cooperation* of grace with the human will that makes human merit possible is founded on the prevenient *operation* of grace in which "the will is the thing moved and God is the mover."[76] Ultimately, grace is something added to human nature from outside, not something that grows from within it. In saying that grace "perfects" or "realizes the potential of" human nature, we should keep before our mind the analogy of a form perfecting matter or an agent perfecting that upon which it acts.[77] If Thomas's thinking has any sort of metaphysical lynchpin, it is that something that is in potentiality can only be actualized by something external to it. In the case of perfections realized within the order of nature, that upon which the agent acts must have some potential that can be realized and thus in some sense "anticipates" its own realization. But in the case of grace perfecting human nature, no such anticipation is possible precisely because the gift of grace realizes something that

74. See, e.g., *Summa theologiae* 1.108.8 ad 1.

75. *Contra Gentiles* 3.148.2.

76. *Summa theologiae* 1-2.111.2.

77. Thomas makes the analogy of form and matter in *Summa contra Gentiles* 3.149 and that of an agent perfecting a potential (in this case, fire perfecting water's potential to be hot) in *Summa contra Gentiles* 3.147.4.

is in excess of human nature's potential. So grace may "respect" human nature in the sense that the beatified human creature remains a human creature, but at the same time, nature is disturbed by grace, like the *aqua turbata* of the pool at Bethsaida (John 5:7), or Mary who, upon hearing the angelic greeting, *turbata est in sermone eius* (Luke 1:29). Thomas, whatever the coolness or dryness of his tone, never forgets that grace is a word at which we are disturbed, a word that stirs us to reach out beyond the confines of our nature.

O'Connor, in the same way, never forgets that grace aims at bringing human nature to fulfillment, not destruction. One might say that grace reveals the truth of our nature that has been obscured by sin. Writing to her friend Betty Hester after Hester left the Church, O'Connor says, "This means a narrowing of life for you and a lessening of the desire for life."[78] In losing that which is beyond our nature, we lose our nature. The difficulty in the culture of nihilism is at root not the loss of a sense of grace but the loss of nature. Just as modern culture wants its mystery without manners, so too it wants its grace without nature. Or, more precisely, it understands nature as an emptiness that is entirely subject to human manipulation; human nature is the object of self-actualization. For O'Connor, this spells death for nature. Cut off from grace, it cannot reach its destiny; cut off from its Creator, it cannot even exist.

At the same time that O'Connor believes that grace serves the flourishing of human nature by piquing our appetite for life, she also believes that "all human nature vigorously resists grace because grace changes us and the change is painful."[79] *Gratia perficit naturam* does not exclude *gratia turbit naturam*; for just as form perfects matter by stirring it to act, "troubling" and "goading" it into actuality, so too grace perfects nature by disturbing it.

78. O'Connor to "A.," October 28, 1961, in *O'Connor: Collected Works*, 1152–53.

79. O'Connor to Cecil Dawkins, December 9, 1958, in *O'Connor: Collected Works*, 1084.

Nature resists, just as matter resists taking on a new form in the artist's hands, but this resistance is not the last word. O'Connor saw her stories as embodying the deeply Catholic view that, unlike the case of angelic natures, grace acts upon human nature independent of whatever natural goodness might be found there. "Grace, to the Catholic way of thinking, can and does use as its medium the imperfect, purely human, and even hypocritical."[80] Grace perfects nature, and the sinfulness of the nature that grace perfects becomes, in O'Connor's hands, a testimony to the radical gratuity of that grace. In her stories, grace appears like the angel who disturbs Mary, in events that stand out in sharp relief: "This would have to be an action or a gesture which was both totally right and totally unexpected; it would have to be one that was both in character and beyond character; it would have to suggest both the world and eternity."[81] The arrival of grace is, for O'Connor as for Thomas, both totally right and totally unexpected because it is both in accord with and beyond our human nature.

HILLBILLY THOMISTIC COMMENTARY: *PRAESTET FIDES SUPPLEMENTUM SENSUUM DEFECTUI*

Flannery O'Connor only quotes Thomas Aquinas once in her fiction. In her story "A Temple of the Holy Ghost," she puts Thomas's Eucharistic hymn *Tantum Ergo Sacramentum* into the mouths of two convent-schoolgirls, who sing it to mock the two teenage boys who have been invited over to entertain them on their weekend away from the convent. The boys, who have just treated the girls to a couple of hymns from the Church of God, are perplexed

80. O'Connor to John Hawkes, April 14, 1960, in *O'Connor: Collected Works*, 1125. In this same letter, O'Connor indicates that she holds the typical Catholic view of the Protestant theology of nature and grace and distinguishes her own view from it: "In the Protestant view, I think Grace and nature don't have much to do with each other."

81. O'Connor, "On Her Own Work," in *Mystery and Manners*, 111. This is from remarks O'Connor made to introduce her reading of her story "A Good Man Is Hard to Find" at Hollins College, Virginia, in 1963.

by Aquinas's hymn, and after a moment of silence, one of them replies, "That must be Jew singing."[82] On the lips of the girls, the sublime theology of Aquinas becomes a tool to assert their own superiority, just as earlier they had, with shrieks of laughter, referred to each other as "Temple One" and "Temple Two," a reference to a lecture from an old nun at their school, who told them that if a boy were to "behave in an ungentlemanly manner with them in the back of an automobile," they were to respond, "Stop sir! I am a Temple of the Holy Ghost!"[83]

At the heart of the story are not the two adolescent girls but the unnamed younger girl whose family they are visiting. When the two girls from the convent return after their evening at the fair with the boys, they tell the girl about the freak show they had seen: a hermaphrodite had exposed himself to the audience, but not before warning them, "God made me thisaway and if you laugh He may strike you the same way. This is the way He wanted me to be and I ain't disputing His way."[84] As the child lies in bed, slipping into sleep, she imagines the scene with the hermaphrodite—the freak show taking on the characteristics of a backwoods revival and blending with the image of the body as a Temple of the Holy Ghost:

> She could hear the freak saying, "God made me thisaway and I don't dispute hit," and the people saying, "Amen. Amen."
>
> "God done this to me and I praise Him."
>
> "Amen. Amen."
>
> "He could strike you thisaway."
>
> "Amen. Amen."
>
> "But he has not."

82. O'Connor, 199.
83. O'Connor, "A Temple of the Holy Ghost," in *O'Connor: Collected Works*, 202.
84. O'Connor, 206.

"Amen."

"Raise yourself up. A temple of the Holy Ghost. You! You are God's temple, don't you know? Don't you know? God's Spirit has a dwelling in you, don't you know?"

"Amen. Amen."

"If anybody desecrates the temple of God, God will bring him to ruin and if you laugh, He may strike you thisaway. A temple of God is a holy thing. Amen. Amen."

"I am a temple of the Holy Ghost."

"Amen."[85]

The story concludes with the girl going with her mother to return Temple One and Temple Two to the school, where she goes into the convent chapel and kneels to pray during the service of Benediction of the Blessed Sacrament as they sing the *Tantum Ergo*. Looking at the Host, ivory colored and pure, she thinks of the freak show and the hermaphrodite saying, "This is the way He wanted me to be." Later, as she is returning home, she looks at the evening horizon: "The sun was a huge red ball like an elevated Host drenched in blood and when it sank out of sight, it left a line in the sky like a red clay road hanging over the trees."[86]

O'Connor offers us here something normally absent from her stories: Catholic ritual and symbolism. And she places it in a complex juxtaposition with images of Protestant revivalism and the grotesque figure of the hermaphrodite. It is as if O'Connor is straining in the story to get at the very heart of the matter in depicting God's disturbing grace. She is reaching for the kind of distortion that will "make the reader feel, in his bones if nowhere else, that something is going on here that counts."[87] The image of the blood-red sun descending like a Host upon the earth

85. O'Connor, 207.

86. O'Connor, 208.

87. O'Connor, "Novelist and Believer," in *Mystery and Manners*, 162.

reflects the pure ivory Host in the service of Benediction, which in turn reflects the freak show in the girl's imagination, where the hermaphrodite claims for himself the dignity of Christ's body: "I am a Temple of the Holy Ghost. Amen. Amen." These images bounce off each other, disorienting us and yet conveying a sense of the immense importance of the identification of the freakish body of the hermaphrodite, whose very flesh violates all rules of order and division, with Christ's Eucharistic body. Faith supplies what the senses fail to perceive: the hermaphrodite's grotesque body is transformed by the grace of acceptance into an icon of purity. Thomas's hymn is freed from the confines of piety and smugness and becomes an exhortation to bow before the graced, freakish body, which has Christ as its head and which extends to the farthest reaches of the horizon. In this single instance, O'Connor takes up the mantle of Thomistic commentator and casts a light upon Thomas's thought that makes its familiar words cast unexpected and luminous shadows.

Why be a hillbilly Thomist? Perhaps because pieties like "grace perfects nature," when found on the cool, dry lips of informed and responsible men, sound to modern ears like religious business as usual and consequently of no interest. The culture of nihilism that O'Connor sought to address believes that it can have its grace without nature, its mystery without manners, its spirit without a freakish body to be transformed. O'Connor knows that for the culture of nihilism, the alleged arrival of God in our world changes nothing, because that world is a void in which the human will plays endlessly. But for O'Connor, it changes everything, to a degree beyond what we can imagine, precisely because the world is not a void but a creation that awaits the unexpected arrival of its maker. Thomas knew this. As highly as he prized human reason, he maintained that the event of the Incarnation, by which creation is brought to its proper end, is beyond the capacity for human deduction; it must therefore be announced in a way that can be heard and seen as a gesture that is both totally right and totally unexpected. In the land of the hard of hearing and the half-blind, where we find ourselves today, it may be necessary to shout and draw large, startling figures if we seek, as Thomas sought, to take every thought captive in obedience to Christ.

Part I

God and Theology

2

Aquinas, Contemplation, and Theology

For Thomas Aquinas, contemplation is an anticipation of the eternal beatitude to which we aspire in hope while now pilgrims but will one day delight in as comprehensors. As Thomas puts it in the *Summa contra Gentiles*, "In this life there is nothing so like this ultimate and perfect happiness as the life of those who contemplate the truth, as far as possible in this life. . . . For contemplation of truth begins in this life, but will be consummated in the future."[1] But what exactly does Thomas mean by "contemplation"? Specifically, is he referring to a prayerful act of mind, the apex of the spiritual life, of which saints and mystics speak, or is he speaking simply of thinking, the kind of mundane wonder with which, according to Aristotle, all philosophy begins? In what follows, I want to draw upon Jonathan Lear's study *Aristotle: The Desire to Understand* to suggest that this is perhaps a false choice because the Aristotelian notion of contemplation, while directed to mundane objects, has a kind of theological *telos*, involving as it does a "spiritualizing" of material substances in which the knower comes to knowledge of world, self, and God. For Thomas, likewise, there is no sharp division between contemplation of

* Originally published as "Aquinas, Contemplation, and Theology," *New Blackfriars* 102, no. 1098 (March 2021): 160–73.

1. *Contra Gentiles* 3.63.7.

mundane realities and the contemplation that is the apex of the life of prayer.

SYSTEMATIC UNDERSTANDERS

As Jonathan Lear puts it, for Aristotle, the human person "is by nature a systematic understander of the world."[2] This will hardly come as news to any reader of Aristotle who understands what it means to say that a human being is a rational animal. It is access to the world in its intelligibility that distinguishes human beings from other sensate beings and characterizes the distinctive human mode of acting, a mode of action beyond the mere reproduction and nutrition by which species and individuals are sustained. Confronted by a frog, we do not see it as something with which to mate, as another frog might, nor simply as something to eat, as a raccoon might, but precisely as a frog—something that is what it is because of its essential frogginess, which it has in common with all other frogs and which is not reducible to its materiality. We might say that, whatever other appetites for frog we may have, our distinctively human appetite for the frog is an intellectual appetite, a desire to know it, to possess its form intellectually by grasping its essence. This activity of accessing the world as intelligible is what Aristotle calls contemplation or *theoria*, and in this activity we simultaneously grasp our own identity as graspers of such intelligible structure, as well as the identity of the first mover—that which accounts for the intelligible structure of the world.

On Lear's account, it is this human activity of grasping essences that reveals the distinctive role of the rational animal in the world. He notes, "When mind comes to understand the essence of flesh it, as it were, lifts form right out of its material

2. Jonathan Lear, *Aristotle: The Desire to Understand* (Cambridge: Cambridge University Press, 1988), 117.

instantiation."[3] Frogginess can exist in a frog only as materially instantiated; in us, however, it can exist immaterially, as a species in the mind. Lear writes, "Mind contemplating an essence is itself that very essence. It is that essence at the highest level of activity."[4] In the act of knowing, the human mind frees frogginess from material potency so that it exists, as Lear puts it, "at its highest level of actuality."[5] Our human contemplation of the world "spiritualizes" material substance through the process of abstraction; our knowledge of frogs is their spirituality.

If contemplation of things raises their essence to their highest level of actuality, then it seems that intelligibility is the *telos* of living substances: "For all natural organisms, the strong desire to survive, to sustain life, flourish, and reproduce is, from another perspective, a striving to become intelligible."[6] What sets human beings apart from other living organisms is that we are, as Lear puts it, "capable of appreciating this other perspective."[7] Contemplation not only brings the essence of the object contemplated to its highest form of actuality, but it is at the same time the contemplator at his or her highest level of actuality, the thinker perfected as thinker. It is, for the rational animal, the highest form of pleasure. And this highest of pleasures, this bliss, is not only a grasping of essences and of ourselves as knowers of essences; it is a grasping, if only partial, of God. Lear notes that, contrary to many standard accounts, for Aristotle, no less than for Kant, knowledge involves not conformity of mind to world but rather conformity of world to mind, but not (as in Kant) to the individual human mind but to the divine mind. "For Aristotle . . . objects must conform to our knowledge not because they must

3. Lear, 121.

4. Lear, 297.

5. Lear, 131.

6. Lear, 298. As he puts it elsewhere, "Essence as such remains a potentiality to be comprehended" (307).

7. Lear, 298.

conform to the human mind, but because they must conform to God or Active Mind."[8] This is why "in coming to understand the world we become like God, we become God-like," because our mind is conformed to God's mind.[9]

So, on Lear's account, Aristotle connects this knowing of the world, ourselves, and God such that one cannot be had without the other. As he summarizes the matter,

> So it is by the very activity of understanding the world that we come to understand ourselves. . . . So it would seem that the desire to understand leads us toward an activity of thinking that is at once an understanding of the world, an understanding of ourselves, and an understanding of God. . . . If we are ignorant of the world's relation to God, we do not know why the world is the way it is. But if we must understand the world in order fully to appreciate what is involved in being a systematic understander of it, it would seem that we must understand God and his relation to the world before we can fully understand ourselves. And in coming to understand God, and thus the world, and thus ourselves, we both fulfill our own essence and imitate God. . . . That is why we must, paradoxically, transcend our own nature in order to realize it.[10]

I am not willing to guarantee that Lear is correct in his presentation of Aristotle; certainly, other interpreters of Aristotle give a

8. Lear, 307–8. In Lear's reckoning, therefore, Aristotle is an "objective idealist." He argues that one of the deep continuities in the history of philosophy is the question of the relationship of the world to the mind and how the intelligibility of the world might be understood to be constituted by mind. The differences are in where world-constituting mind is, as it were, "located." For Aristotle (and, I would argue, in a somewhat different way, Thomas), it is the divine mind; for Kant, it is the individual mind. Lear goes on to note that post-Kantian philosophy can be read as a history of dissatisfaction with the Kantian location of mind: "One of the central responses to Kant's philosophy has been an attempt to relocate the mind to which objects are conforming. Hegel tried to locate mind in the Idea or the Absolute; the later Wittgenstein tried to locate it in the activities and customs of a community—what he called a form of life" (309).

9. Lear, 298.

10. Lear, 302–3.

rather more "secular" account of what is going on in his philosophy. But whatever we think about this as an interpretation of Aristotle, what Lear says about the desire to know as leading to a simultaneous knowing of world, self, and God can cast a helpful light on why Thomas Aquinas does theology in the way that he does, and why theology should be understood as a fundamentally contemplative activity that is not divorced from, indeed illuminates, more mundane human intellectual endeavors.

THE DYNAMISM OF KNOWING

For Thomas, no less than for Aristotle, "contemplation of the divine effects also belongs to the contemplative life, inasmuch as a person is led by this to knowledge of God."[11] The desire to know essences that is so characteristic of the human animal as a systematic understander finds its ultimate orientation and fulfillment in our knowledge of God. This suggests that the mundane contemplation of ordinary things like frogs is for Thomas ordered to contemplation of the divine essence precisely because the essence of the frog is not fully grasped until it is grasped as a divine effect. To see how this is the case, let us look at a much-pored-over-and-debated passage near the beginning of the *prima secundae* of the *Summa theologiae* (1-2.3.8).

To show that human happiness cannot consist in anything other than the vision of God's essence, Thomas says that we must consider two points:

> First, a human being is not perfectly happy as long as something remains for one to desire and seek. Second, the perfection of any power is judged according to the nature of its object.[12]

11. *Summa theologiae* 2-2.180.4.
12. *Summa theologiae* 1-2.3.8.

So perfect happiness—*beatitudo* or, as we might say, "bliss"—is connected with a cessation of our desire, an end to our seeking.[13] What perfection consists in depends upon the object of the particular power: sight, whose object is the visible, is perfected by seeing; touch, whose object is the tactile, is perfected by touching; and so on. What about that most distinctively human power, the power of understanding?

> The object of the intellect is *what a thing is* [*quod quid est*], that is, the essence of a thing. . . . For this reason the intellect attains perfection insofar as it knows the essence of a thing. If therefore an intellect knows the essence of some effect, by which it is not possible to know the essence of the cause (i.e., to know of the cause *what it is*), that intellect cannot be said to reach that cause in an absolute sense, although it may be able to gather from the effect the knowledge *that* the cause is [*an sit*].[14]

The object of the intellectual power is the essences of things, and to know the essence of something we must know its cause—not simply that it has a cause but the essence of the cause, since it is by its essence that the cause brings about the effect. To know merely that there is a cause is profoundly unsatisfying; it leaves the intellect unfulfilled and still seeking in its desire. To put it in

13. The notion that we no longer desire God in the beatific vision seems counterintuitive to many readers, who might prefer the view of another medieval Dominican theologian, Catherine of Siena, to whom God said concerning beatified souls, "They desire me forever, and forever they possess me, so their desire is not in vain. They are hungry yet satisfied, satisfied yet hungry" (*The Dialogue* ch. 4, trans. Suzanne Noffke [New York: Paulist, 1980], 83). It should be noted that Thomas gives a somewhat different account of beatitude and desire in the *Summa contra Gentiles*: "Nothing that is contemplated with wonder [*cum admiratione*] can be tiresome, since as long as the thing remains in wonder it continues to stimulate desire. But the divine substance is always viewed with wonder by any created intellect, since no created intellect comprehends it. So it is impossible for an intellectual substance to become tired of this vision" (3.62.9). This account would seem to bring Thomas's view closer to that of Catherine.

14. *Summa theologiae* 1-2.3.8.

an Augustinian idiom, it leaves us restless in our desire to know. So, Thomas concludes,

> Consequently, in knowing an effect, and knowing that it has a cause, there naturally remains in a human being the desire to know about the cause *what it is.* This desire belongs to wondering, and causes inquiry, as is stated in the beginning of the *Metaphysics* (1.2 982a). . . . Nor does this inquiry cease until he arrives at a knowledge of the essence of the cause.[15]

Thus far we have seen Thomas's views on the natural human desire to know the essences of mundane primary substances and how this involves knowing their causes. His invoking of Aristotle's *Metaphysics* suggests that, at least up to this point, he and Aristotle are singing from the same song sheet. But what if we shift the register, as Thomas does here in a somewhat sneaky way, from the desire to know the essence, and therefore the cause, of this or that mundane primary substance, to the desire to know the essence of the world of primary substances as a whole? What if, beginning from some mundane effect, we stretch the desire to know to extend it across the *totus mundus*—the entire web of effects and causes—such that we desire to know the cause of the world taken, as Peter Geach puts it, "as a great big object"?[16] If the pattern of desire that holds true in the case of knowledge of individual essences holds true in the case of the world as a whole, then knowledge merely that there is a cause of the world as a whole would leave our desire unquenched and our bliss unattained. So, Thomas says,

> If therefore the human intellect, knowing the essence of some created effect, knows no more of God than *that he is,*

15. *Summa theologiae* 1-2.3.8.

16. G.E.M. Anscombe and Peter T. Geach, *Three Philosophers: Aristotle, Aquinas, Frege* (Oxford: Basil Blackwell and Mott, 1961), 112.

> its perfection does not yet reach the first cause in an absolute way, but there remains in it a natural desire to seek the cause. For this reason it is not yet perfectly happy. Consequently, for perfect happiness the intellect needs to reach the very essence of the first cause.[17]

And so, Thomas reaches his conclusion:

> Thus it will have its perfection through union with God as with that object in which perfect human happiness alone consists, as stated earlier (1-2.1.7; 1-2.2.8).[18]

I have spent so long on what may be an extremely familiar passage in order to bring out the congruity of Lear's account of Aristotle with Thomas's account of what we might call the dynamism of human knowing and its orientation toward knowledge of God as first cause. We might say that Thomas and Aristotle continue to sing from the same song sheet even when the register shifts from contemplation of mundane essences to contemplation of the *totus mundus*. As with Aristotle, we know ourselves as knowers in the act of knowing the world since the human intellect, like anything else, is knowable only to the extent it is actual, and the natural object of the act of knowing is the essence of material things.[19] But our knowledge of the world does not simply give us knowledge of ourselves as knowers; it also launches us on a quest to know the first cause of the world that we know. As Thomas says at the outset of his commentary on John's Gospel, "The height and sublimity of contemplation consists most of all in the contemplation and knowledge of God."[20]

If for Thomas, as for Lear's Aristotle, contemplation of God,

17. *Summa theologiae* 1-2.3.8.

18. *Summa theologiae* 1-2.3.8.

19. See *Summa theologiae* 1.87.1, 3.

20. *Super Io.*, prologue, 2.

self, and world are so thoroughly intertwined, this suggests that it is a bit trickier than it might initially appear to separate out contemplation as a theological topic in Thomas. Indeed, "contemplate" proves to be a remarkably plastic term in Thomas's hands. At its broadest stretch, it seems more or less equivalent to thinking itself: to contemplate is to think about some thing so as to know its truth. Natural philosophers who study aquatic life or the motion of heavenly bodies lead contemplative lives of a sort. This is not, obviously, the most perfect form of contemplation, since it is a contemplation of things that are more (aquatic life) or less (heavenly bodies) mutable, and therefore less intrinsically knowable, but it is truly contemplation. What makes it contemplation, however, is not simply the plasticity of the term "contemplate" but the fact that the essence of both frogs and planets cannot be fully grasped until one arrives at contemplation of the first cause, without which there would be neither frogs nor planets. And, we should note, this contemplation of the first cause is not simply the bare knowing that there is a first cause but knowledge of the divine essence.

But this account of Thomas on the mutual implication of mundane and divine contemplation would be incomplete were we not also to note that the knowing of contemplation passes over into loving. Sometimes, in our concern to defend Thomas's "intellectualism" from the depredations of Scotists and others, we underplay the role of the will in contemplation. But Thomas notes that, were our wills not drawn to the good at which the contemplative life aims, we would never embark upon such a pursuit: "Through loving God we are aflame to gaze on his beauty."[21] Moreover, the will delights in that good once it has been attained. Thomas writes:

21. *Summa theologiae* 2-2.180.1.

> Although the contemplative life resides chiefly in the intellect, it has its beginning in the appetite, inasmuch as it is through charity that one is urged to the contemplation of God. And since the end corresponds to the beginning, it likewise follows that the terminus and the end of the contemplative life has its being in the appetite, since one delights in seeing the thing that is loved, and that very delight in the object seen arouses a yet greater love. Therefore Gregory says (*Hom. xiv in Ezech.*) that *when we see one whom we love, we are so aflame as to love him more*. And this is the ultimate perfection of the contemplative life, namely that the divine truth is not only seen but also loved.[22]

Here, it might seem that we have located the point of Thomas's parting of ways with Aristotle. But even though he lacks a developed account of the will, something like love of God is not entirely absent in Aristotle. For Aristotle, the first mover moves the world only by the attractive power it exerts, and so the world we contemplate has the character it does because it is driven by an appetite to imitate the first mover, to replicate in itself the intellectual order of God. We rational animals, we systematic knowers, more than any other beings, are moved to know the world out of a desire to imitate God.[23] Indeed, there is even a sense in Aristotle of a kind of ecstatic transcendence in which contemplation terminates; as Lear puts it in the passage I quoted earlier, "We must, paradoxically, transcend our own nature in order to realize it."[24]

Where Thomas does differ from Aristotle is in his belief that the phrase "love of God" can be read as a subjective genitive as well as an objective genitive—that is to say, the God we desire to imitate is one who has loved us first. The God of Christian faith

22. *Summa theologiae* 2-2.180.7 ad 1.

23. Both Lear and Thomas think that Aristotle's God is not quite so self-enclosed as is often claimed. See Lear, *Aristotle*, 302–3, and Aquinas, *Sententia Metaphysicae* 12.11.2614–16.

24. Lear, *Aristotle*, 303.

causes mundane actuality not simply by being lovable but by loving and by willing to call forth a world from nothing. Such a thought clearly does not—perhaps cannot—enter into Aristotle's understanding of the cosmos. This understanding of God as agent has a dual effect on Thomas's understanding of the relationship between contemplation of the world and contemplation of God.[25]

In one sense, it renders the natural world more opaque as an effect of God. Because God is an efficient cause of mundane essences and not, as with Aristotle, simply a final (and, perhaps, exemplary) cause, this means that the world flows freely from the divine will. Because the world is a contingent effect of God, it is less informative concerning its cause than would be a necessary effect. Since a frog, in reproducing, necessarily produces another frog, the shared frogginess of the effect and cause makes it possible for us to know the essence of the cause, whereas an artifact that an artisan chooses to produce might tell us that there *is* an artisan who is distinct from the artifact and of such a nature as to be able to produce the artifact, but it cannot really give us knowledge of the artisan's essence. Because God, as a free creator, bears an "artisanal" relation to the world, this means that by contemplation of nature, we can know of God "that he is cause of all creatures; and that creatures differ from him, so that he is not any of the things that are caused by him; and that this is not attributed to him on account of any defect in him, but because he surpasses all things."[26] But we cannot arrive at the divine essence itself, and the paucity of the payoff of mundane contemplation perhaps makes the natural world less intrinsically interesting for Thomas than it is for Aristotle.

In another sense, however, God as agent is *more* knowable. Thomas famously said, "No philosopher before the coming of Christ could, solely by the total effort of his own powers, know

25. My thanks to Dr. Zena Hitz for posing a question to me, after a public presentation of some of this material, that prompted the reflections in the remainder of this section.

26. *Summa theologiae* 1.12.12.

as much of God and the things necessary for eternal life as an old woman after the coming of Christ knows by faith."[27] God who freely acts to call the world into being also freely acts to show himself to humanity. Contemplation is not simply the terminus of the natural desire of humans as systematic understanders but is a gracious gift bestowed upon us so that knowledge of God does not remain something "available only to a few, and even then after a long time, and with the mixing in of many errors."[28] If God as agent makes the natural world less interesting to Thomas than it is to Aristotle, it perhaps makes history *more* interesting because it is in the timeful flow of human events that God speaks. Thomas notes, "While in every other *scientia* words refer to things, this *scientia* [of theology] is distinctive in that the things referred to by words also themselves refer to things."[29] The people and events of human history are, for Thomas, a kind of divine speech that shows God to us in a way that nature alone never could.

In contemplating the relationship of God, self, and world, Thomas clearly differs from Aristotle on the relationship of God and world, and consequently on how the world might signify God. But he also differs from Aristotle in his account of the self, for there is yet another thought that seems beyond Aristotle's ken: the damage that sin has wrought upon our contemplative capacity. Why does our mundane contemplation so often fail to lead to contemplation of God? While Aristotle certainly has an account of *akrasia*—a lack of self-mastery that inhibits virtue—he doesn't really have a fully developed notion of willing, which means he likewise lacks an account of that willful wrongdoing that we call "sin." To put it briefly, for Thomas, the natural dynamism of the intellect is diverted from its final end not only by

27. *In Symbolum Apostolorum*, prologue. It strikes me, upon reflection, that Thomas isn't actually famous for saying this; indeed, many people with a passing knowledge of Thomas would be shocked to know he said this. Perhaps I mean that he *should* be famous for having said this.

28. *Summa theologiae* 1.1.1.

29. *Summa theologiae* 1.1.12.

the body's passions, as in the case of Aristotelian *akrasia*, but also by a defective rational appetite, a will that has been wounded by sin. So we are doubly inhibited in what should be our natural passage from contemplation of the world to contemplation of God—not only by the world's timeful contingency but also by our willful perversity—inhibited in such a way that we need not simply self-mastery but also divine grace, not simply elevating but also healing. All of this requires a vision of God, self, and world in which God's act of love has priority, and this seems clearly a thought Aristotle could not think.

CONTEMPLATION IN THEOLOGY

Which at last brings us to the subject of theology. With all that I have said thus far as background, I would like to say something about how this account of contemplation shapes Thomas's understanding of theology.

As is well known, Thomas claims that *sacra doctrina*, holy teaching, is an enterprise that is both speculative and practical, but primarily speculative,[30] and in the *Summa theologiae*, he gives us a model of what this looks like, in which the practical inquiries of the *secunda pars* are framed by and enfolded in the speculative explorations of the *prima pars* and the *tertia pars*. But we should not think that Thomas means by "speculative" what we might mean. He certainly does not mean spinning out theories about God as personal reveries. What Thomas intends by characterizing holy teaching as "speculative" is to highlight the contemplative nature of this undertaking. And the particular nature of theology for Thomas is determined by his understanding of the nature of contemplation as having its beginning in God's effects, those mundane things that we desire to understand.

In asking the question of whether theology is *scientia*, one

30. See *Summa theologiae* 1.1.4.

of the arguments Thomas addresses is that *scientia* is not of particular things, whereas holy teaching deals with particular facts, "such as the deeds of Abraham, Isaac and Jacob and the like."[31] Theology would be, it seems, what he calls in his *Sentences* commentary a "narrative of signs . . . and examples,"[32] which suggests that it is not a science and certainly not a speculative science. But, Thomas responds, the particular facts concerning Abraham, Isaac, Jacob, and so forth are not in fact the principal concern of theology—they are included either as recounting miraculous events that point us toward the truth of revelation or as moral examples for us to follow (since practical reasoning needs examples). They are, in other words, instrumental, directing us toward a truth that exceeds the time-bound narrative of signs and examples, a truth that is nothing less than the timeless essence of God. Thomas speaks of how theology makes use of God's effects, "either of nature or of grace,"[33] so as to move from the effect to the cause. In this way, the narrative of divine revelation witnessed to in Scripture is, like the natural order itself, a created effect that should point us to God as first cause.

We can see how this works in considering the most perfect of all created effects: the sacred humanity of Christ. For as the most actual of God's created effects, it must therefore most clearly point us to the divine essence. In considering devotion, which is the chief act of the virtue of religion, Thomas addresses the question of whether contemplation causes devotion. One of the arguments against the thesis is that if contemplation were the cause of devotion, then the higher object of contemplation—i.e., the divine essence—would cause greater devotion, but in fact it seems that it is often contemplation of the humanity of Christ that causes the greatest devotion. So, the argument concludes, something else must be causing devotion. Thomas replies,

31. *Summa theologiae* 1.1.2 arg. 2.

32. *Super Sent.* 1, prologue, 1.5.

33. *Summa theologiae* 1.1.7 ad 1.

> Matters concerning the divinity are, in themselves, the strongest incentive to love and consequently to devotion, because God is supremely lovable. Yet the weakness of the human mind is such that it needs to be led by hand, not only to the knowledge, but also to the love of divine things by means of certain objects known to us through the senses. Among these the most important is the humanity of Christ, according to the words of the preface, *that through knowing God visibly, we may be caught up to the love of things invisible.* Therefore matters pertaining to Christ's humanity are the chief incentive to devotion, leading us as if by the hand, even though devotion itself has for its object matters concerning divinity.[34]

We see here not only the integral role played by elevating and healing grace in Thomas's account of contemplation but also the Christological character of that grace. For it is through the humanity of Christ as narrative sign that we encounter the preeminent effect of God by which, through the gift of faith, the passage from visible to invisible is brought about. Even in the case of Christ's humanity, it is only through abstracting from the particular created effect that one arrives at the invisible divine essence.

This movement from the visible to the invisible, from humanity to divinity, is seen in Thomas's discussion of the scene in John's Gospel where Thomas the Apostle encounters the risen Christ. He draws upon Gregory the Great's sermon on that scene, especially doubting Thomas's profession of "My Lord and my God," in which Gregory brings out the seeming disjunction between what Thomas's senses see and what his lips profess: "He apprehended a mere man, and testified that this was the invisible God."[35] Aquinas, in his own commentary, writes,

34. *Summa theologiae* 2-2.82.3 ad 2.

35. Gregory the Great, "Homily 26," in Gregory the Great, *Forty Gospel Homilies*, trans. David Hurst (Kalamazoo, MI: Cistercian, 1990), 207.

> It seems that Thomas quickly became a good theologian by professing a true faith. He professed the humanity of Christ when he said, "my Lord" . . . and he professed the divinity of Christ when he said, "and my God." . . . Thomas saw one thing and believed another. He saw the man and the wounds, and from these he believed in the divinity of the one who had arisen.[36]

It seems that what it means to be a good theologian is to be able to pass from knowing Christ after the flesh to being caught up in love of the invisible divine essence that he shares with the Father and the Spirit.

I would like to suggest that what is going on in becoming a good theologian is something analogous to what the marine biologist must do to become a good scientist. If theology is, as Anselm described it, *fides quaerens intellectum*, then what "seeking understanding" involves is something like a process of abstraction by which we move from the particular frog to its essential frogginess. To recount the narrative of God's dealings with the world through Abraham, Isaac, Israel, Jesus, and the Church, as important as that is, is not yet to be doing theology. Like the marine biologist seeking to grasp the intelligible structure of a frog's frogginess, the theologian seeks to grasp the intelligible structure of that narrative—and this intelligible structure is what I believe Thomas means by *convenientia* or "fittingness," the coherent convergence of elements by which the narrative comes together. To grasp this coherence is an activity of the systematic understander. For the narrative of signs and examples to be not merely perceived but to be grasped, there is needed the labor of contemplation, by which the facts of salvation history are "spiritualized" in our seeking to know them, raised to a higher level of actuality by being grasped by the intellect. Of course, the narrative itself can no more be left

36. *Super Io.* 20.6.2562, 2564.

behind for the higher realms of speculation than actual frogs can be left behind by the marine biologist. But the labor of contemplation allows the narrative to be understood with a new depth as the narrative of God.

Of course, "grasping the intelligible structure" is said analogously of frogs and narratives. A narrative, being an artifact woven by humans, does not have a substantial form in the way that a frog does. But Thomas is not interested in just any narrative (indeed, he seems quite uninterested in narrative in general) but in the particular narrative of signs that is God's dealings with the world. This narrative is not simply a human artifact but has God as its author, and it is a story woven not with words but with real people and events.[37] And while it might be odd to speak of a story having a substantial form that the mind grasps, to know the coherence of this particular story is, like knowing a substantial form, to know it as God knows it. It is to see at the center of the story the figure of Christ, the incarnate God to whom all prior history points and from whom all subsequent history flows, the one who is, quite literally, the *logos* or *ratio* of salvation history. Perhaps this is why, when an image of the crucified spoke to him in prayer, saying, "Thomas, you have written well of me; what reward would you have for your labor?" Thomas is reported to have replied, *Non nisi te, Domine*—"Nothing but you, Lord." To possess Christ is to grasp the essence of the narrative of salvation.[38]

So, for Thomas, "contemplation" is not a code word for a kind of mushy mysticism in which thought plays no role. Nor is it solely a nondiscursive beholding of God's essence. Rather, as Thomas notes in his commentary on the *Ethics*, "contemplation" includes both investigation to attain the truth and reflection on

37. See *Summa theologiae* 1.1.10. See also chapter 4, below.

38. See Guillaume de Tocco, *Ystoria sancti Thome de Aquino*, ed. Claire le Brun-Gouanvic (Toronto: Pontifical Institute of Mediaeval Studies, 1996), ch. 34. My thanks to the anonymous reader for *New Blackfriars* who pressed the issue of the disanalogy between narratives and substances, as well as the question of the truthfulness of the narrative in question.

the truth already attained; and while the latter is the superior activity since it is the end toward which investigation is ordered, the hard intellectual work of seeking the truth is no less truly contemplative.[39] Making the same point somewhat more expansively in the *Summa theologiae*, Thomas writes,

> The contemplative life has one act *in* which it is finally completed, namely the contemplation of truth, and from this act it derives its unity. Yet it has many acts *by* which it arrives at this final act. Some of these pertain to the reception of principles, from which it proceeds to the contemplation of truth; others are concerned with deducing from the principles, the truth, the knowledge of which is sought; and the final act, which completes it, is the contemplation itself of the truth.[40]

To contemplate the mysteries of faith is to apply the mind to them—to approach them as the "systematic understander" that we are by nature—by discerning principles and deducing conclusions until we arrive at the point where, Thomas says, "discursive reasoning ceases and the soul's gaze is fixed upon the contemplation of the one simple truth."[41]

This is the first movement of theology. While contemplation of one simple truth may be the crowning act of theological inquiry, it is not the last act of the theologian. There is a second act that follows, for the theological task terminates in sharing with others the fruits of contemplation, a process that might be thought of as the contemplative path run in reverse. For the theologian, fired by love of the divine essence, the discernment of principles and deducing of conclusions that have led to that one simple truth are put on orderly display so that others might retrace the path of that knowledge and love. Thomas is well known

39. See *Sententia Ethic.* 10.10.2092.

40. *Summa theologiae* 2-2.180.3.

41. *Summa theologiae* 2-2.180.6 ad 2.

for saying that when theologians are instructing an audience and "helping them understand the truth they already believe . . . reason should be used to get to the heart of the truth and enable them to know just how it is true." If we determine a theological question by sheer appeal to authority, without argumentation, we may inform people of the truth, but we "leave them empty."[42] The ministry of the teacher is to fill the mind of the student with his or her own discursive path as a systematic understander of the scriptural narrative of signs and examples, now bathed in the light of the teacher's own contemplation of the one simple truth that is the divine essence. But then, in order to become a systematic understander of the truth being taught, the student must non-identically re-enact the teacher's journey—not simply as an intellectual path but as a spiritual itinerary.

Jonathan Lear notes something analogous in seeking to grasp the fruits of Aristotle's contemplation. "We have come to understand his world by working through the very problems and thoughts Aristotle did. Thus our understanding of Aristotle is to some extent a re-enactment of his thinking."[43] We who study Thomas Aquinas can likewise say that as we work through the same problems and thoughts that he did, we seek to re-enact his thinking so that we might catch a glimpse of the one for love of whom Thomas studied, watched, labored, preached, and taught. Through the many questions and articles of the *Summa theologiae*, through the textual divisions and intellectual sifting of his Scripture commentaries, even through the sometimes tediously detailed commentaries on Aristotle, Thomas continues to share with us the fruits of his contemplation. It seems appropriate that the Ambrosian liturgy, in the Eucharistic Preface appointed for his feast day, should praise Thomas with these words:

42. *Quodlibet* 4.9.3.

43. Lear, *Aristotle*, 316.

He turned his back on wealth and honours
and opened his heart to the light of your word,
aspiring to teach with clarity and insight
what he had received in loving contemplation.[44]

44. English translation from *We Give You Thanks and Praise: The Ambrosian Eucharistic Prefaces*, trans. Alan Griffiths (Franklin, WI: Sheed & Ward, 2000), 173.

3

Praeambula Fidei

FAITH AND PROOF

Almost all of the undergraduates I teach think that it is a proposition bordering on the absurd to say that one might be able to demonstrate God's existence. This view is held not only, as might be expected, by unbelievers but by devout believers as well. Typically, when I press them as to why they are so sure of this, most of them will say that we lack physical evidence of God's existence, and in the absence of physical evidence, you cannot prove anything. Some—and this is usually those who are believers—will also say that the whole point is that belief in God cannot be proven—that's why they call it "belief," after all.

It is no secret that Thomas Aquinas thought differently. Thomas quite famously offered in *Summa theologiae* 1.2.3 five ways in which the statement "God exists" might be demonstrated to be true. Each of these argued, based on something that is evident to us (the phenomenon of change or the orderliness by which natural things attained their ends, for example), for the existence of something not evident to us, a transcendent source of what is evident to us that at least some people called "God." Thomas went to some trouble to argue that, while God's existence is not self-evident to us (in the way that a whole being greater than a part or a line being the shortest distance between two points is evident to us), it could be made evident to us (in the way

* Originally published as "*Praeambula fidei*: What is the Purpose of the Proofs of God's Existence?" *Church Life Journal*, September 23, 2021.

that, in a right triangle, the square of the hypotenuse equaling the sum of the square of the two sides can be made evident to us). This would seem to put Thomas in direct opposition to my students, who so fervently believe in the indemonstrability of God's existence.

Thomas sums up the matter of what reason can know with demonstrable certainty about God in this way:

> We know of his relationship with creatures, so that he is the cause of them all; and we know that creatures differ from him, so that he is not any of the things that are caused by him; and we know that this is not attributed to him on account of any defect in him, but because he surpasses all things.[1]

This suggests that it is not merely the bare affirmation "God exists" that we can demonstrate; there are in addition other statements that might also be shown to be true, such as "God is eternal" and "God is good" and "God is wise" and (perhaps most mysteriously) "God is simple." These would seem to add to the affirmation of what people call "God" many of the divine attributes that people traditionally associate with God. So it would seem that Thomas held for a rather capacious body of rationally demonstrable truth claims concerning God.

Yet, at the same time, Thomas also said that what we could know about God by this means was relatively meager. Were human reason left on its own, "the truth about God that reason could discover, would only be known by a few, and after a long time, and with many errors mixed in."[2] In numerous places, Thomas alludes to John of Damascus's statement that we do not know what God is but rather only what God is not,[3] and this seems to be the case especially with what human reason can discover on its

1. *Summa theologiae* 1.12.12.

2. *Summa theologiae* 1.1.1.

3. For example, *Super Sent.* 4.49.2.7 ad 7; *Contra Gentiles* 1.30; *Summa theologiae* 1.1.9.

own. So, Thomas thought, because our whole salvation depends on knowing God, God has not left us to our own devices with regard to knowledge about God but has given us, through divine revelation, knowledge surpassing what reason could discover on its own.

How does Thomas manage to combine what seems to us a quite astonishing optimism about human reason with a realism-bordering-on-pessimism concerning the extent of what we can know concerning God? Also, how might he help us think about how those things that reason *can* discover on its own are related to the life of faith and to those truths about God that we hold on the basis of faith? A chief hint Thomas gives us to how he sees that relation is the term he occasionally uses for the truths that reason can discover: he calls them *praeambula fidei*—literally, "what walks ahead of/before faith"—and he contrasts them with the articles of faith, such as we find in the creed.[4] So we might ask, in what sense do these rationally demonstrable truths about God precede or walk before what we hold on faith?

BUILDING FOUNDATIONS

One perhaps obvious way to think about this is as a kind of temporal priority. That is, we can apply our minds to the question of God, and then, once we have proven what can be proven, we can add to those truths other non-provable truths, such as the Trinity and the Incarnation. We might think of this as the building-foundation approach: you must first have the basis for faith laid in reason, and the truths of faith can then rest securely on truths of reason. I do not think you find many people in the

4. Though the term *praeambula* is associated with Thomas, it is one that he uses relatively infrequently and in the technical sense examined here only in his commentary on Boethius's *De Trinitate* and in the *Summa theologiae*. In a few other places he uses the term in analogous ways that might be helpful for grasping how he uses it in the realm of faith and reason: sense images (*phantasmata*) are preambles to the act of the intellect (*De unitate intellectus* 4; *Super De divinis nominibus* 4.9.414) and *synderesis* is a preamble to the act of virtue (*De veritate* 16.2 ad 5).

tradition who explicitly advocate for this approach. If you look at some older manuals of apologetics, however—which seek first to demonstrate the existence and attributes of God, then the possibility of a divine revelation, and then go on to make probable arguments for the Catholic Church being the bearer of this revelation—you can get the distinct impression that such works presume that one needs to be rationally convinced of some truths concerning God before one can move on to embrace the truths of faith.

This is not the approach of Thomas Aquinas. We might think it is, however, when confronted with statements like this one in his commentary on Boethius's *De Trinitate,* where regarding propositions such as "God exists" and "God is one," he notes that "such truths about God or about his creatures, subject to philosophical proof, faith presupposes."[5] But whatever he means here by "presupposes," he does not mean that such proofs must precede faith in time, nor does he mean that faith cannot be had without a basis in such proofs. Certainly, by the time he writes the *Summa theologiae*, he does not approach the preambles of faith as a distinct body of knowledge that one must establish before one can embrace a quite different body of knowledge contained in the articles of faith. Thomas writes,

> The existence of God and other similar things that can be known about God by natural reason, as Romans says (1:19), are not articles of faith but preambles to the articles. For faith presupposes natural knowledge just as grace presupposes nature and perfections presuppose something that can be perfected. Nevertheless, nothing prevents something that in itself is capable of being demonstrated and known from being

5. *Super De Trinitate* 2.3.

> accepted as worthy of belief by someone who cannot grasp its demonstration.[6]

I will come back to Thomas's statement that "faith presupposes natural knowledge just as grace presupposes nature," but for now I want to focus on the last sentence.

Thomas recognizes three things regarding knowledge of God and salvation.

First, our salvation depends on our knowledge of God because we can only move toward God as the goal of our existing if we have at least *some* knowledge of God. If you walked north from Baltimore, you would, as a point of fact, be walking toward Canada; but you could only be engaged in the activity we call "Being on a journey to Canada" if you had the purpose of arriving in Canada, which involves having some knowledge that there *is* a Canada, even if this is only a dim and cloudy perception of the true nature of that mysterious place. Likewise, if our lives are to be understood as a journey toward God, then we who are on that journey must have some knowledge that there is a God, even if it is only a dim and cloudy perception. So salvation, the culmination of the journey toward God, requires some knowledge of God.

Second, metaphysics is hard. The kind of abstract thinking it calls for—the passage from knowledge of the mundane physical objects that are the natural objects of our human intelligence to the nonmaterial truths that can be deduced from them—is something that not everyone is inclined toward or has time for or is capable of. Moreover, because the natural object of our intelligence is the physical world, metaphysics as a human practice has a certain kind of imprecision to it; it is like trying to do wood sculpting with a chainsaw. It is pretty impressive what some people can achieve with a chainsaw but, let's be frank, it's not exactly

6. *Summa theologiae* 1.2.2 ad 1.

fine art. All of this is why Thomas says, "The truth about God such as reason could discover, would only be known by a few, and that after a long time, and with the admixture of many errors."[7]

Third, God is a gracious and loving God who, as 1 Timothy says, desires that all people be saved and come to knowledge of the truth. This is why God, knowing the difficulty and imprecision of metaphysics, shares with humanity knowledge of himself in divine revelation, so that even those who do not have the inclination or time or ability to engage in metaphysical reflection, as well as those who do but do it in an inadequate way ("I'm sorry, but that sculpture of an owl looks more like a beagle"), might have the knowledge of God needed to journey toward God as the goal of their existence. So, Thomas tells us, the truths about God that can be rationally demonstrated—that God exists and is the cause of all things; that God is not any of the things that are caused by him; that God surpasses all things—are also contained in the deposit of faith. Most people, in fact, accept these truths on the basis of faith and not on the basis of rational demonstration.

All of which is to say that Thomas clearly does not think that faith requires a foundation of rationally demonstrated truths about God. Indeed, for most people, it is faith all the way down, and this is just fine. Not only fine but in some ways better. The knowledge had through faith is not a second-best substitute for knowledge had through demonstration; it is in fact the sublime knowledge of God and the blessed shared with us wayfarers. Thomas says in one of his sermons (and I don't think he was merely pandering to his lay audience) that an old woman with faith knows more about God than the greatest of philosophers.[8] Her knowledge is, of course, more *ex*tensive than the knowledge that the philosopher has wrested from the world via reason—including such mysteries as the triune nature of God

7. *Summa theologiae* 1.1.1.

8. *In Symbolum Apostolorum*, prologue.

and the Incarnation—but it is also more *in*tensive, because faith involves not only intellectual assent to truth but also the will being drawn by the beauty of the truths proposed. Truths held on faith engage the volitional aspect of the human person in a way that demonstrated truths do not. This is why faith is meritorious, while acceptance of a demonstrated truth, in and of itself, is not.[9]

LAYER CAKES

So, for Thomas, the preambles are not a foundation that must be laid before faith can be established. But what about a variation on the building-foundation approach, one that we might call the layer-cake approach? Here, the demonstrated truths of reason do not need to come before the truths embraced in faith in terms of a temporal sequence—you can bake both layers of your cake at the same time, as it were—but they are clearly distinct, and the faith-layer definitely rests on top of the reason-layer. Presumably, you could also have a cake without layers—an all-faith cake—and this may be what most people will do, given the difficulty and opportunities for failure involved in baking the reason-layer. But if you do, for whatever reason, opt for the layer cake, your goal (as the judges on *The Great British Bake Off* would tell you) is to make sure that your layers are distinct and do not bleed into one another.

This might seem closer to Thomas's view, but it still does not quite get it. And to see why it does not quite get it, we can return to Thomas's statements that "faith presupposes natural knowledge just as grace presupposes nature and perfections presuppose something that can be perfected."[10] This is one of a handful of similar statements we find in Thomas about grace and nature that

9. See *Summa theologiae* 2-2.2.10.

10. *Summa theologiae* 1.2.2 ad 1.

have excited intense interest among theologians, particularly in the mid-twentieth century. For my purposes, I would like to focus on the analogy Thomas draws:

natural knowledge : faith :: the perfectible : perfection

It seems to me that the key here is to remember that for Thomas the model of what it means for something to be perfected is the perfection of matter by form. That is to say, a thing's potential to become something in the fullest sense involves the complete transformation of that thing through the reception of a new form. The potential of a tree stump to become, through the agency of the artisan and the instrumentality of the chainsaw, a sculpture of an owl involves the tree ceasing to be a tree and becoming wholly an owl sculpture. There does not remain a "tree layer" over which is laid an "owl-sculpture layer." Metaphysically speaking, it is owl sculpture all the way down. So too with natural knowledge and faith. Even for the philosopher who has attained some natural knowledge of God, through grace that natural knowledge becomes wholly transformed into the meritorious, charity-infused assent we call faith.

But this can't be quite right. After all, Thomas famously says that "grace does not take away nature but perfects it,"[11] and what I am saying here might seem to suggest that the knowledge of faith takes away natural knowledge. Here again, I think the analogy of the perfectible and the perfect, thought of in terms of matter and form, is helpful. In the real world, we never encounter prime matter (which exists only in the realm of thought) but only matter existing under some form. It seems to me that things often, if not always, retain some legacy of the previous forms under which their matter existed, and that legacy gives a distinctive quality to those perfected things. That is to say, an owl sculpture that is

11. *Summa theologiae* 1.1.8 ad 2.

a perfection of a tree stump is going to have certain distinctive qualities not possessed by an owl sculpture that is the perfection of, say, a lump of plasticine. The matter lends to the perfected object something of its prior history as a tree stump: the grain and color of the wood, the inherent possibilities and limitations of the medium, etc. The wooden owl sculpture engages in being an owl sculpture differently than a plasticine owl sculpture does.

In like manner, I think that the metaphysically minded believer engages in believing differently than the non-metaphysically minded believer does. Not, of course, in terms of the content of faith. Both will be believers—and, as it were, believers all the way down—but the believer who has, whether before or after having come to faith, labored at demonstrating those truths concerning God that can be demonstrated, will possess his or her faith in a distinctive way; it will have a particular quality to it. Being metaphysically minded is perfected by faith, not taken away. And being perfected, this inclination to abstraction and rational argument will also serve the faith in ways that go beyond demonstrating things like God's existence, unity, goodness, etc.

For Thomas says that demonstrating such preambles is only one way in which reason serves faith. Reason also serves faith in providing "a clearer notion, by certain similitudes, of the truths of faith."[12] This often works by means of what Thomas calls arguments from "fittingness," which use the tools of reason not to demonstrate truths but to see the patterned coherence of the truths of faith in relation to one another. Reason also serves faith by "resist[ing] those who speak against the faith, either by showing that their statements are false, or by showing that they are not necessarily true."[13] The mind that is skilled in demonstration

12. *Super De Trinitate* 2.3.

13. *Super De Trinitate* 2.3.

ought to be equally skilled in debunking fallacious demonstrations and so serve faith in this way as well.

In some ways, it may be unfortunate that Thomas chose on occasion to use the term *praeambula fidei* to speak of those truths about God that are capable of rational demonstration, since it can suggest something that is a necessary prelude to faith without which faith has no foundation. I hope I have shown that this is not what he meant. But the word "preamble" does still have some value. It has the value of asserting that some truths that most of us hold on faith are in fact capable of rational demonstration, such that faith is the perfection and not the destruction of the reason one possessed before receiving the gift of faith. This is certainly useful in dealing with students, both believers and unbelievers, who think that faith involves embracing the irrational. It is also useful for suggesting that those who labor to grasp the highest reaches of human understanding—whether the great thinkers of antiquity or the honest seekers of today—can be understood as people who are, though perhaps only dimly realizing it, wayfarers walking toward faith, the faith that can give them a truer sense of that toward which they fare.

4

God as Author

Thinking Through a Metaphor

> Metaphor is the dreamwork of language and, like all dreamwork, its interpretation reflects as much on the interpreter as on the originator. . . . Understanding a metaphor is as much a creative endeavor as making a metaphor, and as little guided by rules.[1]

The late Herbert McCabe wrote, "Unless our lives are a story told by God they are not a story at all, and this means they have no final meaning."[2] In what follows, rather than addressing McCabe's claim itself—that God is necessary for our lives to have ultimate meaning—I want to think about the metaphor by means of which that claim is made: God as storyteller or author. Moreover, I will put this metaphor to a somewhat different purpose than McCabe did: rather than using it to think about the meaningfulness of our lives, I will seek to use it to think about the relationship of the world to God, its author. My hope is that thinking through this metaphor, both in the sense of using the metaphor as an instrument for reflection and also in the sense of

* Originally published as "God as Author: Thinking Through a Metaphor," *Modern Theology* 31, no. 4 (October 2015): 573–85.

1. Donald Davidson, "What Metaphors Mean," in *The Essential Davidson* (Oxford: Oxford University Press, 2006), 209.

2. Herbert McCabe, *Faith Within Reason*, ed. Brian Davies (London: Continuum, 2007), 42.

considering the ramifications of that metaphor, will cast a helpful light on how we understand the relationship of God to the world.

As I shall indicate later, not every designation of God as "author" that we find in the tradition is metaphorical, since the Latin word *auctor*, from which our English word derives, has a wide range of meanings, many of which can be non-metaphorically predicated of God. So I should stipulate at the outset that I am thinking of a quite specific use of the term "author": the author who produces a book—a book, moreover, that is in the genre "novel." I shall have more to say about these two stipulations further on, but here I simply want to make the point that speaking about God as author in this sense is clearly metaphorical because it is clearly false.

I am more interested in thinking through the metaphor of God as author than in exploring exactly what we are doing when we "think through a metaphor," and so will not offer even a partial account of the nature of metaphor. But I do need to say something about the falsity of metaphors.[3] Though not all metaphors state something untrue—to use a famous example, the statement "No man is an island" is both true and a metaphor—most do. In this way, they differ from both similes and analogies.[4] Tony

3. For a discussion of metaphor in a theological context that surveys in brief compass the major discussions of the past forty-or-so years, see Jan Muis, "The truth of metaphorical God-talk," *Scottish Journal of Theology* 63, no. 2 (May 2010): 146–62. I remain unconvinced by Muis's distinction between "literal meaning" and "metaphorical meaning" since I think it posits a level of meaning that is not needed in order to claim that metaphors convey something true but rather grows out of an unwarranted fear of subjectivism. When someone asks what a metaphor *means* (as opposed to other things a metaphor might do), we can give a satisfactory account in non-metaphorical discourse. See note 5 below.

4. On similes, see Davidson, "What Metaphors Mean," 218. We might also ask whether this metaphor of God as author is in fact not a metaphor but rather an analogy: God is to the world as an author is to a book. I raise this difficulty because the distinction between metaphor and analogy is often drawn quite sharply, largely based on the fact, as noted at the outset, that metaphors state something that is literally false while analogies state something true. It is true that both a urine sample and a diet can be called "healthy," albeit not in a univocal sense, because they both stand in relation to a healthy body: one as a sign of the body's health and the other as a cause of it. Applying the word "author" to both God and a human being cannot be done analogically in the same sense because there is no third term to which they are related. This does not, however, necessarily mean that metaphor and analogy are utterly opposed. Indeed, Aristotle identifies proportional analogies, such as God-is-to-world-as-author-is-to-book, as a species of

Bennett did not actually leave his heart in San Francisco, and all the world is not in fact a stage. And, in the case of God, that than which no greater can be thought, *esse ipsum subsistens*, is not in fact a novelist. But to say that a metaphor states something false about its subject is not the same as saying that its speaker is mistaken or deceptive, nor that it does not convey something true about that subject. When Tony Bennett tells us that he left his heart in San Francisco, he is neither in error nor lying, and we know something about him that we did not know previously, even though what we now know about him has nothing to do with the state of his circulatory system.[5]

To think through a metaphor, therefore, puts one in the odd situation of seeking truth by means of a statement that is, taken literally, false. Such a procedure, however, seems particularly fitting when one is seeking truths concerning God, for it is a part of the inevitable stammering of human language about God. Catherine of Siena responds to her encounter with God, whom she describes (metaphorically) as a "mad lover," by writing, "And what shall I say? I will stutter: 'A-a,' because there is nothing else I know how to say. Finite language cannot express the emotion

metaphor (*Poetics* 1457a.7–34). Such types of analogy seem to be particularly close to metaphor since they seem to underlie such obvious metaphors as God as an author or the world as a book. So at least for our purposes here, we ought not worry too much about the analogy-metaphor distinction. For a brief account of some of the complexities of the relationship between metaphor and analogy, see Ralph McInerny, "Metaphor and Analogy," in *Studies in Analogy* (The Hague: Martinus Nijhoff, 1968), 67–84.

5. Nor is what we know about him something metaphorical. Though such a view has been unfashionable for a while now, I am inclined to think that what we come to know via a metaphor is not, in terms of cognitive content, irreducible to non-metaphorical knowledge. That is, I think there is much merit to the view of Aquinas that the primary value of metaphors is pedagogical—i.e., that they convey something that at least in principle can be known non-metaphorically (see *Summa theologiae* 1.1.9). But to say that the meaning of a metaphor is reducible to a non-metaphorical meaning is not to say that there might not be an irreducible value to metaphor, since the value of an utterance is not entirely determined by meaning (otherwise, we could not distinguish between, say, a beautiful poem and a lame one). I see no denigration of metaphor in the view that it can help me grasp a point that another (say, the all-knowing God) might grasp without a metaphor, particularly since metaphors can often convey a richness of cognitive content in highly compact form that could not, practically speaking, be conveyed discursively (not unlike the way a picture can be worth a thousand words).

of the soul who longs for you infinitely."[6] So as I try to think through this metaphor, I should not be surprised if my thinking stutters and stammers.

GOD AS "AUTHOR" IN THE TRADITION

The metaphor of God as author would seem at first glance to be closely related to the metaphor of nature as a book by which we come to knowledge of God—a metaphor that is ubiquitous from the Church Fathers, through the medieval period, and persists, though occurring less frequently, even today.[7] Origen, for example, paralleled the difficulties of interpreting Scripture and those of interpreting nature: "We must not therefore blame the Maker of the universe because, say, we cannot discover why basilisks and other venomous creatures were created. Similarly, we should see that the Divine Scriptures also contain many mysteries of which it is hard for us to give an account."[8] Evagrius Ponticus tells us that when Anthony of Egypt was asked by a philosopher how he could survive without books, he replied, "My book, sir philosopher, is the nature of created things, and it is always at hand when I wish to read the words of God."[9] Similarly, Augustine of Hippo wrote,

> Some, in order to find God, read books. But the very appearance of creatures is a kind of book: behold those above you and those below you! Note! Read! God, whom you wish to know, did not make letters with ink; rather, he has placed before your

6. Catherine of Siena, *The Dialogue* ch. 153, trans. Suzanne Noffke (New York: Paulist, 1980), 325.

7. For an overview, see Peter J. Hess, "'God's Two Books': Revelation, Theology and Natural Science in the Christian West," in *Interdisciplinary Perspectives on Cosmology & Biological Evolution*, ed. Hilary D. Regan and Mark Worthing (Adelaide, AU: ATF, 2002), 19–49. For the persistence of the metaphor in the modern period, see the essays in *The Book of Nature in Early Modern and Modern History*, ed. Klaas van Berkel and Arie Johan Vanderjagt (Leuven: Peeters, 2006).

8. Origen, *Philocalia* 2.5.

9. Evagrius Ponticus, *Praktikos* 92.

eyes these things that he did make. Who could seek for a greater voice? Heaven and earth call out to you: God made me![10]

This tradition continues in the Middle Ages: in the seventh century, Julian of Toledo (642–690) noted that "this whole world is somewhat like a book, written by the finger of God,"[11] and five centuries later, Alan of Lille (1128–1202) similarly noted that "the whole created world is like a book and a picture" (*Omnis mundi creatura / Quasi liber, et pictura*).[12] Hugh of St. Victor (1096–1141) spoke in a somewhat different manner of wisdom as a book written internally in us, and both creation and the Incarnation as two external books, the second more perfect than the first.[13] In the thirteenth century, St. Bonaventure (1221–1274) wrote of the book of creation along with the book of Scripture as sources of knowledge of God[14] but also employed Hugh's language of a writing that is both interior and exterior.[15] Adapting the metaphor to new technology, John Calvin (1509–1564) proposed that sin had blurred our vision, so that we need the "spectacles" of Scripture in order to read the book of nature properly.[16] In the early modern period, Francis Bacon (1561–1626) spoke of nature as "the book of God's works,"[17] and recently Pope Francis wrote of how his namesake, Francis of Assisi, "invites us to see nature as a magnificent book in which God speaks to us and grants us a glimpse of his infinite beauty and goodness."[18]

10. Augustine, *Sermones A. Mai* 126.6.

11. Julian of Toledo, *Commentarius in Nahum Prophetam,* incipit expositio 34 (PL 96:723B).

12. Alan of Lille, *De incarnatione Christi rhythmus perelegans* 419 (PL 210: 579A).

13. Hugh of St. Victor, *De Sacramentis* 1.6.5.

14. Bonaventure, *Itinerarium Mentis in Deum* 1.14. Cf. *Collationes in Hexameron* 12.14–17, which speaks of three books: the material creation, the angelic creation, and Scripture.

15. Bonaventure, *Itinerarium Mentis in Deum* 6.7.

16. John Calvin, *Institutes of the Christian Religion* 1.5.1, ed. John T. McNeill, trans. Ford Lewis Battles (Louisville, KY: Westminster John Knox, 1960), 1:52–53, 70.

17. Francis Bacon, *The Advancement of Learning* 1.3 (London: MacMillan, 1876), 10.

18. Francis, *Laudato si'* 6, encyclical letter, May 24, 2015, vatican.va. In using this image, he echoes his immediate predecessors. See, for example, John Paul II, *Fides et Ratio* 19, encyclical

Given the prevalence of the metaphors, similes, and analogies of nature as a book, it is somewhat surprising to find that the presence of the metaphor of God as author is not so easily discerned. First, one is confronted, in the Latin-speaking West at least, with a vertigo-inducing breadth of meanings encompassed by the term *auctor*. The Lewis and Short lexicon gives this definition: "He that brings about the existence of any object, or promotes the increase or prosperity of it, whether he first originates it, or by his efforts gives greater permanence or continuance to it."[19] It goes on to offer as possible translations, "creator, maker, author, inventor, producer, father, founder, teacher, composer, cause, voucher, supporter, leader, head." So when, for example, Augustine in *The City of God* calls God *naturarum omnium auctor*,[20] it is not entirely clear that we are dealing with a metaphor that correlates to the metaphor of nature as a book; we might simply be encountering the non-metaphorical claim that God is the Creator of all natures. While we find both the book of nature and the book of Scripture spoken of frequently in the Fathers, the language of God as author—whether of nature or of Scripture—is not as prominent among them as we might expect.[21] To my knowledge, even those patristic and medieval authors in whom we find reference to nature as a book do not make much of an explicit connection to the notion of God as author, beyond the rather simple point that nature, as well as Scripture, can be "read" in order to attain the knowledge God wishes to convey.

In the later Middle Ages, we seem to find more references to

letter, September 14, 1998, www.vatican.va; Benedict XVI, *Caritas in Veritate* 51, encyclical letter, June 29, 2009, vatican.va. For a recent Protestant example, see the reformed Anglican theologian Alister E. McGrath, *Scientific Theology*, vol. 1, *Nature* (Grand Rapids, MI: Eerdmans, 2001), 117–20.

19. *A Latin Dictionary, Founded on Andrews' edition of Freund's Latin dictionary*, revised, enlarged, and in great part rewritten by Charlton T. Lewis and Charles Short (Oxford: Clarendon, 1879), s.v. "auctor."

20. Augustine, *De civitate Dei* 11.25.

21. With regard to Scripture, see the brief remarks in Denis Farkasfalvy, *Inspiration and Interpretation: A Theological Introduction to Sacred Scripture* (Washington, DC: The Catholic University of America Press, 2010), 180.

God as *auctor*. Perhaps it is with the rise of the notion of theology as an Aristotelian science, with its emphasis on the world's relationship to God as one of efficient causality rather than simply one of reflection, that the notion of God as *auctor*—in the sense of efficient cause—of both nature and Scripture becomes more important.[22] Furthermore, with the proliferation of new and rediscovered philosophical and theological texts beginning in the twelfth century, we see a growth of interest in, and concern about, *auctoritas*. Indeed, the entire Scholastic project might be seen as the harnessing of human reason to the task of showing the *concordia auctoritatum* (harmony of the authorities).[23] Perhaps unsurprisingly, references to God as *auctor* proliferate in writers like Thomas Aquinas.

Thomas teaches clearly that God is the author of Scripture,[24] but he also speaks of God as the author of nature.[25] In addition, for Thomas, God is *auctor* of the intellect,[26] of the influx of the light of grace,[27] of the evil of penalty,[28] and of life and death.[29] Moreover, Christ was not only, following the Vulgate translation of Hebrews 2:10, the *auctor* of our salvation[30] but also of the sacraments[31] and of glory.[32] This variety of uses of the term *auctor*

22. This shift is hinted at in Beryl Smalley, *The Study of the Bible in the Middle Ages* (Notre Dame, IN: University of Notre Dame Press, 1964), 293. The increased emphasis on efficient causality would seem to make God more directly the "author" of Scripture (via the human authors of Scripture as secondary causes) than would a more general notion of "inspiration."

23. See Marie-Dominique Chenu, *Toward Understanding St. Thomas*, trans. A.M. Landry and D. Hughes (Chicago: Henry Regnery, 1964), 126–49.

24. *Summa theologiae* 1.1.10.

25. For example, *Summa theologiae* 1.22.2 ad 3; 1.60.1 ad 2, 3; 1.92.1 ad 1; 2-2.154.12 ad 1.

26. *Summa theologiae* 1.12.2.

27. *Summa theologiae* 1.89.1 ad 3.

28. *Summa theologiae* 1.48.6; 2-2.191 ad 3.

29. *Summa theologiae* 2-2.104.4 ad 2.

30. *Summa theologiae* 1.43.7; 2-2.114.6; 3.7.3 ad 2. In his commentary on Hebrews, Thomas makes nothing of the possible metaphorical resonances of "author" in this passage. See *Super Heb.* 1.3.128.

31. *Summa theologiae* 3.72.1 ad 4.

32. *Summa theologiae* 3.53.3 ad 3.

indicates that we are still in something of a quandary with regard to knowing whether we are dealing with a metaphor in which God is presented as the one who writes the story of the world or simply the non-metaphorical claim that God causes these things. I am inclined to think the latter is the case. Even in the claim that God is the *auctor* of Scripture, the focus is more on authority and causality than on what we might think of as creative authorship. Moreover, perhaps somewhat surprisingly, unlike his contemporary Bonaventure, Thomas speaks rarely of the book of nature or creation.[33] We do find, in his discussion of God as the *auctor* of Scripture, the claim that God can signify his meaning not only with words but also with events, which suggests that perhaps we might think of history as a kind of story.[34] But this suggestion, however intriguing it might be, is not put to further theological use by Thomas. It is not, in other words, a metaphor he thinks through.

Why, given the prevalence of the metaphor of nature as a book, do patristic and medieval authors not attempt to exploit the theological possibilities latent in the metaphor of God as author in relationship to the book of creation? Why does a theologian like Aquinas, who does speak of God as signifying meaning by historical events, not exploit this idea further, or even speak of creation as the book God writes? I suggest that the author-metaphor as a way of speaking and thinking about God's relationship to creation did not seem like a particularly interesting or fruitful one prior to the advent of modernity for at least two reasons.

First, the Middle Ages, for all their interest in *auctoritas*, still had a relatively humble conception of the author of a book. Though there are exceptions, such as Abelard or Dante, authorship was not generally thought of as involving much in the way

33. The closest he comes is in *De veritate* 7.5 ad 6, where, in speaking of the "book of life," he says that "God can be called the book of creatures and vice versa" (i.e., creatures can be called the book of God).

34. *Summa theologiae* 3.1.10.

of creativity. Indeed, many of the most important authors were more compilers than creators of new texts. While writers such as Bede and Peter Lombard perhaps took a certain amount of pride in their literary works, their activity was in some ways more akin to scrapbooking than to what we today think of as authorship. Though creativity—and, in the case of Bede, perhaps a bit of fiction writing—was no doubt involved,[35] the author was seen more as a demiurge shaping preexistent material than as a true creator. This not-unintended lack of novelty that characterized so much premodern writing probably made the title of "author" seem like meager praise of the God who created the world *ex nihilo*. Perhaps Western culture needed the modern romantic notion of the author-as-creative-genius before the metaphor could come alive as a way of speaking about the Creator God.

Second, the metaphor of God as author needed a further invention of modernity: the novel—specifically, the so-called "realistic" novel, which, again allowing for some exceptions, is generally thought to arrive on the scene with Defoe's *Robinson Crusoe*. Let me stipulate that by "realistic," I mean not a correspondence to the way things actually are or were but rather the creation of a more-or-less complete narrative world in which the plot—as the interaction of individual characters and events over time within a given space—provides a plausible matrix of causes for explaining the action of the novel.[36] A novel is realistic not because of its gritty subject matter or hard-nosed pessimism, nor even because it presents to us a world that bears a close similarity to our own, but rather because it is a self-consistent world, one that makes

35. On the use of fiction in medieval histories, see Nancy F. Partner, "Medieval Histories and Modern Realism: Yet Another Origin of the Novel," *MLN* 114, no. 4 (1999): 857–73.

36. Though written in the middle of the last century, Ian Watt, *The Rise of the Novel: Studies in Defoe, Richardson and Fielding* (London: Chatto and Windus, 1957) remains a standard touchstone in defining the genre of the realistic novel. See especially pp. 9–34. My own views on "realism" have obviously been influenced by Hans Frei and his notion of realistic narrative as "cumulative rendering of persons and reality through narrative continuity in time" (*The Eclipse of Biblical Narrative: A Study in Eighteenth and Nineteenth Century Hermeneutics* [New Haven, CT: Yale University Press, 1974], 147).

sense on its own terms. One might say that I am taking "realism" to be more a matter of coherence than of correspondence. In this way, both *The Grapes of Wrath* and *The Hunger Games* are realistic novels, whereas *Alice's Adventures in Wonderland* and Kafka's *The Castle* are, by design, not.[37] Even modernist novels such as *To the Lighthouse* and *Ulysses*, which seem to subvert the traditional novelistic rendering of reality through the interaction of character and event by such techniques as stream of consciousness and multiple narrative perspectives, do so in order to render, as Erich Auerbach argued, "nothing less than the wealth of reality and depth of life in every moment to which we surrender ourselves without prejudice."[38] At the same time, while the world of the realistic novel need not correspond to any actual world that is or was, the characters and events of the novel must correspond closely enough to those that are familiar to its readers that they can perceive the coherence of the interactions that drive the plot (which is why the characters in so many science fiction novels set in the far future or on distant planets seem so much like people of our own time and place). The author of the novel is not simply a creative genius but the creator of a fictional world. As I hope becomes apparent, it is really only once we have this sort of book and, consequently, this sort of author that the metaphor of God as author becomes truly useful.

Having now made some preliminary moves in thinking through the metaphor of God as author, I would like to attempt to deploy that metaphor.

THE WORLD AS GOD'S NOVEL

When we as readers enter the world of a realistic novel, we expect to find a narrative "space" in which there exists sufficient

37. This, however, must be qualified by what I say below concerning "magical realism."

38. Erich Auerbach, *Mimesis: The Representation of Reality in Western Literature*, trans. Willard R. Trask (Princeton, NJ: Princeton University Press, 1953), 552.

motivation on the part of characters to make their actions comprehensible. It is this that allows us to "lose ourselves" in the story: the story provides us with a plausible network of causes that enables us to remain within the narrative space. Even in a post-apocalyptic fantasy world, if we want to know why Katniss Everdeen, the protagonist of *The Hunger Games*, hunts with a bow rather than a rifle, we need to have sufficient knowledge of the historical and political events that provide the setting in which the character lives, as well as a character whose personality is rendered with sufficient richness, in order for the actions of the character to be believable, to be "realistic." Presumably, in a perfectly realistic novel, perhaps one like that described by Jorge Luis Borges in his story "The Garden of Forking Paths," every question about every character's actions—indeed, any question about any event whatsoever—would be explicable in terms of what is found in the novel itself (indeed, multiple explanations of any action would be possible). It would presumably be something of a novelistic failure if, in asking why Katniss hunts with a bow rather than a rifle, the best answer one could produce was that Suzanne Collins, the author of *The Hunger Games*, was herself a bow-hunting enthusiast. Ideally, we want an answer to any conceivable question asking "Why?" about any conceivable plot element to be something contained within the world of the novel itself, without having recourse to the claim that the book merely mirrors the author's predilections. As Aristotle said about drama, long before the advent of the novel, "Whenever such-and-such a personage says or does such-and-such a thing, it shall be the probable or necessary outcome of his character; and whenever this incident follows on that, it shall be either the necessary or the probable consequence of it."[39]

This, of course, is presuming a *perfectly* realistic novel, which no actual novel is; every novel is limited by length and by the

39. Aristotle, *Poetics* 1454a.35–38.

capacities of the author. But even for a perfect novel, an infinite novel such as Borges might imagine, there is one question that is, by its very nature, not answerable in terms of the novel itself. That is the question of why there is a novel at all.[40] The question of why a novel called *The Hunger Games* exists cannot be answered completely in terms of any element or set of elements within the plot, not even the sum total of elements within the plot; in Aristotelian terms, such elements could only address the formal and material causes of the novel, not its efficient or final cause. The question of how the story came to exist and the ends for which it has been written must be found outside the story, by reference to an author. That is, we know that who- or what-ever it is that is the answer to the question "Why is there a story rather than no story?" is something outside the story itself, and this is what we normally call "the author."

Even if the text were anonymous, we would still know that there was an author. Moreover, even with an anonymous author, we would know certain things about the author in addition to the bare affirmation of his or her existence. Some of these things would amount to "negative" knowledge: as indicated, we would know that the author is not a character in the novel, even if there were a character in the novel with the same name and many of the same characteristics as the author. Part of what it means to identify a novel as a novel is to identify its inability to generate itself. We would also have some "positive" knowledge of the author. Leaving aside complicating scenarios of co-authorship, dictation to an amanuensis, or self-publication, we would know that the author possesses the wherewithal to produce a novel, such as literacy and perhaps connections in the publishing world. We might not know where the author acquired his or her literacy or connections, but we would be warranted in asserting that the author

40. Thus, Aquinas argues that even a temporally infinite world would still require a creator. See chapter 13 below.

possessed these attributes. We would not, I should note, be warranted in claiming that because the book contains bow hunting, the author must possess the attribute of being a bow hunter.

My point is perhaps too obvious to need stating: God is not the answer to the question of why there is this or that feature of the world but rather to the question of why there is a world at all. Just as every plot element in a novel is ideally accounted for by something else within the novel, so too everything in our world can, at least in principle, be accounted for by something else within the world. What cannot be accounted for by something in the world, or some set of things in the world, or even by the totality of things in the world, is the existence of the world itself. The principle that nothing moves or causes itself, which we discover from our observation of the world, applies to the world taken as what Peter Geach calls "a great big object."[41] The only difference between asking "Why?" about something in the world and asking "Why?" about the world as a whole is that our answer, however we name it (many people call it "God"), cannot be something in the world. Beyond simply affirming the existence of that which accounts for a world that cannot account for itself, we can say—as we can say concerning a book and its author—that whatever it is that accounts for our world must possess the wherewithal to produce a world like ours, and from this such attributes as divine aseity, eternity, omnipotence, and so forth are derived.

The inability of the world to explain its existence, like the inability of a novel to explain its existence, should not be thought of as being the result of something missing from the world. It is not a "lack" in the novel's plot that requires that it have an author. Even the most convincing narrative world, in which each and every event can be accounted for from within the plot, would still require an author. This does not mean that the need for an

41. G.E.M. Anscombe and Peter T. Geach, *Three Philosophers: Aristotle, Aquinas, Frege* (Oxford: Basil Blackwell and Mott, 1961), 112.

author is obvious within the world of the story. Indeed, one of the things that measures the skill of the author as author is the degree to which the rich detail of setting and the convincing motivation of agents make the author's hand seem to disappear, so long as the reader remains within the novelistic world. Reflection on the author is, we might say, more the business of the critic than of the reader, who, like the characters in the novel, is fully justified in not thinking about the author at all. The critic, however, steps back from the emplotted world of the novel in a reflexive act, and in so doing, becomes aware of the book as something created by an author.[42]

The world, too, is self-explicable on the level of its temporal and spatial "emplotment" of everyday events. With a few exceptions, the Christian tradition has rejected the "occasionalist" metaphysics that sees God alone as exercising genuine causality. Occasionalism is the view, to use the classic example, that when fire encounters cotton, it is a special act of God, not the fire, that makes the cotton burn. The burning of the cotton is, on every occasion, nothing less than a miracle. Rejecting this occasionalist metaphysics, many Christian theologians have preferred to distinguish the primary causality of God from the secondary, but no less real, causality of creatures. While the idea that even an event that seems as natural as fire burning cotton is in fact a miracle specially wrought by God might seem to enhance God's power, it actually diminishes it. Thomas Aquinas can stand for the consensus of the Christian tradition as a whole in saying that a denial of causal efficacy to creatures "would imply a lack of power in the creator: for it is due to the power of the cause that it bestows active power on its effects."[43] Just as characters with ultimately inexplicable motives, whose actions were unconnected to the other elements in the plot, would mar the realism of a novel and imply a lack of skill

42. I should add, however, that a sensitive reader might, at various points in the novel, slip into the mode of "critic" and pause to admire the author's artistry, or lament the lack thereof.

43. *Summa theologiae* 1.105.5.

on the part of the author, so too a world in which creatures lack a genuine causal capacity to act upon other creatures would reflect poorly upon its creator. In particular, just as the choices made by characters in a novel should be intrinsic to the explanation of their actions, so too the free choices of rational creatures should have a genuine causal effect in the world. That is, just as a skilled author can make his or her characters "come to life" by making them act in spontaneous ways, so too the Creator of the world can will the free action of rational creatures without compromising that freedom. The world is still the story God wants to tell, but that story is one that is the story of free creatures acting freely.

This use of the metaphor of God as author and world as novel runs somewhat counter to the often-encountered notion that the novel is a distinctively "secular" genre because it eschews all *deus ex machina* plot resolutions. Ian Watt famously argued,

> The novel's usual means—formal realism—tends to exclude whatever is not vouched for by the senses; the jury does not normally allow divine intervention as an explanation of human actions. It is therefore likely that a measure of secularization was an indispensable condition for the rise of the new genre.[44]

For Watt, the rise of the novel coincides with the growth of empiricism and the secularization of everyday life. If what I am arguing is correct, however, the "realism" of the novel is in no way at odds with the traditional Christian view of the relationship of God to the world. God makes a world that, in its exercise of secondary causality, makes itself. The absence of divine intervention in the plot of the novel fits well with a world in which creatures are self-motivated.

And yet, there is something slightly unsatisfactory about all this. After all, Christians believe that the world's author has been

44. Watt, *Rise of the Novel*, 84.

involved in rather visible ways in the world's plot: calling Abraham into a covenant through which all the families of nations would be blessed; freeing the people of Israel from slavery and leading them to a promised land; speaking through the prophets of future plot developments; and, in these last days, entering into the story of creation as a creature, taking on a human nature in Jesus Christ—God, as it were, becoming a character in the story God is telling. This all seems rather strange from the perspective of the realistic novel, in which the author has the role of explaining the whole but not any particular part.

Therefore, perhaps I need to modify the metaphor of God as author by suggesting that the world of which God is the author is not simply in the genre of "realistic novel" but rather in the subgenre of "magical realism." The term "magical realism" is typically associated with Latin American literature, though it has precursors in European writers such as Kafka, about whom André Gide wrote, "I could not say what I admire more: the 'naturalistic' notation of a fantastic universe, but which the detailed exactitude of the depiction makes real in our eyes, or the unerring audacity of the lurches into the strange."[45] Practitioners of magical realism seek, as one critic put it, the "transformation of the common and everyday into the awesome and the unreal" without abandoning "the well-knit plot."[46] Or, as another critic puts it, "Magic realists present familiar things in unusual ways (flying carpets, Nabokovian butterflies, mass amnesia, and so on) to stress their innately magical properties. . . . Through a process of supplemental illusions, these textual strategies seem to produce a more realistic text."[47] We might say that magical realism works upon its readers

45. André Gide, *Journal* (New York: Knopf, 1951), 4:42, entry for August 28, 1940, quoted in Angel Flores, "Magical Realism in Spanish American Fiction," *Hispania* 38, no. 2 (May 1955): 189. Flores's essay is, to my knowledge, the first application of the term "magical realism" to Latin American literature.

46. Flores, "Magical Realism in Spanish American Fiction," 190, 192.

47. Scott Simpkins, "Magical Strategies: The Supplement of Realism," *Twentieth Century Literature* 34, no. 2 (Summer 1988): 145. Simpkins, it should be noted, is dubious about whether the textual strategy of magical realism actually works.

by getting them to see the story *as* a story, as being the artifice of an author, and yet as somehow more real, more saturated with meaning, than a non-magical reality.

With regard to God as the world's author, the presence of God in the world's story, as both unseen intervening agent and as visible character, serves to remind us that the story that is the world is ultimately a story that God is telling; it has a meaning bestowed by God. Though the creaturely characters in that story drive the plot forward, there is no story apart from its divine author. Without the element of magical realism in the world's story, we, as characters, might all too easily miss the fact that it is a story—an artifice—that we are living in. This is particularly the case since sin has, as it were, ripped the cover and frontispiece off of the text of the world, making our inquiry into the world's author more difficult than it would be otherwise. Moreover, by writing himself into the story, God allows us to have a deeper knowledge of our author than we could possess simply by reflecting on the existence of the story itself. Indeed, in Jesus, God has chosen to subject himself to the vicissitudes of a world emplotted by sinful characters, and because it is as *human* that Christ redeems us, as Anselm argued, God has won the victory over sin from within the plot of our world. The story has been set back on course not via a *deus ex machina*, but by a character who emerges within the plot itself, albeit in a magically realist series of plot twists involving miraculous births and vacated tombs.

DIFFICULTIES

How useful has this metaphor proven? Because all metaphors are literally false, they all limp to one degree or another and have the potential to mislead. Just as the metaphor of God as author might illuminate God's relationship to the world, it might also cast shadows that obscure that relationship. For example, the characters in a book have the appearance of autonomy and self-motivation, but that is a novelistic illusion; in fact, their actions are wholly determined by the decisions of the author. Christians, however, want to maintain that our freedom is not an illusion but something genuinely bestowed on us by our author. Indeed, in the metaphor, we are both readers and characters, and so can become aware of the story as story in a way that actual characters cannot. We even sometimes move from being readers to being critics, as when we engage in theological reflection.

Furthermore, the book, once written, has an independence in relation to its author that the world never has in relation to God. This is true both with regard to the existence of the book itself—*The Grapes of Wrath* continues to exist even though John Steinbeck does not—and with regard to the meaning of the plot. That is, God knows the fullness of the world's meaning in a way that no author knows the meaning of his or her novel, which always contains possibilities of meaning that extend beyond the author's intention. Moreover, whereas the act of writing is a discursive process, extended in time and space, the divine Author is eternal, such that from God's perspective, the plot of the world is always already complete, contained within the simultaneity of the divine mind, although temporally extended in history. As Dante wrote:

> O grace abounding and allowing me to dare
> to fix my gaze on the Eternal Light,
> so deep my vision was consumed in It!
> I saw how it contains within itself
> all things bound in a single book of love
> of which creation is the scattered leaves.[48]

48. Dante Alighieri, *Paradiso* 33.82–87, trans. Mark Musa, in *The Portable Dante*, ed. Mark Musa (New York: Penguin Books, 1995).

Such concerns, however, do not mean that we should avoid the metaphor of God as author any more than we should avoid any other metaphor. These difficulties remind us that while metaphors might open up possibilities of insight that would otherwise be closed to us and can often say in short compass what it would take an endless expanse of time to explicate, they also never say everything that needs to be said. Indeed, precisely because metaphors in theology speak of the eternal, infinite God in time-bound and matter-constrained terms, we must be particularly careful in our employment of metaphor to be vigilant in recognizing the untruths involved, to tune our ear to the stuttering of our utterance.

There is a different sort of difficulty involved in the metaphor of God as author that has nothing to do with the general problem of metaphorical language about God but rather with the perilous status of authors today. I refer, of course, to the supposed "Death of the Author." This was the title of an essay published by the literary critic Roland Barthes in 1967, for whom it signaled the end of the Author as the privileged locus of meaning for the text and the advent of the reader—or, perhaps better, the act of reading—as the true locus in which the multiplicity that the text is finds a sort of rough unity. As Barthes puts it in concluding his essay, "The birth of the reader must be at the cost of the death of the Author."[49] In particular, the tyranny of the Author as the possessor of the text's meaning is now replaced by the reader as the one who constructs meaning. One might see a somewhat different articulation of the same fundamental impulse in Michel Foucault's famous essay "What Is an Author?" originally given as a lecture in 1969, in which he argues that the author as creative subject "must be stripped of its creative role and analyzed as a complex

49. Roland Barthes, "The Death of the Author," in *Image—Music—Text*, ed. and trans. Stephen Heath (London: Fontana, 1977), 148.

and variable function of discourse."[50] In other words, the author, now redesignated as the "author-function," is no longer the one who produces discourse but is rather that which is produced *by* discourse.[51] Foucault speaks somewhat more gently than Barthes of the "disappearance" of the author rather than his death, but the net effect is the same inasmuch as the author as source of meaning is replaced, in this case not by the reader but by the anonymous working of power in the production of discourse. To seek meaning in the author, Foucault says, makes no more sense than seeking meaning in the fictional narrator.[52]

Barthes is not shy about drawing out the theological implications of the death of the Author:

> In precisely this way literature (it would be better from now on to say *writing*), by refusing to assign a 'secret,' an ultimate meaning, to the text (and to the world as text), liberates what may be called an anti-theological activity, an activity that is truly revolutionary since to refuse to fix meaning is, in the end, to refuse God and his hypostases—reason, science, law.[53]

It seems that for Barthes—paying a backhanded compliment to the metaphor I have been attempting to think through—the ultimate refusal of the Author is the refusal of God.

Regarding what will take the place of the author, it is interesting to play out the positions of both Barthes and Foucault as metaphors for thinking through the relationship between the world and the divine. For though Barthes explicitly identifies his

50. Michel Foucault, "What Is an Author?" in *Language, Counter-Memory, Practice: Selected Essays and Interviews*, ed. Donald F. Bouchard, trans. Donald F. Bouchard and Sherry Simon (Ithaca, NY: Cornell University Press, 1980), 138.

51. For an instructive comparison and critique of Barthes and Foucault, see Adrian Wilson, "Foucault on the 'Question of the Author': A Critical Exegesis," *The Modern Language Review* 99, no. 2 (April 2004): 339–63.

52. Foucault, "What Is an Author?" 129.

53. Barthes, "Death of the Author," 147.

announcement of the death of the Author with atheism, it seems to me that both he and Foucault still retain some account of the "genesis" of the meaning of the book. For Barthes, the book's meaning finds its genesis in multiple acts of reading: exalting readers over the Author, he offers us what we might think of as a kind of interpretive polytheism, in which there are as many "gods"—i.e., sources of meaning—as there are readers (or acts of reading). For Foucault, the book's meaning finds its genesis in an immanent "author-function" dispersed in discourse. Making the author coextensive with the discursive working of social power, he offers something like pantheism, in which the author-function is immanently diffused throughout the text: *auctor sive sermo*.

If what the advocates of authorial death are offering us, in the context of thinking through the metaphor of God as author, is not simply atheism but something like a renewed version of polytheism or pantheism, perhaps past debates with polytheists and pantheists could offer resources for response. Can polytheism and pantheism adequately answer the question of "Why" asked about the world as a whole—the question of why there is something rather than nothing? Or do they, rather, simply amount to a refusal of the question in favor of rival forms of divine immanence? Ancient polytheisms and pantheisms, while positing the divine as a way of speaking of the cause of events within the world, seemed incapable of (or uninterested in) conceiving of a radical origination of the world, instead presuming an eternal world already populated by the divine. Is the same not true of the postmodern advocates of the death of the author, who simply presume acts of reading or power-generated discourse that can generate meaning? How do we address those who refuse the question of radical origination? Perhaps there is no single argument to answer such a refusal. Perhaps our best recourse is the one had by the Christians who confronted the polytheisms and pantheisms of late antiquity: to live lives of such radical faith, hope, and love that one provokes in response the most radical sorts of questioning. In doing so, we become the means, as it were, by which an element of "magical realism" is interjected into the plot of the world, which makes the refusal of the world's author just that much more difficult.

In pondering these possibilities, it is important to keep in mind that God-as-author is simply a metaphor that, like all metaphors, casts both light and shadow upon the mystery of God. If, as I suggested earlier, it is a metaphor that became useful only with modern conceptions of authorship and of novels as realistic narratives, then the death of those conceptions might require that we abandon the metaphor as useless. But, *pace* Barthes, the truth of God is hardly imperiled if we find that we must cast aside a literal falsehood that once proved somewhat useful in speaking and thinking about God but does no longer. I suspect, however, that the metaphor still has some life in it, still retains its utility, and is still worth thinking through in part because people still presume that the novels they are reading have a meaning that they do not themselves impart, and that a skilled author can render a world that is convincing in its own terms, a world in which we can lose (and find) ourselves. And if this is the case, then the metaphor of God as author can still cast light on how our own lives are emplotted in a story in which we are genuine agents of the plot's unfolding, yet the final meaning of which we do not ourselves generate and about the existence of which we still want to ask the question "Why?"

5

Imagination and Theology

IMAGINATION AND THE INNER SENSES

Thomas Aquinas's account of the imagination is somewhat frustrating in its austerity. If one combs through his works looking for the term *imaginatio*, or its synonym *phantasia*, one finds little or no reference to that creative faculty so prized by modern people, what Wordsworth called "Reason in her most exalted mood." One finds rather what seems a pedestrian account of one of the "inner senses," that by which we retain images that we have received through the outer senses. I hope to show that, while *imaginatio* is not really what we today would call "imagination," it is not without interest and can in fact point us in a helpful direction in the doing of theology. Furthermore, I will suggest that Thomas's theological practice is a lot more "imaginative," in the modern sense, than his account of *imaginatio* might at first suggest.

Aquinas's basic account of *imaginatio* is derived from that of Aristotle. As Thomas summarizes Aristotle's view, "Those animals have imagination in the precise sense of the term which retain a distinct image of things even while they are not actually sensing things."[1] More specifically, imagination takes its place among the "inner senses" that medieval Aristotelians developed out of remarks made by Aristotle in the third book of *De Anima*. These were faculties that were thought to work along with our five exterior senses, which Aristotle discussed in the second book of *De*

* Originally published as "Imagination and Theology in Thomas Aquinas," *Louvain Studies* 34, nos. 2–3 (2009–10): 169–84.

1. *Sententia De anima* 3.5.644.

Anima, so as to provide a kind of nonrational cognition that is common to human beings and other animals. Furthermore, in human animals, these inner senses provide the soul with the knowledge of the material world that is the prerequisite for reasoning. Thus, in order to get a sense of what Thomas means by *imaginatio*, it is helpful to locate it within the ensemble of the inner senses.[2]

In Thomas' reckoning, the inner senses were four: common sense (*sensus communis*), imagination (*imaginatio*), the "estimative" or (in the case of humans) "cogitative" faculty (*vis aestimativa* or *cogitativa*), and the sense-memory (*memoria*).[3] Thomas arrives at these four inner senses by means of two distinctions: the distinction between reception and retention, and the distinction between sensation and what I would call "evaluation." The distinction between receiving—or, perhaps better, *per*ceiving—and retaining is a fairly obvious one: we must be able not only to take in sense data but also to retain it; this calls for distinct powers of the soul because what is apt for receiving is not typically apt for retaining (one might think of the difference between wet cement and dry cement). The distinction between sensation and evaluation is a bit more difficult to grasp but has to do with the difference between being drawn to or repelled by something because of the immediate pleasure or displeasure it affords the senses, and being drawn to or repelled by a "sense" of that thing's usefulness or harmfulness. The following figure might be of some assistance in grasping how Thomas coordinates these inner senses:

2. For a brief general account of Aquinas's understanding of human knowing, with copious references to primary texts, see Edward P. Mahoney, "Sense, Intellect, and Imagination in Albert, Thomas, and Siger," in *The Cambridge History of Later Medieval Philosophy*, ed. Norman Kretzmann, Anthony Kenny, Jan Pinborg, and Eleanore Stump (Cambridge: Cambridge University Press, 1982), 602–22.

3. For the account of the inner senses in this paragraph and the following ones, see *Summa theologiae* 1.78.4 and *Q. d. de anima* 13. There were various ways of reckoning the "inner senses" in medieval philosophy. For an in-depth account, see Harry Austryn Wolfson, "The Internal Senses in Latin, Arabic, and Hebrew Philosophic Texts," *Harvard Theological Review* 28, no. 2 (1935): 69–133.

The Inner Senses	Perception	Retention
Sensation	*sensus communis*	*imaginatio*
Evaluation	*vis cogitativa*	*memoria*

Let us take up first the perception and retention of sensation. The *sensus communis*, which we might translate as "common sense" (though in modern English, this is somewhat misleading), is the power of the soul to receive as a coordinated *Gestalt* what has been taken in by the five exterior senses. Thomas notes that while the eyes might distinguish between white and black, and the tongue between sweet and bitter, it is the *sensus communis* that allows us to distinguish between white and sweet.[4] Furthermore, it is also the *sensus communis* that allows us to perceive sugar and not simply the whiteness and the sweetness perceived by the eyes and the tongue.[5] The *Gestalts* perceived by the *sensus communis* are called by Thomas *phantasmata*.[6] *Imaginatio*, as mentioned previously, is the power of the soul to retain and recall those *Gestalts*.[7] It is also, in human beings, though not in lower animals, able to perform, at the command of the intellect, certain operations of composition and division upon them, disaggregating and recombining, as it were, the *Gestalts*. For example, *imaginatio* can separate the goldness of the golden chalice that I saw the priest using at last Sunday's Mass and join it to the mountain that I saw six years ago in the Pyrenees so as to form the image of a golden mountain, an image that I "experience" with my inner

4. See *Sententia De anima* 3.3.600–605.

5. On the *sensus communis* as that which receives *Gestalts*, see Herbert McCabe, *On Aquinas*, ed. Brian Davies (London: Burns and Oates, 2008), 123–27.

6. Anthony Kenny suggests that we might think of these *phantasmata* as "experiences," though I am not sure that one can properly speak of experience without also including the evaluative role of the *vis cogitativa* and *memoria*. See Anthony Kenny, "Intellect and Imagination in Aquinas," in *Aquinas: A Collection of Critical Essays*, ed. Anthony Kenny (Notre Dame, IN: University of Notre Dame Press, 1969), 278.

7. *Sententia De sensu* 2.2: "that first stimulation of our senses by which they sense leaves in us a sort of secondary change [*secundario motu*] which persists even in the absence of what has been sensed and is located in the imagination [*phantasiam*]."

senses even though I have no exterior sensual experience of it.[8] In Avicenna, the retention of sense experience and the construction of new experiences were divided between two different powers, the former called *hayâliyyah* (often translated as *phantasia* or *imaginatio*) and the latter called *mutahayyila* (often translated as *imaginativa*).[9] Aquinas, however, ascribes both to the single inner sense *imaginatio*.[10]

Turning now to the perception or retention of evaluation, we see that what Aquinas calls, in non-human animals, the *vis estimativa* (estimative power) or, in human animals, the *vis cogitativa* (cogitative power)[11] is the receptive power of the soul by which material things are evaluated as desirable or undesirable, not because of their direct effect on the senses, but because of their potential benefit or harm to the animal as a whole. This is something that is instinctual in non-human animals but learned through trial and error in human beings. Aquinas offers the examples of birds gathering straw for nests or lambs fleeing wolves. We might also think of how a human being might find the sensation of a lamb's fleece or a wolf's fur equally pleasurable, while still evaluating the wolf, though not the lamb, as something to be avoided. This power is still tied to sensation, however, since it has to do with the evaluation of something that I have experienced through my senses: a wolf. Moreover, I avoid the wolf, despite its pleasant furriness, because of the not yet—and, one

8. For the "golden mountain" example, see, e.g., *Summa theologiae* 1.12.9 ad 2 and 1.78.4; *Quodlibet* 8.2.1; *De veritate* 8.5; *De malo* 16.11 ad 9.

9. Wolfson, "Internal Senses," 115–16. The distinction is not unlike the one made by Coleridge centuries later between "imagination" and "fancy." See Samuel Taylor Coleridge, *Biographia Literaria*, ed. John T. Shawcross (Oxford: Clarendon, 1907), 1:304–5.

10. Serge-Thomas Bonino ascribes this "creative" power of *imaginatio* to its proximity to the intellect and the intellect's influence on it: *imaginatio* is "impregnated with reason" and takes on certain of reason's characteristics. See Serge-Thomas Bonino, "Le rôle de l'image dans la connaissance prophétique d'après saint Thomas d'Aquin," *Revue thomiste* 89, no. 4 (1989): 550–51.

11. Thomas notes that the *vis cogitativa* is sometimes called "particular reason" because "it correlates individualized notions, just as the 'universal reason' correlates universal ideas" (*Sententia De anima* 2.13.396). How this relates to what he says elsewhere about the *vis cogitativa* is unclear.

would hope, never—experienced sensation of its teeth tearing my flesh. Whether instinctual or learned through trial and error, these are evaluations that all animals, including humans, can make, and they do not seem to be dependent upon reason's ability to form abstract notions such as "lamb" or "wolf." Memory or, more specifically, "sense-memory" is the power of the soul to retain these evaluations.[12] It is that by which I recall not just the look and sound and smell of a wolf, but the fear I experienced upon seeing it. In human beings, Aquinas notes, this is a capacity that can be exercised at will and thus is not simply memory but "reminiscence." This reminiscence is not like remembering a fact that has been learned but rather like reliving in memory a past experience.

If we focus on imagination in isolation from the intellect and the other inner senses, we see why Thomas's account of *imaginatio* might, at least at first, prove to be somewhat disappointing for those who want to make imagination central to the task of theology, indeed to the task of thought itself.[13] *Imaginatio*, rather than being the wonderful productive power of the human mind, seems simply a kind of storage facility for sense images; rather than being a factory churning out marvelous (or dangerous) products, it is a humble warehouse of forms (*thesaurus formarum*).[14] Aquinas would seem to fall into what Douglas Hedley, for example, sees as the "empiricist" tradition of Aristotle and Hobbes, which sees imagination as simply "a form of faded perceptual experience: decaying sense."[15]

12. There is also, according to Thomas, a memory of the intellect in which is retained not our estimation of sense objects but the intelligible species abstracted from *phantasmata*. See *Summa theologiae* 1.79.6.

13. See the wonderful contrasting accounts of the imaginative genius (in the modern sense) of Albert Einstein and what we might call the "memorative genius" of Thomas Aquinas with which Mary Carruthers begins her study of medieval memory practices (*The Book of Memory: A Study of Memory in Medieval Culture* [Cambridge: Cambridge University Press, 2008], 1–9).

14. *Summa theologiae* 1.78.4.

15. Douglas Hedley, *Living Forms of the Imagination* (London: T&T Clark, 2008), 52.

Such disappointment with Aquinas's account of *imaginatio* only arises, however, if we isolate it from the ensemble of inner senses that operate together and that in turn are the basis for the operation of the intellect. We must remember that the inner senses perceive the world not as discrete bits of sense data (patches of color, isolated lines and curves, etc.) but as *Gestalts*. This is particularly true if we take into account the evaluative faculties, which encode our sense perceptions with a fundamental "attitude" toward that which is perceived, an attitude that is in a sense "prior" to thought and akin to the instinctual responses of other animals. The inner senses, as Timothy McDermott puts it, "presents the animal not with a picture to look at, but with a three-dimensional world to walk into, to occupy, and in which to take a stance."[16]

In the case of human animals, however, this three-dimensional sensorium is subjected to a yet higher level of perception. This is the level of intellectual perception or, more properly, intellectual *con*ception, which allows us to know the world not simply as it impinges on *me*—what I sense or evaluate as pleasing or displeasing, useful or harmful—but as something that is a thing in its own right. I see the wolf outside my door not simply as the pleasingly furry yet dangerous threat to me but also as "a wolf," something that takes its place within the species *lupus*, which is in turn within the genus *canis*. I conceive of *this* wolf in relation to other wolves, and wolves in general in relation to other canines, and canines in relation to other animals, and animals in relation to other sentient beings, and sentient beings in relation to all created beings.

Some recent interpreters of Aquinas associate this passage from sensual perception to intellectual conception with the human capacity for language, our ability to transcend our private sense-world into the commonly shared world created by

16. Timothy McDermott, *How to Read Aquinas* (London: Granta Books, 2007), 24.

linguistic communication. As Anthony Kenny puts the matter, "If we want 'intellect' to mean a characteristically human capacity then it seems most helpful to regard the intellect as the capacity for thinking those thoughts that only a language-user can think."[17] While one cannot, in interpreting Aquinas, simply collapse reason into language use—after all, I can identify the sound of a clarinet even if I cannot describe it in words, except to call it "the sound of a clarinet"[18]—it is undeniable that Aquinas sees thought as structured in a way that we might call "linguistic": we think by composing and dividing, just as we form sentences by combining subjects and predicates. The structure of both language and thought, in turn, conforms to the structure of things themselves.[19]

It is precisely by means of this linguistically structured thinking that the material world of the senses becomes, for the human animal, not simply *per*ceivable but *con*ceivable. Yet human thought is only possible so long as it remains tied to that material world of the senses. Thus, it is the *phantasmata* that provide the raw material for the conceptual activity of the intellect.[20] My sensual perception of *this* wolf is the basis for my intellectual conception of a wolf. But it is not simply that the intellect needs sensual

17. Anthony Kenny, *Aquinas* (Oxford: Oxford University Press, 1980), 67. See also McDermott, *How to Read Aquinas*, 24–26; McCabe, *On Aquinas*; and Roger Pouivet, *After Wittgenstein, St. Thomas*, trans. Michael Sherwin (South Bend, IN: St. Augustine's, 2006), 39–42. But see also the cautionary remarks in Anthony Kenny, *Aquinas on Mind* (London: Routledge, 1993), 49.

18. See Ludwig Wittgenstein, *Philosophical Investigations*, 4th ed., trans. G.E.M. Anscombe (Hoboken, NJ: Wiley-Blackwell, 1998), 1.78.

19. *Summa theologiae* 1.16.2. A century before Aquinas, John of Salisbury drew a parallel between the structure of language and the structure of nature, noting that adjectives "depict the force and nature of nouns in the same way that properties of substances indicate their differences." Similarly, the tense of verbs reflects the way in which "there is no movement independent of time." From these and like examples, John concludes that language is "a clear footprint of nature impressed on human reason." See John of Salisbury, *Metalogicon* 1.14, in *The Metalogicon of John of Salisbury: A Twelfth-Century Defense of the Verbal and Logical Arts of the Trivium*, trans. Daniel D. McGarry (Berkeley: University of California Press, 1955), 39–41.

20. See *Summa theologiae* 1.84.6: "It cannot be said that sensible knowledge is the total and perfect cause of intellectual knowledge, but rather it is in a way the material cause." Thomas says in the *Summa contra Gentiles* that the imaginative and cogitative powers prepare the phantasm "in such a way as to facilitate its being made actually intelligible by the agent intellect" (2.73.28).

perception to get it started; in this life, the intellect of human beings needs sensual perception to sustain it throughout its activity.[21] Thomas writes, "For the intellect to understand actually, not only when it acquires fresh knowledge, but also when it applies knowledge already acquired, there is need for the act of the imagination and of the other [sensual] powers."[22] The human intellect, by its very nature as an embodied intellect, finds the "proper object" of its activity in the nature of material things—not simply the concept "wolf" but *this* wolf. Because of this, the intellect must constantly revert to the *phantasm*, the sensual world in which we take our stance, in order to carry out its proper activity.[23] If we think of this in terms of language, we might say that it is only *within* our activity of talking about this or that particular wolf that human talk of wolves-in-general continues to make sense. Viewed in this way, the much-discussed *conversio ad phantasmata* (i.e., the need of the mind to "turn to the phantasm") in Aquinas is not so much about occult mental operations as it is about the fact that human language does not find its end in airy abstractions or ideal logical structures but in everyday use. Our language about wolves-in-general becomes unmoored unless we constantly return to talking about particular wolves. The entire apparatus of human language and thought, including such abstractions as wolves-in-general, is entirely oriented toward knowing objects in the world in the fullest way possible.

My point here is to suggest that the constant recourse of the intellect to the world of sense as contained in the *imaginatio* is an indication of how thoroughly embedded in the material world and bodily life Aquinas's account of human knowing is. Indeed,

21. The human soul that has been separated from its body by death can still know singulars, but knowledge of these must be directly infused by God and can be possessed by the separated soul only as "a confused knowledge" (see *Summa theologiae* 1.89.4).

22. *Summa theologiae* 1.84.7.

23. *Super De Trinitate* 6.2 ad 5: "An image . . . remains as the foundation of intellectual activity, just as the principles of demonstration must remain throughout the whole process of science."

Thomas is adamant that knowing is not a matter of grasping a concept but rather a matter of grasping the nature of some material thing by means of a concept.[24] And in this act of grasping the *quidditas* ("whatness") of a material substance, the *phantasmata* contained in the *imaginatio* have a crucial role. *Imaginatio* is not, like modern imagination, the means by which human thought takes flight but rather that which keeps our thought grounded in this world. As Iris Murdoch put it, "We use our imagination not to escape the world but to join it."[25]

THE IMAGINATION AND KNOWLEDGE OF GOD

While crucial in our mind's grasp of material things, *imaginatio* also has a role to play in our attempt to grasp nonmaterial realities, even the reality of God. Thomas rejects the view, which he identifies with Averroes, that the human intellect can know non-material realities, or "separated substances," by being united with one of them, called the "agent intellect."[26] For Thomas, our knowledge of nonmaterial realities is rather more indirect and cloudy. As he says, "From material things we can rise to some kind of knowledge of immaterial things, but not to the perfect knowledge, for there is not a sufficient parallel [*comparatio*] between material and immaterial things."[27] The lack of proportion between material and immaterial is stretched to infinity when it comes to the case of God, for while material substances and

24. See *Summa theologiae* 1.85.2 ad 3 and *De veritate* 2.6. Roger Pouivet writes that the concept is "a *function* by means of which objects are characterized. The function is a *means*, not an object. It is an intellectual tool revealed in linguistic activity. It is not an intentional entity" (*After Wittgenstein, St. Thomas*, 17).

25. Iris Murdoch, *The Sovereignty of Good*, 2nd ed. (London: Routledge, 2001), 88.

26. *Summa theologiae* 1.88.1. Thomas's differences with Arabic philosophers over the agent intellect are not simply a matter of how we know separated substances but also have to do with questions of individual identity and the immortality of the soul.

27. *Summa theologiae* 1.88.2 ad 1.

immaterial substances have at least the commonality of being placed in the genus "substance," God is outside of any genus whatsoever.[28]

If our thinking is rooted in *imaginatio* and the other inner senses, and the natural object of the human intellect is the nature of material things, how then could we ever arrive at any knowledge of God? Here, we must note the well-known distinction that Thomas makes, in company with the Christian tradition as a whole, between what we can know of God through the natural powers of our intellect and what we can know through grace. And in both forms of knowing, *imaginatio* has a role to play.

First, in terms of what we can know through the natural powers of our intellect, Thomas notes that "we can use the senses and the imagination as the starting points but not as the termini of our knowledge of divine things."[29] The material substances that we know through the senses and that we recall through *imaginatio* can serve as our starting point because they are, when subjected to the deepest sort of probing by the human intellect, so utterly inadequate at explaining themselves and thus point beyond themselves to the Other who infinitely transcends them. And so, by natural reason, we come to a knowledge not, of course, of God's essence but of God as the source of all that makes up the world in which we take our stance, a source that is not one of the things in that world but infinitely exceeds the world.[30] We might even hesitate to call such natural knowledge "knowledge of God" at all, so indirect is it. Perhaps we might better think of it as a particular sort of judgment that we make with regard to the world: the judgment that this world cannot account for itself, that this world is not its own source. And in this judgment, *imaginatio* has a vital role to play. Thomas writes, "Clearly, we cannot know that God causes bodies, or transcends all bodies, or is not a

28. *Summa theologiae* 1.88.2 ad 4.

29. *Super De Trinitate* 6.2.

30. See *Summa theologiae* 1.12.12.

body, if we do not form an image of bodies." But, he goes on to note, "our judgement of what is divine is not made according to the imagination."[31] The natural knowledge of God begins in imagination, but it ends in the act of judgement, an act by which the contents of *imaginatio* become diaphanous, transparent to their transcendent source.

Second, in terms of what we can know of God through grace—that is, in the phenomenon of prophecy—*imaginatio* has an even more important role to play.[32] Again, the contrast with the Arabic Aristotelian tradition is instructive. Avicenna, for example, saw prophets in what we might call a "naturalistic" light: prophecy did not involve any particular act of God but was simply the perfect exercise of natural human reason by which it came to know separated substances by union with the universal agent intellect.[33] In contrast, Thomas, while acknowledging a sort of natural prophecy in the sense of insight into the future through knowledge of secondary causes,[34] saw prophecy-strictly-speaking as a supernatural gift that is formally similar to, but materially distinct from, natural human knowledge. Thomas notes that normal human cognition involves both the images of sensible objects as well as "the natural intelligible light" by which we derive general concepts from these images. In the case of the knowledge of God that we have by prophecy, both of these are affected. Not only is the natural light of reason strengthened by "the infusion of gratuitous light," but also, at least sometimes, images are formed by God in the *imaginatio* "to express divine things better than the images that we receive naturally from sensible objects are able to

31. *Super De Trinitate* 6.2 ad 5.

32. For a comprehensive treatment of prophecy and *imaginatio* in Aquinas, see Bonino, "Le rôle de l'image."

33. See Majid Fakhry, *A History of Islamic Philosophy*, 2nd ed. (New York: Columbia University Press, 1983), 142–45, and Serge-Thomas Bonino, "Charisms, Forms, and States of Life," trans. Mary Thomas Noble, in *The Ethics of Aquinas*, ed. Stephen J. Pope (Washington, DC: Georgetown University Press, 2002), 342.

34. *De veritate* 12.3.

do."[35] Thomas gives chief importance to this infusion of divine light, so much so that someone like Joseph, who can by this light properly interpret the images in someone else's imagination—in this case, Pharaoh—can rightly be called a prophet.[36]

At the same time, we speak of prophecy in its fullest sense when it involves both divine illumination and the reception of a new species. Thomas does not seem to be completely consistent in his terminology and classification of the kinds of prophecy, but broadly speaking, we can distinguish between prophecy that involves the reception of a sensible species into the *imaginatio* and prophecy that involves the reception of an intelligible species into the intellect. The former case might involve either images received through the senses in a normal fashion,[37] or "reception by the imagination, as when images are formed by divine power in the spirit of the prophet,"[38] or it might take the form of a divine coordination of *phantasmata* already received in *imaginatio* from the senses.[39] Any of these instances, according to Thomas, is prophecy according to the strict definition of the term, since "prophecy" involves a certain obscurity of knowledge, a seeing in the mirror of the imagination.[40] In the latter case—the reception of intelligible species into the intellect—"prophecy" can involve "naked intelligible truth" (*nude intelligibilis veritas*) being received

35. *Summa theologiae* 1.12.13.

36. *Summa theologiae* 2-2.173.2.

37. *Summa theologiae* 2-2.173.2. Thomas offers as an example Daniel seeing the hand that is writing on the wall of Belshazzar's palace (see Dan. 5:5–30), something that the others present see as well. In the following article, he mentions Moses and the burning bush as another example (see Exod. 3:2).

38. *De veritate* 12.12. Cf. *Summa theologiae* 2-2.173.2. In reference to this latter passage, Torrell notes that Thomas offers no example from the Bible, and that one is at pains to find such an example. This leads Torrell to conclude that while this is a possible form of prophecy, it is not a possibility that has ever been actualized by God in history. See *Somme Théologique: La prophétie, 2a-2ae, Questions 171–178*, 2nd ed., translated and annotated by Paul Synave and Pierre Benoit, with a new introduction by J.-P. Torrell (Paris: Cerf, 2005), 69–70*.

39. *Summa theologiae* 2-2.173.2. Thus, Jeremiah might have a vision of Jerusalem burning because God brings together in his *imaginatio* the *phantasm* of fire and the *phantasm* of Jerusalem.

40. *Summa theologiae* 2-2.174.2 ad 3.

by the intellect. Though conforming less strictly to the definition of prophecy, this latter sort is a higher form of knowledge through grace.[41]

What is interesting to note is that even in this latter sort of prophecy, in which an intelligible rather than sensual species is received in the mind from God, *imaginatio* is still involved. When God infuses an intelligible species into the mind of the prophet, "the understanding is so clearly flooded with knowledge of the truth that it does not grasp the truth from the likeness of any images, but in fact can form images for itself from the truth it has seen." Thomas goes on to note, "It uses these [images] because of the nature of our understanding."[42] In other words, in this life, divinely given knowledge always involves images, because, though divinely given, it must remain *human* knowledge, and human knowledge in this life always involves *phantasmata*.[43] The difference between the two forms of prophecy is that in the case of imaginative reception, the divinely given *phantasmata* are the raw material from which the light of reason strengthened by prophetic light abstracts intelligible truth, while in the case of intellectual reception, the divinely given intelligible truth in turn gives rise to the formation of new images. What is clear in both cases is that prophetic knowledge itself, and not simply its communication, involves sensuous images.

Serge-Thomas Bonino, while recognizing the importance of the image in prophetic knowledge, also underscores the importance of the infusion of prophetic light, which Thomas calls the divinely given prophetic capacity for "judgment" (*judicum*).

41. *Summa theologiae* 2-2.174.2 ad 1. For a discussion of Thomas's categorization of the various types of prophecy, see the explicative notes by Synave and Benoit in *Somme Théologique: La prophétie*, 2a–2ae, 243–47.

42. *De veritate* 12.12.

43. *Summa theologiae* 2-2.174.2 ad 4, *De veritate* 12.7 ad 2 and 18.5. Jean-Pierre Torrell notes that "the divine intervention that assures the prophetic revelation does not structurally modify the laws of the human spirit and therefore, despite its peculiarities, prophetic knowledge remains human knowledge" (*Somme Théologique: La prophétie, 2a-2ae*, 64*). See also Bonino, "Charisms, Forms, and States of Life," 351n17.

Bonino goes so far as to say that "the specificity of prophecy is contained entirely on the side of the gift of a new and supernatural light, which explains adequately the entire process of prophetic knowledge."[44] In other words, prophetic revelation is no less supernatural when it is a matter of a judgment made through the divinely infused "gratuitous light" regarding an image or idea obtained through ordinary natural means. Though this claim perhaps does not fully reflect Thomas's emphasis on the divinely given images, Bonino does seem to be true to Thomas in his concern that divine revelation be seen as a supernatural event that can take place from *within* natural human knowledge and not be seen as an extrinsic implanting of images and ideas in the prophet. Likewise, in underscoring the significance of the divine light by which the prophet judges *phantasmata*, we see clearly the parallel between the natural knowledge of God and the prophetic knowledge of divine things: both begin in imagination but end in the act of judgment.

IMAGINATIO, SCIENTIA, CONVENIENTIA

Thus far, I have indicated why some people have found Aquinas's account of imagination so unsatisfying, suggesting that it is because they looked at what he had to say about *imaginatio* for something like modern accounts of the imagination and went away disappointed because they did not find what they hoped for. I have also tried to offer some reasons why I think that Thomas's account of *imaginatio*, while not really what a modern person means by "imagination," is in fact quite interesting, not just philosophically, but also theologically, because it takes seriously the sensuous nature of human knowing, even with regard to knowledge of God.

But I think there is perhaps a deeper source of dissatisfaction

44. Bonino, "Le rôle de l'image," 568.

for the modern reader who looks to Thomas for an "imaginative theology." Thomas attempts to reconceive theology along the lines of an Aristotelian science (*scientia/epistēmē*), in which, as Aquinas puts it, "from things already known conclusions about other matters follow of necessity."[45] The engine that drives this science of necessary conclusions is the syllogism, and it is here, I think, that many difficulties arise for those who would value the kind of "lateral thinking" that we associate today with the religious imagination.[46] It is not simply that Thomas's account of *imaginatio* does not measure up to our modern expectations regarding imagination but rather that his account of theology as *scientia* seems to confine the theologian to the plodding pace of the syllogism, leaving no room for the intuitive leaps and logical *aporiae* that seem to lie at the heart of religious thinking. Furthermore, Thomas's commitment to his theological forebears and the dogmas of the Church, his unwillingness to abandon authoritative formulations, might seem indicative of a lack of theological originality and imagination (though the same critics are usually willing to grant Thomas some philosophical originality). Here, I think, is the real difficulty: it seems that Thomas has not only an impoverished theological account of the imagination but in fact that he has an impoverished theological imagination.

Such a charge has just enough plausibility to sting a lover of Aquinas and call for a response. After all, as Cornelius Ernst pointed out, it is undeniable that Thomas's theological practice "is almost bare of metaphor,"[47] and he seems constitutionally incapable of coming up with helpful examples, typically recycling those he finds in Aristotle. Acknowledging that such evidence

45. *Super De Trinitate* 2.2. On Thomas's account of theology as *scientia* in general, see John I. Jenkins, *Knowledge and Faith in Thomas Aquinas* (Cambridge: Cambridge University Press, 1997), particularly chapters 1–3.

46. I borrow this phrase from Herbert McCabe, who in turn has borrowed it from Edward de Bono. See *On Aquinas*, 130.

47. Cornelius Ernst, *Multiple Echo: Explorations in Theology*, ed. Fergus Kerr and Timothy Radcliffe (London: Darton, Longman and Todd, 1979), 66.

calls for a reply, in the last part of this essay, I will offer three points by way of response.

First, one must properly locate Aristotelian science within the field of human intellectual activity as a whole. *Scientia* is not the whole of thinking, despite the importance it has in both Aristotle and Aquinas.[48] Thomas knows that most human thought is of an intuitive, associative kind. Particularly in the realm of religion, people typically do not try to order their beliefs according to the schema of an Aristotelian science, and they are no worse for not doing so. Indeed, Thomas said an old woman with faith—which is certainly the most intuitive, associative form of thinking known to humanity—knows more about God and the things necessary for life than any of the philosophers who lived before the coming of Christ.[49] The role of *scientia* is to provide some sort of check on the other ways of human knowing that form, as it were, the background for *scientia*. The goal of Aristotle's logic is, as Herbert McCabe puts it, "not to help people to make rational arguments, but to hinder them from making bogus arguments."[50] In the case of what Thomas calls *sacra doctrina*—which we would call dogmatic or systematic theology—he uses the logical tools bequeathed to him by Aristotle not to figure out how Christians ought to talk but to help Christians make sense of the sometimes messy and misleading ways in which they are always already talking. He does not want to replace statements like "God is a human being" or "The body of Christ is made from bread"[51] with "better" ones that are suited to serve as syllogistic premises. He simply wants to make sure that one does not draw false conclusions from such statements.

48. Though in his commentary on Aristotle's *Posterior Analytics* Thomas calls logic "the art of arts" (*ars artium*), he also goes on to list a variety of other ways of ordering thought, including rhetoric and poetry. See *Expositio Posteriorum* 1.1.3.

49. *In Symbolum Apostolorum*, prologue.

50. McCabe, *On Aquinas*, 130.

51. *Summa theologiae* 3.16.1; 3.75.8. For a full discussion of the latter, see chapter 13 below.

Second, along with Thomas's acknowledgment that the *scientia* of *sacra doctrina* is not the whole of human religious thinking, one should also note that Aquinas considers *sacra doctrina* to be *scientia* of a very particular, and somewhat peculiar, sort. Theology is a "subaltern" *scientia*, in the sense that it borrows its first principles from another *scientia*—that of God and the blessed.[52] This subalternation, of course, is not something unique to theology. Just as the biologist might begin from principles taken from the chemist without having "scientific" (i.e., rationally certain) knowledge of those principles, and be no worse a biologist for doing so, so too the theologian who engages in *sacra doctrina* begins from principles given by God through divine revelation and articulated in the creeds. The theologian can no more prove these starting principles than any scientist can prove his or her starting principles (as he notes, one argues *from* first principles, not *to* them).[53] Yet what is peculiar about this *scientia*, and what makes it nobler than any other *scientia*, is the odd way in which it is simultaneously *more* certain, because it is derived from the pellucid reason of God, and yet seemingly unmoored from human reason, treating "chiefly of those things which by their sublimity transcend reason."[54] This is why Thomas says that faith falls somewhere between *scientia* and opinion: "With science and understanding it has in common unerring and firm assent. . . . With opinion it shares the fact that it has to do with matters that are not clear to the mind, in which respect it differs from science and understanding."[55] So theology seems to be something that is both a science and not a science, Thomas's claims for its scientific status notwithstanding.

Third, and finally, as Cornelius Ernst noted, "St. Thomas's actual practice, like Aristotle's own, was fortunately a good deal

52. *Summa theologiae* 1.1.2.

53. *Summa theologiae* 1.1.8.

54. *Summa theologiae* 1.1.5.

55. *Super De Trinitate* 3.1.

less rigid than his epistemological theory."[56] Though when reflecting on the nature of *sacra doctrina*, Thomas tries mightily to fit theology into the mold of an Aristotelian science, in his actual theological practice, one does not always find him arguing in syllogistic fashion. Thomas seems to operate often not by means of the syllogism but rather by the careful drawing of distinctions and that odd form of reasoning that is the *argumentum ex convenientia*. This latter is hardly syllogistic but is rather a process by which we judge something "fitting" because of the way in which it makes to come together (*con-venire*) a host of factors that aid in the attaining of a particular end. Thus, we might judge an axe a more fitting tool for cutting a log than either a sword or a sledgehammer because in the axe the sharpness of the sword and the weight of the sledgehammer come together to form the most fitting tool for log cutting. In a similar fashion, Thomas judges the Incarnation to be the most fitting means of our salvation, since in the event of God becoming flesh there comes together both our advancement in goodness and our withdrawal from evil.[57] This is not in any sense a syllogistic argument for the Incarnation, though in the far background one might find lurking a syllogism of the sort: God acts in the best way possible; what is most fitting is the best way possible; therefore, God acts in the most fitting way. Yet the power of such argumentation does not derive from a deeply buried syllogism but from what we might call the aesthetic appeal of that which is fitting, the same appeal that draws mathematicians to "beautiful equations."

With the *argumenta ex convenientia*, which pervade the Third Part of the *Summa theologiae*, Thomas has moved well beyond anything resembling Aristotelian science. Indeed, one might describe such arguments as highly imaginative inasmuch as they involve an ability to see matters "whole" and to imagine connections that

56. Ernst, *Multiple Echo*, 83.

57. *Summa theologiae* 3.1.2. See chapter 10, below.

might not at first appear. Though Thomas himself does not seem to consider originality a theological virtue, he ends up with strikingly original positions on any number of theological issues.[58] It is an originality that does not require any rejection of the received doctrinal tradition but rather a deeper intellectual appropriation of that tradition by seeing its wholeness.

Though one might be predisposed to take any hagiographical account with at least a small grain of salt, it is worth noting that Bernard Gui's early-fourteenth-century life of Thomas speaks of how he, "when perplexed by a difficulty . . . would kneel and pray and then, on returning to his writing and dictation, he was accustomed to find that his thought had become so clear that it seemed to show him inwardly, as in a book, the words he needed."[59] Such stories give us a sense of how, on particularly difficult questions, Thomas's theological practice was less a matter of constructing syllogisms than it was a matter of seeing a kind of theological *Gestalt.* The sort of originality embodied in Thomas's practice might offer us an alternative to certain modern approaches that seek theological originality in the endless cycle of critique and re-critique of received tradition. While such critique is no doubt necessary at times, it can become as formulaic and stale as the most rigid traditionalism. The true originality of the theological imagination is found not in novel doctrines but in the ability, after reflection, to turn back to the tradition of the Church in a kind of *conversio ad phantasmata*, so as to see it anew and to think it anew.

58. My own view is that those who see Thomas's theology as simply repeating the positions of the councils and of past theologians such as Augustine and Anselm have simply not read his theology with much care. On any number of issues—ranging from his transformation of Augustine's "psychological analogy" of the Trinity to his views to the single *esse* of Christ to his understanding of the instrumental causality of the sacraments—Thomas offers positions that are startling in their originality.

59. Bernard Gui, "The Life of St. Thomas Aquinas" 15, in *The Life of St. Thomas Aquinas: Biographical Documents*, ed. and trans. Kenelm Foster (London: Longmans, Green, 1959), 37.

Part II

Virtue and Vice

6

The Unity of the Virtues and the Journeying Self

In an early essay, Stanley Hauerwas wrote, "I do not pretend to say anything that Aristotle or Thomas did not say as well or better. But perhaps this essay will at least provide the impetus to read their work with fresh eyes."[1] From the outset, Stanley Hauerwas has carried on a sustained engagement with the thought of Thomas Aquinas.[2] In works ranging from *Character and the Christian Life* (1975) to his Gifford Lectures, published as *With the Grain of the Universe* (2001), we find him returning again and again to engage St. Thomas in dialogue. This dialogue, while critical, is at the same time fruitful, since Hauerwas's interests and concerns prod us to see Aquinas in new ways. One case of this is the way in which Hauerwas's emphasis on character and narrative prompts a reengagement with the question of the unity of the

* Originally published as "Thomas Aquinas: The Unity of the Virtues and the Journeying Self," in *Unsettling Arguments: A Festschrift on the Occasion of Stanley Hauerwas's 70th Birthday*, ed. Charles R. Pinches, Kelly S. Johnson, and Charles M. Collier (Eugene, OR: Cascade Books, 2010), 25–41.

1. Stanley Hauerwas, "Toward an Ethics of Character," in *Vision and Virtue: Essays in Christian Ethical Reflection* [1974] (Notre Dame, IN: University of Notre Dame Press, 1981), 52.

2. I should make clear that while I am Hauerwas's student, I am not really a student of Hauerwas. That is, while Hauerwas was my teacher and I have learned much from him over the years, I have not made a careful study of all his writings. Thus, those who are students of Hauerwas will have to forgive me if I miss some of the more subtle points of his thought or overlook some obvious text. For a brief survey of Hauerwas's Thomistic engagements, see Nicholas M. Healy, "Three Theological Appropriations of Analytic-Philosophical Readings of Thomas Aquinas," in *Analytical Thomism: Traditions in Dialogue*, ed. Craig Paterson and Matthew S. Pugh (Aldershot, UK: Ashgate, 2006), esp. 47–53.

virtues and the nature of the human person as a *viator* or "wayfarer."

CHARACTER AND THE UNITY OF THE VIRTUES: AN EARLY OBJECTION

Among professional ethicists, Hauerwas is probably best known for his role in refocusing attention on the importance of "character" in ethical analysis. In his earliest work, Hauerwas focused on the idea of "character" as "the qualification or determination of our self-agency, formed by our having certain intentions (and beliefs) rather than others."[3] This understanding of character was heavily influenced by philosophical action theory and sought a way of speaking of the self's settled orientation toward a particular set of goods that did not compromise the freedom of the agent.[4] Hauerwas subsequently expressed misgivings about his early formulation of the notion of "character," noting that it "still suggests a kind of dualism insofar as a 'self' seems to stand behind our character," and in later writings, he thinks it preferable to say "that character is not so much the qualification but the form of our agency."[5] In other words, the self does not "have" a particular character, but rather "character" is simply another way of talking about selfhood—one that highlights the self as an agent who acts with a particular orientation.

Hauerwas's attention to "character" as a category of analysis has always been of a piece with his larger concern to turn ethics away from fruitless debates between deontologists and utilitarians and back toward a more classical account of morality as the pursuit of the good life: a pursuit that is made possible by the

3. Stanley Hauerwas, *Character and the Christian Life: A Study in Theological Ethics* [1975] (Notre Dame, IN: University of Notre Dame Press, 1994), 115.

4. This is how Hauerwas retrospectively describes his motivation in "Going Forward by Looking Back: Agency Reconsidered," in *Sanctify Them in the Truth: Holiness Exemplified* (Nashville, TN: Abingdon, 1998), 93–103, esp. 94.

5. From Hauerwas's preface to the 1994 reissue of *Character and the Christian Life*, xx.

cultivation of virtues. This approach, which Hauerwas from the outset identified with Aristotle and Thomas, "is not concerned primarily with how the observer determines whether specific actions are good or bad but rather how the agent becomes good or bad through his activity."[6] The return to this more classical account, which in the English-speaking world was initiated by G.E.M. Anscombe's essay "Modern Moral Philosophy,"[7] has come to be described as "virtue ethics." Though Hauerwas would undoubtedly not find much kinship with some of those who describe themselves as "virtue ethicists," his work has been a significant force in the revival of interest in virtue and, concomitantly, has contributed to something of a shift in how Thomas's ethics are viewed.

Though Catholic theologians had never entirely forgotten the place of the virtues in Thomas's theology, there was, for much of the modern era, a tendency among both Catholics and Protestants to see Thomas's approach to the moral life predominantly in terms of natural law and its casuistic application. This has changed in recent years with the recognition of the significance of the detailed attention Thomas pays in the *Summa theologiae* both to virtue in general and to discussion of particular virtues and vices, as well as the rather modest place natural law occupies in those discussions.[8] Throughout his life as a theologian, Hauerwas has returned to Thomas as a dialogue partner, precisely because he, perhaps more than any other, has rethought the classical tradition of the virtues from within the perspective of Christian faith.

Hauerwas's dialogue with Thomas has not been an uncritical

6. Hauerwas, *Character and the Christian Life*, 37.

7. G.E.M. Anscombe, "Modern Moral Philosophy," in *Human Life, Action and Ethics: Essays by G.E.M. Anscombe*, ed. Mary Geach and Luke Gormally (Exeter, UK: Imprint Academic, 2005), 169–94.

8. To take but a single example, see Stephen Pope's statement, "The *Summa* assigns primacy of place to the virtues and to personal character formation, and a subordinate role to law" (Pope, "Overview of the Ethics of Thomas Aquinas," in *The Ethics of Aquinas*, ed. Stephen J. Pope [Washington, DC: Georgetown University Press, 2002], 30–53 at 49). See also Thomas S. Hibbs, "Interpretations of Aquinas's Ethics Since Vatican II," in *The Ethics of Aquinas*, 412–25.

one. In particular, he has on a number of occasions expressed reservations about Thomas's (and Aristotle's) view that the virtues form a unity, such that you cannot have one virtue without possessing all virtues. Hauerwas, at least in his early work, sees this as an attempt to ground the unity of character or selfhood in the unity of the virtues: Thomas had to posit a fundamental harmony of the virtues in order to secure the stability of character necessary to be a self. Hauerwas, in contrast, wished to argue that it is the unity of the self—what we call "character"—that gives direction to the virtues. The virtues cannot provide unity for the self because the self pursues goods, and thus requires virtues, that at any given moment might be incommensurable and even in conflict.[9] It is only within the self as temporally extended over the course of a lifetime and unified through a developmental narrative that the incommensurable goods can be unified. Thus, the unity of the self is a "narrative" unity—that is, the orientation of the self as agent is shaped by the narratives in which we live and develop our character.[10] The coherence of the self—its "character"—depends upon "having a narrative that gives us skills of interpretation sufficient to allow us to make our past our own through incorporation into our ongoing history."[11] Thus, the virtues of the narrative-self can be acquired in a piecemeal fashion, whereas Thomas's non-narrative view of the self depends for its unity on the rather incredible idea that the virtues must be acquired all at once.[12]

9. See Stanley Hauerwas, "Character, Narrative, and Growth in the Christian Life," in *A Community of Character: Toward a Constructive Christian Social Ethic* (Notre Dame, IN: University of Notre Dame Press, 1991), 141–43.

10. "The moral life is not simply a matter of decisions governed by publicly defensible principles and rules; we can only act in the world we see, a seeing partially determined by the kind of beings we have become through the stories we have learned and embodied in our life plan" (Hauerwas, "The Self as Story: A Reconsideration of the Relation of Religion and Morality from the Agent's Perspective," in *Vision and Virtue*, 69).

11. Hauerwas, "Character, Narrative, and Growth in the Christian Life," 147.

12. This criticism is similar to that of Alasdair MacIntyre in *After Virtue: A Study in Moral Theory*, 2nd ed. (Notre Dame, IN: University of Notre Dame Press, 1984), 179–80. MacIntyre

ON THE UNITY OF THOMAS'S ACCOUNT

How convincing is this as a description and critique of Thomas? It is undoubtedly true that Thomas, like Aristotle, holds that one cannot have prudence unless one has the other moral virtues and that one cannot have the other moral virtues without having prudence.[13] But it is not entirely clear to me that Thomas's purpose here is to account for "the unity of the self," as Hauerwas puts it.[14] Indeed, it is not entirely clear that Thomas is particularly concerned with the "self" at all—a point that Hauerwas recognizes in some of his later writings.[15] If this is the case, we might also ask whether the notion of "character" as Hauerwas uses it is not somewhat alien to Thomas's way of thinking.[16] Can we find in Thomas a unified disposition that determines the orientation of the person as agent? In thinking of human agency, what we discover in Thomas is something that looks not so much like Hauerwas's "character" as it does a nexus of forces that collaborate to move the person toward his or her ultimate end. What Peter King writes in reference to Thomas's account of the passions might also be said with regard to his depiction of the human agent in general: "All in all, things are fairly messy, and a good deal more interesting for it."[17]

One way in which we might get some sense of this messy/

later retracts his criticism of Thomas on the question of the unity of the virtues. See *Whose Justice? Which Rationality?* (Notre Dame, IN: University of Notre Dame Press, 1988), 197–98.

13. See *Summa theologiae* 1-2.58.5 and 1-2.65.1.

14. Hauerwas, "Character, Narrative, and Growth in the Christian Life," 143.

15. "What MacIntyre helped me see is that you do not need an account of agency in itself to understand our ability to acquire character. Rather character is the source of our agency, that is, our ability to act with integrity. Interestingly enough, this puts me much closer to my other conversation partners in *Character and the Christian Life*, that is Aristotle and Aquinas. We often forget that they had no account of agency or the 'self' as such" (Stanley Hauerwas, "Going Forward by Looking Back: Agency Reconsidered," in *Sanctify Them in the Truth*, 95).

16. The term "character" is only ever used by Thomas in a sacramental context, to speak of the indelible spiritual seal brought about by Baptism, Confirmation, and Holy Orders. Likewise, in Aristotle, there really is no term that corresponds to our term "character," the closest approximations being *êthos* or *hexis êthikê*, which we might translate as "moral disposition."

17. Peter King, "Aquinas on the Passions," in *Thomas Aquinas: Contemporary Philosophical Perspectives*, ed. Brian Davies (Oxford: Oxford University Press, 2002), 359.

interesting account of the self is to consider the various forces at play in a person's journey to his or her ultimate end. There are intrinsic principles of action: the soul's powers (vegetative or nutritive, sensitive, appetitive, locomotive, and intellectual) and habits (virtues—which may be moral, intellectual, or theological—and vices). There are also extrinsic principles of action: law (both divine and human) and grace (both that which makes us holy and that which gives us a particular gift for the upbuilding of the Church). In addition to the principles of the soul's actions, there are also the passions or emotions to be taken into account, which can be broadly categorized as those of the concupiscible appetite and those of the irascible appetite (roughly speaking, those emotions related to physical pleasure and those related to violent action). Then, there are those things connected with virtue as it is transformed by grace: infused moral virtues, the gifts of the Spirit, the Beatitudes, and the fruits of the Spirit.[18] It is the burden of the *prima secundae* of the *Summa theologiae* to lay out all these factors, yielding a very rich account of human action. If Hauerwas is correct that Thomas needs the unity of the virtues in order to unify the agent's character, then it would seem that he would need to claim a similar unity for all of these other forces.

What sort of unity can be found amidst these various principles of action? It seems at first glance that Thomas lays them out in a very orderly manner. Within the self, there are actions and passions, and actions derive either from intrinsic or extrinsic principles, and intrinsic principles are either the soul's natural powers or its virtues, which are a sort of "second nature," and these in turn are either naturally acquired or infused by God; the acquired virtues are either intellectual or moral, with the various moral virtues gathered under the headings of the four cardinal virtues of prudence, justice, temperance, and courage. Likewise,

18. For the enumeration of the soul's powers, see *Summa theologiae* 1.78.1. For the rest of these factors, see *Summa theologiae* 1-2, passim.

extrinsic principles can be further subdivided into law and grace and so forth. The image is of a sort of Porphyrian tree branching out from a unified self into ever finer degrees of analysis, each set of distinctions deduced according to some rational principle.

Upon closer inspection, however, the various principles of action that Thomas explores in the *prima secundae* and elsewhere do not actually fit together in any single classificatory scheme. The pattern described in the previous paragraph is one possible way of unifying some of the principles of action Thomas discusses—one that certainly has grounding in the text. But there are principles of action that do not seem to fit into this scheme. How are the gifts of the Spirit and the Beatitudes related to the virtues?[19] How are the infused moral virtues related to the identically denominated acquired moral virtues?[20] Why does prudence seem to belong both to the intellectual virtues and to the moral virtues?[21] How can the cardinal virtues be both particular virtues and, at the same time, generic virtues under which other virtues are gathered?[22] If external principles of action are divided into law and grace, what sense can we make of the evangelical law, which is "chiefly the grace itself of the Holy Spirit, which is given to those who believe in Christ" and only secondarily a written law?[23] It is not that Thomas lacks good answers to these questions, but his answers require him to use a number of different schemata when addressing them.

To take one particular issue: How are the virtues related to

19. See, e.g., *Summa theologiae* 1-2.68.1, 8; 1-2.69.1; *Super Is.* 11.2.360–365; *Super Mt.* 5.2.

20. See *Summa theologiae* 1-2.63.3–4; *De virtutibus* 1.10. See also John Inglis, "Aquinas's Replication of the Acquired Moral Virtues: Rethinking the Standard Philosophical Interpretation of Moral Virtue in Aquinas," *The Journal of Religious Ethics* 27, no. 1 (Spring 1999): 3–27.

21. Cf. *Summa theologiae* 2-2.47.1, 4, and 5.

22. See *Summa theologiae* 1-2.61.3 and *Sententia Ethic.* 2.8.337–339. See also István P. Bejczy, "The Cardinal Virtues in Medieval Commentaries on the *Nicomachean Ethics*, 1250–1350," in *Virtue Ethics in the Middle Ages: Commentaries on Aristotle's "Nicomachean Ethics," 1200–1500*, ed. István P. Bejczy (Leiden, NL: Brill, 2008), 199–221.

23. *Summa theologiae* 1-2.106.1.

the gifts and the Beatitudes? Thomas inherits from Augustine a correlation of the Beatitudes and the gifts of the Spirit, a correlation that he adopts in his commentary on Matthew and that he employs throughout the *secunda pars* of the *Summa theologiae*.[24] In the *secunda pars*, he also links the gifts of the Spirit to particular virtues: as the virtues are perfections according to which we are moved from "within," in accordance with our nature, the gifts are perfections that dispose us "to become amenable to divine inspiration" such that we are moved "by divine instinct." In this way, "the gifts perfect humans for acts that are higher than acts of virtue."[25] Consequently, when Thomas discusses each of the theological and cardinal virtues, he includes a question on the correlative gift. Thus, we seem to have a three-way correlation of Beatitudes, gifts, and virtues: those who are poor in spirit have the gift of fear, which correlates to the virtue of hope; those who are meek have the gift of piety, which correlates to the virtue of justice; those who mourn have the gift of knowledge, which correlates with the virtue of faith; those who hunger and thirst for righteousness have the gift of courage, which correlates with the virtue of courage; those who are merciful have the gift of counsel, which corresponds to prudence; those who are pure of heart have the gift of understanding, which also correlates with the gift of faith; and the peacemakers have the gift of wisdom, which correlates with the gift of charity. The Beatitudes name the actions possible when a virtue is strengthened by the correlative gift.[26]

Yet this neat scheme begins to fray a bit, since Thomas assigns two gifts to the virtue of faith: knowledge and understanding.[27] This means that one of the virtues must lack a gift, and indeed

24. See *Super Mt.* 5.2, where Thomas adopts the Augustinian correlation of gifts and Beatitudes. See also *Summa theologiae* 2-2.8.7, 2-2.9.4, 2-2.19.12, 2-2.52.4, 2-2.121.2, 2-2.139.2. On Augustine's correlations and their subsequent influence in the tradition, see now Rebekah Eklund, *The Beatitudes through the Ages* (Grand Rapids, MI: Eerdmans, 2021), 53–59.

25. *Summa theologiae* 1-2.68.1.

26. *Summa theologiae* 1-2.69.3.

27. Discussed in questions 2-2.8 and 2-2.9, respectively.

there is no correlative gift discussed under the virtue of temperance. However, in *Summa theologiae* 1-2.68.4, he says that the concupiscible appetite, which naturally is perfected by the virtue of temperance, is also the subject of the gift of fear.[28] Yet this correlation of the virtue of temperance with the gift of fear doesn't really help matters, since this correlates fear with both temperance and hope, which is the virtue under which he actually discusses the gift of fear. The difficulty is not simply that we have a dual correlation of fear with two different virtues but that this gift seems to reside in two different faculties: the concupiscible appetite in the case of temperance and the will in the case of hope.[29] Furthermore, in 1-2.69.3, Thomas associates the perfection of the concupiscible appetite with the Beatitude of mourning, correlated by Augustine with the gift of knowledge.

The fraying continues when we look at some of the other correlations. For example, in 1-2.68.4, Thomas associates the perfection of the irascible faculty, quite logically, with the gift of courage. This is consistent with his discussion in 1-2.56.4, which sees this faculty as the subject of the virtue of courage. In 1-2.69.3, however, he associates the perfection of this faculty with an unnamed virtue and gift that he connects to the Beatitude "Blessed are the meek," which the Augustinian tradition associates not with the gift of courage but with the gift of piety. Of course, Thomas is aware that he has a problem here. In his discussion of the gift of piety in the *secunda secundae*, under the virtue of justice, he asks whether the traditional Augustinian correlation is correct. He notes that Augustine's correlation is achieved by simply matching the Beatitudes as they are found in Matthew with the gifts of the Spirit taken in the reverse order that they are

28. This solution to the problem of the missing gift correlated to the virtue of temperance is suggested by Stephen Pope in "Overview of the Ethics of Thomas Aquinas," 37.

29. On the will as the subject of hope, see *Summa theologiae* 2-2.18.1. To my knowledge, Thomas never discusses whether a gift can be in two different faculties, but he does state that one virtue cannot be in two faculties "equally" (*aequo*) but only by residing in one principally and in another secondarily (*Summa theologiae* 1-2.56.2).

found in Isaiah 11:2. He says that a different set of correlations might be established "in keeping with the special nature of each gift and beatitude," and in that case, piety would fit better with hungering and thirsting for righteousness—the Beatitude associated with courage in the Augustinian tradition.[30] This would seem to be supported by 1-2.69.3, in which hungering and thirsting for righteousness is associated with justice, the virtue under which the gift of piety falls.

What can we make of all of this? One who has suffered through my parsing of the seeming inconsistencies in Thomas's correlations might be tempted simply to dismiss Thomas as profoundly confused and confusing, a case of a mind fallen victim to the Scholastic mania for categorization, though a mind that was not quite up to the task. Aside from the *prima facie* implausibility of this, I have already noted that Thomas evinces an awareness of his inconsistencies in a number of places.[31] More plausible is the view that we see here one of the negative results of the Scholastic desire to harmonize an irreducibly diverse tradition. That is, Thomas inherits from Augustine a set of correlations between the Beatitudes and the gifts that he feels compelled to use. But this correlation, as one commentator puts it, "was more an invention of Augustine's kerygmatic rhetoric than a solid theological construction."[32] Thomas does have a solid theological scheme of relating both the gifts and the Beatitudes to the various faculties of the soul, which he spells out in 1-2.68.4 and 1-2.69.3, respectively.[33] When combined, however, these constructions do not fit with the traditional Augustinian correlations.

30. *Summa theologiae* 2-2.121.2.

31. See, e.g., *Summa theologiae* 1-2.69.3 ad 3.

32. In Thomas Aquinas, *Summa Theologiae*, vol. 24, *The Gifts of the Spirit*, ed. Edward D. O'Connor (London: Eyre and Spottiswoode, 1973), 56, note n.

33. O'Connor states that in his judgment, it is a mistake to see *Summa theologiae* 1-2.69.3 as making a correlation between the Beatitudes and the seven gifts and seven particular virtues. Rather, "the author means to speak simply of whatever virtue or Gift may be pertinent in the case" (*Gifts of the Spirit*, 52, note h).

Certainly, the difficulties engendered by Thomas's loyalty to the inherited tradition are a factor here, as elsewhere. But if the unity of the human agent's character were dependent on giving a unified account of the virtues, gifts, and Beatitudes, one would expect Thomas to be willing to jettison the Augustinian tradition so that order might be restored.[34]

Another possibility exists: perhaps Thomas is *not* seeking to ground the unity of the agent's character in the unity of the virtues, gifts, and Beatitudes. Even if we excise the Augustinian account of the gifts' relation to the Beatitudes, the sprawling account of the principles of human action that we find in the *secunda pars* does not seem to be a very suitable way of rendering a unified self. But if Thomas is not, as Hauerwas claimed, seeking the unity of the self in the unity of the virtues, how else might he account for the coherence of agency?

The answer, I believe, is to look to the beginning of the *secunda pars.* Thomas's discussion of the principles of human action is prefaced by five questions on happiness (*beatitudo*). It is only in light of these questions, which in turn presuppose the account of God the Creator and the human being as creature found in the *prima pars*, that the discussion of the virtues can be seen as having any coherence, a coherence that is not really apparent if we look simply at the various schemes by which the soul's powers are associated with various gifts, Beatitudes, and virtues. I would also suggest that it is here that any sort of "coherence of the agent" is to be sought—though only indirectly. For in these questions, Thomas is not concerned primarily with the agent but

34. With regard to accounting for the order and significance of the Beatitudes, Thomas is in places quite unattached to the Augustinian account. In his commentary on Matthew, he gives two different accounts of the structure of the Beatitudes, one as a kind of preface and one *en passant* as he discusses each Beatitude. Neither of these pays much attention to the Augustinian tradition of correlating gifts and Beatitudes, even though that correlation is mentioned in his discussion of each Beatitude. See Jeremy Holmes, "Aquinas' *Lectura in Matthaeum*," in *Aquinas on Scripture: An Introduction to his Biblical Commentaries*, ed. Thomas G. Weinandy, Daniel A. Keating, and John P. Yocum (London: T&T Clark, 2005), 73–97, esp. 79–83. In addition, Thomas's sermon *Beata gens* discusses the Beatitudes but makes no use of Augustine's correlation with the gifts of the Spirit.

with the end toward which all of the various powers and passions of the person are ordered. As Thomas says in introducing the first question of the *prima secundae*, one must discuss the end before discussing the means of attaining that end, "for the end is the measure [*ratio*] of whatever is ordered to the end."[35]

WHY GOD MATTERS MORE THAN THE SELF

In criticizing Thomas's account of the unity of the virtues, Hauerwas writes that Thomas "assumes that perfect moral virtue necessarily provides a unity to the self" and that this assumption is possible "only because he asserts that all men have a single last end which orders the various virtues appropriately."[36] If I understand this argument correctly, it seems to say that Thomas posits a single last end for human beings precisely in order to secure the unity of the self as agent, which unity is an assumption that Thomas cannot do without. If this is in fact the argument, I think it gets the matter precisely backward. Thomas's discussion of God and creation in the *prima pars* has rendered for us a picture of reality that makes plausible the view that there is a single ultimate end for human beings, and the picture of human beings as unified agents flows as a consequence from their having an ultimate end. It is not that Thomas asserts a final end because he needs to secure the unity of the self; rather, we can find something that looks to us like a unified agential self (i.e., "character") in Thomas precisely because he sees a single end for human beings: supernatural happiness or *beatitudo*. The various forces at play in what we call "human action" only fully coalesce into agency or selfhood or character when they are properly ordered to the ultimate end. Thus, the burden of establishing the coherence of agency falls on the account given of God as first cause and final end that we find

35. *Summa theologiae* 1-2.1.

36. See Hauerwas, "Character, Narrative, and Growth in the Christian Life," 142.

in the *prima pars* and the first five questions of the *prima secundae*, and not on the account of virtues given in the *secunda secundae*. This allows there to be a certain "looseness" in the various ways in which Thomas relates the virtues to the gifts, the Beatitudes, the powers of the soul, as well as to each other. What drives Thomas's account of the virtues is his understanding of God as the source and object of human beatitude, not a particular account of the unity of the self.

On this reading, Thomas begins to look a bit more like Augustine. Thomas's facility with the Aristotelian idiom, as well as an overly simple historiography of high medieval thought that employs a facile distinction between "Thomists" and "Augustinians," can lead us to overlook the profound debt Thomas has to Augustine—not just on particular points of doctrine but also in the overall shape of his thought.[37] In particular, Thomas is heir to the fundamental Augustinian conviction that, in the end, it is our love that gives our life its moral orientation. For Augustine, it is the orientation of love—whether toward God or toward ourselves—that distinguishes the city of God from the earthly city. Thomas's view that *caritas* is the form of all the virtues conveys this same conviction.[38] Apart from charity that is motivated by the grace of Christ, the self as agent remains in a sense inchoate, a chaotic and conflicting set of forces that cannot really be called a self. The unity of the self finds its source in our participation as creatures in God's own simplicity. It is only in this light that we can make sense of what Thomas says about the unity of the

37. See chapter 14 below.

38. Edward O'Connor notes, "Along with the sensitive appreciation of natural values which makes Thomas a humanist in comparison with mainstream Augustinianism, there is an Augustinian radicalism in his understanding of the exigencies of the following of Christ" (*Gifts of the Spirit*, 52–53, note i). Thomas's account of the virtues, however, is vastly more complex—and, dare I say, more subtle—than Augustine's, for whom all the virtues seem, in the end, to be simply modes of charity. One might say that Thomas's account relates to Augustine's the way that polyphony relates to chant, with charity being the melody in both. In Augustine, this melody can be pitched high or low, but it is only ever one melody, while in Aquinas the melody is the organizing center of a variety of distinct harmonies (my thanks to Charlie Pinches for suggesting a musical metaphor here).

virtues. To see the unity of the virtues as a way of securing the unity of the self is to see the matter from the wrong end. The virtues have a unity because our end as creatures is the one God; to the degree that our virtues lack unity, they are mere inclinations and cannot serve as means to our final end.[39] But Thomas goes further: only those virtues that are infused by God's grace "deserve to be called virtues simply."[40] Without God's assistance, we fall short in our sharing in the divine nature, and thus, even if we possess all of the acquired virtues, we do not possess perfect virtue in the proper sense of the term. In this way, the unity of the virtues is less an account of the unity of the self and more a correlate of an Augustinian theology of grace.

While Hauerwas's early reflections on "character" seem to be driven more by a particular philosophical account of the self than by a properly theological account of the end of creatures, his later writings seem to reflect a shift to a more resolutely theological starting point and, not coincidentally, a greater willingness to accept some form of the notion of the unity of the virtues, as well as a greater focus on happiness as the *telos* of the Christian life.[41] Indeed, Hauerwas's insistence on the importance of narrative in the Christian life, properly understood, can help us understand how, for Thomas, human beings can only be properly understood in light of the end toward which we journey, a journey enabled by God's grace.

39. *Summa theologiae* 1-2.65.1.

40. *Summa theologiae* 1-2.65.2.

41. "We do not mean to deny the unity thesis flat out. . . . If Christians do go on to affirm an ultimate unity of the virtues, they do best to follow Aquinas rather than Aristotle, who finally calls charity (not prudence) the form of the virtues" (Stanley Hauerwas and Charles Pinches, *Christians among the Virtues: Theological Conversations with Ancient and Modern Ethics* [Notre Dame, IN: University of Notre Dame Press, 1997], 188–89). Yet doubts seem to linger: "There certainly seems to be something right about the insistence on the interrelation of the virtues, since, for example, courage depends to some degree on temperance. Yet as MacIntyre suggests, strong accounts of the unity of the virtues have difficulty accounting for their acquisition over time" (Hauerwas and Pinches, 206). With regard to happiness, Hauerwas writes in the preface to the 1994 edition of *Character and the Christian Life*, "I am increasingly convinced that happiness, virtue, and friendship are crucially interrelated in a manner necessary for any adequate account of character" (xxv).

THE CHRISTIAN AS *HOMO VIATOR*

There seems to be something fundamentally right about Hauerwas's point concerning the role of "narrative" in thinking about character. Particularly in his later writings, when the language of "narrative" is increasingly replaced by that of "journey," we can see points of contact with Thomas's account of human beings as *viatores*, journeying to their final end of beatitude.[42] Thomas, no less than Augustine, sees the human person as a wayfaring stranger:

> The natural longing of a human being cannot rest in anything else except in God alone. For human beings have an innate longing that moves them from the things that have been brought into being to seeking their cause. Therefore this longing will not rest until it reaches the first cause, which is God.[43]

The image of Christians as "wayfarers" (*viatores*) or "pilgrims" (*peregrini*) is, of course, an ancient one, employed with great facility by Augustine in *The City of God* and other works. Gerhart Ladner argued that the image of the human person as *viator* was, in the hands of orthodox Christian theologians, a way of reconciling the themes of "alienation" and "order" that run through the Christian tradition. According to Ladner, in Christianity, there is a dual sense of alienation: "estrangement from God and estrangement from the world."[44] On the one hand, through sin, human beings have become alienated from the divine order of things; on the other hand, the solution to this alienation is for Christians to live as aliens, sojourners in this fallen world. It is important to see how these two types of alienation are related to each other and to the notion of divine order. As Ladner puts it, orthodox early

42. See, for example, Hauerwas and Pinches, *Christians Among the Virtues*, 17–20.

43. *De virtutibus* 1.10.

44. Gerhart Ladner, "*Homo Viator*: Mediaeval Ideas on Alienation and Order," *Speculum* 42, no. 2 (April 1967): 238.

Christians (in contrast to the Gnostics) "seem to have felt that the type of alienation which meant detachment from this world somehow belonged together with man's attempts to establish the disturbed terrestrial order of creation in such a way that it would reflect, however imperfectly, the celestial order."[45] Thus, there is a sort of alienation from the fallen world that has become alienated from God—a sort of counter-alienation that establishes a counter-order to the sinful "order" of the world. For Ladner, the meticulous ordering of life that we find in a document like *The Rule* of St. Benedict has the purpose of securing alienation from the world of sin by instantiating a life of true order in opposition to the pseudo-order of the world. "One might perhaps describe the monastic intention paradoxically as follows: no alien order must alienate the monk from his alienation from an alienated world."[46] The asceticism of the interior pilgrimage of the monk, the physical pilgrimage of the Irish penitent, the wandering of the mendicant friars, and even the legends of the knights-errant are all seen by Ladner as forms embodying this idea of the *viator* who is detached from the world for the sake of the world. "Medieval men asserted ever anew that the order of the world would become spiritually lifeless if it did not transcend itself through various modes of alienation from what seemed the ordinary scheme of things."[47]

Ladner explicitly connects the idea of the human person as wayfarer to Thomas's statement that "grace perfects and does not destroy nature," seeing in it "a new formulation of hope for *Homo Viator*, the wayfarer on this earth."[48] Because grace is a perfection and not a destruction of nature, I can understand my life not simply as a matter of disjunction but of some sort of genuine moral

45. Ladner, 238. For a similar idea of pilgrimage as the journey toward a restoration of cosmic order, in this case applied to Dante's *Divine Comedy*, see John Freccero, "Dante's Pilgrim in a Gyre," *PMLA* 76, no. 3 (June 1961): 168–81.

46. Ladner, "*Homo Viator*," 242.

47. Ladner, 244–45.

48. Ladner, 250.

development. One might say that Thomas excludes any Gnostic interpretation of alienation: the alienation of the *viator* from the world is not a radical rupture from an inherently sinful creation but is rather a journey toward happiness along a distinctive path, a happiness that involves the perfection-through-reordering of the person.[49] I take Hauerwas to be making much the same point about grace perfecting and not destroying nature when he writes, "The gospel does not require that we doubt everything we believe but that everything we believe be reordered."[50]

It is worth noting that the description of the human person as a *viator* is not itself something neutral but is already a description redolent of the Christian story. Indeed, we might say that the first step of one's wayfaring is to come to see oneself as a wayfarer. For once we see ourselves as wayfarers, we see ourselves as those whose identities are determined by their goal. We come to see our journey as one undertaken by means of acts of love, through which we are conformed to the divine order of things. We see that even if our love falls short of the perfection of love, in the very struggle itself is our perfecting. Thomas writes, with regard to the religious who seek to live Christ's counsels of perfection, "Although the perfection of the blessed is not possible to us in this life, we ought, nevertheless, to endeavor, as far as we can, to emulate it: and it is in this that the perfection in this life consists, to which we are invited by the counsels."[51] We also come to see that this journey of reordering is a process that requires not only our actions but God's grace, and we come to see that God's grace is not something that we merit by our acts of love but is in fact

49. M. Michèle Mulchahey, summarizing the view of one early Dominican author, writes, "The Dominican novice who learns to regulate his exterior conduct according to the Preachers' *ordo*, and who learns to match conduct with interior disposition, will see the divine order fully expressed in himself" (*"First the Bow Is Bent in Study": Dominican Education before 1350* [Toronto: Pontifical Institute of Mediaeval Studies, 1998], 123).

50. Stanley Hauerwas, *With the Grain of the Universe: The Church's Witness and Natural Theology* (Grand Rapids, MI: Brazos, 2002), 211n11.

51. *De perfectione* 6.

the source of those acts. To know ourselves as *viatores* who struggle is itself an act of grace.

Hauerwas's emphasis on the story-formed character of the person as agent gives us "fresh eyes" to see the importance of Thomas's picture of the human person as *viator*. What Thomas says about the powers of the soul and its passions, its virtues, and its gifts is both interesting and important in understanding human action. But the proper starting place for understanding the character of the self is the one that Thomas himself gives us at the outset of the *prima secundae*: the self as a wayfarer on the journey to beatitude. The human person cannot rest in any created good but "goes forth to the universal font of good itself, which is the universal object of happiness of all the blessed, as being the infinite and perfect good."[52] As any pilgrim will tell you, the journey is often a messy affair, filled with distractions and diversion. It is the goal that gives both the journey and the journeyer their unity. It is in this context of the person as journeyer that we ought to see how the virtues form a unity, how acquired virtues are related to infused virtues, how grace is related to freedom, and how an insistence on the primacy of divine grace is not at odds with a belief in the moral development of the person.

52. *Summa theologiae* 1-2.2.8 ad 1.

7

Conversion, Coercion, and Persuasion

Thomas Aquinas on the Will

In the middle of the thirteenth century, what seems to have been a new question arose for debate in the theological schools: whether the child of Jewish parents, or of other infidels, should be baptized against the wishes of the parents.[1] Thomas Aquinas held that such baptisms were not permissible, appealing to the natural rights of parents and the striking image of the child being enveloped in the care of its parents as in a "spiritual womb" (*spirituali utero*), in which, we might say, it is knit together as a moral agent. He goes on to note that when the child has attained the use of reason, emerging, as it were, from the spiritual womb of its parents, the child should be "brought to faith not

* Originally given as a lecture at the Catholic Theological Society of America, Miami, FL, June 2013 and in revised form at Yale Divinity School, New Haven, CT, March 2019.

1. In Thomas's writings, it seems first to appear in his second Parisian regency as a quodlibetal question, which is then taken over almost verbatim into the *secunda secundae* of the *Summa theologiae* in the discussion of *infidelitas*. The issue reappears in the *tertia pars* in the discussion of Baptism, with many of the same arguments (see *Summa theologiae* 2-2.10.12; 3.68.10; *Quodlibet* 2.4.2). On the novelty of this question, see Manfred Svensson, "A Defensible Conception of Tolerance in Aquinas?" *The Thomist* 75, no. 2 (April 2011): 291–308, at 305. For a comprehensive discussion of the issue of the baptism of Jewish children, along with coerced baptism of adults, in the Middle Ages, see Marcia L. Colish, *Faith, Fiction and Force in Medieval Baptismal Debates* (Washington, DC: The Catholic University of America Press, 2014), especially 227–318. One thing Colish's study makes clear is that while this question might be new to Scholastic debates, it had a long prehistory in the mission field and among canonists.

by coercion, but by persuasion" (*inducendus ad fidem non coactione, sed persuasione*).[2]

While we may wish to commend Thomas's conclusion as plain common sense—though, let it be noted, it was not universally seen that way in his own day—we might also worry that it begs the question of so neat a distinction between coercion and persuasion. Given the analysis of Foucault and others of disciplinary regimes and the hidden workings of power, it is today difficult to accept the distinction as an obvious one.[3] While it might be clear that tying someone up and submersing them in water while reciting the baptismal formula is a coerced, unfree act, the case is maybe a little less clear if I induce someone to embrace the Christian faith by threatening burning at the stake (since physical force itself is not involved) and still less clear if I do so by threatening the fires of hell. In these latter two cases, is it entirely clear that I have acted coercively in the first but only persuasively in the second? At best, the distinction between coercion and persuasion seems a fuzzy one, and at worst, a specious one, a part of the way in which power masks itself.

I would argue, however, that we do have reasons to maintain the distinction, so that we might commend those who persuade others to become Christians while condemning those who use coercion to attain the same ends. It seems not a merely Scholastic distinction, nor one that is relevant only to infidel babies, but one that might help us to think about the nature of the will and its freedom, and to lay a bit of groundwork for questions pertaining to the spiritual life.

In what follows, I will first give a brief overview of what Thomas thinks about the will and its freedom of action

2. *Summa theologiae* 2-2.10.12. Thomas consequently holds that adult Jews and infidels ought not be compelled to believe, though heretics and apostates can be so compelled, since at one time they freely embraced the faith. See *Summa theologiae* 1-2.10.8.

3. See, e.g., Michel Foucault, *Discipline and Punish: The Birth of the Prison*, trans. Alan Sheridan (New York: Vintage Books, 1979).

vis-à-vis faith. Then, I will look at his claim that God's grace acts non-coercively in the justification of the sinner. After this, I will examine the role of human agents in persuasion toward faith and whether this, too, can be understood as non-coercive. Finally, I will look at his analysis of fear and how it does and does not compromise freedom. I will conclude with some brief remarks about lessons we might draw from this and raise the question of whether and how one might accept the distinction between coercion and persuasion without accepting Thomas's account of the will.

THOMAS ON THE WILL AND FAITH

Thomas's consistent teaching is that turning to God in faith must be a free act of the will. To understand this claim, however, it is important first to recall that Thomas sees "will" not primarily as a faculty by which we make choices but as "rational appetite"—the specifically human capacity to be drawn to something because of our mind's apprehension of its goodness. The main role of the will is not exercised in making a choice between, say, building a house or building a boat but in my attraction to shelter or transport as goods to be sought.[4] As long as I act in accordance with what reason perceives as good, I act freely.[5] And this is in spite of the fact that the willing of the good is not something I choose, since I cannot help but be drawn toward that which I understand to be good, just as a heavy object cannot help but be drawn downward by gravity. This is why Timothy McDermott writes, "For Aquinas will is not willpower but willweakness: it is a weakness or attraction for anything that fulfills, anything good, anything happy."[6] To say that the act of faith is a free act of the will is

4. See *Summa theologiae* 1-2.8.1.

5. See *Summa theologiae* 1-2.10.3 on how passions, for example, might make the will unfree.

6. Timothy McDermott, *How to Read Aquinas* (London: Granta Books, 2007), 47.

not to say that I "choose" to have faith but that my will is drawn by a natural inclination to the perceived good of assenting to the truth of God. If the will is moved in a way contrary to its natural inclination toward good, then its motion is not free but coerced or violent. Thomas writes, "Just as it is impossible for a thing to be at the same time violent and natural, so too it is impossible for a thing to be coerced or violent in an absolute sense, and at the same time voluntary."[7] Or, more succinctly, "By its nature, the will is free from coercion."[8]

Second, while an act of the will cannot be coerced, a willed act can be. That is to say, my will cannot be drawn to something that my intellect does not perceive as good, but my will can move me to act in a way that I would not otherwise act due to the influence of an external agent—say, someone holding a gun to my head.[9] From this, we get some idea of the range of things that might count as coercion. Coercion is a matter of an external agent acting upon a person precisely as agent and not simply as end (i.e., it must be a moving cause and not simply a motivating goal) and must make the person act in a way contrary to his or her natural inclination. Because what is natural to the will is to desire a perceived good, a person cannot act willingly, but only under coercion, to achieve an end that he or she does not perceive as good.[10]

Third, we can see the unique role played by the will in the act of faith by way of contrast with other cognitive acts. In ordinary knowing, the mind assents to evident truths without any need

7. *Summa theologiae* 1.82.1. For the full context: "Necessity of coercion is altogether repugnant to the will. For we call something violent when it is against the inclination of a thing. But the movement of the will is itself an inclination to something. Therefore, just as a thing is called natural because it is according to the inclination of nature, so too a thing is called voluntary because it is according to the inclination of the will. Therefore, just as it is impossible for a thing to be at the same time violent and natural, so too it is impossible for a thing to be coerced or violent in an absolute sense, and at the same time voluntary."

8. *De veritate* 17.3. Cf. *Summa theologiae* 1-2.6.4.

9. *Summa theologiae* 1-2.6.4.

10. *Summa theologiae* 1-2.6.5.

for the will to act: to grasp a proof for the Pythagorean theorem, for example, simply *is* to assent to that theorem; you can't grasp it without assenting to it. This is because in such cases one, as it were, sees its truth. In such knowing, the will is not so much overridden as it is irrelevant; it has no role to play. The truth of those things to which faith assents, in contrast, is something unseen—and here Thomas appeals to the words of the Letter to the Hebrews: faith is "proof [in the Vulgate, *argumentum*] of things not seen"—which is why the will has a crucial role to play in moving the intellect.[11] Because in matters of faith the intellect's assent cannot be elicited by the evidence of truth, the will must move the intellect to such assent. Therefore, faith is, in contrast to other forms of certain knowledge, by its very nature a free act because it is a willful act, an act of the will inclining the intellect. We might call it "willed knowing."

THE WILL AND GOD'S GRACE: CAN GRACE MOVE THE WILL NON-COERCIVELY?

While the will cannot be moved coercively, this doesn't mean that it cannot be moved at all. As we have seen, the will is moved by the natural object of its desire: the good as perceived by the intellect. This is intrinsic to the will's nature and so is non-coercive. For Thomas, it would make no sense to speak of the desired end "coercing" the will's desire for it.

In the case of the act of faith, however, the will that moves the intellect is itself moved by God not only as end but as agent—that is, as a moving cause and not simply a motivating goal. God causes us to will not only by endowing us with rational appetite but also by causing our will to act.[12] In an act of faith, the will moves freely, but it is still a moved mover, moved by God. This is,

11. See *Summa theologiae* 1-2.17.6; 2-2.1.4.

12. *Contra Gentiles* 3.89.4: "Divine causality is not only extended to the power of the will but also to its act."

in addition to the general principle that God is the first mover, a result of two things. First, the sublimity of the object of faith. As we have noted, the object of faith is "unseen," which means that the intellect is not sufficient to perceive its true goodness. Thus, Thomas says, "free will is inadequate for the act of faith since the contents of faith are above human reason."[13] Second, the disordering of human nature by sin. While the natural goodness of the will is not taken away entirely by the fall, it is corrupted by malice and diverted by the passions, inhibiting the will from turning to God as its good.[14]

Thomas frequently invokes Lamentations 5:21: "Convert us, O Lord, to you, and we shall be converted" (DRB). He notes, "It is clear that our conversion to God is preceded by God's help that converts us."[15] Turning to God in faith—converting—is really a matter of being turned by God. Thomas is resolute, however, in maintaining that this action is not "violent," that it is not contrary to the natural inclination of the will, even though God moves the will as an efficient or agent cause. While the will is moved externally by the good that it apprehends as by a final cause, the efficient or agent cause of any free movement of the will must come from within the will itself. God, "who alone is the cause of [the soul's] being and who sustains it in being," is "joined to the intellectual soul in regard to its inner parts."[16] In short, "the only agent that can cause a movement of the will, without violence, is that which causes an intrinsic principle of this movement, and such a principle is the power of the will itself. Now, this agent is God, who alone creates a soul."[17] In other words, God can move the will, not only as an end but also as an agent,

13. *Super Eph.* 2.3.95.

14. See *Summa theologiae* 1-2.109.7.

15. *Contra Gentiles* 3.149.6.

16. *Contra Gentiles* 3.88.5.

17. *Contra Gentiles* 3.88.6. Cf. *De veritate* 22.9: "From the point of view of the will only what works inside the will can change the act of the will. This is the will itself and that which is the cause of the being of the will, which according to the faith is God alone."

in a non-coercive manner because God creates the principle of the will's movement, working not over and against the will but, as it were, within the will. Thomas notes, "Although it is part of the meaning of 'voluntary' that an action's principle is within the agent, nevertheless, that this intrinsic principle being caused or moved by an extrinsic principle is not contrary to the meaning of voluntariness, because it is not part of the meaning of a voluntary act that its intrinsic principle be a first principle."[18] God as first principle is, we might say, the source of the internal source of human action.

Grace works noncoercively and nonviolently because God, while remaining an external agent, moves the will from within and in a way entirely in accord with its nature, and this is because God is the author both of nature and of grace. Indeed, as Thomas puts it, "the infusion of grace is a kind of creation" [*infusio gratiae est quaedam creatio*].[19] God can, therefore, convert the hearts of sinners—in the strong sense of acting so as to turn them—in a way that does not compromise human freedom by doing violence to the will.[20]

HUMAN AGENTS OF CONVERSION: CAN PERSUASION MOVE THE WILL NON-COERCIVELY?

All of this seems well and good when we are speaking of God's role vis-à-vis the sinner in the work of conversion. But conversion typically involves human agents as well, and here we come to speak of persuasion. Thomas says that faith requires that the object of faith be proposed for belief and that the believer assent to the truth proposed. In both respects, God is the ultimate cause of faith, but in such a way as not to exclude the action

18. *Summa theologiae* 1-2.6.1 ad 1.

19. *Super II Cor.* 5.4.192.

20. We might see this as a specific application of the principle that grace perfects and does not destroy nature.

of human beings as secondary causes, whether as transmitters of the revealed truth proposed for belief or as those who induce others to assent by means of convincing words or miraculous signs.[21] Thomas always emphasizes the secondary and external character of the human role in conversion. In commenting on Paul's discussion of charismatic graces in 1 Corinthians, he notes that one human being can procure the salvation of another, "not by working within, for this belongs to God alone, but only by persuading outwardly."[22] Whereas the justifying work of grace is internal and instantaneous, the human activities through which grace works—including "thoughts, conversations, and other such motions"—are part of our external, time-bound world.[23]

If we compare persuasion to coercion and to grace, we see that persuasion is like coercion and unlike grace inasmuch as it is external to the will. Persuasion, however, is unlike coercion and like grace inasmuch as it does not move the will violently. Unlike both coercion and grace, persuasion's action upon the one being moved is not immediate but mediated by an appeal to what is most natural to the will: the desire for a perceived good. In the *Summa contra Gentiles*, Thomas writes,

> No created substance can move the will except by means of a good that is understood. Now, this is done by showing it that something is a good thing to do: this is the act of persuading. Therefore, no created substance can act on the will, or be the cause of our act of choice, except in the way of a persuading agent.[24]

21. *Summa theologiae* 2-2.6.1. Glossing Song of Songs 7:11, "Come, my beloved, let us go out in the field," Thomas notes in a sermon that "a particular familiarity of God with the preacher is indicated: 'Let *us* go out: I by inspiring, and you by preaching'" (*Serm.* 9: *Exiit qui seminat*).

22. *Super I Cor.* 12.2.727.

23. *De veritate* 28.2 ad 10.

24. *Contra Gentiles* 3.88.2; cf. *De malo* 3.3.

To persuade someone is to offer a convincing account of an end *as* good so that the will is drawn to that good through its own natural desire. In persuading someone to belief in the true sense, one must present a captivating vision of the object of beatitude or those things that lead to it: "Just as the origin of bodily love lies in the vision accomplished through the bodily eye, so also the beginning of spiritual love ought to lie in the intellectual vision of an object of spiritual love."[25]

We forget at our interpretive peril that Thomas Aquinas was a Dominican friar, a member of a religious order dedicated to preaching. The mission of the preaching friars was, in a phrase coined by Thomas and adopted as a motto by his order, "to hand on to others the fruits of contemplation" (*contemplata aliis tradere*).[26] The task of the preacher as persuader is precisely to convey to his audience his or her own "intellectual vision of an object of spiritual love." Note that it is precisely as "loved," as desirable, that the object of faith must be presented. Thus, preaching often takes the form of wooing the audience with descriptions of the benefits conferred by the virtues of faith, hope, and love by which one is united to God.[27]

This is a feature of Thomas's own sermons, particularly those given in the vernacular to lay audiences. In the very first of his series of sermons on the Apostles' Creed, he begins with a description of the "goods" (*bona*) of faith: the soul is wedded to God; eternal life is begun in us; we are guided in this life; and we are able to conquer the temptations posed by the world, the flesh, and the devil.[28] In his sermons on the Ten Commandments, he likewise notes that charity powerfully produces in human beings four desirable things (*desiderabilia*): spiritual life (understood as

25. *Contra Gentiles* 3.118.2.

26. *Summa theologiae* 2-2.188.6; cf. *Serm.* 9: *Exiit qui seminat.*

27. Thomas notes in his commentary on 1 Thessalonians, "It is the practice of a good preacher to use as an example the blessings coming to others" (*Super I Thes.* 1.1.18).

28. *In Symbolum Apostolorum*, prologue.

the indwelling of God), the ability to promptly carry out God's law, a stronghold against adversity, and a pathway to happiness.[29] Note that persuasion here is not toward God *simpliciter*, the final good in itself, but toward a specific benefit, which is, as Thomas puts it, "something similar to or oriented toward the final end that is naturally desired" (*aliqua similitudo vel ordo respectu ultimi finis naturaliter desiderati*).[30]

Someone—perhaps a particularly strict and joyless kind of Kantian—might object that a conversion that grows from a desire for reward, even a spiritual one, is somehow tainted: one desires the benefit more than God and one's freedom is in some way compromised by the desire to attain a benefit for oneself. To proffer such benefits is to manipulate people's emotions and thereby compromise their freedom. Indeed, Thomas himself says that demons learn "from people's acts . . . to which passions they are more subject, so that accordingly they more effectively impress on people's imagination what they intend."[31] Is the preacher who excites his audience with promised benefits following the example of the demons? To think this would be to misunderstand Thomas's entire view of human action. Far from holding that concupiscence, in the sense of passionate longing for something, necessarily detracts from our freedom with regard to that thing, Thomas holds that concupiscence can in fact enhance our willing, inasmuch as the will, the intellectual appetite, is given, as it were, a tailwind by the passions, while still moving in its natural direction toward the perceived good.[32]

At the same time, persuasion cannot be simply a matter of moving the passions: "Persuasion is always accompanied by rational inference [*ratio secundum ordinem illationis*], for one must

29. *De decem praeceptis*, prologue, 2.

30. *De veritate* 22.9.

31. *De malo* 3.4.

32. *Summa theologiae* 1-2.6.7.

have some reason for being persuaded of anything."[33] Faith remains, for Thomas, an intellectual act, and much of his own preaching, to both the educated and the uneducated, takes the form of an appeal to the intellect, particularly by making distinctions and showing the fitting connections between the mysteries of faith. Indeed, by our standards, Thomas's sermons are notably cerebral and un-affective. Were the passions appealed to entirely apart from the intellect, then the will would not be fully engaged in the act of faith and voluntariness would be compromised.

FEAR AND FREEDOM

So, the preacher should draw the will of listeners through "the intellectual vision of an object of spiritual love." But, as we know, sometimes preachers seek to persuade not through attraction toward a good but through fear of some evil. Commenting on Luke 14:23—"compel them to come in"—which was often given as a proof text for religious compulsion, Thomas notes that "the compelling mentioned there is not that of coercion [*coactionis*] but that of efficacious persuasion, either by harsh or gentle means."[34] Thomas's discussion of persuasion and coercion takes place against the background of ongoing medieval discussions. Rufinus of Bologna, in his mid-twelfth-century commentary on Gratian's *Decretum*, had introduced the important distinction in regard to baptism between *coactio absoluta* or "absolute coercion," which involved physical force, and *coactio conditionaliter* or "conditional coercion," which involved the threat of physical harm. The former was almost universally rejected as a practice (though there were disagreements as to the sacramental validity of such baptisms), while the latter was seen by many as acceptable, if not ideal, because it preserved a measure of freedom (one could choose death

33. *Sententia De anima* 3.5.650.

34. *De veritate* 22.9 ad 7.

rather than baptism). The line between these two was constantly shifting, often depending on the level of physical resistance that the one being baptized put up, and the line between any sort of coercion and simple persuasion was similarly unclear.[35]

Thomas joins the general consensus in holding that an unbeliever should never be made to convert by means of physical force (e.g., forcibly dunked in water three times while the baptismal formula is recited), since an action that is physically forced (*simpliciter violentium*) is in no sense a free act. Such prohibition extends beyond physical manipulation of the body to include the actual inflicting of pain, since this is simply physical manipulation at one remove. He seems even to hold that such a baptism would be not only illicit but invalid.[36] So neither physical manipulation nor torture would fall under "efficacious persuasion either by harsh or gentle means."

But what about the threat of torture? What of fear? Does fear compromise the voluntary nature of an act of faith, making persuasion lapse into coercion, or is it simply a tool of persuasion, if perhaps a harsh one?

Thomas does not offer a simple answer. He does say that an action done out of fear is not necessarily an unfree act. It is, he says, of mixed character: it is voluntary absolutely speaking (*simpliciter*) but involuntary in a certain sense (*secundum quid*). If, in a particular set of circumstances, we do an act in order to avoid something that we fear, we are feely doing that act because we

35. See Colish, *Faith, Fiction and Force*, 314–17. Durandus of Saint-Pourçain (c. 1275–c. 1332) seems to have been alone (as he so often was on theological matters) in holding that not only coercion but even persuasion was to be excluded in inducing adults toward baptism. See Colish, 307–10.

36. See *Summa theologiae* 3.68.7 ad 2, where he says that an adult who was baptized without the intention of being baptized ought to be rebaptized. On the other hand, Thomas holds that vows that are coerced are morally binding inasmuch as they are made to God. One is not obligated with regard to the human being to whom the promise was made, but one remains obligated to God, though Thomas seems to allow and even encourage prelates to release people from such coerced vows (*Summa theologiae* 1-2.89.7 ad 3). Why Thomas holds Baptism and vows to different standards is not clear, though it is perhaps related to the different roles he allows for compulsion in the case of Jews and heathens, on the one hand, and heretics and apostates on the other. See *Summa theologiae* 2-2.10.8.

are naturally inclined to avoid the feared evil, even if we would not will that act under other circumstances. To use Thomas's example, which he takes from Aristotle, the sailor who jettisons cargo in order to avoid sinking does so willingly, though he or she might think, "I would never do this if the circumstances were not what they are." But, given that the action is done in these circumstances and not some other, the act is treated as voluntary since it "conforms somewhat" (*aliquid confert*) to the will.[37]

Given Thomas's views on voluntariness and fear, he would seem to hold that someone who converts out of fear is engaged in a free act, even if it is not as clearly free as someone who converts out of a passionate desire. Therefore, it seems there can be conversion born out of fear. But before reaching this conclusion, we should note the distinctions he draws regarding fear, distinctions taken over from Peter Lombard's synthesis of the prior tradition, particularly Augustine.[38]

First, there is "worldly fear" (sometimes called "human fear"), which refers to a fear of loss of life or property. If such fear turns us away from God, it is always evil.[39] It is interesting that Thomas never, to my knowledge, discusses how worldly fear might turn us toward God; he presumes that it only serves to turn us away from God, since it implies that we love something, whether life or property, more than we love the object of our spiritual love.[40]

Second, there is "servile fear," which fears the evil suffered (*malum poenae*) in turning from God. This fear might motivate the will to move the intellect to assent, but such assent would seem to fall short of a genuine act of faith because it is a result of

37. *Summa theologiae* 1-26.6. Cf. *Sententia Ethic.* 3.1.389–90.

38. See Peter Lombard, *Sententiae* 3.34. For Thomas's discussion of the different sorts of fear, see *Summa theologiae* 2-2.19.2 and *Super Rom.* 8.3.638–641.

39. *Summa theologiae* 2-2.19.3.

40. Thomas disallows compulsion in bringing unbelievers to faith but not in restraining them from harming the faith "by blasphemies or evil persuasions or even open persecutions," and suggests (either disingenuously or naively) that this is what is happening when Christians wage war against unbelievers. See *Summa theologiae* 2-2.10.8.

being repelled by eternal punishment rather than being attracted by eternal life. Thomas suggests that while such assent is good in itself, it is not a genuine act of faith because it is not free: "Even if a person, under the influence of such fear, does something good, he does not act well, because he does not act spontaneously [*sponte*] but is coerced [*coactus*] by fear of punishment, which is proper to slaves."[41] In servile fear, one is not drawn to God himself, since God is seen as the source of punishment. One's will is still drawn to worldly things, but it is restrained by fear of punishment. This sort of fear might make one more persuadable,[42] but would not itself be persuasive, since it presents God under an aspect that is, in a literal sense, repulsive.

Third, servile fear is contrasted with "chaste fear," also called filial fear or holy fear, which Thomas compares to the reverent love one has for a parent or a spouse and the concomitant fear of doing any evil (*malum culpae*) that would diminish that reverent love. Chaste fear is a gift of the Holy Spirit,[43] an unalloyed good—indeed, it is a good that persists in the heavenly homeland.[44] It involves an attraction to God that repels us from anything that would separate us from God. As Thomas says, "Filial fear must increase when love [*caritas*] increases. . . . For the more one loves another, the more one fears offending and being separated from that person."[45] This sort of fear could be an instrument of persuasion, though not as fear per se, but as a desirable spiritual good that might draw the will.

Between servile and chaste fear, Thomas inserts a fourth, mediating category: "initial fear." Such fear involves both a repulsion from eternal punishment and a desire for eternal life.[46] It relates

41. *Super Rom.* 8.3.639.
42. See *Summa theologiae* 1-2.44.2, 4.
43. See *Summa theologiae* 2-2.19.9.
44. See *Summa theologiae* 2-2.19.11.
45. *Summa theologiae* 2-2.19.10.
46. See *Summa theologiae* 2-2.19.8.

to chaste fear as the imperfect to the perfect, such that it is the same kind of fear as chaste fear but not yet perfected by love. Instilling this sort of fear would seem to be not only allowable but even desirable as an instrument of persuasion, so that as one is repelled from worldly desires by fear of punishment one is simultaneously being drawn by hope of heavenly reward toward spiritual good, with fear of the evil of punishment (*malum poenae*) being gradually transformed into fear of the evil of sin itself (*malum culpae*), a fear of the evil of violating the bond of love by which we are united with God as our final end.

So, while preaching that instills initial fear might be a harsh form of persuasion, it is, for Thomas, still persuasion and not coercion. Just as the sailor who jettisons cargo does so not simply as repelled by the evil of sinking but also as drawn by the good of completing the journey, so too the person who—moved by a sermon that presents both the eternal consequences of sin and the eternal rewards of faith—jettisons a life of sin, does so not only out of fear of punishment but as positively attracted by the goods of faith. In both cases, the presence of fear does not take away the voluntary character of the act because it is ultimately the good sought, and not the evil feared, that motivates the action.

SO WHAT?

I hope I have made a plausible case that Thomas Aquinas's distinction between coercion and persuasion is a coherent one, given his understanding of the will's freedom, as well as shown why he thinks that genuine conversion can never be obtained via coercion. What are the implications of this view?

The view that faith is a willful, and therefore free, act should provoke a certain caution with regard to the means used in conversion. Even apart from overt coercion—the use or threat of physical violence—there are, Thomas suggests, more subtle forms of coercion that subvert the will's freedom. The surest way to ensure that conversion is a free act is to attract the will through, as Thomas puts it, "the intellectual vision of an object of spiritual love."[47] This kind of persuasion involves not simply the will being moved by the passions but also a process of rational inference such that we have reasons for being persuaded. Put differently, the will is moved to conversion in a manner most clearly free when it is moved by the beauty of a sound argument, so the preacher's task is to hand on to others the fruits of one's own contemplation.

In the context of a modern university, the idea that people ought to be persuaded by the intellectual beauty of argumentation is, I would hope, an easy sell. Thomas, however, knows that we are often unmoved by even the soundest of arguments. We have a variety of attachments that are nonrational and that cause our wills to be immune to reason's suasion. The process of conversion might therefore also involve inspiring examples of the lives of holy people—the so-called *exempla* that medieval Dominican preachers assiduously collated and copied (but that are, oddly, largely lacking from Thomas's own preaching). But it also can involve the harsher means of fear, though only fear of a particular sort. It cannot be worldly fear of loss of life or property, nor can it be the servile fear that is solely focused on eternal punishment (whatever social utilities either of these might have). It can, however, be initial fear, the simultaneous recoiling from eternal punishment and attraction to eternal life with God that still leaves the will free. Perfect love may cast out fear, but often we must work with imperfect love. The harsh persuasion of a certain kind of fear might be needed to separate us from the nonrational attachments of the will. Jesus's proclamation of God's reign was also a call to repent (see Mark 1:15). While this may seem less palatable than a conversion void of all fear except chaste fear, I think anyone

47. *Contra Gentiles* 3.118.2.

familiar with the psychological dynamics of conversion will at least have to give Thomas points for realism.

Finally, while Thomas's distinction between coercion and persuasion might be coherent given his account of the will, are we today willing to buy Thomas's account of the will? Thomas's account of the will's freedom, and therefore his distinction between coercion and persuasion, depends on teleological notions of the will's "natural desire" and its orientation toward "the good"—notions of which many today are suspicious. Perhaps the reason that writers like Foucault blur the distinction between coercion and persuasion is not because they haven't thought as rigorously as Thomas about the implications of the will's freedom but because they have a rather different account of the will, one in which the will has no natural inclination toward a good that stands over and against it but is rather a force that creates its own good.[48] Which leaves us with the question of whether we can distinguish coercion from persuasion on the basis of a non-teleological account of the will or whether, in order to sustain the distinction, we might need to look again at notions like "natural desire" and "the good."

48. See, for example, Nietzsche: "My brother, if you have a virtue and she is your virtue, then you have her in common with nobody. . . . If you must speak of her, then do not be ashamed to stammer of her. Then speak and stammer, 'This is *my* good; this I love; it pleases me wholly; thus alone do *I* want the good. I do not want it as divine law; I do not want it as human statute and need'" (*Thus Spake Zarathustra*, "On Enjoying and Suffering the Passions," in *Thus Spake Zarathustra*, part 1, in *The Portable Nietzsche*, ed. Walter Kaufmann [New York: Penguin Books, 1954], 148). On this understanding of the will's freedom, not even a god could move the will non-coercively.

8

Sin

A Reading of *Summa theologiae* 1-2.71.6

Thomas Aquinas was a member of the Order of Preachers, founded by Dominic de Guzmán at the beginning of the thirteenth century to preach doctrine and to care for souls through the administration of the sacrament of Penance. When Thomas came to composing a comprehensive account of theology that the "teacher of catholic truth" could use to train Dominican friars for these tasks, the *Summa theologiae*, he devoted the second of its three parts—arguably, the heart of the whole work—to a treatment of virtue and vice that could enable friars to be wise and compassionate spiritual guides.[1] Though handbooks to help confessors in "handling sin" (the title of one such work from the early fourteenth century) were common both before and after Thomas, the *Summa* offered something that was different from the typical manual inasmuch as, rather than being a standalone guide to various sins, it integrated the practical task of the care of souls within the more speculative task of unfolding the logic of Christian doctrine.[2] In this way, it not only drew together the two primary

* Originally published as "Thomas Aquinas" in *The T&T Clark Companion to the Doctrine of Sin*, ed. Keith L. Johnson and David Lauber (London: T&T Clark, 2016), 199–216.

1. See Leonard Boyle, *The Setting of the "Summa Theologiae" of Saint Thomas* (Toronto: Pontifical Institute of Mediaeval Studies, 1982); M. Michèle Mulchahey, *"First the Bow Is Bent in Study": Dominican Education before 1350* (Toronto: Pontifical Institute of Mediaeval Studies, 1998).

2. See John Inglis, "Aquinas's Replication of the Acquired Moral Virtues: Rethinking the Standard Philosophical Interpretation of Moral Virtue in Aquinas," *Journal of Religious Ethics* 27, no. 1 (Spring 1999): 3–27; Mark D. Jordan, *Rewritten Theology: Aquinas after His Readers* (Oxford: Blackwell, 2006), 116–53.

tasks of the Dominican friar, but it also offered an account of sin embedded within an account of the God who creates, redeems, and brings to consummation.

Thomas was also one of the thirteenth century's greatest interpreters of Aristotle. More than a mere interpreter, Thomas was also an appropriator: following a venerable Christian tradition, he treated the truth found in Aristotle's thought as Egyptian gold that rightly belonged to God's people, to be used for the tasks of preaching, teaching, and the care of souls. But more even than interpreter and appropriator, Thomas was an original thinker who performed a kind of alchemy on the gold of Aristotle. Or, to shift the metaphor to one that Thomas himself uses, rather than diluting the wine of theology with the water of philosophy, he transformed that water into the wine of Christian teaching.[3] This can be seen perhaps most clearly in the Second Part of the *Summa theologiae*, where Aristotle's account of moral excellence is fused with an Augustinian account of sin and grace to produce a rich and nuanced picture of the Christian life. It is within this account of the Christian life that we find one of Thomas's most extensive treatments of sin.[4]

So, in reading Thomas on sin, we need to keep in mind both the practical, pastoral intent of his writing as well as grappling with the Aristotelian subtleties and complexities of his account. While it would be possible to give an account of what Thomas thinks simply by reporting his views, a sense of *how* Thomas thinks can best be had by reading Thomas himself. But reading Thomas can be difficult for those unfamiliar with both the content of his thought and the Scholastic style of his writing. So in what follows, I will look at a single article from the *Summa*

3. *Super De Trinitate* 2.3 ad 5.

4. While here I focus on the *Summa theologiae*, other extended accounts can be found in *Super Sent.* 2.30–44 and *De malo*. The *Summa contra Gentiles* has discussions relevant to Aquinas's theology of sin scattered throughout the third book, as well as in chapters 50–52 of book 4.

theologiae and offer commentary on it that will, I hope, unfold the basics of Thomas's thinking on sin.

The specific article is the sixth and final one in the seventy-first question of the first part of the Second Part of the *Summa*, which is the first question dealing with sin. In this article, having worked toward a basic account of what sin is, Thomas is struggling with a definition of sin that had been extracted from Augustine's *Contra Faustum*—a definition that had achieved quasi-canonical status by the mid-thirteenth century in large part because of its inclusion in Peter Lombard's *Sentences*.[5] As we shall see, it is a definition that Thomas wishes to affirm, while recognizing that it poses a number of difficulties, which the opening arguments or "objections" will serve to point out. Since these difficulties often have to do with the ways in which the Augustinian definition seems to depart from other things Thomas has already said about human action and sin, I shall use the article's objections to establish the broader intellectual context in which Thomas understands sin. Of course, Thomas's goal is to find a way of understanding this venerable definition that is compatible with his overall view of sin, so in his "response" and the "replies" to the objections, we will see how he goes about rescuing the Augustinian definition from possible misunderstanding.

> *Objection 1*: It appears that sin is defined unfittingly by saying: "Sin is a word or deed or desire, contrary to the eternal law" [*peccatum est dictum vel factum vel concupitum contra legem aeternam*], because "word" or "deed" or "desire" involve an action. But not every sin involves an act, as stated earlier (2.71.5). Therefore this definition does not include every sin.

The first objection concerns the possibility of a sin of omission: sinning not only in what I have done but also in what I have

5. Peter Lombard, *Sententiae* 2.35.1.1.

failed to do. Thomas argued in the immediately preceding article that sins of omission are sometimes *not* actions. Yet the Augustinian definition focuses on actions, whether of speaking or doing or desiring, and therefore seems unable to account for sins of omission. The objection, in pointing us to sins of omission, also points us to how Thomas sees the need for the broader context of a life narrative in order to identify virtue or vice.

In *Summa theologiae* 2.71.5, Thomas sketches two views of sins of omission. The first view says that there is always some act involved in a sin, even if it is only the interior act of willing not to do something or to do something else instead of the thing one ought to do. The second view says that there is no need to posit such an act of the will, since the mere omission of the good act suffices for sin. So, on the first view, if I fail to go to church on Sunday, it is either because I willed not to go or I willed to do something else, such as going out to brunch with friends; in either case, there is an act of will that constitutes the sin. The second view, in contrast, says that one need not concern oneself with what the will is or is not doing; the failure to go to church when I ought is, in itself, a sin.

As he often does, Thomas finds an element of truth in both views. If one is thinking of sin in terms of a particular act in itself, then the second view seems correct. If I stay up late drinking and sleep through church the next day, then at the moment I commit the sin, I am not willingly doing a sinful act—indeed, I am not willingly doing anything at all, since I am asleep. At the same time, if we consider the sin of omission in a more extended sense, then it must be related to *some* act, for our omission must be caused in *some* way. If the cause of the omission is not something that I will (say, an illness that prevents me from getting out of bed), then there is no sin involved at all, since for Thomas it is only those acts that are voluntary that are subject to praise or blame (as we shall see below). If the cause of my omission is an earlier act of my will—such as my choice to go out drinking on a Saturday night—then that act is the cause of the omission, even though I am not actively willing it at the time of the omission (since I am passed out). But, he concludes, the act that causes my sin of omission—excessive drinking—is not the same thing as the non-act in which my sin consists, since excessive drinking is obviously not the same as failing to go to church. So, speaking most strictly, there are sins of omission that are not acts.

The larger implications of the discussion of sins of omission to which the objection points is that sin is a more complex reality than simply doing or saying things contrary to God's law, and more complex even than desiring things contrary to that law. I can sin even when, at the point in time when the sin occurs, I am not saying or doing or desiring anything. This is because sin is not a matter of punctiliar words or deeds or desires but of a life that is extended through time. Understanding this aspect of sin is crucial for those who seek to care for souls in the sacrament of Penance, such as the Dominican friars for whom Thomas wrote the *Summa*. The skilled confessor, while attending to particular acts (and non-acts), also attends to the patterns of action and inaction in which particular acts find their place. This is also one reason why the Aristotelian account of virtue proves so useful to Thomas, since it speaks of moral goodness in terms of habits and dispositions acquired over the course of a life. My sin of omission is, as it were, a "gap" that appears only within the context of a series of prior and subsequent words, deeds, and desires: promises that have been made, drinks that have been drunk, goods that have been yearned for. It is partly for this reason that the Augustinian definition's focus on deeds, words, and actions could pose a problem.

> *Objection 2:* Augustine says in the book *On the Two Souls*: "Sin is the will to retain or obtain what justice forbids" (11.15).

> But the will is included under desire [*concupiscentia*], in so far as "desire" can be taken in a broad sense to mean any appetite. Therefore it would have sufficed to say "sin is a desire contrary to the eternal law," and it was not necessary to add "word or deed."

The force of this objection is as follows: since a definition aims at what is essential rather than accidental (i.e., contingent) about a thing, and since it is the orientation of the will that is the essential element in sin, there is, therefore, no need to include "words or deeds" in our definition of sin, because willing is a form of desire or "concupiscence." The objection points to an important aspect of the Augustinian tradition indicated by the quotation from *On the Two Souls*: the significance of the will in determining the morality of an action or a desire.[6] Whether he was discussing the origin of sin in the Garden of Eden or the distinction of the two cities in history, Augustine gave primacy to the orientation of the will. As Augustine says in his *Retractions*, "It is by the will that we sin."[7] In this, Thomas follows Augustine, noting, for example, how the act of almsgiving, while good in itself, could be sinful if motivated by the vain desire for glory.[8]

The emphasis on the will found in both Augustine and Thomas departs from the Platonic tradition, for which evil actions arise from a cognitive error concerning the good. While Thomas does believe that human beings have by nature an appetite for the good (see below), he also believes that our appetite can be corrupted, not only due to a defect of the intellect (as when we sin through ignorance, thinking something good when it is not) or to a defect of our sense appetites (as when we sin through weakness, controlled by our emotions or "passions") but also due

6. For the importance of the will in Augustine's account of sin, see, e.g., *De civitate Dei* 14.6.

7. Augustine, *Retractiones* 1.9.

8. *Summa theologiae* 1-2.19.7 ad 2.

to a defect of the will. In this last case, which Aquinas calls "malice" (*malitia*), the will still has an appetite for the good, but it knowingly chooses a lesser good over a greater one.[9] All three sorts of defects—ignorance, weakness, and malice—are "wounds" in human nature, consequences of original sin that damage human nature without entirely taking away its goodness.[10]

In discussing original sin, Thomas is the inheritor of two traditions: that found in Lombard's *Sentences*, which, drawing on Augustine, focuses on concupiscence as the essence of original sin;[11] and a tradition flowing from St. Anselm, which, also drawing on Augustine, talks about original sin as the loss of "original justice."[12] The former sees the essence of original sin as the will's inherited tendency to ignore due measure in desiring, a tendency that mirrors the first sin's preference for created good over uncreated good and that is passed on by the concupiscence involved in the act of sexual reproduction. The latter says that what is essential in original sin is not disordered desire itself but humanity's deviation from its original status as just before God, a justice that consisted of the subordination of human reason to divine wisdom.

Following Alexander of Hales and others, Thomas splits the difference between these two approaches, saying that "formally" original sin is the loss of original justice, but "materially" it is concupiscence. What does this mean? Thomas develops Anselm's notion of original justice so as to see it as the original graced state of humanity characterized by the fitting subordination of human reason to God, the will to reason, and the body to the will.[13] When human beings turned from God and suffered the loss of grace, our nature was wounded by this loss of proper order,

9. *Summa theologiae* 1-2.78.1.

10. *Summa theologiae* 1-2.85.1–3.

11. Peter Lombard, *Sententiae* 2.30.

12. See Anselm, *De conceptu virginali* 1.

13. *Summa theologiae* 1.95.1.

suffering ignorance, weakness, malice, and, eventually, death.[14] Original sin is, Thomas says, "an inordinate disposition arising from the destruction of the harmony which was essential to original justice."[15] This harmony's destruction plays itself out in the powers of the soul turning away from the eternal good of God toward the lesser good of creatures, a disorder that "may be called by the general name 'concupiscence.'"[16]

In identifying original sin as a disordered disposition that issues in disordered acts, Thomas once again locates sin primarily in a life story and only secondarily in particular acts. Even in his account of the transmission of original sin, Aquinas downplays (but does not eliminate entirely) the role of lust in sexual intercourse, focusing more on the unity of the human race: "All those born of Adam may be considered as one person, inasmuch as they have one common nature, which they receive from their first parents. . . . So original sin is not the sin of this person except inasmuch as this person receives his nature from his first parent."[17] As with a sin of omission, original sin is not an action that we engage in but emerges from within a story of words, deeds, and desires. Only, in this case, it is not the words, deeds, and desires of an individual but of the human race as a whole. We might say that it is because human beings share a single story—the story of creation in the image of God and of primal human disobedience—that every person shares in the sin of Adam and Eve and suffers the wounds of ignorance, weakness, and malice that it effects.

14. *Summa theologiae* 2-2.164.1.

15. *Summa theologiae* 1-2.82.1.

16. *Summa theologiae* 1-2.82.3. For a concise discussion of views of original sin in the thirteenth century, see Pierre J. Payer, *The Bridling of Desire: Views of Sex in the Later Middle Ages* (Toronto: University of Toronto Press, 1993), 43–50.

17. *Summa theologiae* 1-2.81.1. For a discussion of how Thomas, particularly in his mature theology, differs from Augustine on the question of the transmission of original sin, see Mark Johnson, "Augustine and Aquinas on Original Sin: Doctrine, Authority, and Pedagogy," in *Aquinas the Augustinian*, ed. Michael Dauphinais, Barry David, and Matthew Levering (Washington, DC: The Catholic University of America Press, 2007), 145–58.

> *Objection 3:* It appears that sin consists specifically in turning away from the end, for good and evil are considered chiefly with regard to the end, as explained above (1-2.18.6). Therefore Augustine, in book 1 of *On Free Will* (ch. 11), defines sin in relation to the end, saying that "sin is nothing else than neglecting eternal things and pursuing temporal things": and in the book *Eighty-three Questions* (q. 30) he says that "all human evil is a matter of using what we should enjoy and enjoying what we should use." But the proposed definition makes no mention of turning away from our appropriate end. Therefore it is an insufficient definition of sin.

As is well known, Thomas's approach to morality is a "teleological" one, meaning that he interprets the goodness or badness of human action in terms of the end at which that action aims. Central to Thomas's understanding of sin, and seemingly missing from the Augustinian definition found in the *Contra Faustum*, is the natural orientation of human beings toward the good as their proper end and the disastrous consequences of turning away from that good. But this teleological morality is part of a larger interpretation of reality that sees all things as moved by an appetite for divine goodness.

Thomas, following Aristotle, defines goodness as "that which all things desire" (*quod omnia appetunt*).[18] While we might think of "appetite" or "desire" as something had only by sentient beings, Thomas sees everything that exists as having an appetite. Most fundamentally, all things desire or have an appetite to be the kind of being that they are and to behave in ways that accord with that being: a stone desires to move downward so as to rest on the ground, an eye desires to see things, a human desires to know things. In other words, the "appetite" of all things for the good serves Thomas as a way of talking about why it is that all things

18. *Summa theologiae* 1.5.1.

tend to act in ways characteristic of the beings that they are. To have that desire or appetite fulfilled—for the stone to rest on the ground, for the eye to see, for the human being to know—is to be "perfected" or fulfilled as a particular sort of being.

Here, we can see the close connection Thomas makes between goodness and existence. In Thomas's terminology, what all things desire is the actualization of their potential to *be* what they are by nature. The goodness of a thing is a function of its possession of the "fullness of being" that a thing of its kind ought to have: the resting stone, the seeing eye, the knowing person. The most fundamental perfection of any being is the very act of existing, and in this sense, "to be" (in Latin, *esse*) is the most universal good, since every thing that is has an appetite for existence. Entailed in the particular goods of particular things—resting on the ground, seeing, knowing—there is the universal good of existing, and the source of this universally desirable good is what people call "God."[19] Thus all things, no matter how they seek to realize their particular kind of existence, have an appetite for God, who bestows upon each creature its *esse*. Thomas, therefore, says that God is the highest (or, we might say, most fundamental) good that all beings desire, the "last end" that each being seeks to attain in its own distinctive way.[20] All other things, while good and therefore desirable, are, in view of this highest good, means to be used and not ends to be enjoyed.

Evil, simply put, is the failure of a thing to be perfected in the way that is appropriate to the kind of thing that it is. Evil is a *privatio boni* or "privation of good."[21] An eye that cannot see is bad at being an eye because it fails to actualize its potential as an eye. The evil of blindness that is suffered by an ailing eye is simply the privation of the good that an eye should possess. "Sin" names

19. Cf. Thomas's "fourth way" of demonstrating God's existence in *Summa theologiae* 1.2.3.

20. *Summa theologiae* 1-2.1.8.

21. *Summa theologiae* 1.5.3 ad 2; 1.48.1.

the kind of evil specific to human beings, how they fail to act in such a way so as to attain the perfection or actualization or fulfillment of existence that is proper to them: the perfection of intellect and will that comes from knowing and loving God.[22] It is the distinctively human way in which evil is done. As the objection points out, it involves not simply a failure to attain the end but a willful turning away or "aversion" from the end. Inasmuch as the Augustinian definition is not framed in terms of this aversion, it seems inadequate as a definition of sin.

> *Objection 4:* Something is said to be prohibited because it is contrary to the law. But not all sins are evil because they are prohibited; some are prohibited because they are evil. Therefore sin in general should not be defined as being against the law of God.

We might hear in this objection a kind of reverse echo of the question of Plato's *Euthyphro*: Is something evil because it is forbidden by God or is something forbidden by God because it is evil? The view proposed in the objection is that at least in some cases sins are forbidden because they are evil and would still be evil whether they were forbidden or not, so the Augustinian definition under examination fails because it defines sin in terms of a transgression of divine law.

While the objection makes no explicit reference to earlier arguments by Thomas, it is clear that Thomas is not one who thinks that the law in itself determines the rightness or wrongness of an act. Martin Luther King cited Thomas in his famous "Letter from Birmingham Jail" in support of the view that an unjust law is not binding but can, and in some cases must, be disobeyed.[23] Not only is the human good not determined by human laws; it

22. See *Summa theologiae* 1-2.3.8; 1-2.21.1.

23. Martin Luther King Jr. cites *Summa theologiae* 1-2.96.4 in "Letter from Birmingham Jail," in *Why We Can't Wait* (New York: Harper and Row, 1964), 76–95 at 82.

is also not determined by brute divine decree (as if God could decree that it is good for human beings to dishonor their parents or murder each other) but by the nature of what it means to be a human being. Therefore, so the objection goes, Augustine's definition is problematic because of its focus on law. Though, as we shall see, Thomas will in his reply offer a defense of the Augustinian definition's reference to eternal law, the objection usefully draws our attention to the fact that it is evil as a privation of the human good and not as the violation of law that is the primary framework within which Thomas understands sin.

> *Objection 5:* "Sin" denotes a bad human act, as is clear from what has been said (1-2.71.1). But "the evil of humans is to be against reason," as Dionysius states in chapter four of *On the Divine Names*. Therefore it would have been better to say that sin is against reason than to say that sin is contrary to the eternal law.

This objection builds upon the previous one, proposing that rather than seeing sin as a violation of law, we should see it as a violation of reason. As with the previous objection, Thomas will in his reply offer a corrective to the view espoused here, but at the same time, this objection gets something right about the general tenor of Thomas's thought, particularly with regard to his understanding of the nature of human action. If evil is a privation of good, and sin is an evil human act, then we need to understand the distinctive way in which human beings are fulfilled or fail through their actions. In other words, to determine the nature of the human good we must ask, what makes a human act distinctively human?

A human action is not simply any action that a human being engages in—such as having one's pupils dilate or stumbling down a flight of stairs—but rather precisely those actions that are rooted in the distinctive human capacities of reason and will.[24] As we have already seen in discussing Thomas's use of the term "appetite," while the good is that which all things desire, the terms "desire" and "appetite" are used analogically by Thomas, which means that they are applied in related but non-identical ways to different sorts of beings, as a way of speaking of how they incline toward that which fulfills them. Human beings (and angels) incline toward good things precisely because their intellects grasp them as good, and this inclination is what Thomas calls "rational appetite" or "willing."[25] Of course, not every action of a human being is a result of rational appetite and not every way in which a human might fail to act is a sin. If, because of some neurological failure, I cannot sense the flea that is biting me and so fail to scratch myself, this might indicate that I am an ill-functioning organism, but not that I am a bad human being, since my neurological failure is not a failure of that which distinguishes me as human—i.e., my reason and my will. It is not, in other words, a "moral" failure. To fail morally is to fail in a distinctively human way, as a thinking and willing being; it is the failure to will in accord with right reason, to incline toward that which the intellect accurately identifies as good. Above all, it is the failure to incline toward God as that which reason grasps as the highest good, in relation to which all other goods are subordinate.[26] To fail to be united with God through knowing and loving God as our highest good is to fail as a human being, which for Thomas is to be a sinner.

The Augustinian definition, by focusing on the eternal law, seems to leave reason out of the equation. As we shall see, however, Thomas thinks of law as an expression of reason and, therefore, sees Augustine as implicitly including it in his definition.

24. *Summa theologiae* 1-2.1.1.

25. See *Summa theologiae* 1.59.1.

26. *Summa theologiae* 1-2.1.8.

On the contrary, the authority of Augustine is sufficient.

The *sed contra* of an article of the *Summa theologiae* is typically quite brief and often simply cites an authoritative opinion. But this is even terser than usual. That the naked invocation of Augustine's authority would suffice speaks both to the importance of authorities in theological argumentation[27] and to the specific importance of Augustine. It serves to remind us that as much as he values reason, Thomas sees theology as grounded in our faithful assent to an authoritative word revealed by God, and as much as he values the insights of Aristotle into virtue and vice, Thomas knows that these pale in comparison with Augustine's insights into the human heart wounded by sin and healed through grace.

I respond: as is clear from what was said earlier (1-2.71.1), sin is nothing other than a bad human act. But, as was also said earlier (1-2.1.1), an act is human based on the fact that it is voluntary, either voluntary in the sense of being elicited by the will (e.g., willing or choosing), or in the sense of being commanded by the will (e.g., the exterior actions of speech or deeds). But a human act is evil if it lacks its due measure, and every measure of something is attained through a comparison to some standard [*regula*], and if the thing deviates from that measure, it will be incommensurate. But the standard of the human will is twofold. One is proximate and homogeneous: human reason itself. The other, however, is the primary standard: the eternal law, which is as it were God's reason. Therefore, Augustine puts two things in the definition of sin. One pertains to the substance of a human act, which is something like the "matter" of sin, and this is when he says, "word or deed or desire." The other pertains to the idea of evil, which

27. See *Summa theologiae* 1.1.8 ad 2.

is something like the "form" of sin, and this is when he says, "contrary to the eternal law."

In developing his justification of Augustine's definition, Thomas rehearses a number of points already alluded to in the objections. His argument unfolds as follows:

1. A human action is a voluntary action.
2. A voluntary action can either be entirely internal—what we might call "an act of will"—or be an external action that we will to do—what we might call "a willed act."
3. The goodness or badness of any act is determined by the degree to which it conforms to or deviates from some *regula* or standard.
4. The standard for human action is twofold:
   a. human reason, which is in a sense "closest" and more readily apparent to us because it is our own; and
   b. divine reason (eternal law), which is logically and ontologically primary, though less readily apparent to us.
5. The Augustinian definition therefore fittingly includes both human actions (the "matter" of sin) and the eternal law as the standard by which those actions are judged (the "form" of sin).

While Thomas's response is fairly clear, there are a few points that call for comment.

First, in choosing to translate *regula* as "standard" rather than "rule," I have sought to convey how Thomas thinks of sin first and foremost not as transgression of a command but as a deviation from a norm, which is set simultaneously by eternal law and human reason. The standard of action as present in human reason has a certain kind of priority, inasmuch as it is what we know first, though the standard of eternal law has primacy as the source of all order in creatures. It is important to underscore both that these two standards operate simultaneously and harmoniously, and that human reason's right functioning depends upon its proper orientation toward and participation in the eternal law, which is nothing other than divine wisdom itself. What matters here is that, in speaking of the eternal law, Augustine's definition obliquely includes human reason. I shall say more about this below in discussing Thomas's reply to the fourth objection.

Second, what does Thomas mean when he speaks of action as "matter" and the *regula* as "form"?[28] Thomas's use of the term *quasi* (i.e., "something like") indicates that he is using "matter" and "form" by way of analogy, and the analogy appears to be this: just as matter is undetermined potential that is actualized by form so as to be this or that sort of thing, so too a human action is determined as good or evil through its conformity with or deviation from the eternal law. Just as a particular human being is human on account of possessing the form of humanity, so too a particular human action is a good action—a fully human action—on account of its conformity to the eternal law. To put it in terms of logic, "human action" is the genus that is specified as good or evil by its conformity or non-conformity to eternal law. Because Augustine's statement gives us both the matter of sin (human action) and its form (deviation from the eternal law), it suffices as a definition since matter and form are analogous to genus and species.

> *Reply to Objection 1:* Affirmation and negation are traced back to a single genus. For example, in the Godhead "begotten" and "unbegotten" are traced back to the genus "relation," as Augustine states in *De Trinitate* (5.6–7). And so what is "said"

28. Note that Thomas's use of "matter" and "form" here does not map seamlessly onto his use of "matter" and "form" in speaking of the essence of original sin.

and "unsaid," what is "done" and "undone," should be taken in the same way.

In his reply to the first objection, Thomas invokes a point of logic to rescue the Augustinian definition. His reasoning, as stated here, however, may not exactly be clear. His point is made perhaps a bit clearer in his *Disputed Questions on Evil*, where he notes that two things within the same genus might be related to that genus in different ways.[29] They might equally participate in the genus, as in the case of cows and horses in the genus "animal": neither a cow nor a horse is more an animal than the other, and thus the genus is "univocal." But some genera are "analogical," in which case things within that genus can have a relationship of priority and posteriority to each other. The example Thomas gives is the way that the genus "being" can be divided into "substance" and "accident": the former belonging most properly to the genus of "being" and the latter belonging, as it were, due to its relationship to substance. We might also think of the way in which a human body and a urine sample might both be described as "healthy": the urine sample belongs to the genus "healthy things" not because it is itself a well-functioning organism but because of its relation to a well-functioning organism—namely, a human body.[30]

A similar thing might be said of affirmation and negation. Earlier in the *Summa*, Thomas notes, "Negation is reduced to the genus of affirmation, as 'not a human being' is reduced to the genus of substance, and 'not white' to the genus of quality."[31] In other words, an affirmation and a negation are understood by means of the same genus, but the negation is understood only *after* (logically speaking) the affirmation is understood. The key point is that Thomas seeks to defend Augustine's definition from

29. *De malo* 7.1 ad 1.

30. See *Summa theologiae* 1.13.5.

31. *Summa theologiae* 1.33.4 ad 3.

the objection by arguing that, by supplying the affirmative actions that can be sins (words, deeds, and desires), Augustine has implied and given one all one needs to understand the negation of those actions in sins of omission.

> *Reply to Objection 2:* The first cause of sin is in the will, which commands all voluntary acts, for only in these kinds of acts is sin to be found. This is why Augustine sometimes defines sin in terms of the will alone. But, as has been said (1-2.20.1–3), because external acts also pertain to the substance of sin when they themselves are evil, it was necessary in defining sin to include something pertaining to external action.

As I noted earlier, Augustine taught that it is by the will that we sin. But the medieval figure most associated with the teaching that sin is a matter of the will and intention is Peter Abelard (1079–1142). Abelard argued that it was the will's consent to sin—not the desire to sin or the external action—that made one a sinner. He writes, "The sin isn't said to be the willing itself or the desire to do what isn't allowed, but the consent. . . . Adding on the performance of the deed doesn't add anything to increase the sin."[32] As he puts it, "It isn't a sin to lust after someone's wife, or to have sex with her; sin is rather the *consent* to this lust or to this action."[33] For Abelard, one who intends to commit adultery is as guilty of the sin as someone who follows through on that intention, and someone who engages in an act of adultery without intending to commits no sin. While Abelard's position, on the one hand, seems to be simply drawing out the consequences of Augustine's emphasis on will, on the other hand, it seems counterintuitive to say that the act of adultery or theft is irrelevant

32. Peter Abelard, *Ethics* 29–30, in Peter Abelard, *Ethical Writings: "Ethics" and "Dialogue Between a Philosopher, a Jew and a Christian"*, trans. Paul Vincent Spade (Indianapolis: Hackett, 1995), 7.

33. Abelard, *Ethics* 49, pp. 10–11.

to the act of sin. Abelard himself notes the oddness of saying that those who crucified Jesus committed no sin because they intended to honor God by their actions.[34]

Thomas, while agreeing with Abelard (and Augustine) that it is by the will that we sin, rejects Abelard's sharp distinction between intention and action. Indeed, he argues that the act of the will and the external action form a single moral act.[35] He notes that with regard to the external aspect of the act, we can discern a twofold goodness: the goodness of the action in itself and the relation of that action to its intended end. The latter goodness is due entirely to the goodness of the will, while the former is due to the action's conformity to the standard of reason.[36] Thomas's account of what makes an action good or evil appears quite complex compared to Abelard's fairly simple account. In evaluating the merit or blame attached to an act, one must take account not only of the act itself but also of the circumstances, object, and end of the act.[37] For an act to be good, it must be good in every way, and if it fails to be good in any way, it is a bad act. Thus, it might be praiseworthy if, on a Tuesday, Abraham cut wood to build a boat in order to trade with the Phoenicians; but if he performed the act of wood-cutting on the sabbath (a change of the action's circumstance) or to fashion an idol (a change of the action's object), then the praiseworthy intention of trading with the Phoenicians would not be sufficient to make the action a good one.

To put this in the pastoral context that Thomas saw his analysis in service of, it is not sufficient for a priest hearing confessions to know what the penitent did. The confessor might have to ask not only *why* the penitent did the act (i.e., its end) but also the specific nature of the act (i.e., its object) and other factors

34. Peter Abelard, *Expositio in Epistolam ad Romanos* 14:23, in *Commentary on the Epistle to the Romans*, trans. Steven R. Cartwright (Washington, DC: The Catholic University of America Press, 2011), 365–66.

35. *Summa theologiae* 1-2.17.4.

36. *Summa theologiae* 1-2.20.1.

37. *Summa theologiae* 1-2.18.4.

concerning when and where the act occurred (i.e., its circumstances). These provide context for determining not only whether a particular act is a sin but also the severity of the sin and, therefore, the healing penance that the confessor should assign.[38] As I noted in discussing the first objection, the confessor must try to see not simply single actions or intentions but the way in which intentions are enacted in particular circumstances, bringing about particular consequences, having particular objects, and so forth.[39]

> *Reply to Objection 3*: The eternal law first and foremost orients a human being to his or her end, but as a consequence of this it makes one well-disposed concerning things that are means to the end. Therefore when he says, "contrary to the eternal law," he includes both turning away from the end and all other forms of disorder.

The objection argued as if the only thing that mattered in defining sin was turning away from the end. In his reply, however, Thomas notes that an adequate definition of sin requires attention to both means and ends. In some cases, we may simply reject our final end, whether due to ignorance or weakness or malice. This is what Thomas identifies by the traditional term "mortal sin." In other cases, we retain our orientation toward the end but in a disordered way, choosing inadequate means to attain that end. This is how Thomas understands the traditional notion, found as early as Augustine, of "venial sins."[40] Since mortal sins and venial sins are both sins in a true though analogous sense,[41] Thomas's reply to the objection is that Augustine defines sin not as turning

38. See *Contra Gentiles* 4.72.9, 14.

39. See *Summa theologiae* 1-2.73.

40. See, e.g., Augustine, *On the Spirit and the Letter* 48, in *The Works of Saint Augustine: A Translation for the 21st Century*, pt. 1, vol. 23, *Answer to the Pelagians I*, trans. Roland J. Teske, ed. John Rotelle (Hyde Park, NY: New City, 1997), 173–74. For Thomas, see *Summa theologiae* 1-2.72.5.

41. *Summa theologiae* 1-2.88.1.

away from our final end but as contradiction of the eternal law, which governs not only the end but also the means, thus making the definition applicable to venial sins and not just mortal ones.

Again, we can perceive the practical intent behind Thomas's careful distinctions. He holds that while it is possible with God's grace to avoid all mortal sin, it is not possible for us to avoid all venial sin. Though one might avoid any one particular venial sin, our nature wounded by sin is such that we cannot possibly avoid all venial sins.[42] He describes vividly how someone feeling the initial temptations of lust might seek to redirect his thoughts to abstract philosophical considerations, only to become so impressed with his own cleverness that he feels a twinge of pride.[43] While one is not bound to confess venial sins, in administering the sacrament of Penance, the confessor must attend not only to the mortal sins of the penitent but also the venial sins that dispose one to sin mortally by accustoming us to love things that are not directed to our final end.[44]

> *Reply to Objection 4*: In saying that not every sin is evil because it is forbidden, this must be understood of a prohibition made by positive law. But if one speaks with reference to the natural law, which is contained primarily in the eternal law but secondarily in the natural judgment of human reason, then *every* sin is evil because it is forbidden, for it is precisely because it is disordered that it conflicts with natural law.

Though Thomas is not a "legalist" in his understanding of sin, he still maintains that Augustine is correct to define sin as an act contrary to divine law. He is able to do this because he

42. *Summa theologiae* 1-2.109.8. It is not unlike the way that on any given coin toss the odds of heads coming up is 1/2, while the odds of tossing heads 100 times in a row is 1/1,267, 650,600,228,229,401,496,703,205,376.

43. *Summa theologiae* 1-2.74.3 ad 2.

44. *Summa theologiae* 1-2.88.3.

understands law as an expression of divine reason and human nature's participation in that reason.[45] Thomas distinguishes several sorts of law, which are closely interrelated to one another. As noted, "eternal law" is simply divine reason itself, which is the *regula* or standard of all action. "Natural law" is human reason's participation in the eternal law, which is less what we might think of as a legal code and more a general sense of what is desirable, given the kinds of creatures that we are. In this sense, we might say that God is a lawgiver because he is a nature-giver: God legislates via the natural law by endowing us with our human nature. From this natural law derive specific laws that govern human conduct—what Thomas here calls "positive law" and elsewhere calls "human law." Thus, the natural law directs human beings to provide for their offspring, while human law specifies how this is done by requiring, for example, that children be made to ride in car seats, that they be sent to school at a particular age and for a particular period of time, that parents provide a dowry for their daughters when it is time for them to marry, and so forth. This human law can vary according to culture and historical era, so long as it conforms to the general principles of the natural law. God also legislates via what Thomas calls "divine law," by which he means the way in which God reveals laws to human beings, as in the Torah of the Old Testament or the evangelical law of the New Testament. I shall say more about this in discussing Thomas's reply to the fifth objection.

So, there is a sense in which, for Thomas, sin always involves a violation of law, inasmuch as it is a violation of the created order that is an expression of divine wisdom. When Thomas says that it is not always a sin to break a law, he is thinking of the human or positive law that gives specificity to natural law. In a case where the law requires that a child be made to ride in a car seat or provided with a dowry, it is no sin to violate this law, so long as the

45. See *Summa theologiae* 1-2.91.

natural law's requirement that parents care for their offspring is not violated. If a human law violates the natural law, say by denying human dignity on the basis of race or enshrining a tyrannical rule, then not only is it not a sin to break that law, but it would be a sin to obey it. So Thomas's non-legalistic approach to sin turns out to be rooted in a more profound sense of law as an expression of divine wisdom.

> *Reply to Objection 5*: Theologians consider sin chiefly in terms of it being an offense against God; moral philosophers consider it in terms of it being contrary to reason. Therefore Augustine more fittingly defines sin in terms of its being "contrary to the eternal law," than in terms of its being contrary to reason, especially since we are ruled and guided by the eternal law in many things that exceed human reason, as in the case of those things that are matters of faith.

In his reply to the final objection, Thomas reminds us of the difference between the philosophical and theological perspectives. Because Thomas often operates at a very high level of abstraction, and so frequently appeals to Aristotle in analyzing virtue and vice, one can easily forget that he sees himself as a Christian theologian who is attempting to help preachers and confessors do their jobs more effectively. Indeed, in discussing Thomas's understanding of sin, I have had little occasion to mention the drama of the Genesis narrative of the fall,[46] or Paul's reflections on sin and righteousness, or Jesus's prodigal bestowal of divine mercy on those who have so prodigally squandered their divine inheritance. In this final reply, however, Thomas reminds us that what the Christian theologian can and must say about sin far surpasses what the moral philosopher (a term Thomas only ever applies to

46. In the *Summa theologiae*, Thomas's discussion of the fall occurs not as a part of his general discussion of sin but as part of his discussion of the virtue of temperance (2-2.163–65).

non-Christian thinkers) can say, precisely to the extent that the truth that faith can know surpasses the truth that unaided human reason can grasp.

On the one hand, Thomas thinks that human beings can know through reason the moral truths that they need in order to live well in this life, just as they can know through reason certain truths concerning God. On the other hand, just as the truths known about God through reason can only be "known by a few, and after a long time, and with many errors mixed in,"[47] so too with our knowing and doing of the good. Moreover, even if we know and do the good to the fullest extent of our natural powers, this would suffice only for the attaining of the imperfect and fragile happiness of this life; it could in no way enable us to attain the perfect eternal happiness to which human beings are called by God.[48] To attain this happiness, human beings must be guided by the eternal law, which is given to us not only through the divine law of the Torah and the Gospel but above all through the grace of the Holy Spirit, which becomes a standard or rule that is written in our hearts, an internal principle of action graciously bestowed on us in Christ.[49]

Seen in the light of grace, sin too takes on new contours. More than simply the product of vicious habits that thwart our flourishing, sin appears as a rejection of the gift of divine love. In a sermon from a series on the Ten Commandments preached to a popular audience, Thomas captures well the difference between the philosopher's account of vice and what the theologian means by sin. There, rather than defining the rightness or wrongness of human actions in terms of their conformity to reason (whether divine or human), Thomas says, "Any human work is right and virtuous when it is in accordance with the standard of divine love; when it is not in accordance with the rule of charity it is not good,

47. *Summa theologiae* 1.1.1.

48. *Summa theologiae* 1-2.4.5–8.

49. *Summa theologiae* 1-2.106.1.

right, or perfect."[50] Sin is a deviation from the rule of divine love, which we share in through grace that forms the created disposition of charity within us.

The fact that we arrive at divine love only at the end of this account of what Thomas has to say about sin should not obscure the primacy that Thomas assigns to charity. Indeed, the primacy of charity has been presumed throughout this account. Only a free action is subject to moral evaluation because it is through grace's movement of the will to love that the soul is joined to God. Original sin is formally the loss of original justice and materially concupiscence because loving any creature more than God is a derangement of our very being. Venial sins are distinguished from mortal sins because the latter destroy the bond of charity between the sinner and God while the former do not. And the Passion of Christ is the undoing of sin because it is the supreme act of love, which Christ effects on our behalf.[51] For Thomas, the Christian language of divine love and the loss of that love through sin speaks far more eloquently of the human condition than the Aristotelian language of virtue and vice—as useful as that Aristotelian language is—because the end for which we have been created is the God who is revealed in Jesus Christ to be love. Thomas wrote the *Summa* so that Dominican friars and others could more effectively proclaim the truth of this God and offer his mercy to penitent sinners.

50. *De decem praeceptis*, prologue, 2.

51. *Summa theologiae* 3.47.2 ad 1; 3.48.2–3.

9

Wine, Women, Kings, and Truth

The ethical and political thought of Thomas Aquinas has, in recent decades, been of interest both to those concerned with the "ethics of virtue"[1] and to those concerned with the role of "natural law," including legal and political theorists,[2] as well as some liberation theologians.[3] In what follows, I will argue for the contemporary relevance of Aquinas for political theology, though not primarily on the basis of his appeals to natural law. Rather, by examining some texts from Aquinas that do not appear at first glance to have much at all to do with his moral theology, much less his political theory, I hope to show that the chief importance of Aquinas for political theology is his belief that truth is stronger

* Originally published as "Aquinas" in *The Blackwell Companion to Political Theology*, ed. William T. Cavanaugh and Peter Scott (Oxford: Basil Blackwell, 2003 [revised 2nd ed. 2019]), 48–61.

1. See, e.g., Jean Porter, *The Recovery of Virtue: The Relevance of Aquinas for Christian Ethics* (Louisville, KY: Westminster John Knox, 1990); Alasdair MacIntyre, *Three Rival Versions of Moral Enquiry: Encyclopaedia, Genealogy, and Tradition* (Notre Dame, IN: University of Notre Dame Press, 1991); Servais Pinckaers, *The Sources of Christian Ethics*, trans. Mary Thomas Noble (Washington, DC: The Catholic University of America Press, 1995); David Decosimo, *Ethics as a Work of Charity: Thomas Aquinas and Pagan Virtue* (Stanford, CA: University of Stanford Press, 2014); Thomas J. Bushlack, *Politics for a Pilgrim Church: A Thomistic Theory of Civic Virtue* (Grand Rapids, MI: Eerdmans, 2015).

2. John Finnis, *Aquinas: Moral, Political, and Legal Theory* (Oxford: Oxford University Press, 1998).

3. Gustavo Gutiérrez, *Las Casas: In Search of the Poor of Jesus Christ*, trans. Robert R. Barr (New York: Orbis Books, 1993).

than kings, and his identification of truth with the God of Israel, incarnate in Jesus Christ.

THE CONTOURS OF THOMAS'S THOUGHT: EXEGESIS OF A TEXT

Let me begin by sketching three formal contours of Thomas's thought.

First, Thomas is concerned with *both logic and metaphysics*, seeking clarity of thought and speech in order to help our thought and speech conform to the order inherent in things. He combines precise analysis of how we use words with deep metaphysical speculation in a way not usually found in modern philosophy. This combination arises from Thomas's concern to find the clearest way in which to convey the content of the Christian faith, which he does by way of making distinctions and ordering those distinctions in terms of a comprehensive vision of reality.

Second, Thomas thinks as a participant in the give and take of *a living tradition*. Though Thomas is concerned to move from things better known to things less known, he does so as a participant in a complex conversation that is already underway. The *quaestio* format, which is at the heart of the *Summa theologiae*, as well as other texts, situates Thomas's own arguments in the context of initial arguments and counterarguments that represent that conversation.

Third, Thomas's thought is *scriptural*. The tradition to which Thomas belongs is a conversation initiated by God with humanity, as recorded in the Bible. It is true that Thomas freely employs the treasures of philosophy (Platonic as well as Aristotelian) in order to enrich the Christian conversation. But it is the voice of Scripture that predominates,[4] both in posing questions and in answering them. The philosophical tradition is both plundered

4. See *Summa theologiae* 1.1.8 ad 2.

for its riches and transformed into something that would seem quite odd to either Plato or Aristotle.

In order to see how these formal contours function in practice, let us look at a specific text, since Thomas, as a *magister sacra pagina* (a teacher of the sacred page), was above all an interpreter of texts. This minor text represents one of the random questions (*quaestiones quodlibetales*) with which Thomas dealt on a regular basis in his role as a teacher. In addition to displaying the formal contours of his thought, it can also serve as an introduction to some of the possibilities and problems of Thomas's thought for today. A clear problem raised by this particular text is that, to modern sensibilities, Thomas's treatment of "woman" as an example of "sensual causality" is at best patronizing and at worst overtly misogynist. Thomas's identification of woman with "sensuality" and man with "intellect" indicates that he, like all of us, is a product of his culture, in this case imbibing certain notions that make "woman" a natural metonym for "sexual attraction." This raises the question, to which I will return toward the end of this chapter, of how social and political power can shape our perception of the natural order of things, upon which so much of Thomas's political thought relies.

> QUODLIBETAL QUESTION 12.13.1: Whether truth is stronger than wine, a king, or a woman.
>
> *Obj. 1:* Wine, since it can change the greatest of men.
>
> *Obj. 2:* A king, since he compels a person to that which is most difficult, i.e., to that which exposes one to mortal danger.
>
> *Obj. 3:* Woman, since she dominates even a king.
>
> *Against this:* 3 Esdras 4:35: "Truth is stronger."
>
> *I reply:* This is a question proposed for solution to the youths in Esdras. Now it must be observed that if we consider these four in themselves (namely, wine, a king, a woman and truth),

> they are not comparable because they are not of the same genus. However, if they be considered in relation to some effect, they concur in one regard and may thus be compared. This effect in which they concur and according to which they can be compared is the changing of the human heart. Therefore, whichever among them brings about the greatest change in the human heart would seem to be the strongest.
>
> It must be observed that change in human beings concerns sometimes the body and sometimes the soul, and this latter change can be in two ways: regarding the senses and regarding the intellect. Furthermore, the intellect is also two-fold: practical and contemplative [*speculativum*].
>
> Among those things, however, that pertain to natural change according to bodily disposition, the best is wine, which makes people talkative by drunkenness. Among those things that pertain to change in the appetite of the senses, the best is pleasure, especially sexual pleasure, and thus woman is stronger. In practical matters and human affairs that we can accomplish, the king has the greatest power. In contemplative matters the highest and most powerful thing is truth.
>
> Now bodily powers are subordinate to animal powers, animal powers to intellectual powers, and practical intellectual powers to contemplative ones. Therefore, all other things being equal, truth is most worthy and excellent and strong.

As he begins his reply, Thomas takes four candidates for "strongest" and points out the difficulty of comparing them if we simply take them as what they are in themselves. However, he goes on to say that they are all causes of change in the human heart and thus may be compared on that level. Thomas, therefore, locates them within the context of his understanding of human beings, observing (1) that human beings are both bodily and spiritual (or, as he puts it here, "animal"—from *anima* or "soul"); (2) that our spiritual natures consist in our capacity for sensation, which we share with other animals, and our capacity for thought, which distinguishes us from other animals; and (3) that our capacity for thought can be further divided into thought oriented toward action (practical reason) and thought oriented toward knowledge (speculative or contemplative reason).

Having made these distinctions, we can see that the human heart can be moved in various ways. Wine can affect us on a physical level by means of a chemical reaction, turning an otherwise taciturn person into a talkative one. A beautiful woman (or man) affects us not simply on the level of a physical change but through sensation, specifically pleasurable sensation. Both a king and the truth act on the level of thought but in distinct ways. A king can command the will to move us to perform some action, but he cannot command the mind to desire something or to assent to something. Only the truth can do that. So, there are different kinds of causes of human action and consequently different kinds of human actions: those of the body, those of the senses, those of the willed acts, and those of practical and speculative reason. These distinctions are crucial to the articulation of Thomas's overarching vision of reality. Thomas claims not only that we can distinguish different kinds of causes of change in the human heart but that these kinds have a proper ordering, one to another. This ordering is implicit in his initial description of the different kinds of changes. The most basic (or "lowest") kind of change is that which human beings share in common with all existing things: change brought about by physical causes. Change brought about by things that act through the senses is distinctive to sensate beings (i.e., animals), but again is not distinctively human. Thus, the *less* distinctive causes of action are lower than or "subordinate to" (ordered below) *more* distinctive causes of action.

But what about the two kinds of causes of action that are equally distinctive of human beings: those that act upon practical reason and those that act upon speculative reason? How are these ordered in relation to each other? The practical intellect and the speculative intellect are not two different powers of reason so much as the application of reason in two different ways: in the former case, about the good that is to be pursued (i.e., what we should do), and in the latter case, about the truth that is known (i.e., what is the case). And these distinct objects turn out not to be so distinct, since "truth and good include one another; for truth is something good, otherwise it would not be desirable; and good is something true, otherwise it would not be intelligible."[5] Yet a difference remains: practical reason is reasoning about the good that is the cause of *human* action, whereas speculative reason reaches beyond the human to God, the cause of all that is and thus of all truth.[6] Therefore, causes that operate through the practical intellect are subordinate to those that operate through the speculative intellect. We might say that it is easier to cause behavior than belief. Thus, "truth is stronger" because the hierarchy of causes exemplified by wine, woman, king, and truth corresponds to the ontological hierarchy of inanimate beings, animate beings, intellectual beings, and God, who is the act of existing itself (*esse ipsum subsistens*).

So far, so logical and metaphysical. But what about Tradition and Scripture? Some have taken this quodlibetal question to be a student's joke, posed to baffle the professor, and perhaps it was (though it is not a particularly funny one). More importantly, however, the question is rooted in the text of Scripture, specifically the deuterocanonical book of 3 Esdras,[7] in which three young Jewish servants of the Persian king Darius debate

5. *Summa theologiae* 1.79.11 ad 2.

6. *Summa theologiae* 2-2.47.2 ad 1.

7. This book, also known as "Esdras A," was rejected by Jerome as part of the canon, so perhaps one should not consider it part of the "text of Scripture." It was, however, integrated with the canonical books in the so-called "Paris Bible" used at the University of Paris in the thirteenth century. See Edmon L. Gallagher, "Deuterocanonical Books in Latin Tradition," in *The Oxford Handbook of the Latin Bible*, ed. H.A.G. Houghton (Oxford: Oxford University Press, 2023), 91–105. We do not know whether or not Thomas viewed it as canonical, but his

this question before their master. Darius's predecessor, Cyrus, had defeated the Babylonians, who had fifty years before destroyed Jerusalem and taken many of its people off into exile. Cyrus had allowed the Jewish exiles to return to their homeland, but many had remained in Babylon, where they had established themselves. At this time, the temple in Jerusalem remains in ruins because Darius has yet to fulfill the vow he made to rebuild it.

The first of the three servants argues that wine is strongest, not least because "it makes equal the mind of the king and the orphan, of the slave and the free, of the poor and the rich" (3 Esdras 3:19). The second young man, more inclined to flattery than wit, argues that the king is stronger since "all his people and his armies obey him" (4:10). The third defends the proposition that "women are strongest, but truth is victor over all things" (3:12). This young man is Zerubbabel, the grandson of King Jehoiachin, who was the last king of Judah before the exile in Babylon. Zerubbabel is not interested in impressing Darius with wit or flattery. He argues that women are stronger than wine since they give birth to the men who plant the vineyards, and also stronger than kings, pointing to Darius's own fawning behavior with his concubine Apame, who would "take the crown from the king's head and put it on her own, and slap the king with her left hand" (4:30).

Then Zerubbabel abruptly shifts gears, announcing that "truth is great, and stronger than all things" (4:35). What justifies this shift? Zerubbabel's mockery of the king and his concubine points to their pettiness and makes ridiculous their claims to importance. Zerubbabel continues, speaking of truth as a woman (perhaps echoing the figure of "lady wisdom" in the book of Proverbs), a woman who is in striking contrast to Darius's concubine: "With her there is no partiality or preference, but she does what is righteous instead of anything that is unrighteous or wicked"

use of it in the *sed contra* ("against this") of his quodlibetal question suggests that it had at least a "Scripture-ish" aura.

(4:39). The implicit appeal to Darius is that he pursue the powerful and righteous Lady Truth, rather than the fickle and untrustworthy Apame. But the punchline to Zerubbabel's encomium to truth comes at the end: "To her belong the strength and the kingship and the power and the majesty of all the ages. Blessed be the God of truth" (4:40). In this final turn, Zerubbabel makes it clear that to dedicate oneself to the pursuit of truth is to dedicate oneself to the God of Israel.

Darius is won over, smitten by Zerubbabel's portrayal of Lady Truth. He says, "Ask what you wish," and Zerubbabel replies, "I pray therefore that you fulfill the vow whose fulfillment you vowed to the King of heaven with your own lips" (4:43–46). Darius, confronted with truth, a power greater than his own power as king, agrees to Zerubbabel's request that he rebuild the temple.

Relocating Thomas's discussion in its biblical source helps us see that, though he employs the tools of philosophy, his answer to the question is saturated with biblical understandings of the relationship between power and truth, and the subordination of earthly rulers to God's eternal law. In the story of Zerubbabel, we see displayed a fundamental narrative pattern that repeats itself throughout the Old and New Testaments, a pattern that is central to Thomas's thoughts on political order and that is summed up in the verse that Thomas quotes in his quodlibetal question: "Truth is stronger."

SPEAKING TRUTH TO POWER

The confrontation between truth and other claimants to the throne of power is expressed perhaps most acutely in the Gospel of John's account of Jesus's appearance before Pilate, the representative of earthly power (see John 18:33–19:22). Thomas's own commentary on this narrative is instructive. While Thomas casts Pilate in as favorable a light as possible—he is a "just judge" who wishes to know the truth[8]—he still sees Pilate as one who cannot understand what Christ says because he is thoroughly bound to "worldly" ways of thinking, unable to imagine a kingdom that is not "physical"—that is, one of external coercion. Even though Pilate is willing to accept Jesus as a "teacher of the truth,"[9] he never understands the real relationship between truth and kingship; he never understands that "truth is stronger."

Pilate further misunderstands Jesus's statement that his kingdom is not of this world in an error that Thomas characterizes as "Manichean," in that the material world is seen as a realm of irredeemable darkness ruled by the forces of brute coercion. Against this, Thomas maintains that while Christ does not reign "in the physical way that those of the earth do"[10]—namely, by external coercion—this does not mean that he does not rule this world. Indeed, Christ's kingdom "is here, because it is everywhere."[11] While law is often coercive, operating through the threat of punishment,[12] it is not inevitably so. The eternal law by which God guides creation operates from the *interior* of things, not by external coercion; and even in the case of earthly laws, these are coercive to the wicked, because they run contrary to the inclination of their wills, but not to the good, because their wills are in harmony with truth.[13] Pilate presumes, in common with the Manichean worldview, that power is always and merely the power of coercion, operating (like wine) on the level of physical force, and that any power that is "not of this world" must not be real power.

Thomas notes Jesus's care in replying to Pilate's questions. When Pilate says, "So you are a king?" Jesus replies, "You say that I am a king." Thomas says, "Our Lord tempered his response

8. *Super Io.* 18.6.2344.
9. *Super Io.* 18.6.2365.
10. *Super Io.* 18.6.2350.
11. *Super Io.* 18.6.2354.
12. See *Summa theologiae* 1-2.90.3 ad 2.
13. See *Summa theologiae* 1-2.96.5.

about his kingship so that he neither clearly asserted that he was a king—since he was not a king in the sense in which Pilate understood it—nor denied it—since spiritually he was the King of Kings."[14] The Manichean worldview would have it that if Christ's kingship is "worldly," then it must partake of the darkness of coercion; if it is "unworldly," then it is utterly different from and irrelevant to this realm of darkness. Thomas rejects such an alternative. He denies that Christ is a king according to the mode of physical kingship but asserts that he is king in another way, the way of righteousness.[15]

Thomas says that Christ then reveals the "mode and order" (*modum et rationem*) of his kingdom in the statement, "For this I was born and for this I have come into the world, to bear witness to the truth" (John 18:37).[16] The kingdom of Christ is "unworldly," yet exercised from the very heart of the world. Those he rules, because they have seen the truth manifested by Christ, set their affections not on earthly things but on heavenly ones; yet (as Augustine would put it) they live as pilgrims in this world in order to witness to the truth. Similarly, the authority he receives from the Father is the true power and pattern of the world's creation.[17]

Pilate proves a somewhat tragic figure in Thomas's estimation. He asks Jesus in all sincerity, "What is truth?" (John 18:38), but he does not wait for the answer.[18] He is interested in truth, but it is a dilettante's interest; he does not realize that real strength resides in finding the truth. He still trusts in his ability to manipulate the Jews in order to free Christ, whom he has decided is harmless (because powerless). Rather than waiting to hear the truth from Christ, he tries to exploit the Jewish custom of

14. *Super Io.* 18.6.2358.
15. *Super Io.* 18.6.2358.
16. *Super Io.* 18.6.2359.
17. See *Super Io.* 18.6.2351.
18. *Super Io.* 18.6.2364.

releasing a prisoner at Passover time.[19] As Thomas continues to describe Pilate's bargaining with those who seek Christ's death, Thomas becomes uncharacteristically passionate in chiding Pilate: "Why then, unrighteous Pilate, was there this shameful bargaining if there was no crime in him?"[20] From the human perspective, Pilate has the power to release Jesus, but he continues to pretend that he does not really have the authority to do so, even while boasting of his own power. Tangled in this knot of self-deceit, "he has condemned himself."[21]

The final act of this confrontation comes when the Jews threaten Pilate with Caesar's displeasure because "they thought that Pilate would prefer the friendship of Caesar to the friendship of justice."[22] They are right. Pilate cannot ignore such a threat because he believes that his power in this matter comes from Caesar. Pilate's capitulation before the threat of Caesar's power shows both his moral failings and his inability to grasp the power of truth. And so truth goes to the cross: "Christ bore his cross as a king does his scepter; his cross is the sign of his glory, which is his universal dominion over all things."[23]

Thomas's commentary on the encounter between Pilate and Jesus reveals the precise way in which "truth is stronger." Speaking truth to earthly power is no guarantee that you will not be killed, for the power of "physical" rulers is essentially the power of coercion, which reaches its extreme measure in the death of those who will not comply. But the noncoercive power of truth accomplishes the purposes of truth more inexorably than the purposes of any earthly rule. A martyr for truth can resist an earthly ruler to the point of death and thus beyond the limits of the ruler's power, but the power of truth has no limits. So, as Aquinas says,

19. *Super Io.* 18.6.2367.
20. *Super Io.* 19.2.2380.
21. *Super Io.* 19.2.2393.
22. *Super Io.* 19.3.2399.
23. *Super Io.* 19.3.2414.

Christ's cross becomes the sign of his "universal dominion over all things."[24]

LAW, ORDER, BEAUTY

To those familiar with the standard account of Aquinas's political thought, what I have written above must seem strange because I have not mentioned natural law. I have postponed discussing natural law because when it is taken as "foundational" for Thomas's political thought (as it is, for example, by John Finnis), one can miss the theological context in which Thomas frames his relatively brief discussion of natural law and the limited, but not unimportant, role it plays in his account of the political life of Christians.

In the *Summa theologiae*, Thomas's discussion of natural law (1-2.94) occurs in the context of a cluster of questions (1-2.90–108) concerned with law as one of the "external principles" of human action, matched by another cluster of questions concerning grace (1-2.109–114), the other external principle of human action. These questions occur in the larger context of Thomas's discussion of human action in the second part of the *Summa*, which in turn is located in the larger context of the *Summa* as a whole, with its structure of creation coming forth from God and returning to God through Christ. Of the 512 questions in the *Summa theologiae*, Aquinas devotes only one, consisting of six articles, to natural law. By way of contrast, he devotes seven questions, a total of forty-six articles, to the Torah. While such quantitative information can be misleading since the notion of natural law crops up throughout the questions on law and in various other places in Aquinas's work, it raises the question of whether the importance of natural law in Aquinas's thought has been overestimated. Our

24. *Super Io.* 19.3.2414.

evaluation, however, must ultimately rest on a careful reading, in context, of Thomas's account of natural law.

After a general discussion of "law" (1-2.90–92), Thomas begins not with natural law but with the basis of all law in the "eternal law," by which "the whole community of the universe is governed by divine reason."[25] This law is a *ratio* (in this sense, an idea or exemplar, but also an "order" or a "standard") existing in God eternally, by which all of the world's actions and movements are directed: the eternal law is both the pattern of divine order within the uncreated being of God and the pattern of order in which all created things participate and by which they are governed and led to their end. This eternal law is "appropriated" to the divine Word, the second person of the Trinity, by which the Father expresses himself.[26]

The natural law is the participation of rational creatures in the eternal law through sharing in divine wisdom.[27] While all creatures are guided by the eternal law, rational creatures are guided by God precisely through their intellects. Thomas's initial emphasis is not on natural law as an autonomous human faculty for discovering right and wrong but on how the human ability to discern good and evil is "nothing else than the imprint on us of the divine light."[28] This participation in divine reason provides rational creatures with "first principles" of moral reasoning. These first principles are not conclusions about particular actions but rather what one might call the basic "grammar" of such reasoning.[29] The first precept of moral reasoning—"Good is to be done and pursued and evil is to be avoided"[30]—does not tell us whether any particular action is good or evil but that no

25. *Summa theologiae* 1-2.91.1.

26. *Summa theologiae* 1-2.93.1, 4.

27. *Summa theologiae* 1-2.91.2.

28. *Summa theologiae* 1-2.91.2.

29. See *Summa theologiae* 1-2.94.2.

30. *Summa theologiae* 1-2.94.2.

action can be simultaneously good (and therefore to be pursued) and evil (and therefore to be avoided) at the same time and in the same way. In other words, all reasoning about action must begin with a recognition of the "grammatical" or logical distinction between good and evil.

However, Thomas thinks that natural law can also yield something more than simply the principle that good is to be pursued and evil is to be avoided. Human beings "naturally" (i.e., by virtue of their rational natures) incline toward those things that they apprehend as good, and therefore our knowledge of what it means to be a human being can yield a skeletal account of those goods we ought to pursue. Thus, we have the goods that we pursue in common with all beings, such as self-preservation; goods that we pursue in common with other living beings, such as nutrition, reproduction, and the nurture of young; and, finally, pursuits peculiar to us as human beings, such as life in community and truth.[31]

Thomas follows Aristotle in claiming that the human being is by nature a "social animal"—that is, human society and all it entails is part of what it means to be human.[32] Given the relative complexity of human needs and the poverty of human instinct relative to other animals,[33] human beings need some sort of structured way of living and flourishing *together*. This flourishing together is based on what Thomas calls "the common good." This is neither the aggregate of all individual goods nor those goods that a given group of individuals happen to have in common. Rather, it is *God* who is the common good of all creatures, both as the source of all created goods and as the end toward which they are drawn.[34] Beings are drawn to God through what Thomas describes as "the beauty of order": the good of ordered diversity

31. *Summa theologiae* 1-2.94.2.

32. *Summa theologiae* 1-2.61.5; 1-2.95.4.

33. *Summa theologiae* 1-2.95.1.

34. *Summa theologiae* 1.60.5; 1-2.19.10.

reflecting in a finite way the infinite, simple goodness of God.[35] Thus, we might say that, on the level of human community, the common good is the good of ordered common life itself, a goodness that is a participation in the goodness of God.

While social life is natural to human beings, this does not mean that untutored human impulse will inevitably lead to the forsaking of individual goods for the common good. Human beings have a "natural aptitude" to pursue good and avoid evil in particular ways, but this aptitude is not sufficient in itself for leading a good life precisely because those particular goods must be coordinated to reflect the "beauty of order." Thus, particular human laws must be instituted in order to train and direct human beings in community to properly order the goods that they pursue by natural inclination.[36] Thomas is remarkably undogmatic about which form of government is best suited to this purpose, though he tends to identify pure democracy with mob rule and expresses a preference for a "mixed" form of government incorporating elements of monarchy (one clear head of government), aristocracy (the powers of government distributed among a group), and democracy (those who govern being chosen from the people and by the people).[37] Whatever the polity, however, a government is judged as good or bad according to its ability to properly order human life together in view of its supernatural end.

The presence of the beauty of order in human societies is what we call "justice," and the lack of such order is what we call "tyranny." Aquinas says that "justice, by its nature, implies a certain rightness [*rectitudinem*] of order."[38] A just society is one that is rightly or beautifully ordered by imitating God, who, according to his eternal law, "gives to each thing what is due to it by

35. *Summa theologiae* 1.96.3 ad 3.

36. *Summa theologiae* 1-2.95.1.

37. *Summa theologiae* 1-2.105.1.

38. *Summa theologiae* 1-2.113.1.

its nature and condition."[39] Human communities participate in the beauty of God's order when, for example, they give to children the nurture and education due to them on account of their nature. However, when those entrusted with the leadership of a community fail to render to each what is his or her due, we have tyranny, which is a kind of perverse imitation of law.[40] Indeed, if justice truthfully mirrors the ordering action of God by caring for each and every one, tyranny is a false representation because it is an exercise of power that ignores the common good.

The task of justice, understood as our participation in the divine beauty of order, is something to which human beings are called, both as individuals and as communities, but at the same time is a task to which they are in no way adequate. This inadequacy is rooted in human creaturely finitude and exacerbated by human sin. Thus, beyond natural law and human law, it was necessary that there be a law given to human beings by God, which Aquinas calls "divine law."[41] This divine law is intended both to strengthen the dictates of natural law and to supplement them by uniting human beings in the right worship of God.

This divine law is first manifested in the Torah of the people of Israel, which in the Decalogue clearly articulates the natural law for God's people and in the ceremonial and judicial precepts gives shape to the common life of that people.[42] Indeed, Thomas says that "the people of Israel is commended for the beauty of its order."[43] That beauty lies in part in the relative clarity with which the Torah renders God's eternal law, but above all in its "figurative" quality by which it points to the new law of Jesus Christ.[44] The new law surpasses the old by bringing it to perfection. Whereas

39. *Summa theologiae* 1.21.1 ad 3.

40. *Summa theologiae* 1-2.92.1 ad 4.

41. *Summa theologiae* 1-2.91.4.

42. *Summa theologiae* 1-2.99.4.

43. *Summa theologiae* 1-2.105.1 sed contra.

44. *Summa theologiae* 1-2.104.2.

the old law directed and ordered human action through external means—promises and punishments—the new law directs and orders human action from within, through the infusion of grace.[45] Indeed, Thomas says that the new law first and foremost simply is the grace of the Holy Spirit, ruling (in the sense both of directing and of measuring) our hearts.[46] We find here echoes of Thomas's comments on the distinction in his *Commentary on John* between Christ's kingship and "physical" kingship. However, the new law also commends certain physical actions: the sacramental rituals that are a source of grace and the visible acts of human love that are consequences of divinely imparted love.[47] Thus, the new law, no less than the old, imparts a visible "shape" to the community of God's people, though without recourse to physical coercion. At this point, Thomas's discussion of law in the *Summa* merges seamlessly into his discussion of grace.

Attempts to reduce Thomas's views on law to the few articles that he devotes to natural law stumble over the fact that his account of law is irreducibly theological. In fact, it is not simply *theological* but *Christological.* It begins by rooting all law in the eternal law expressed by the Father in the generation of the Son and ends with the new law of Christ, given through the Spirit to his disciples. In between these Christological bookends, we do indeed find discussions of natural and human law, and Thomas clearly holds the view that certain particular goods can be realized by societies established on the basis of the natural law written in our hearts. He rejects the position that the seemingly good things that people do apart from grace—such as building houses or having friends—are somehow not actually good.[48] But they do remain incomplete, and radically so, because such natural goodness can only dimly glimpse the eternal law, the divine truth

45. *Summa theologiae* 1-2.107.1 ad 2.

46. *Summa theologiae* 1-2.106.1.

47. *Summa theologiae* 1-2.108.1.

48. *Summa theologiae* 1-2.109.2, 5.

manifested in God's incarnate Word.[49] Though human societies apart from divine law can instantiate particular goods and even partially order them to the common good, they cannot ultimately attain the truly common good, which is God.

To make this same point from a different angle, let us return to Jesus standing before Pilate. Pilate's human nature has retained sufficient goodness for him to recognize Jesus as a teacher of the truth; it has retained sufficient goodness for him to value the truth enough to want to release Jesus; but because he has not recognized "the gift of God which enables us to believe and love the truth,"[50] he has not recognized Jesus himself as the truth, the embodiment of the eternal law. Pilate has retained just enough goodness to be morally responsible, and thus, in his condemnation of Christ, "he has condemned himself."[51] Like all embodiments of human law and authority left to their own devices, Pilate can be held accountable to justice, but he can implement it only imperfectly. He cannot enact the beauty of order.

THOMAS TODAY

The reading I have offered of Thomas on politics has suggested that what some modern interpreters see as his greatest strength—namely, the autonomy he gives to secular politics through his notion of natural law—is in fact not Thomas's position at all. While Thomas believed that the goodness of human nature is not entirely vitiated by sin, and that just human societies are ordered toward the common good, he also shared the views of his culture that in any rightly ordered society, the Gospel would be welcomed and promoted by the laws of that society. He argued that unbelievers should not be allowed to establish their rule over

49. See Decosimo, *Ethics as a Work of Charity.*

50. *Super Io.* 18.6.2363.

51. *Super Io.* 19.3.2393.

believers,[52] that heretics were an illness of the body politic and could under certain circumstances be killed,[53] and that an apostate prince could be deprived by the Church of his dominion over his subjects.[54] He was not, as Lord Acton would have had it, "the first Whig."

Any proposed use of Thomas today must accept the fact that his views are not easily separable from the ecclesial-political situation of his day; and it must equally accept that Thomas's ecclesial-political situation no longer obtains in our day. In order to avoid any facile or distorted applications of what Thomas has to say on politics, we must look carefully at the assumptions of Thomas and his day and at those of our own. Thomas does not share our assumptions. He does not think of the common good as equivalent to the greatest good for the greatest number. He does not think of human societies as primarily instruments by which individuals pursue their private ends. He does not think that questions of ultimate truth must be bracketed in order for societies to function. Indeed, because "truth is stronger," a truly human society can be established only on the basis of eternal truth.

This last point indicates the greatest difference between Thomas's assumptions and contemporary assumptions, which is exemplified by his treatment of Pilate's question, "What is truth?" As noted above, Thomas takes Pilate to be making a serious inquiry. Pilate retains a goodness in his nature that still desires the truth. But contrast Thomas's reading of Pilate with the one given by Nietzsche in *The Antichrist*:

> Need I add that in the whole New Testament there is only a single figure who commands respect? Pilate, the Roman governor. To take a Jewish affair seriously—he does not persuade himself to do that. One Jew more or less—what does it matter?

52. *Summa theologiae* 2-2.10.10.

53. *Summa theologiae* 2-2.11.3.

54. *Summa theologiae* 2-2.12.2.

> The noble scorn of a Roman, confronted with an impudent abuse of the word "truth," has enriched the New Testament with the only saying *that has value*—one which is its criticism, and even its *annihilation*: "What is truth?"[55]

Thomas's benign reading of Pilate's question seems to miss the irony in it that is so obvious to Nietzsche. It is almost as if Thomas could not imagine that Pilate was not genuinely interested in the truth, an eternal and universal truth. The question of Nietzsche's Pilate, on the other hand, is redolent of the corrosive irony that relativizes all truth, turning it into, in Nietzsche's phrase, "a mobile army of metaphors, metonyms, and anthropomorphisms—in short, a sum of human relations, which have been enhanced, transposed, and embellished poetically and rhetorically, and which after long use seem firm, canonical, and obligatory to a people."[56] Whatever "truth" Pilate may be concerned with, it is a Roman truth, established by Caesar's rule and the greatness of the Roman people; he is supremely *un*concerned with the *Jewish* truth of which Jesus speaks.

Pilate's "noble scorn" embodies for Nietzsche the reversal of the hierarchy of power that is at the heart of Thomas's politics. For Aquinas, the truth is more powerful than the king because it is God, eternal truth, who creates the king; for Nietzsche, the king—at least, a "noble" king—is more powerful than truth because it is he who creates gods for his people. A Roman like Pilate might choose to ignore a Jewish truth or to destroy it on a cross, but he would never bow before it as being more powerful than Caesar. And indeed, it seems that Nietzsche understood Pilate better than Aquinas did, for it was the reminder of the power of

55. Friedrich Nietzsche, *The Antichrist* 46, in *The Portable Nietzsche*, ed. and trans. Walter Kaufmann (New York: Viking, 1954), 626–27.

56. Nietzsche, "On Truth and Lie in an Extra-Moral Sense," in *The Portable Nietzsche*, 46–47.

Caesar, the "truth" that Caesar can create, that strengthened the resolve of Pilate.

While few today approach Nietzsche's subtlety with regard to the relationship among politics, truth, and power, his conviction that "truth" is a product of human making and is malleable in the hands of whoever has the most coercive power is widespread, as a practical attitude if not a theoretical position. Liberal societies seek to bracket questions of truth not simply because they seem unresolvable but because they seem so subject to manipulation by the powerful. And in this, they are capable of posing some difficult questions to a thinker like Aquinas, who at times accepts certain cultural assumptions as truths of nature. For example, in the quodlibetal question with which we began, Thomas is convinced that he knows the place of "woman" in the order of things. A recognition of the role of human making in our understanding of the truth can lead us to be more critical than Aquinas was in his construal of the "natural" relations of men and women or masters and slaves.

But the corrosive question "What is truth?" can be turned back upon liberal societies themselves. The question that liberal societies must face is whether their bracketing of truth makes them more or less subject to ideological manipulation. Does suspicion of overt truth claims liberate one from covert truth claims? Could it be that the forces that shape our lives—forces that shape what we buy, how we earn our living, what we watch and listen to, whom and for whom we will kill in war, whom we see as "us" and whom we see as "them"—are no less absolute in their claims upon us, even if they have abandoned the language of "truth" for the language of "freedom"?

It is perhaps here that Thomas can be genuinely helpful for Christian thinking about politics. The ideal of a Christian prince withers before the Nietzschean understanding of what Pilate is saying when he asks, "What is truth?" Particularly when rule, even democratic rule, takes the form of empires, truth must always be subordinate to the rulers. But Thomas's conviction that truth is stronger than kings—or presidents or prime ministers—can still undergird a political vision for Christians. Indeed, it was precisely Thomas's understanding of a natural law that is rooted in God's eternal law to which Martin Luther King Jr. appealed in his 1963 "Letter from Birmingham Jail" in order to justify his civil disobedience against unjust laws.[57] The example of King suggests that today, the conviction that truth is stronger will not be manifested in laws proscribing heresies or in popes deposing princes, nor in overly confident claims about the "natural" ordering of relations between slaves and masters or women and men. But it will be manifested by a Christian community that forms people to resist the functional idolatries of the state and the market, that makes its members disobedient subjects of tyrannical regimes, that displays in its common life the beauty of order. It will be manifested by a Church that emulates Zerubbabel before Darius and Jesus before Pilate, a Church that speaks truth to kings in the conviction that truth is stronger and that a ruler who does not serve the truth is a tyrant. Such a political vision will have at its heart Thomas's claim that the cross, the instrument of state-sanctioned murder, has become the sign of Christ's "universal dominion over all things," a sign of the power of God's truth by which all earthly polities will be judged.

57. Martin Luther King Jr., "Letter from Birmingham Jail," in *Why We Can't Wait* (New York: Harper and Row, 1964), 76–95.

Part III

Divine and Human

10

Incarnation, Redemption, and the Character of God

If one follows the standard accounts of the matter, the kind that appear in theological textbooks, there are in Catholic theology two positions regarding the answer to the question, "Whether, if human beings had not sinned, God would have become incarnate?" Thomas and Thomists answer in the negative, Scotus and Scotists answer in the positive. Thomas sees the Incarnation as a remedy for sin, and therefore Christ's predestination was conditional: no sin, no Incarnation. Scotus, on the other hand, sees the Incarnation as the perfection of creation, something that would have occurred even if sin had never entered the world, and therefore Christ's predestination was absolute or unconditional.[1] Further, theology in the last hundred years seems to be tilting in Scotus's direction; there seems to be a growing agreement that one ought to think of the Incarnation first in terms of perfecting creation for the glory of God rather than repairing it. Perhaps the most prominent proponent of this view among twentieth century

* Originally published as "Incarnation, Redemption, and the Character of God," *Nova et Vetera* 3, no. 3 (Summer 2005): 459–72.

1. This account can be found especially in any number of theological handbooks or textbooks in the last century. See, for example, Adolphe Tanquerey, *A Manual of Dogmatic Theology*, trans. John J. Byrnes (New York: Desclée, 1959), 2:92–93; Ludwig Ott, *Fundamentals of Catholic Dogma*, ed. James Canon Bastible, trans. Patrick Lynch (Cork: Mercier, 1958), 175–76; Albert Schlitzer, *Redemptive Incarnation: Sources and Their Theological Development in the Study of Christ* (Notre Dame, IN: University of Notre Dame Press, 1956), 317–29; John P. Galvin, "Jesus Christ," in *Systematic Theology: Roman Catholic Perspectives*, ed. Francis Schüssler Fiorenza and John P. Galvin (Minneapolis, MN: Fortress, 1991), 1:280; Gerhard Ludwig Müller, "Incarnation," in *Handbook of Catholic Theology*, ed. Wolfgang Beinert and Francis Schüssler Fiorenza (New York: Crossroad, 1995), 378.

Catholic theologians was Karl Rahner, who identified his own view with that of "the 'Scotist' school" that "the first and most basic motive for the Incarnation was not the blotting out of sin but . . . [rather] the Incarnation was already the goal of divine freedom even apart from any divine foreknowledge of freely incurred guilt."[2]

I think that this turn to the purportedly "Scotist" view on the Incarnation is related to a more general shift in Catholic theology toward a closer integration between the order of nature and the order of grace. Just as grace is no longer seen as an extrinsic and theoretically optional addition to human nature, so too the Incarnation of the Word is no longer seen as an extrinsic and theoretically optional addition to God's work in creation. Just as grace perfects nature, so too Incarnation perfects creation. The fundamental purpose of the Incarnation, therefore, is not to repair and, perhaps, "add-on" to human nature but to elevate human nature to participation in the divine nature, something that would have occurred even if Adam and Eve had managed to resist the allurements of the serpent. In this view, were the Word never to become incarnate, creation would be incomplete, human nature would be frustrated, and God would be deprived of his proper glory. We find this view not only in the writings of theologians like Rahner but also in Church documents, most notably in *Gaudium et Spes.* As *Gaudium et Spes* §22 puts it: "It is only in the mystery of the Word incarnate that light is shed on the mystery of humankind. For Adam, the first human being, was a representation of the future—namely, of Christ the lord. It is Christ, the last Adam, who fully discloses humankind to itself and unfolds its noble calling by revealing the mystery of the Father and the Father's love."[3] Here, we see the view that it is only

2. Karl Rahner, *Theological Investigations,* vol. 5, *Later Writings,* trans. Karl-H. Kruger (New York: Crossroad, 1983), 184–85.

3. In *Decrees of the Ecumenical Councils,* ed. Norman P. Tanner (London: Sheed & Ward, 1990), 2:1081.

in the light cast by the Word-made-flesh that the human person becomes intelligible; therefore, unless we would be willing to embrace the possibility that God could create the universe without willing its completion and perfection, we seem to find endorsed here the view of Scotus that God wills the Incarnation primarily and absolutely for the crowning of creation, and only secondarily and contingently as a remedy for sin.

The text just quoted, *Gaudium et Spes* §22, runs like a red thread through the writings of John Paul II. Indeed, beginning with his first, programmatic encyclical, *Redemptor Hominis*, John Paul returned again and again to what he called "this stupendous text from the Council's teaching"[4] in order to underline his conviction that "through the Incarnation God gave human life the dimension that he intended man to have from his first beginning."[5] So it would seem that the answer to the question of the motive of the fundamental purpose of the Incarnation is the completion and crowning of God's creative work.

But things are not always as they would seem. In what follows, I propose that the question of what God would have done had humanity not sinned is not really of interest to either Aquinas or John Paul II. Rather, their shared concern is to stress the redemptive nature of the Incarnation, without ignoring its other purposes, in order to render for us the character of God as rich in mercy. Further, John Paul enriches Thomas's account of the redemptive purpose of the Incarnation by seeing it not only as a revelation of the divine nature but also of human nature.

CUR DEUS HOMO?

It is remarkable how long it took Christian theologians to get around to asking explicitly the question of whether Christ would

4. John Paul II, *Redemptor Hominis* 9, encyclical letter, March 4, 1979, vatican.va.

5. *Redemptor Hominis* 1.

have become incarnate apart from human sin. Despite the reputation that the Greek Fathers have of holding a view of Christ that is more "cosmic" than later Western theologians,[6] they do not really raise the question.[7] Anselm, of course, raises the famous question *Cur Deus homo?* though he does not consider the counterfactual situation of an unfallen world.

It is only when we get to Rupert of Deutz in the early twelfth century that we find an explicit formulation of the question, to which he answers that the Incarnation was part of God's original intention for creation and thus would have occurred even if humanity had not sinned. Rupert's contemporary Honorius of Autun raised the speculative stakes somewhat, arguing that God would have become incarnate in an impassible form had there been no sin for which to atone.[8] In the thirteenth century, similar views were put forward by Robert Grosseteste, Alexander of Hales, and Albert the Great. The great champion of this view, as already noted, was John Duns Scotus, after whom the position becomes associated with the Franciscan order, though it was also held by such non-Franciscans as Denis the Carthusian and Gabriel Biel, as well as, in the early modern period, Francis de Sales and Nicolas Malebranche.[9] The first to pose the question and give a negative answer was the early Dominican Master at Paris

6. See, for example, George A. Maloney, *The Cosmic Christ: From Paul to Teilhard* (New York: Sheed & Ward, 1968), and, more recently, Ilia Delio, "Revisiting the Franciscan Doctrine of Christ," *Theological Studies* 64 , no. 1 (February 2003): 3–23.

7. In fact, they presume a close link between the Incarnation and human redemption, and indeed make arguments for the divine identity of the Incarnate One on the basis of his role as redeemer. See Georges Florovsky, "*Cur Deus Homo?* The Motive of the Incarnation," in *Collected Works of Georges Florovsky*, vol. 3, *Creation and Redemption* (Belmont, MA: Nordland, 1976), 163–70. Florovsky's essay provides a succinct summary of the history of the question. For a comprehensive and compelling account of the medieval Western development of this issue and its theological ramifications, see Justus H. Hunter, *If Adam Had Not Sinned: The Reason for the Incarnation from Anselm to Scotus* (Washington, DC: The Catholic University of America Press, 2020).

8. On Rupert and Honorius, see Florovsky, "*Cur Deus Homo?*," 165, as well as J. McEvoy, "The Absolute Predestination of Christ in the Theology of Robert Grosseteste," in *Sapientiae doctrina*, ed. H. Bascour et al. (Leuven: Peeters, 1980), 212–30, at 220–21.

9. See Florovsky, "*Cur Deus Homo?*," 166–67, for citations and illustrative texts.

Guerric of Saint-Quentin in the thirteenth century.[10] Bonaventure and Aquinas also answer in the negative, and subsequent Dominican theologians tended to side with Aquinas, as well as such non-Dominicans as Robert Bellarmine. Suárez attempted to reconcile the two approaches, arguing for a twofold, coordinated purpose for the Incarnation. From the mid-nineteenth century to the mid-twentieth century, interest in the issue revived, with theologians tending to identify themselves as "Thomist" or "Scotist" in inclination.[11]

Yet before we happily line up these figures on opposing sides (with Suárez, perhaps, in the middle), we ought to actually attempt to gain a bit more clarity regarding the theological point at issue. It is not immediately clear that there *is* a single point at issue in the question *Cur Deus homo?* An indication of this is the variety of labels that are used to describe what is being argued about. Is it a question about the motive of the Incarnation, or are we considering an alternative, hypothetical universe without sin? Are we discussing the predestination of Christ or his primacy? We are confronted here with a tangle of issues, and it is not at all clear how they are related. What is clear is that the theological world does not clearly divide into Thomists and Scotists.

For example, the hypothetical question "What if humanity had not sinned?" is certainly one way of approaching the question of the motive of the Incarnation, if we presume that the Incarnation would have the same motive no matter what the contingencies were—indeed, presuming that speaking of "motivations" in regard to divine actions makes any sense at all. But if we do not make such presumptions, then the question looks like idle speculation. Likewise, we might be concerned with understanding the

10. See Guerric of Saint-Quentin, "*Quodlibet* 7.1 *(Utrum Filius fuisset incarnatus si homo non peccasset),*" in *Quaestiones de quolibet,* ed. Walter H. Principe, rev. Jonathan Black (Toronto: Pontifical Institute of Mediaeval Studies, 2002), 307–17.

11. For a brief overview of some of these figures, see Jean-François Bonnefoy, *Christ and the Cosmos,* ed. and trans. Michael D. Meilach (Paterson, NJ: St. Anthony Guild, 1965), 3–6.

relationships among God's various "decrees" (i.e., the election of Christ, the election of individual human beings, etc.) without having any particular concern to see Christ as the "crown" of creation, and vice versa. Disputants on all sides seem to quote the *Exsultet—O felix culpa, quae talem ac tantum meruit habere Redemptorem*—with the implication that it supports their own view.[12]

THOMAS ON FITTINGNESS

We cannot sort this tangle out here. But we should at least be led to wonder if Thomas himself held a "Thomist" position. Gilbert Narcisse writes that on the question of the motive of the Incarnation, we can discern three positions: that of Scotus and his followers, that of the Thomists, and that of Thomas himself.[13] I am inclined to think that Narcisse oversimplifies a bit here and that there are actually more than three positions in play; in particular, I am not convinced that Scotus's position is "Scotist."[14] Yet Narcisse's basic point is an extremely important one. In answer to the question of whether Christ would have become incarnate if human beings had never sinned, Thomas's answer is not the flatfooted "No" that some have identified as the "Thomist" position.

In looking at what Thomas has to say on this question, it is striking how *little* he in fact says. The texts that deal with the question constitute but a handful. It is only in his commentary on

12. Thomas quotes this in support of his position in *Summa theologiae* 3.1.3, as does Robert Jenson, who apparently believes himself to be in disagreement with Thomas. See Robert Jenson, "For Us He Was Made Man," in *Nicene Christianity: The Future for a New Ecumenism*, ed. Christopher R. Seitz (Grand Rapids, MI: Brazos, 2001), 76.

13. Gilbert Narcisse, *Les raisons de Dieu: Arguments de convenance et esthétique théologique selon saint Thomas d'Aquin et Hans Urs von Balthasar* (Fribourg, CH: Éditions Universitaires de Fribourg, 1997), xxii.

14. It is noteworthy that in outlining Scotus's position on the question, Richard Cross comments that "the whole argument has to be gleaned from several passages" (*Duns Scotus* [Oxford: Oxford University Press, 1999], 128); in other words, the "Scotist" argument is not something that is found as such in Scotus. Of course, Cross and others are fully justified in connecting the dots that they find in Scotus, but it is possible that those same dots might be connected in a way somewhat different from traditional Scotism.

Lombard's *Sentences*[15] and in *Summa theologiae* 3.1.3 that we find anything approaching a systematic treatment of the hypothetical question of whether or not Christ would have become incarnate apart from sin, and in both these cases, Thomas devotes only a single article to the question. He also mentions it very much in passing in *De veritate* 29.4 and discusses it briefly in his commentary on 1 Timothy, where he says, "This question is not of great importance, because God ordained things to be done in the way that they were to be done, and we are ignorant of what would have been ordained if he had not foreseen sin."[16]

Thomas's essential argument in both the *Sentences* commentary and in the *Summa theologiae* is that the hypothetical question is really a question about the divine will and, as such, is beyond our capacity to answer. This approach should come as no surprise to any careful reader of Aquinas. Despite the image that some have of him as one who believes that human reason can prove quite a number of things about God, Thomas in fact thinks that unaided reason not only cannot grasp what God is—it also cannot deduce *a priori* what God wills to do. These two things are related, since in God, being and doing are the same thing. Thus, God's acting is always in conformity with God's nature, but since we cannot grasp God's nature, our thinking about God's actions must always be, as it were, after the fact. To put it in modern terms, there can be no deduction of salvation history. Though each and every event of that history is enfolded within the divine decree, we have no access to that decree except as it unfolds before us in time. So hypothetical questions about what *would* have happened if history had unfolded in some other way are for Thomas simply veiled attempts to grasp what is ungraspable: the divine essence. At the same time, to say that events *had* to unfold in precisely the way that they did

15. *Super Sent.* 3.1.1.3

16. *Super I Tim.* 1.4.40: "Haec quaestio non est magnae auctoritatis, quia Deus ordinavit fienda secundum quod res fiendae erant. Et nescimus quid ordinasset, si non praescivisset peccatum."

is equally a reduction of God's essence to the graspable, as if the infinite mystery of God were exhausted in those events.

While Thomas always seeks to affirm God's freedom, at the same time, he is careful not to make that freedom arbitrary. Though God's nature is not graspable by created intellect, God's actions are still an expression of that nature, and through those actions, we can gain some inkling of the character of God. God's freedom is not contentlessness willing, and in God's actions, human reason is able to discern patterns that shape our understanding of who God is.

Thomas's chief tool for inquiring into God's character while still respecting divine freedom and incomprehensibility is the category of *convenientia* or "the fitting." Gilbert Narcisse writes that "fittingness is a realized possibility."[17] To inquire into the fittingness of something is first of all to acknowledge that it is contingent and not a matter of strict necessity: We wouldn't say that it is "fitting" for a circle to be round or for 2 plus 2 to equal 4, since these are matters of logical necessity. However, fittingness carries with it its own kind of necessity—one that is a matter of the relationship of means to ends.[18] Thus, we might say that it is "necessary" for parents to feed their child or for citizens to pay taxes, not in the sense of a logical necessity (as if "child feeder" were part of the definition of "parent" or "taxpayer" were part of the definition of "citizen"), but rather in the sense that these are the most fitting means of achieving certain ends. While the result could be achieved in a number of possible ways (the child could be hooked up to an IV in order to nourish it; the government could employ privateers in order to raise revenue), a certain path toward that result is the most fitting one.

However, reasoning about fittingness is a matter of *realized* possibility, which is why it is largely a retrospective activity. It

17. Narcisse, *Les raisons de Dieu*, 109.

18. See *Summa theologiae* 3.1.1.

is only when presented with a certain way of proceeding that we can discern the way in which various factors come together (*con-venire*) to make that way the most fitting one. At the same time that judgments of fittingness are largely retrospective, there *is* a certain prospective element to them, which is related to the notion of "character." When we say that it is characteristic of a parent to feed their child or of a citizen to pay taxes, we are not saying that these sorts of things are definitive of parenthood or citizenship, but rather that these are the sorts of things that we could expect a good parent or citizen to do. We are making a claim not so much about the definition or nature of a parent or citizen as we are about the "second nature" that is character. Our discernment of the fittingness of a certain type of action is a discernment of the character of the agent. And while discernments of character, as a "second nature," do not bring the kind of knowledge that accompanies discernments of essence or "first nature," they can give us a reasonable hope that someone will act in a certain way in the future.

Of course, in speaking of God's "character," we are speaking analogously. As an agglomeration of "habits," a human being's character, no matter how constitutive of their personal identity, remains "accidental," and the radical simplicity of God allows for no accidental properties. But my fundamental point is that the category of *convenientia* or "fittingness" provides Aquinas—and us—a way of "reasoning from revelation" in order to discern the character of the God whose nature reason cannot comprehend. In thinking about how the ensemble of divine acts converge so as to fit into a decorous pattern, we do not grasp God's essence, but we receive the revelation of God's character in a way appropriate to rational creatures, in a way that allows our hope not to be irrational.

THOMAS ON INCARNATION

In the specific case of the Incarnation, we can see how Thomas is clear that there is nothing external or internal that necessitates the Incarnation in the strict sense of logical necessity.[19] Nothing in the divine nature, or in the nature of creation, compels God to enter into personal union with creatures. As an uncompelled act of divine love toward humanity and all creation, the Incarnation cannot be deduced a priori, but can only be revealed to us. As Aquinas writes in his *Sentences* commentary, "Only he who was born and was offered up can know the truth concerning this question, because he willed it."[20] However, once we accept that God *did* will to become flesh, we can reason from this revealed truth in order to gain insight into God's character so as to deepen our grasp of how the truth that God took flesh fits with other things we believe about God and what this tells us about God's character.[21] In other words, the hypothetical question of whether Christ would have become incarnate apart from sin is located within a larger context of seeking to discern the fittingness of the Incarnation in order to hope appropriately in God. It is not an inquiry into possible worlds but a jumping-off place for a deeper understanding of what God's taking flesh says about who God is for humanity and the cosmos.

Thomas thinks that, on the whole, the witness of revelation

19. See *Summa theologiae* 3.1.2.

20. *Super Sent.* 3.1.1.3.

21. Note that seeing the fittingness is not the same thing as seeing the "necessary reasons" for the Incarnation. Thomas's view can be distinguished from two other possible views of how reason might be used in relation to the Incarnation. One view would be to say that unaided human reason can arrive at the truth that God must become incarnate apart from divine revelation. I cannot think of any medieval who held such a view, but this might well describe the view of Hegel. Another view, which is found in medieval writers such as Anselm, would be to say that unaided human reason cannot arrive at the Incarnation, but once one holds the truth of the Incarnation on the basis of faith, one can use reason to grasp the "necessary reason" for the Incarnation. Thomas's view can also be distinguished from the fideist view that reason is of no use whatsoever in grasping the truth of the Incarnation. For this delineation of possible positions, I am indebted to the discussion (with reference to the Trinity, not the Incarnation) of Gilles Emery, "The Threeness and Oneness of God in Twelfth- to Fourteenth-Century Scholasticism," in *Trinity in Aquinas,* trans. Matthew Levering et al. (Ave Maria, FL: Sapientia, 2003), 1–32.

is that, as 1 Timothy 1:15 says, “Christ Jesus came into the world to save sinners.” At the same time, he is somewhat tentative in his voicing of this view: In the *Sentences* commentary, he notes that this is “said probably” (*probabiliter dicunt*),[22] and in his commentary on 1 Timothy, he says that the view that God would not have become incarnate apart from sin is “the view to which I am more inclined” (*in quam partem ego magis declino*).[23] In the *Summa theologiae,* having said that, in light of Scripture, it was “more fitting to say” (*convenientius dicitur*) that the Incarnation was ordained by God as a remedy for sin, he then adds, “And yet the power of God is not limited to this; even if sin had not existed, God could have become incarnate.”[24]

Thomas's seeming hesitation, and even equivocation, is not a matter of him being unable to make up his mind; rather, it is the precisely appropriate rhetorical stance to take when speaking of the fittingness of realized divine possibilities. Thomas is unwilling to adopt the apodictic tone that one finds in some later Thomists when they speak on this issue because, as noted earlier, he wishes to guard the incomprehensibility of God from those who are sure they can deduce what God's nature must entail in a given possible order of things. Of course, God could become incarnate even if sin had not existed; there is no logical contradiction involved in the idea. But we have no way of knowing if God *would* have become incarnate, and equally, we have no way of knowing that God *would not* have become incarnate.

In the *Sentences* commentary, Thomas goes so far as to say that the alternative view—that, in addition to freeing humanity from sin, the Incarnation of the Son of God exalts human nature and consummates the whole universe—can be maintained as a

22. *Super Sent.* 3.1.1.3.

23. *Super I Tim.* 1.4.40.

24. *Summa theologiae* 3.1.3.

probable cause of the Incarnation.[25] Such a comment might at first surprise us since Thomas seems to take his firm stand on the biblical datum that "Christ Jesus came into the world"—this actually existing order of things—"to save sinners." But Thomas in no way restricts the purpose of the Incarnation to the remedying of original sin. It is a serious distortion of his view to say, as one author does, that Aquinas—and "Western Christology" in general—"maintains a strict correlation between the Incarnation, sin, and redemption"[26] or to accuse him of "hamartiocentrism." Thomas repeatedly makes the point that the Incarnation, and the sacramental economy flowing from it, has the twofold purpose of freeing us from sin and advancing us in goodness,[27] and in his discussions, he sometimes seems to highlight the first purpose and sometimes the second.

If we look at the brief discussion in chapters 199–201 of book 1 of the *Compendium theologiae*, we get some sense of the richness of Thomas's understanding of the purpose of the Incarnation. He first sketches the way in which the Incarnation liberates us from sin by making satisfaction to God, recalling us to the spiritual life, and freeing us from the power of demons by showing us the dignity of our human nature. He then goes on to speak, in Abelardian fashion, of how the Incarnation displays the greatness of God's love for humanity, inciting a mirroring love in us. In addition, in the union of humanity and divinity in the person of Christ, we catch a glimpse of our union with God in glory, a glimpse that helps us to have faith. Finally, sounding what some might think a "Scotist" note, Thomas says that God's whole work in creation is "perfected" (*perficitur*) or brought to fulfillment by

25. *Super Sent.* 3.1.1.3: "Alii vero dicunt, quod cum per Incarnationem filii Dei non solum liberatio a peccato, sed etiam humanae naturae exaltatio, et totius universi consummatio facta sit; etiam peccato non existente, propter has causas incarnatio fuisset: et hoc etiam probabiliter sustineri potest."

26. Delio, "Revisiting the Franciscan Doctrine of Christ," 23.

27. For example, *Contra Gentiles* 4.54; *Summa theologiae* 3.1.2, 5; 3.53.1; 3.63.l; 3.65.1; *De rationibus fidei* 5; *Compendium theologiae* 1.199–201.

the Incarnation, which brings human beings—the last of God's creatures to be made—back into union with the Creator from whom they came forth.

Even in this brief treatment, Thomas offers us an example of how reflection on the realized possibility that is God's free action in our history yields a rich picture of God's character, a picture that grounds Christian hope. Thomas is in fact little concerned with how God's character might have been manifested in a hypothetical world without sin. Instead, he wishes to direct our eyes to God's character as both just and merciful, a God who invites his creatures into communion with himself and who never ceases to work to bring creation to perfection. This character of God cannot be deduced by human reason; it can only be shown to us in the event of Incarnation itself. Yet our reason *can* see how the character of this incarnate God, who loves us freely in drawing us to himself, is not incompatible with the God who creates the world. The dim knowledge that we have from creation of God as self-diffusive goodness itself is entirely consonant with the God who shares himself with us by becoming incarnate. Revealed knowledge of God perfects and does not destroy natural knowledge of God.

JOHN PAUL II AND HUMAN REDEMPTION

Though John Paul II spoke warmly of Duns Scotus, "with his splendid doctrine on the primacy of Christ,"[28] I know of no text where he weighs in on the hypothetical question of whether Christ would have become incarnate if humanity had never sinned. One can certainly find statements by John Paul that present the Incarnation of Christ as the completion and crowning of God's creative activity. "Paul pointed out that the goal of history

28. John Paul II, "Address of John Paul II to the Members of the Scotus Commission" 2, February 16, 2002, vatican.va.

lies in the Father's plan to 'unite all things in [Christ], things in heaven and things on earth' (Eph 1:10). Christ is the center of the universe, who draws all people to himself to grant them an abundance of grace and eternal life."[29] In particular, John Paul presents the Incarnation as a uniting of time and eternity: "By becoming man, the Son of God embraced human time with his humanity, to guide man through all the measures of this time towards eternity and to lead him to participation in the divine life, the true inheritance of the Father, the Son and the Holy Spirit."[30] In his first encyclical, *Redemptor Hominis*, he writes, "Through the Incarnation God gave human life the dimension that he intended man to have from his first beginning."[31]

Such purposes seem to have no necessary connection to liberation from sin, and thus such texts can give the impression that John Paul would answer our hypothetical question with a clear "yes"—the Incarnation serves the eternal intention of God to unite creation with himself and would have occurred even if we had not fallen into sin. But if we continue reading *Redemptor Hominis*, we find John Paul saying that God fulfilled his eternal intention for humanity

> in the way that is peculiar to him alone, in keeping with his eternal love and mercy, with the full freedom of God—and he has granted it also with the bounty that enables us, in considering the original sin and the whole history of the sins of humanity, and in considering the errors of the human intellect, will and heart, to repeat with amazement the words of the

29. John Paul II, "Second Coming of Christ at the End of Time" 4, general audience, April 22, 1998, vatican.va.

30. John Paul II, "Program for Year 2000 Must Help Us Discover Glory of God Revealed in Christ" 1, homily, November 30, 1996, https://www.ewtn.com/catholicism/library/program-for-year-2000-must-help-us-discover-glory-of-god-revealed-in-christ-8837. See also John Paul II, *Fides et Ratio* 12, encyclical letter, September 14, 1998, vatican.va.

31. *Redemptor Hominis* 1.

> Sacred Liturgy: "O happy fault . . . which gained us so great a Redeemer!"[32]

Here, the picture has grown a bit more complex. John Paul shares some of the same concerns as Aquinas in trying to hold together God's freedom with God's nature. God's freedom is of a sort that is "peculiar to him alone" because it is not constrained by contingencies, nor is it contentless willing, but is entirely oriented toward love and mercy. Also, like Aquinas, John Paul is not speaking of some hypothetical world order but of the concrete order in which we find ourselves, the order marred by human sin.

For John Paul, no less than Thomas, the Incarnation is a redemptive Incarnation.[33] Yes, Christ is the New Adam, but he is the one who comes to "cancel the work of devastation, the horrible idolatries, violence and every sin that rebellious Adam sowed in the age-old history of humanity and in the created realm."[34] The approach John Paul employs is not unlike Thomas's way of *convenientia.* It is a reasoning from God's actions in history toward God's character through the discerning of patterns of fittingness, which takes reason outside of itself so as to see the typological structure of human history. As he puts it in *Fides et Ratio*,

> the fundamental conviction of the "philosophy" found in the Bible is that the world and human life do have a meaning and look towards their fulfillment, which comes in Jesus Christ. The mystery of the Incarnation will always remain the central point of reference for an understanding of the enigma of human existence, the created world and God himself. The challenge of this mystery pushes philosophy to its limits, as reason

32. *Redemptor Hominis* 1.

33. See John Paul II, *Crossing the Threshold of Hope*, trans. Jenny McPhee and Martha McPhee (New York: Alfred A. Knopf, 1994), 68: "Christianity is a religion of salvation."

34. John Paul II, "All Creation Will Be 'Recapitulated' in Christ" 3, general audience, February 14, 2001, vatican.va.

> is summoned to make its own a logic which brings down the walls within which it risks being confined.[35]

For John Paul, the "philosophy" of Scripture is oriented toward the love of Wisdom incarnate, and in the light of that Wisdom, human reason is, as it were, "colonized" by the light of glory. It is not that this light replaces human wisdom, but it elevates it and transforms it so as to allow us to discern the character of the God who is always beyond reason's grasp. Or, as John Paul puts it at the beginning of the encyclical *Dives in Misericordia*, "It is 'God who is rich in mercy' whom Jesus Christ has revealed to us as Father."[36]

This emphasis on divine mercy is fundamental to John Paul's understanding of how the Incarnation leads us to characterize God. Mercy is "love's second name and, at the same time, the specific manner in which love is revealed and effected vis-à-vis the reality of the evil that is in the world."[37] In the cross and Resurrection, we experience the love that is God, pouring itself out without counting the cost so that we may be freed from evil and share in the goodness of God's own life. An Incarnation in a hypothetical world without sin (perhaps, as Scotus speculates, by a Christ with an impassible body)[38] would not offer us the same characterization of God. This is not, of course, to say that sin is necessary; such a claim would require that we could somehow characterize God apart from how God has acted in our present world order. But it is to say that, in our actual world, we cannot fully understand God's character apart from the cross, and it is the divine character as revealed in the cross that grounds our hope.

So, we see a very similar approach in Aquinas and John Paul to Incarnation, redemption, and the discerning of God's

35. *Fides et Ratio* 80.

36. John Paul II, *Dives in Misericordia* 1, encyclical letter, November 30, 1980, vatican.va.

37. *Dives in Misericordia* 7.

38. See John Duns Scotus, *Ordinatio* 3.7.3.

character. However, John Paul is distinctively modern in comparison with Thomas in the role that theological anthropology plays in his thought. Like much modern theology, John Paul adopts an anthropological approach—seeing in the mystery of the human person the starting point for theological inquiry—that is quite alien to Aquinas.[39] Yet John Paul's specific anthropological approach is in some ways equally alien to much modern theology, not least because it remains a thoroughly Christocentric anthropology. Most striking is his emphasis, inspired by *Gaudium et Spes* §22, on people as mysteries to themselves, mysteries that only become clear in the light cast by the Incarnation. In a sense, as fully divine and fully human, Christ accomplishes at the same time the revelation of God and the revelation of true humanity.

We see here an insight that renews and genuinely enriches Thomas's thinking about the Incarnation. Though Thomas's account of the human person is theological through and through and casts light on his Christology, that light is not reflected back so that Christology illumines anthropology. While Thomas discerns in the Incarnation certain truths about human beings, such as their dignity and their destiny, one does not find in him the strong emphasis on the Incarnation as a revelation of the character of humanity as well as of the character of God. At times, one gets the impression that Thomas thinks that it is pretty obvious what a human being is and is supposed to be. Because of this, Thomas seems to have been insufficiently critical in his thinking about what was and was not "natural" for human beings (slavery and the subordination of women come to mind as obvious

39. It is difficult to imagine Aquinas making a statement like this:

> Man in the full truth of his existence, of his personal being and also of his community and social being—in the sphere of his own family, in the sphere of society and very diverse contexts, in the sphere of his own nation or people (perhaps still only that of his clan or tribe), and in the sphere of the whole of mankind—this man is the primary route that the Church must travel in fulfilling her mission: he is the primary and fundamental way for the Church, the way traced out by Christ himself, the way that leads invariably through the mystery of the Incarnation and the Redemption. (*Redemptor Hominis* 14)

examples). What John Paul offers is the insight that human nature cannot simply be "read off" of conventional social or cultural patterns, not only because our nature has been distorted by sin, but also because our nature is itself paradoxical: we are the "thinking reed" (Pascal) created in time but destined for eternity. Therefore, our understanding of what authentic human existence is must be clarified and purified by our discernment of the human character of Christ. As John Paul writes in *Redemptor Hominis*,

> The man who wishes to understand himself thoroughly—and not just in accordance with immediate, partial, often superficial, and even illusory standards and measures of his being—he must with his unrest, uncertainty and even his weakness and sinfulness, with his life and death, draw near to Christ. He must, so to speak, enter into him with all his own self, he must "appropriate" and assimilate the whole of the reality of the Incarnation and Redemption in order to find himself.[40]

John Paul indicates that in our thinking about human beings, no less than in our thinking about God, we ought to accept the fragmentariness of our knowledge. In seeking to discern what is "fitting" for human beings, we ought to look to Christ. For if we need Christ to know what we should hope for *from* God, no less do we need Christ to know what we should hope for *as* human beings. For only Christ can give us the "realism of hope," the realism that, as John Paul put it, "knows that the world, in spite of everything, is instilled with that paschal grace which sustains and redeems it."[41]

40. *Redemptor Hominis* 10.

41. John Paul II, "Only Christ Can Fulfill Man's Hopes," general audience, November 8, 1995, https://www.ewtn.com/catholicism/library/only-christ-can-fulfill-mans-hopes-8341.

11

Taking Up and Taking Down

Ellacuría, Aquinas, and the Crucified People

Writing in 1973, the Jesuit philosopher and theologian Ignacio Ellacuría (1930–1989) stated:

> Today we need a new christology. Our major concern cannot be to quiet our intellectual unrest by somehow effecting a conceptual reconciliation between the oneness of Jesus' person and the duality of his nature. Today we must explore how Jesus realizes his salvific mission to man in a full and perfect way. . . . Our new christology must give the history of the flesh and blood Jesus its full weight as revelation.[1]

As a key element in the development of this new Christology, Ellacuría began in a series of essays in the 1970s and 80s to develop what he called a "historical soteriology," grounded in a view of salvation history that refused the division between "sacred" and "profane" histories, arguing instead for a unified history in which God is at work to counter the effects of sin. For Ellacuría, the cross of Jesus cannot be segregated in a "sacred" realm where it serves some exclusively religious purpose, such as the expiation of

* Originally given as a lecture at the Society of Christian Ethics, New Orleans, LA, January 2017.

1. Ignacio Ellacuría, *Freedom Made Flesh: The Mission of Christ and His Church*, trans. John Drury (Maryknoll, NY: Orbis Books, 1976), 26.

the sins of individuals, but must be located within the history of social and political violence that God seeks to redeem. Located within that history, the cross of Jesus is seen by Ellacuría as being in continuity with the ongoing crucifixion of the oppressed masses, the "crucified people," in whom God's saving activity continues. Underscoring the cross as Christ's solidarity with the suffering, Ellacuría clearly saw himself as departing from traditional soteriologies that viewed the cross as an expiatory sacrifice making satisfaction for our sins and reconciling us to the God whom our sins have offended.

But do traditional soteriologies really offer no resources for connecting the cross of Jesus to the ongoing suffering of the oppressed—except, perhaps, pietistic platitudes about how the wretched of the earth must embrace the cross in order to wear the crown of glory? Despite Ellacuría's own sense of making a break with traditional approaches, I wish to argue that that putatively most traditional of traditional theologians, Thomas Aquinas, offers in his own soteriological reflections a voice that can be fruitfully brought into dialogue with Ellacuría, specifically on the question of the theology of the cross.[2] I will first present a sketch of Ellacuría's project of historical soteriology, then point to areas of Aquinas's thought that are particularly relevant to Ellacuría's project, and then suggest areas of convergence and divergence that place Aquinas and Ellacuría in fruitful conversation. In the end, I wish to suggest that an adequate soteriology will be one that will lead Christians both to take up the cross of Jesus and to take down from the cross those who are victims of injustice.

2. It is not entirely clear to me whether Ellacuría saw the traditional Christologies of the past as achievements that can simply be presumed as we move forward (in the manner of Rahner) or as obstacles to be overcome in the forging of a new Christology; I suspect that at different times and in different contexts he thought both things.

ELLACURÍA: HISTORICAL SOTERIOLOGY

Ellacuría's historical soteriology addresses the question, "What do human efforts toward historical, even sociopolitical, liberation have to do with the establishment of the Reign of God that Jesus preached."[3] A key component of this soteriology, by which he seeks to cut the Gordian knot of the question, is Ellacuría's rejection of any "two-tiered" account of historical reality. In particular, he rejects the idea that there is a history of salvation that somehow floats above ordinary history, perhaps intersecting at key moments in supernatural events like the parting of the Red Sea or the raising of Jesus from the dead, but which is essentially segregated from mundane human activities. For Ellacuría, the issue of how to relate what human beings do in profane history to what God is doing in sacred history is based on a false dichotomy of the sacred and the profane that is the result of "pernicious philosophical influences" on Christian thinking that identify transcendence with separateness.[4] By employing "Hellenic, Platonic, and Aristotelian philosophy" as the framework, traditional theology had "profoundly dehistoricized" salvation: "In the transition from what was fundamentally a biographical and historical experience, with its own theoretical interpretation, to a metaphysical formulation, historicity was diluted in favor of static essentialism."[5] The "static

3. Ignacio Ellacuría, "The Historicity of Christian Salvation," in *Ignacio Ellacuría: Essays on History, Liberation, and Society*, ed. Michael E. Lee (Maryknoll, NY: Orbis Books, 2013), 140. In some ways, this is a question that is perennial in Catholic theology, but it has been asked by theologians in this form since the 1950s, when encounter with the secular "eschatologies" of Marxist dialectic and Darwinian evolution led those with "incarnational" approaches to stress the continuity of the Reign of God with intra-historical development and those with "eschatological" approaches to stress the discontinuity of the in-breaking of God's Reign with any human progress. These debates fed into the debate over *Gaudium et Spes* at the Second Vatican Council (often seen as a victory for the "incarnational" camp), which then flowed into the developing liberation theology of Latin America as it sought to address how movements of liberation among the oppressed might be understood to contribute to the coming of the Reign of God.

4. Ellacuría, "Historicity," 142.

5. Ellacuría, "Salvation History," in *Essays*, 170; cf. the criticism of the "Greek *logos* employed by the Church fathers in developing classical Christology" in *Freedom Made Flesh*, 25–26. Typically, Ellacuría registers not at all the fact of incredible diversity in Greek thought, with philosophical schools often differing from each other as much as any one of them differs from modern ways of thinking. This ahistorical essentializing of "Greek" ways of thinking may have been a habit Ellacuría picked up from his teacher Xavier Zubiri (see Zubiri, *The Fundamental*

essentialism" of Greek thought passed into Scholasticism, leading to an overwrought distinction between an essentially fixed nature and an "ontic" understanding of grace that, even if it did not entirely obliterate the biblical worldview, was the "prevailing tendency" of theology.[6]

This two-tiered view, whether expressed in the language of nature and supernature or of sacred and profane histories, is rejected by Ellacuría, who argues instead that

> salvation history and so-called profane history both belong to a single history that they serve: God's history; what God has done with all of nature; what God has done in human history; and what God wants to result from God's constant self-giving, which can be imagined as going from eternity to eternity.[7]

The term "salvation history," which enshrines a potential misunderstanding of transcendence as separateness, is replaced in Ellacuría by "salvation *in* history."[8] Drawing upon his teacher Karl Rahner's notion of a "supernatural existential," Ellacuría argues that this single history is "transcendentally open" such that "God is already present, at least in an inchoate way, in that transcendentality."[9] And just as God is present, at least inchoately, in the

Problems of Western Metaphysics, trans. Joaquín Redondo, rev. Thomas Fowler [Lanham, MD: University Press of America, 2009], 21–22). Michael Lee notes both the problems caused by Ellacuría's reliance on Zubiri's sometimes idiosyncratic philosophy and his polemical tendency when dealing with other positions, whether contemporary or historical, from which he wished to distinguish his own.

6. Ellacuría, "Salvation History," 173.

7. Ellacuría, "Historicity," 146.

8. Ellacuría, *Freedom Made Flesh*, 15–18; Lassalle-Klein tries valiantly to parse the relationships between "salvation," "salvation history," and "salvation in history" but, in my judgment, does not achieve much clarity. See Robert Lassalle-Klein, *Blood and Ink: Ignacio Ellacuría, Jon Sobrino, and the Jesuit Martyrs of the University of Central America* (Maryknoll, NY: Orbis Books, 2014), 296–97.

9. Ellacuría, "Salvation History," 175. For a general account of the influence of Rahner on Ellacuría, see Lassalle-Klein, *Blood and Ink*, 253–84, and Martin Maier, "Karl Rahner: The Teacher of Ignacio Ellacuría," in *Love That Produces Hope: The Thought of Ignacio Ellacuría*, ed. Kevin F. Burke and Robert Lassalle-Klein (Collegeville, MN: Liturgical, 2006), 128–43.

transcendental openness of that one history to the offer of divine self-communication, so too that offer is embraced or rejected by human beings. This leads to Ellacuría framing his theology according to the division neither of nature and supernature, nor of sacred and profane, but according to the dialectic of sin and grace.[10]

This way of framing matters locates theology within the history of God's concrete offer of grace and humanity's graced acceptance or sinful rejection of that offer. Ellacuría is suspicious of the appropriation of what he takes to be a "Greek" emphasis on "nature," understood as a static and conceptually graspable essence that could yield "objective, fundamentally closed intellectual formulations" in which "the fullness of revelation was terribly impoverished, breaking its spontaneous communication with human history."[11] He goes on to note, "This absolutizing and reductionist reification is most blatant in the dehistoricization of Jesus himself."[12] While not rejecting dogmatic formulations concerning Christ's two natures or the hypostatic union, Ellacuría worries that in overemphasizing such formulations,

> the historical becomes natural, the existential becomes essential, and thus they cease to be decisive elements enabling Jesus' followers, in their personal life or in the community of the church, to historicize his life, knowing that what is important is not some ontic transformation, which is hard to prove and whose effectiveness in history is entirely accidental.[13]

10. Ellacuría does not reject the question of nature and supernature, but he does not see it as the primary question ("Historicity," 150); see also Lassalle-Klein, *Blood and Ink*, 258–59.

11. Ellacuría, "Salvation History," 171.

12. Ellacuría, 172.

13. Ellacuría, 172–73. It is important to note that Ellacuría is more interested in "historicity" than in historical investigation itself. Michael E. Lee notes, "Ellacuría's focus on Jesus' historical reality has less to do with the attempts of German biblical scholarship to secure the *geschichtlich* or *wirklich* Jesus, and more to do with *la realidad histórica* of Jesus as portrayed in the Gospels, understanding the weight that this term carried in Ellacuría's philosophy of historical reality. It represents a hermeneutic perspective that, acknowledging that human existence is intrinsically constituted by historical, social, and political factors, claims that interpretation of

In other words, static conceptual formulations couched in terms of "natures" and "persons" can never capture the life-changing existential significance for believers of Jesus as an event within history. Such significance cannot be grasped conceptually but is a reality that is encountered by persons in their embodied historicity. In this, Ellacuría seems to have been influenced not only by Rahner but also by the view of his teacher Xavier Zubiri that traditional Scholasticism was interested more in concepts than reality,[14] and he rejects the medieval ideal of knowledge as *scientia*—a knowledge that concerns itself only with the universal and unchangeable, not with the particular realities of history.[15]

Ellacuría's worries about "nature" emerge with particular clarity in relation to the necessity of the death of Jesus. He states that Jesus's death can be accepted as necessary for salvation, "but only if we speak of a necessity in history and not a merely natural necessity."[16] While acknowledging that the Scriptures tell us that Jesus "had to die" (e.g., Luke 24:26), Ellacuría rejects the idea that this "had to" was either a matter of strict theological necessity (Jesus had to die in order to atone for sins), or a prophetic necessity (Jesus had to die because it was foretold in the prophets), or a natural necessity (Jesus had to die in order to enter into new life).[17] The *historical* necessity of Jesus's death, on the other hand, like all historical necessity, "forces us to emphasize the determining causes of what happens. . . . Passing from death to glory is

the Gospel portrayal of Jesus cannot be complete without taking these into account" (*Bearing the Weight of Salvation: The Soteriology of Ignacio Ellacuría* [New York: Crossroad, 2009], 78).

14. See Zubiri, *Fundamental Problems of Western Metaphysics*, 45–82. I cannot help but note that Zubiri's reading of Thomas, particularly his emphasis on the role of the "concept of being" and his ignoring of the role of the spiritual senses in Thomas, is seriously flawed.

15. See Ellacuría, "Salvation History," 171. Cf. Ellacuría, *Freedom Made Flesh*, 13: "Classical theology was too 'scientific' to concern itself with the accidental and the changing, and it could not even verify the fact of salvation history because of its profound ignorance of the biblical data." It is not clear to me what "biblical data" refers to in this case since premodern theologians display a profound knowledge of the content of Scripture.

16. Ellacuría, "Crucified People," 203.

17. See the discussion in Kevin F. Burke, *The Ground Beneath the Cross: The Theology of Ignacio Ellacuría* (Washington, DC: Georgetown University Press, 2000), 177–78.

necessary only given the fact of sin, a sin that takes possession of the human heart, but especially a sin in history that collectively rules over the world and over peoples."[18] The determining cause of Jesus's death is not the divine will but the sin of the world, manifested in the powers of oppression, both political and religious. These powers could not tolerate Jesus's proclamation of the Reign of God and so *had to* eliminate him. Ellacuría writes, "Jesus's way of behaving before the public authorities could not help but lead to the cross—the punishment for political rebels."[19] It was because of human sin, which is neither natural nor divinely willed, that Jesus's proclamation of the kingdom was rejected and he was crucified. And because this sin was not simply a matter of the personal failings of individuals but of the collective forces that oppress humanity, this was a political execution. As Ellacuría strikingly puts it, to claim that Jesus's death is a matter of historical and not natural necessity is to replace the question "Why did Jesus die?" with the question "Why was Jesus killed?"[20]

To say that the cross is historically necessary and not naturally necessary is in fact to say, somewhat paradoxically, that it is necessary only presuming a contingency—human rejection of Jesus's proclamation of God's Reign—and not essential to Jesus's mission as such. As Ellacuría puts it:

> There is no certainty to the view that we are to see the example of Christ as a bloody quest for the cross as such. Christ did not come to be crucified. He came to convert, to save people by offering them a message of conversion. The message was not accepted by those in power. Because Christ remained faithful

18. Ellacuría, "The Crucified People: An Essay in Historical Soteriology," in *Essays*, 204.

19. Ellacuría, *Freedom Made Flesh*, 67.

20. Ellacuría, "The Church of the Poor, Historical Sacrament of Liberation," in *Essays*, 232. See also Michael E. Lee, *Bearing the Weight of Salvation*, 82, citing Ellacuría's essay "¿Por qué muere Jesús y por qué lo matan?" *Misión Abierta* 10 (1977): 176–86. The importance of the question of why Jesus was killed, as opposed to simply dying, is discussed from a quite different perspective in Khaled Anatolios, *Deification Through the Cross: An Eastern Christian Theology of Salvation* (Grand Rapids, MI: Eerdmans, 2020), 381.

> to his mission, their repudiation transformed salvation into a bloody redemption that is embodied in the notions of sacrifice, cross, and bloodshed.[21]

While Jesus does not go to the cross with the intention of being an expiatory sacrifice, by God's will and work the cross does become a means by which the sins of the world are borne away. "God accepts as having been wished by himself, as salutary, the sacrifice of someone who has concretely died for reason of the sins of human beings."[22] Yet Ellacuría sees this as something quite distinct from traditional substitutionary accounts of the cross. He notes that the idea that Jesus's death is necessary due to the need for "expiation and sacrifice," while it "may have some validity for particular mindsets" and "expresses some valid point," can also "turn into an evasion of what must be done in history in order to eliminate the sin of the world."[23] By holding strictly to Jesus's death as a historical necessity, occasioned by sinful human choices and subsequently redeemed by God in Resurrection, Ellacuría foregrounds the political significance of the cross.

Finally, we might note that another element in Ellacuría's resolute rejection of any nonhistorical necessity of the cross is his use of the notion of "the crucified people." Ellacuría drew inspiration for this phrase from the homily Archbishop Óscar Romero preached at the parish of Aguilares, El Salvador, after the state-sanctioned murder of their pastor, Rutilio Grande. Speaking of a passage from the prophet Zechariah—"And I will pour out a spirit of compassion and supplication on the house of David and the inhabitants of Jerusalem, so that, when they look on the one whom they have pierced, they shall mourn for him, as one mourns for an only child, and weep bitterly over him, as one weeps over a firstborn" (Zech. 12:10 NRSV-CE)—Romero told

21. Ellacuría, *Freedom Made Flesh*, 216; cf. Ellacuría, "Crucified People," 206.

22. Ellacuría, "Crucified People," 217.

23. Ellacuría, 205.

the people of Aguilares: "You are an image of the wronged Divinity that is spoken about in the first reading in prophetic and mysterious language—language that represents Christ nailed to the cross and pierced by a lance. You are the image of all people, who like yourselves, have been pierced and abused."[24] Ellacuría takes up this notion of those who have been "pierced and abused" by sinful oppression as an image of crucified divinity, a "continuation" in history of the crucified Jesus, and defines "crucified people" as

> that collective body that, being the majority of humanity, owes its situation of crucifixion to a social order organized and maintained by a minority that exercises its dominion through a series of factors, which, taken together and given their concrete impact within history, must be regarded as sin.[25]

But more than simply identifying the "crucified people" with Jesus in his suffering the effects of sin, Ellacuría, like Romero, sees this collective body as sharing in Christ's redemptive mission. The crucified people is both "victim" of the world's sin and "bearer" of the world's salvation[26] through "active participation in gradually turning the proclamation of the Reign into a historically palpable fact."[27]

In addition to the influence of Romero, we might also detect in the background here the Christology of Karl Rahner, for whom the Incarnation and hypostatic union form the apex of the ongoing activity of divine self-communication that we call "grace." This means that, as Rahner puts it,

24. Óscar Romero, "A Torch Raised on High," homily delivered Sunday, June 19, 1977, Archbishop Romero Trust, http://www.romerotrust.org.uk/sites/default/files/homilies/ART_Homilies_Vol1_16_TorchRaisedOnHigh.pdf.

25. Ellacuría, "Crucified People," 208.

26. Ellacuría, 223–24.

27. Ellacuría, "Historicity," 155.

> nothing stands in the way theologically of the assumption that grace and hypostatic union can only be thought together, and as a *unity* signify the one *free* decision of God for the supernatural order of salvation. . . . This very communication which is aimed at by this "assumption" [of humanity in the Incarnation] is *the* communication by what we call grace and glory—and the latter are intended for all.[28]

Rahner, in a sense, makes God's identification with Jesus via hypostatic union continuous with God's identification with all people through grace. Ellacuría reflects a similar line of thinking when he writes, "The uniqueness of Jesus is not in his standing apart from humankind, but in the definitive character of his person and its saving omnipresence."[29] This enables him to see the crucified people, like Jesus himself, as a "real symbol" or, as he prefers to say, "sign" of God's redeeming presence in history.[30] Rahner's commitment to the universality of divine self-communication and the ubiquity of grace, albeit often in an "anonymous" form, is reflected in Ellacuría's insistence that this crucified people is not found simply among those who are within the visible bounds of the Church but includes all those suffering from political oppression. He notes that it is in their suffering itself that they unmask and pass judgment on sin, and that "this judgment is salvation insofar as it unveils the sin of the world by standing up to it; insofar as it makes possible redoing what has

28. Karl Rahner, "Christology within an Evolutionary View of the World," *Theological Investigations*, vol. 5, *Later Writings*, trans. Karl-H. Kruger (London: Darton, Longman and Todd, 1966), 182, emphasis modified.

29. Ellacuría, "Crucified People," 207.

30. See Ellacuría, *Freedom Made Flesh*, 87–126. For a discussion of Ellacuría's appropriation and modification of Rahner's theology of symbol, see Lassalle-Klein, *Blood and Ink*, 277–88.

been done badly; insofar as it proposes a new demand as the unavoidable route for reaching salvation."[31]

Ellacuría goes on to note that, as with Jesus, "the oppression of the crucified people derives from a necessity of history: the necessity that many suffer so a few may enjoy, that many be dispossessed so that a few may possess."[32] To make the cross of Jesus either a theological mandate or a natural necessity would be to disempower the crucified people who share in that cross; it would be to tell them to accept and embrace their suffering as inevitable, as God's will; it would be to accept an "ascetic and moralizing" account of the cross;[33] it would be to indulge in "an expiatory masochism of a spiritualizing sort."[34] Ellacuría insists that because the suffering of both Jesus and the crucified people is neither a natural necessity nor a divine mandate but a historical necessity occasioned by sin, working for the coming of God's Reign involves "taking the crucified people down from the cross" by combating the forces of oppression.[35] At the same time, the identification of the cross as a historical necessity occasioned by opposition to Jesus's proclamation of the Reign of God invites the crucified people to undertake the salvific mission of proclaiming that Reign themselves, to be in their crucifixion not simply victims of sin but agents of salvation. Alluding to Paul's statement in Colossians 1:24 about filling up "what is lacking in Christ's

31. Ellacuría, "Crucified People," 223.

32. Ellacuría, 209.

33. Ellacuría, 201.

34. Ellacuría, 203.

35. This phrase is used by Ellacuría's colleague Jon Sobrino, and he describes them as the words of Ellacuría. See Jon Sobrino, *The Principle of Mercy: Taking the Crucified People from the Cross* (Maryknoll, NY: Orbis Books, 1992), 188. The phrase worded in this precise way does not seem to be in Ellacuría's extant writings; the closest I have found is in Ellacuría's development of Ignatius of Loyola's colloquy before the crucified Jesus from the First Week of the *Spiritual Exercises*, in which Ellacuría directs the exercitant, "Set your eyes and heart upon these people who are suffering so much, some from misery and hunger, others from oppression and repression, and then, before this people thus crucified, to make the colloquy . . . by asking, What have I done to crucify them? What am I doing in order to un-crucify them? What ought I do so that this people be raised?" ("Las Iglesias latinoamericanas interpelan a la Iglesia de España," *Sal Terrae* 826 [1982], 219–30, quoted in Lee, *Bearing the Weight of Salvation*, 74).

afflictions," Ellacuría notes, "There is only one redemptive sacrifice, it is true, but much is still wanting in the passion of Christ and in his resurrection as well."[36] By his life, Jesus denounces sinful oppression, unveiling it in his death and overcoming it in his Resurrection; this redemptive work is continued in the life, suffering, and triumph over evil of the crucified people.

We might say that whereas traditional soteriology, at least since Anselm, has operated with a logic of "substitution," in which Jesus suffers in our place to take away our sin, Ellacuría suggests a soteriology that operates with a logic of "solidarity," in which Jesus suffers with the oppressed in bearing the effects of sin, and by this the sin of the world is overcome.[37] This points us toward an answer to the question that framed Ellacuría's exploration of historical soteriology: "What do human efforts toward historical, even sociopolitical, liberation have to do with the establishment of the Reign of God that Jesus preached?" The crucified people, in solidarity with the crucified God, is both the victim of and the victor over oppression through its actions within history.

AQUINAS: THE FITTINGNESS OF THE CROSS OF JESUS

Like Ignacio Ellacuría, Thomas Aquinas concerned himself with the question, "In what sense can the cross be spoken of as necessary?" His concerns in asking this question are, however, quite different than Ellacuría's. He is not concerned with the debilitating political effects of theories that "naturalize" the cross or the "expiatory masochism" fostered by sacrificial accounts of atonement. His concerns seem more to focus on the questions of divine freedom vis-à-vis God's works *ad extra* and how it is possible for human beings to have true knowledge of such freely

36. Ellacuría, *Freedom Made Flesh*, 245.

37. For a discussion of "solidarity" and "substitution" in soteriology, see Jean Galot, *Jesus, Our Liberator: A Theology of Redemption* (Rome: Gregorian University Press, 1982), 286–93.

undertaken divine works. Thomas, like all medieval Scholastics, accepted the Aristotelian notion of *scientia* as his ideal of certainty and accepted the view that theology, in order to be a matter of genuine knowledge, had to approximate *scientia*.[38] For Thomas, the problem posed by the acts of God *ad extra* is that, on the Aristotelian model, *scientia* could only be of things that were necessary and unchanging; so it would seem that in order to be the subject of *scientia*, divine acts *ad extra* must be necessary, not free. With regard to events in the order of salvation, his chief conceptual tool for addressing this concern is *convenientia*, typically translated as "fittingness."[39] For Thomas, to claim that something is "fitting" is to claim for it a certain kind of necessity and thus make it a proper object of the knowledge that is *scientia*, but it also registers that something possesses a kind of necessity that does not compromise God's freedom.

Thomas's first pass at explicating *convenientia* in the *Summa theologiae* comes at the outset of the Third Part in discussing the question of "whether it was necessary for the restoration of the human race that the Word of God should become incarnate?"[40] Here, he makes a simple twofold distinction between what is absolutely necessary in order to attain a certain end (in the way that eating is necessary to sustain human life) and what is relatively necessary because it allows a certain end to be attained in a "better and more fitting [*melius et convenientius*]" way (in the way that a horse might be said to be necessary for a long journey). Thomas invokes the authority of Augustine, who said with regard to the Incarnation, "Other ways were not wanting to God, to whose power all things are equally subject," yet "there was not a more fitting way of healing our misery."[41] Thus, Thomas says, it is this

38. See *Summa theologiae* 1.1.2.

39. As in many philosophical matters, Thomas draws inspiration on this from Aristotle. See *Sententia Metaphysicae* 5.6.827–835 and 12.7.2532.

40. *Summa theologiae* 3.1.2. See chapter 10 above. This is not, however, the first time he employs the notion in the *Summa*.

41. Augustine, *De Trinitate* 12.10.

second kind of necessity—the necessity of the fitting means to an end—that pertains with regard to the Incarnation. He then proceeds to spell out the various ways in which the Incarnation both promoted the human good and took away human evil, reflecting the root meaning of *convenientia*: *con-venire,* to come together. A means is *conveniens* or fitting to an end if it brings together a variety of correlative means directed to obtaining that end. The Incarnation is a fitting means to the end of human salvation because in it both our advancement in good and our removal from evil are accomplished, and each of these in a variety of ways: increasing in us the virtues of faith, hope, and love; providing a moral example; divinizing human nature; revealing human dignity; humbling human pride; and expiating sin.

Thomas revisits the question of necessity and *convenientia* later in the Third Part of the *Summa*, in this instance specifically with regard to the necessity of the Passion of Jesus, asking "whether it was necessary for Christ to suffer for the liberation of the human race" (*utrum necesse fuerit Christum pati pro liberatione hominum*)?[42] Here, Thomas gives a more elaborate analysis of different sorts of necessity than he does when addressing the necessity of the Incarnation. He first distinguishes between what we might call "strict necessity" and what we might call (to invoke a paradoxical term already used in connection with Ellacuría) "contingent necessity." The former is, Thomas says, that "which of its nature cannot be otherwise," in the way that a triangle necessarily has three sides, or that God is necessarily *ipsum esse subsistens*, or that a human being is necessarily a rational animal. This would perhaps approximate to what Ellacuría calls "natural necessity" (or at least some of his uses of that term). Thomas states that with regard to this sort of necessity, "it is clear that it was not necessary, either on the part of God or on the part of human beings,

42. *Summa theologiae* 3.46.1.

for Christ to suffer."[43] That is to say, there is nothing about either God's nature or human nature that would in principle make it impossible for human beings to be liberated without the suffering of Christ. It would seem then that Thomas would be at one with Ellacuría in rejecting any "natural necessity" of the cross.

With regard to what I have called "contingent necessity," Thomas notes that an act might be necessary not due to any intrinsic feature of an agent's nature but due to some extrinsic factor. Such an extrinsic factor might either be a force acting upon an agent or an end that the agent desires to attain. The first of these, which Aquinas identifies as the "necessity of coercion" (*necessitas coactionis*), and for which he gives the example of "when someone cannot get away owing to the violence of someone else detaining him," does not obtain in the case of Christ, either on the part of God or on the part of Christ's humanity, because God cannot be coerced by creatures and because Jesus willingly submitted to his suffering. The second of these, which Thomas identifies as "necessity from a presupposed end" (*necessitas ex suppositione finis*), does obtain in the case of Jesus's cross, by means of which humanity is raised up to God, Jesus merits salvation for us, and God's predestining will is fulfilled. Yet even in this case, we ought to bear in mind Thomas's earlier distinction, with regard to necessity from a presupposed end, between that which is absolutely necessary in order to attain a certain end and that which is relatively necessary because it allows a certain end to be attained in a more fitting way. Thomas argues in subsequent articles that the end of the forgiveness of sins could have been obtained in some way other than the cross, say by God simply forgiving humanity.[44] The suffering of Jesus, however, was the most fitting means of obtaining the end of our salvation because a means is fitting to an end when "the various concurring means employed are themselves helpful

43. *Summa theologiae* 3.46.1.

44. *Summa theologiae* 3.46.2.

to such an end," and in Christ's suffering, "many other things besides liberation from sin concurred for human salvation."[45]

Thomas then proceeds to sketch the various concurring means, in addition to the expiation of sins, by which the suffering of Jesus brings about salvation.[46] First, the depths of divine love are revealed to us in Jesus's willingness to suffer, and we are thereby stirred to love God in return. Second, he provides a moral example, displaying "obedience, humility, constancy, justice, and the other virtues" that are necessary to human flourishing. Third, Christ's suffering not only frees us from sin but merits grace and glory for us, making salvation not simply a matter of forgiveness of sin but of the restoration and perfection of the image of God in us. Fourth, the suffering of Christ shows us the costliness of our salvation, making us prize it all the more. Finally, since it was by a human action that the human race became subject to the devil and death, it was appropriate that a human being free us from death by dying.

So, the picture that Thomas paints for us of the suffering of Jesus on the cross is of an event in no way subject to any sort of natural necessity, but rather an act freely willed both as a divine act *ad extra* and as a human act that Jesus does for us and for our salvation. Moreover, Thomas's employment of *convenientia* to explain the "necessity" of Christ's suffering yields what we might call a very "weak" form of necessity, but one that is still robust enough to allow reasoned inquiry into the "why" of the cross. Though the cross may be foolishness to the Greeks, it is not so foolish that rational reflection can yield no insight into how the sufferings of Christ are "for us and for our salvation." Moreover, the multiplicity of effects that must be considered in order to grasp the fittingness of the cross yields an extraordinarily rich account of salvation as something involving not only the removal

45. *Summa theologiae* 3.46.3.

46. *Summa theologiae* 3.46.3.

of evil but also our advancement in good: the expiation of sins as well as providing a moral example, not to mention the divinization of human nature, the defeat of evil and death, the meriting of sanctifying grace, and so forth. The logic of *convenientia* lends itself to an inclusive, multifaceted understanding of what the cross does rather than a single-minded focus on expiation. Indeed, for Thomas, the saving work of Jesus extends beyond the cross to encompass "everything that the incarnate word did and suffered in the flesh"[47] because "all Christ's actions and sufferings operate instrumentally, by virtue of his divinity, for the salvation of human beings."[48] This leads Thomas in the *Summa* to pay what is, for a Scholastic, an unusual amount of attention to the mysteries of the life of the incarnate Word, addressing questions such as Jesus's embrace of poverty, his obedience to the law, his manner of teaching, and so forth.[49]

Yet within this multifaceted understanding of salvation, we do not seem to find what we might call a "political" element. That is to say, while Thomas certainly sees the suffering and death of Jesus to be caused by human sin—not only the original sin of humanity that he died to take away but also the actual sins of those who arrested, condemned, and executed him[50]—he never identifies what Ellacuría calls "structural violence" (and what Thomas might call "tyranny") as a cause of Jesus's death. In commenting on Jesus's exchange with Pilate in John's Gospel, Thomas registers no sense of a confrontation between the kingdom of God and imperial power. Indeed, he interprets Jesus's words "My kingdom is not of this world" in such a way as to mitigate any conflict:

47. *Summa theologiae* 3.27, prologue.

48. *Summa theologiae* 3.48.6.

49. Thomas's discussion in *Summa theologiae* 3.27–59 seems to treat these questions of Jesus's public ministry as forming a single unit with Christ's coming into the world and his Cross, Resurrection, Ascension, and Second Coming in judgment.

50. *Summa theologiae* 3.47.1, 6.

> There was no reason for Pilate to fear, because Jesus was not setting himself against Caesar. Christ had no purple, no scepter, no diadem, no chariots, no soldiers to indicate that he was seizing a kingdom. Christ always sat alone with his disciples, plain in food, in clothing, and in dwelling.[51]

For Thomas, the political realm is the sphere of natural ethics, and just as there is no in-principle conflict between grace and nature, so too there can be no in-principle conflict between Christ's kingdom of grace and any polity that conforms to the natural law. What conflicts may arise are not conflicts between the Reign that Jesus proclaimed and the structural violence of empire but conflicts within the realm of nature, when tyrannical rulers exceed the bounds of right reason. Thomas acknowledges that governments may be oppressive, and might even be resisted,[52] but sees this as a question of natural justice and its proper exercise, which is something quite distinct from the supernatural justification before God that Christ came to bring through his cross.

In a similar way, Thomas's understanding of how Christians share in the Passion of Christ, "filling up what is lacking" in his suffering, does not seem to register what we might call "political suffering" borne by a crucified people. Commenting on Paul's Letter to the Colossians, Thomas first notes that speaking of there being anything "lacking" in Christ's suffering "can be misunderstood to mean that the passion of Christ was not sufficient for our redemption, and that the sufferings of the saints were added to complete it." This, he notes, "is heretical, because the blood

51. *Super Io.* 19.3.2402. See essay 9, above.

52. See *Summa theologiae* 2-2.42.2 ad 2, where Thomas is discussing the sin of sedition: "A tyrannical government is not just, because it is directed, not to the common good, but to the private good of the ruler, as the Philosopher states (*Polit.* 3.5; *Ethic.* 8.10). Consequently, there is no sedition in disturbing a government of this kind, unless indeed the tyrant's rule be disturbed so inordinately, that his subjects suffer greater harm from the consequent disturbance than from the tyrant's government. Indeed, it is the tyrant rather that is guilty of sedition, since he encourages discord and sedition among his subjects, that he may lord over them more securely; for this is tyranny, being conducive to the private good of the ruler, and to the injury of the multitude."

of Christ is sufficient to redeem many worlds." In this sense, the cross of Christ is not to be identified with any other human suffering. But if we take into account the unity of the Church as "one mystical person, whose head is Christ, and whose body is all the just," then we can understand Paul to be saying that God has ordained that merits exist throughout the body, by what it does and what it suffers, and that "among these merits, the sufferings of the holy martyrs occupy a prominent place." For Thomas, it is not simply the sign-value of innocent suffering that makes it salvific but the willingness with which it is embraced out of a desire to witness to Christ. Thus, "all the saints suffer for the Church, which receives strength from their example."[53]

Thomas's soteriology then seems to be at one with that of Ellacuría in rejecting any "natural necessity" to the cross. He likewise concurs with Ellacuría in not focusing exclusively on salvation as the expiation of sin and seeing all of the acts of Jesus in his life as salvific, not simply the cross. And, without using the language of a "crucified people," he affirms with Ellacuría that martyrs and others share in the cross of Christ in a way that incorporates their suffering into the work of salvation. What we do not find in Thomas is Ellacuría's animating question: "What do human efforts toward historical, even sociopolitical, liberation have to do with the establishment of the Reign of God that Jesus preached?" Or, to put it slightly differently, for Thomas the question remains "Why did Jesus die?" and not "Why was Jesus killed?" Even so, these two thinkers can be fruitfully brought into conversation as we reflect upon the cross of Jesus.

53. *Super Col.* 1.6.61.

AQUINAS AND ELLACURÍA CONVERSING AT THE CROSS

Perhaps the first thing that must be said at the outset of any conversation between Thomas and Ellacuría is that much of what the latter says about the Scholastic tradition and the role of Greek thought in that tradition is simply a caricature. Were this not the case, it would be difficult to imagine what might be gained from entering into conversation with someone firmly within that tradition, such as Thomas. At the same time, Ellacuría's failure to understand Scholasticism does not mean that he brings nothing to the conversation. Indeed, Ellacuría's shift from the question "Why did Jesus die?" to "Why was Jesus killed?" reframes soteriology in a quite radical way that should make us rethink what Thomas says about the cross.

As I have argued, neither Thomas nor Ellacuría presents the cross as an absolute or natural necessity. Ellacuría distinguishes "historical necessity" from "natural necessity" as a way of saying that the "had to" of the claim that "Jesus had to die" arises from forces within history—specifically the clash between Jesus's proclamation of God's Reign and those social and political forces that embody the sin of the world. This puts to the fore the political meaning of the cross and identifies Jesus with other victims of political oppression. Thomas's analysis of necessity is considerably more detailed than Ellacuría's. While he, like Ellacuría, rejects any "natural necessity," his chief interest in doing so is the freedom both of the divine will and of Christ's human will, rejecting any necessity of constraint, as well any necessity imposed by an inability to bring about salvation in any other way. For Thomas, God could have chosen a variety of means to save us but chose incarnation and the cross as the most "fitting" means. Likewise, Christ freely embraced this fitting means; as John's Gospel puts it, "No one takes [my life] from me, but I lay it down of my own accord" (10:18). Commenting on this verse, Thomas notes that at least in one very important sense, Jesus was not a victim of violence: "Did not the Jews use violence against Christ? They did insofar as it was in them; but this violence was not in Christ, because he laid down his life voluntarily, when he willed."[54] For this reason, Thomas says elsewhere in his *Commentary on John*, "[Jesus] carried his cross as a victor carries the trophy of his victory."[55] While it is true that Jesus's killers used violence against him, through his willing embrace of that death as a consequence of his mission, he is not a victim of violence but a victor over violence.

Ellacuría and Thomas, therefore, have two somewhat different motivations for their rejection of "natural necessity" with regard to the cross. Ellacuría proposes "historical necessity" as a way of locating Jesus's Crucifixion within a history of oppression, emphasizing his solidarity with all of the crucified peoples of history. Thomas's "necessity of fittingness" seeks to allow for enough necessity to make the cross the subject of theological *scientia* while still allowing for God's freedom with regard to the means of salvation and for the freedom with which Jesus embraces the cross "for us and for our salvation." The aims of Thomas and Ellacuría are not necessarily mutually exclusive, however, and I will argue that both are needed for an adequate theology of the cross. At the same time, it is worth noting at this point that Thomas's "necessity of fittingness" places emphasis on the cross as an act of God in Christ, while Ellacuría's "historical necessity" focuses on sinful human agency in the event of the cross.

Contrary to Ellacuría's depiction of traditional soteriology, Thomas sees the Incarnation as a fitting means to the end of human salvation not because it does one thing—provide a victim to die on the cross for the expiation of sins—but because it does a variety of things, all of which "come together" (*con-venire*) in the

54. *Super Io.* 10.2.1424. Thomas means that Jesus's killers acted violently but he did not suffer violence, since he willingly laid down his life. Cf. *Summa theologiae* 3.47.1 on the question of whether Jesus was slain by himself or by others.

55. *Super Io.* 19.3.2414.

life of the incarnate Word. Thomas consistently speaks of salvation in terms both of our advancement in good as well as our removal from evil. He sees no need to choose between Jesus as sacrificial victim and Jesus as moral teacher; between Jesus as revealer of God's love for humanity and as the one who merits salvation for us; between Jesus as the one who in the Incarnation divinizes that nature and as the one who by his example humbles human pride. Among the ten ways that Aquinas gives at the outset of the Third Part of the *Summa* for how the Word made flesh advances us in good and removes us from evil, the cross only figures directly in one of them: the making of satisfaction for sin.[56] Thomas is well known for saying that, since Scripture teaches that "Christ Jesus came into the world to save sinners" (1 Tim. 1:15), Jesus would not have become incarnate if humanity had not sinned.[57] But Thomas clearly sees purposes of the Incarnation other than the expiation of sins on the cross and saving effects of the life of Jesus other than satisfaction. For Thomas, salvation requires not only the restoration of the image of God that has been obscured by sin but also the perfection of that image, a perfection that would have been necessary even if there had been no sin.[58]

Ellacuría in fact echoes Thomas's twofold purpose of salvation as removing evil and advancing good.[59] He notes that "the first gift of salvation to history is the overcoming of sin" and that this includes the presence of sin in both personal and collective life, which is "not only forgiven but taken away from the world, not only through the transformation of hearts but also

56. *Summa theologiae* 3.1.2.

57. *Summa theologiae* 3.1.3.

58. Thomas thus does not say definitively that there would have been no Incarnation apart from sin; indeed, since the Incarnation is a free divine act *ad extra*, God could certainly have willed to become incarnate apart from sin, and the need for image perfection, even apart from image restoration, would seem to provide sufficient motive for such a divine action. See chapter 10 above. For the language of "image restoration" and "image perfection," see Romanus Cessario, *The Godly Image: Christ and Salvation in Catholic Thought from Anselm to Aquinas* (Petersham, MA: St. Bede's, 1990), 128.

59. For what follows, see Ellacuría, "Salvation History," 180–82.

through the creation of new structures." He goes on to say, "From a more positive angle, a new human being and a new earth are what salvation brings to humanity so that all will be reconciled and definitively recapitulated, so that God will be all in all." He couches this in terms of conversion: "Conversion is not only the absence and even the rejection of sin, but it is a superabundance of grace: where sin reigned, grace now reigns; where the power of sin and evil prevailed, the power and grace of the Spirit now prevail." There is, however, a sense in which Ellacuría makes sin and the cross more central to his soteriology than does Thomas. As mentioned before, Ellacuría replaces the Scholastic distinction between nature and grace with a dialectic of sin and grace. This means that whereas Thomas can see salvation in terms of the perfecting of human nature, Ellacuría, while not entirely abandoning the notion of nature,[60] restricts its importance in his project of historical soteriology, meaning that grace is thought not by way of contrast with nature but primarily as the antithesis of sin. This gives his theology as a whole not only a more Christocentric character but also what we might call a more "hamartiocentric" and "staurocentric" character. This emphasis certainly underscores historicity and avoids abstract notions of nature, but it also seems to lead to the positive pole of soteriology—becoming partakers of the divine nature and God becoming all in all—receiving relatively little attention in Ellacuría's writings. Perhaps a more robust account of nature is required to strike the right balance between salvation as image restoration and salvation as image perfection.

While focusing on the cross, Ellacuría is careful to emphasize the connection between Jesus's life and his cross. Kevin Burke puts it this way: "Ellacuría . . . accents the continuity of Jesus's life with his death. His death, of course, represents a historical rupture, but not by way of imposing a new meaning on his life.

60. See, for example, his intriguing but somewhat cryptic remark that "history is the supernature of nature" (Ellacuría, "Salvation History," 193).

The rupture of his death confirms the irruption, in and through his life, of the Reign of God."[61] If the cross is isolated from the life of Jesus, then it is robbed of its political meaning and becomes merely a means of expiation, something that would have been effective even if Jesus had never proclaimed liberty to captives and good news to the poor—even if, in Ellacuría's sense, he merely *died* and was not *killed*. We can only properly grasp the necessity of Jesus's cross if we keep in sight his proclamation of the Reign of God and the threat it posed to the human forces of oppression. When the herald of the Reign encounters the sin of the world, it is unimaginable that he would not take up the office of suffering servant, both because of his fidelity to his mission and because the forces of oppression would find it necessary to eliminate him. The cross is not sought by Jesus for its own sake but is embraced as a consequence of the kind of life he lives.[62]

Thomas also presents an "inclusive" soteriology in which *everything* done and suffered by the incarnate Word is part of his saving work. We do not find in Thomas, any more than in Ellacuría, a sense that the suffering of the cross was sought by Jesus for its own sake. What Jesus does on the cross is not primarily a matter of bearing the penalty that is owed on account of sin (though it is that, in a secondary sense) but of restoring to God what human sin has taken away. What sin has deprived God of is the love and obedience that human beings owe to their creator; what matters in Christ's suffering and death, as in the living of his life as a whole, is that it is done as an act of love and obedience that Christ performs both as one of us and on our behalf. That Jesus's love and obedience ultimately led him to his death is significant because such love unto death is the highest form of human

61. Burke, *The Ground Beneath the Cross*, 180.

62. Ellacuría is not, of course, the first to pursue this line of argumentation. Adolf von Harnack, critiquing the soteriology of Anselm, wrote at the beginning of the twentieth century, "The death of Christ is entirely severed from His life-work on earth, and isolated. This God-man need not have preached, and founded a kingdom, and gathered disciples; He only required to die" (*History of Dogma*, trans. Neil Buchanan [New York: Dover, 1961], 6:76).

love, but it is the loving obedience that is saving, not the death. Thomas presumes that the love and obedience that Christ shows on the cross are the same love and obedience that characterize his life as a whole, but he does not bring out the political resonances of that life (either for Jesus's day or for Aquinas's own), nor link the opposition that his proclamation of the Reign of God aroused directly to the Crucifixion as a cause, and in this, Ellacuría's soteriology marks a clear advance over Thomas's in highlighting this aspect of the Gospel story.

If the cross must be linked back to Jesus's life, it must also be linked forward to his Resurrection. Thomas, in his mature theology, gives more emphasis to the Resurrection than most of his Scholastic contemporaries, emphasizing its genuinely causal efficacy with regard to salvation,[63] but it still seems something of an addendum: while the Resurrection as a mystery of salvation is not ignored, the heavy soteriological lifting is done by the cross. Ellacuría, on the other hand, does say that "Jesus's death is inseparably connected to the eschatological and historical coming of the Reign, and for that purpose the resurrection means not only a verification or consolation but the assurance that the work must continue and thus he remains alive to continue it."[64] To flesh this out, it would be necessary to make a link between Christ's Resurrection and his death that is as strong as the one between that same death and the life of Jesus. Ellacuría writes,

> The Crucified One rises, and rises because he was crucified; since his life was taken away for proclaiming the Reign, he receives a new life as fulfillment of the Reign of God. Thus, the resurrection points back toward the passion, and the passion points back toward Jesus's life as proclaimer of the Reign of God."[65]

63. *Summa theologiae* 3.53.1.

64. Ellacuría, "Crucified People," 200.

65. Ellacuría, 202–3.

The linkages between life, cross, and Resurrection are therefore more clearly indicated by Ellacuría than by Thomas. But the linkage cannot be made in the same way in the two cases. In the case of the life of Jesus and the cross, the link is the historical necessity of sinful human resistance to God's reign. In the case of the cross and Resurrection, however, since the Resurrection is an act of God and in no sense the act of sinful humans, the link cannot be understood in terms of Ellacuría's historical necessity, which focuses on human agency, but is better thought of in terms of Thomas's necessity of fittingness: it is only fitting that God would greatly exalt the one who emptied himself in his proclamation of the kingdom so as to take the form of the suffering servant.

Even if we are careful to locate the cross within an inclusive account of salvation, and even if we are careful to connect the cross to Jesus's proclamation of the Reign of God and to his Resurrection, at some point we need to grasp the nettle and attempt to articulate what it is that the cross does. Thomas has a fairly clear account of the efficacy of the cross in terms of what we might call the master-metaphors of merit, satisfaction, sacrifice, and redemption. It is noteworthy that Thomas begins with merit, which depends on the unity of Christ and his Body, the Church. The real unity between Jesus and his followers is such that the works of Jesus can be meritorious for us in the same way that one's own works can merit for oneself. And since Jesus merits salvation as one who suffers for the sake of justice, he makes us who are joined to him to be numbered among those of whom he said, "Blessed are they that suffer persecution for justice's sake."[66] In other words, Jesus's solidarity with us plays a significant role in Thomas's account of the efficacy of the cross. Yet his account moves from solidarity to substitution as his discussion moves toward the metaphor of Christ as our redemption, in which Jesus offers himself in our place for our salvation, making satisfaction

66. *Summa theologiae* 3.48.1.

"by bestowing what was of greatest price—himself—for us."[67] Christ does for us on the cross what we cannot do for ourselves, but he does this precisely to the degree that we have become one with him. For Aquinas, therefore, the efficacy of the cross derives both from Jesus's solidarity with and his substitution for us.

We do not find any such developed account of the efficacy of the cross in Ellacuría. Indeed, Michael Lee suggests that Ellacuría has difficulty explaining "how and why the manner of Jesus's death was salvific."[68] In his desire to distance himself from what he takes to be ahistorical expiatory accounts of the cross, Ellacuría leaves something of an explanatory vacuum. As I mentioned earlier, Ellacuría does speak of how the crucified people unveils and reveals the hidden workings of the world's sin, offering what we might call an "apocalyptic" or "unveiling" account of the cross by which the world's sin is exposed, judged, and ultimately defeated. Ellacuría writes that "the case of Christ and of many others reveals the underlying dynamic of much history and the tremendous effectiveness of established violence."[69] The difficulty here, however, is in discerning what—if any—unique role the cross of *Jesus* plays, as opposed to the crosses of the "many others" with whom he is in solidarity.[70]

It is difficult not to feel that here the logic of solidarity is overwhelming the logic of substitution, so that the crucified Jesus as a particular figure disappears into the crucified people. While an apocalyptic account of the cross such as we find in Ellacuría perhaps offers a new master-metaphor for soteriological thinking, one that is vital for recovering the political dimension of the

67. *Summa theologiae* 3.48.4.

68. Lee, *Bearing the Weight of Salvation,* 153.

69. Ellacuría, *Freedom Made Flesh*, 216.

70. Perhaps this apocalyptic element in Ellacuría's soteriology could be pressed in the direction developed by René Girard, for whom the cross of Jesus is unique because, by God's vindication of him through resurrection, his innocence is made manifest, casting a revelatory light upon all other innocent victims. See, among Girard's many works, *I See Satan Fall Like Lightning*, trans. James G. Williams (Maryknoll, NY: Orbis Books, 2001).

cross, it is insufficient apart from metaphors of merit, satisfaction, sacrifice, and redemption to account for what the cross—not the cross in general but the particular cross of this specific man, Jesus of Nazareth—accomplishes.[71] Perhaps if we closely link the cross to Jesus's proclamation of the Reign of God, we do not need to share Ellacuría's allergy to more traditional, "substitutionary" accounts of the cross.

At the heart of Ellacuría's soteriology is his striking image of "the crucified people." Yet there is an ambiguity in this image regarding whether the crucifixion of these suffering servants is salvific or whether it is a manifestation of the world's sin that must be brought to an end. I believe some of this ambiguity is a result of Ellacuría's failure to account for the cross of Jesus as not only an act of identification with those who suffer the effects of sin but also as a unique act freely undertaken by Jesus as a particular individual. As Jean Galot puts it, "The texts of Scripture as well as the testimony of Tradition agree in saying that Christ suffered and died *for* us, and did not merely suffer and die *with* us."[72] In our theology of the cross, we must allow both the logic of substitution and the logic of solidarity to operate, and if we fail to do so, then we blur the distinction between Christ freely taking suffering and death upon himself and the unwilling suffering of victims, and so risk—clearly contrary to Ellacuría's intentions—sacralizing the effects of sin and undercutting the mission of Jesus's disciples to alleviate suffering. The mystery of Christ's expiatory suffering *for* us is replaced by the mystique of the crucified people suffering *with* Jesus.

What Ellacuría wishes to avoid is evident: robbing the crucified people of any agency with regard to salvation. He writes,

71. Ellacuría at times registers this, as when he remarks on how Matthew 25 "entails a dialectical vision of Jesus in history; he has been poor and yet it is he who helps the poor. Seen from the Pasch, Jesus appears as the Son of Man, who suffers in the wretched of the earth, yet is likewise also the Lord who comes to their aid" ("Crucified People," 223).

72. Galot, *Jesus, Our Liberator*, 290.

"It is easy to regard the oppressed and needy as those who are to be saved and liberated, but it is not easy to see them as saviors and liberators."[73] But morally significant agency requires intention.[74] In Ellecuría's writings, it seems at times as if anyone who suffers political violence becomes thereby a salvific figure—a real symbol of salvation, unveiling the world's sin—regardless of their intention, regardless of whether they seek to identify their own suffering and death with the cross of Jesus. Michael Lee remarks,

> With its reading of the contemporary poor as a "Suffering Servant," Ellacuría's theology must account more clearly for the suffering victims who do not demonstrate the volitional character of the servant's suffering. At most, it seems, the victims of history serve as a principle of salvation in their power to call for conversion. Their bearing of sin beckons those who would listen to take up the path of following Jesus and carrying forward his mission.[75]

Whether intending to or not, the "apocalyptic" account of the cross, when thought of exclusively in terms of solidarity and not substitution, can suggest that it is the manifestation of violence upon the crucified people that is in itself salvific.

The danger here is that it can tempt us to instrumentalize such suffering, to see it as something necessary to move history forward to a more just society. But there is clearly something wrong with taking victims of violence and making them unwitting agents of the realization of utopia, whether we are talking about the death of a *campesino* at the hands of a death squad in

73. Ellacuría, "Crucified People," 199.

74. This point is fundamental to Thomas's account of human agency; see *Summa theologiae* 1-2.1.1.

75. Lee, *Bearing the Weight of Salvation*, 153. This ambiguity in Ellacuría's thought is further explored by Daniel P. Castillo in "Reconfiguring Ignacio Ellacuría's Symbolic Conception of 'the Crucified People': Jesus, the Suffering Servant, and Abel," *Theological Studies* 84, no. 1 (March 2023): 8–29.

El Salvador or the death of another black man at the hands of the police in our own country.[76] It is true that such deaths can serve to unveil and reveal the structural violence of a society, but to make this the sum total of salvation is to sacralize these deaths, to treat them as sacrifices that are efficacious for salvation, and to perversely embrace tragedy as divine providence. It is to claim that victims are victors simply by the fact of being victims.

If we lose the uniqueness of the cross of Jesus, if we make it only one instance—even the most important instance—of the suffering of the crucified people, then we diminish our ability to distinguish between the disciple who willingly bears that cross in imitation of Jesus and the victim who unwillingly suffers the cross. The disciple's bearing of the cross of his or her own suffering is transformed when it becomes a willing participation in the unique cross of Jesus. And the disciple who takes up the cross of Jesus must share in the mission of Jesus not simply by suffering but also by taking the crucified people down from the cross, relieving the suffering of those who are victims, not victors. Ellacuría makes gestures in this direction, noting that "the death of Jesus avoids the danger of extolling salvifically the mere fact of the crucifixion of the people, as though the brute fact of being crucified of itself were to bring about resurrection and life."[77] But because he interprets the death of Jesus almost exclusively in terms of solidarity with the suffering and not as a unique free action of Christ as divine and human, an act done on our behalf, he has difficulty distinguishing the willing embrace of the cross by disciples from the unwilling crucifixion of the oppressed.

In this regard, I believe that Thomas has something to offer. As I have said, Thomas employs the logics both of solidarity and substitution in his theology of the cross, seeing Christ's

76. See Brittany Shammas, "Pelosi Faces Backlash after Thanking George Floyd for 'Sacrificing Your Life for Justice'," *Washington Post*, April 21, 2021, https://www.washingtonpost.com/politics/2021/04/21/nancy-pelosi-george-floyd/.

77. Ellacuría, "Crucified People," 210.

meritorious suffering united to the suffering of his Body but also seeing in the cross of Jesus a unique efficacy by which he suffers on our behalf. The interplay of these two logics suggests a way in which the disciple who willingly takes up the cross of Jesus can be distinguished from the crucified people who must be taken down from the cross. When we willingly take up the cross, we identify ourselves with the one who willingly suffered in our stead, and in so doing, we take up the task of ending the suffering of those whom Ellacuría calls "the crucified people."

Yet while Thomas's soteriology might strike a better balance between solidarity and substitution, it is Ellacuría's transformation of the question "Why did Jesus die?" into "Why was Jesus killed?" that shows us the importance of striking that balance. It seems, Thomas says, that Pilate had nothing to fear from Christ. *Sed contra*, Christ so threatened the kind of power wielded by Rome that Pilate had to use that power to kill him. Foregrounding the death of Jesus at the hands of the principalities and powers of this world, staring unflinchingly at the historically unique shape of the imperial power that put him to death while seeing analogies with the play of power in our own day—all this helps us discern the identity of the crucified people and recognize what discipleship demands in our place and time. It also helps us understand why Jesus must be both victim and victor: one who is united in solidarity with victims and one who does for victims what they cannot do for themselves; one who takes up the cross of salvation for us and our salvation so that the crucified people can be taken down from the cross of sinful degradation.

If liberation theology has taught us nothing else, it has taught us that we must take context seriously in our study of theology. At first glance, it might seem that the contexts of Ignacio Ellacuría and Thomas Aquinas could not be more different, making dubious the prospect of a mutually enriching exchange. While both were academics, and both belonged to new ecclesial movements that were suspect in many ecclesiastical and political quarters (in Thomas's case, the mendicant Order of Preachers, and in Ellacuría's case, the theology of liberation), the thirteenth-century University of Paris was a quite different sort of institution than the twentieth-century University of Central America, and the medieval Dominicans were not exactly founding base communities among the laity (though this might be an interesting angle from which to study communities of Dominican tertiaries).

Yet we must still take the gamble that such an encounter can bear fruit. And we take this gamble on the basis of the fact that Thomas Aquinas and Ignacio Ellacuría both stood on what Kevin Burke has called the ground beneath the cross, looking to the crucified as revealing the truth of history. The story is told of Thomas that at the end of his life, while praying in front of a crucifix, the figure of the crucified spoke to him, saying, "You have written well of me, Thomas; what will you accept as a reward for your labor?" Thomas replied, *Domine, non nisi te*—"Lord, nothing but you."[78] Certainly, in his own life and death, Ignacio Ellacuría answered the crucified Christ's question in the same way.[79] If we find our solidarity in the unique cross of Jesus, if that cross is the context in which we live and do our theology, then distances of time and place and culture cannot prevent Jesus's disciples from engaging in a mutually enriching dialogue of love that bridges those distances. Standing on the ground beneath the cross, we too can join in the conversation of the saints.

78. Guillaume de Tocco, *Ystoria sancti Thome de Aquino*, ed. Claire le Brun-Gouanvic (Toronto: Pontifical Institute of Mediaeval Studies, 1996), ch. 34. For further reflection on this saying from Thomas, see the homiletic Coda to this volume.

79. Ellacuría, who was working for a negotiated peace between the government of El Salvador and rebel forces, was killed, along with five other Jesuits and two laywomen, in his home on November 16, 1989, by members of the Salvadoran military.

12

"That the Faithful Become the Temple of God"

The Church Militant in Aquinas's *Commentary on John*

Where *did* Thomas Aquinas put his ecclesiology? Theologians today generally accept the claim that Thomas has no "ecclesiology" as we would understand that term, by which I mean that he never takes up the Church as a distinct locus for comprehensive theological discussion.[1] Did the famously absent-minded saint simply misplace it? One searches the *Summa theologiae* in vain for a treatise *de ecclesiae*.[2] The situation seems even less promising in his *Commentary on the Gospel of St. John*, where the commentary genre itself does not tend to the systematic treatment of anything. Yet this does not mean that Thomas's commentary has nothing to do with the Church. In his introduction, Thomas writes, "The end of this Gospel is also clear, and it is that the faithful become

* Originally published as "'That the Faithful Become the Temple of God': The Church Militant in Aquinas's *Commentary on John*," in *Reading John with St. Thomas Aquinas: Theological Exegesis and Speculative Theology*, ed. Matthew Levering and Michael Dauphinais (Washington DC: The Catholic University of America Press, 2005), 293–311.

1. See, e.g., George Sabra, *Thomas Aquinas' Vision of the Church: Fundamentals of an Ecumenical Ecclesiology* (Mainz, DE: Matthias-Grünewald, 1987), 19.

2. This of course begs the question of whether any of the so-called treatises of the *Summa* are intended to be comprehensive treatments. For example, if the discussion of the Trinity in the First Part is supposed to be comprehensive, it is decidedly lopsided, focusing entirely on the intra-Trinitarian processions and relations and giving scant attention to the missions (or, to use modern terminology, focusing on the "immanent Trinity" to the detriment of the "economic Trinity"). For a balanced discussion of the Trinity, one must also take into account, *inter alia*, the discussions of the Incarnation in the Third Part and of the gifts of the Spirit in the Second Part. See Herwi Rikhof, "Aquinas' Authority in the Contemporary Theology of the Trinity," in *Aquinas as Authority*, ed. Paul van Geest, Harm Goris, and Carlo Leget (Leuven: Peeters, 2002), 213–34.

the temple of God and be filled with the majesty of God; and so John says below (20:31), 'These things are written so that you may believe that Jesus is the Christ, the Son of God.'"[3] In what follows, I wish to argue that Thomas's reading of John's Gospel is one that is throughout concerned with the "edification" or "up-building" of the Church as a community of disciples who follow the risen Lord—what Thomas and the tradition typically call "the Church Militant."[4] Indeed, Thomas sees John's aim in writing his Gospel to be the formation and hallowing of that community. Further, Thomas's own purpose in writing his commentary on John is the continuing formation of a community of disciples.

While Aquinas did not think the Church theologically uninteresting, he also does not appear to have approached it as a topic to be treated systematically. Rather, he saw theological reflection on the Church to be what we might call an "occasional" enterprise, something to be discussed as need arose but not itself a major topic of discussion.[5] Remarks about the Church are scattered throughout the *Summa theologiae*, cropping up in some obvious places (e.g., the discussion of the sacraments in the Third Part) and in some not so obvious ones (e.g., the discussion of duties and states of life that concludes the Second Part). One must therefore do a bit of excavating and piecing together in order to come up with anything like what we would call an ecclesiology.

This is no less true in Aquinas's *Commentary on John*. Indeed, his remarks on the Church are here, if anything, *more* occasional, prompted as they are by the specific requirements of textual exposition. If one combs through the text looking for references to the Church, the result seems like nothing more than an unpromising

3. *Super Io.* prologue 10.

4. In this essay, I am concerned primarily with the Church Militant and not the Church Suffering (the souls in purgatory) or the Church Triumphant (the saints and angels).

5. On the "occasional" nature of Aquinas's ecclesiology, see Nicholas M. Healy, *Church, World and the Christian Life: Practical-Prophetic Ecclesiology* (Cambridge: Cambridge University Press, 2000), 56–58. In this entire essay, I am much indebted to Healy's "practical-prophetic" approach to ecclesiology for helping me to understand what Thomas is up to in his *Commentary on John*.

pile of scraps: a remark from the story of the wedding at Cana of Galilee, bits from the Last Supper discourse, and so on. Perhaps it is possible to cobble these together into some sort of ecclesiology, particularly if one were to supplement them with bits from the *Summa theologiae.* But is that the best this text has to offer?

While the scattered remarks Aquinas makes about the Church in the *Commentary on John* are not without interest, one must look at his overall interpretation of the narrative if one wishes to fully grasp what he has to say about the nature of the Church. And the first thing that one must see is that, for Thomas, the whole purpose of John's Gospel is not simply the instruction of individuals but the edification and sanctification of the Church as the new Temple of Jesus's Body.[6] In his comments on John 2:19–21—"Destroy this temple, and in three days I will raise it up"—Aquinas refers to Origen's ecclesiological interpretation of the "Temple" in this passage, and goes on to note that, interpreted in this way, the "three days" refer to three phases of divine pedagogy: the law of nature, the written law, and the law of grace.[7] It is through this process of pedagogy that God forms his household, "built upon the foundation of the apostles and prophets, Christ Jesus himself being the cornerstone" (Eph. 2:19–20). One might say that, through this threefold pedagogy (i.e., the natural law, the old law, and the new law), God creates and hallows a space within the fallen world in which an acceptable sacrifice—doing

6. George Sabra's survey of ecclesiological images and metaphors in Aquinas (*Thomas Aquinas' Vision of the Church,* 34–71) mentions "temple" only in passing (40) and focuses on *congregatio fidelium* and *corpus mysticum* as the dominant descriptions of the Church (69). While his comments are an accurate representation of Aquinas's work as a whole, they do not take into account the importance that a particular terminology (i.e., temple) might have in a particular context (i.e., a commentary on John).

7. *Super Io.* 2.3.404. See Origen's *Commentary on John* 10.20 ("Now, both of these two things, the temple and the body of Jesus, appear to me, in one interpretation at least, to be types of the Church, and to signify that it is built of living stones, a spiritual house for a holy priesthood, built on the foundation of the Apostles and prophets, Christ Jesus being the head cornerstone; and it is, therefore, called a temple"), which Aquinas excerpts in the *Catena Aurea,* 2.5. As far as I have been able to determine, the interpretation of the three days as three phases of ecclesial pedagogy comes not from Origen but from Aquinas himself, perhaps reflecting a particular Dominican interest in teaching.

good, seeking justice, rescuing the oppressed, defending the orphan, pleading for the widow—can be offered to God.[8]

Thus, when Aquinas says that John's purpose in writing his Gospel "is that the faithful become the temple of God," he is indicating that the ecclesiological importance of John's Gospel (and of his commentary on it) is found not so much in what it says about the Church but in the way in which the Gospel (and his commentary) functions as a means of ecclesial edification for the Church Militant. In fact, the Gospel is not really *about* the Church at all; Thomas says that the "matter" of the Gospel is the humanity and divinity of Christ.[9] But the *goal* of the Gospel is the formation of the Church as a community of disciples, a goal that is achieved through the proclamation of the humanity and divinity of Jesus.

***

One might object that, however important Aquinas thinks the Church is, such an interpretation of his commentary is trying a bit too hard; that a much more obvious approach is to begin where Aquinas begins, with John as the contemplative *par excellence.* Comparing John to the other evangelists, Thomas notes that whereas they instruct us on the active life (or, as he also puts it, about the humanity of Jesus), John in addition instructs us on the contemplative life (or, as he also puts it, about the divinity of Christ).[10] Whereas the other evangelists are symbolized by such earthbound figures as an ox, a lion, and a human being, John's symbol is a lofty eagle, which flies "above the cloud of human

8. See Isaiah 1:16–17. Thomas says in *Summa theologiae* 2-2.188.2, "Those services which we render to our neighbor, in so far as we refer them to God, are described as sacrifices." In the *Commentary on John*, he quotes Isaiah 1:16 in his discussion of the cleansing of the temple (*Super Io.* 2.2.389).

9. *Super Io.* prologue 10. Jesus Christ, not the Church, is (as Hans Frei would put it) the "ascriptive subject" of the narrative.

10. *Super Io.* prologue 1, 9.

weakness and looks upon the light of unchanging truth with the most lofty and firm eyes of the heart."[11] Thus John's Gospel is, in Thomas's eyes, preeminently a *contemplative* text: a text that is the fruit of and food for contemplation.

I have no counter-objection to any of this, provided we guard against the resonances that the word "contemplation" has in modern ears. Particularly as used in the religious context, contemplation (and its cousin "mysticism") is often portrayed as a universal, trans-confessional phenomenon practiced by individuals who are connected only accidentally to any particular religious tradition or body. Therefore, it ought to be stressed that this is emphatically *not* what Aquinas means by contemplation. The contemplative life is not equivalent to some sort of non-ecclesial "mysticism." To be a contemplative is to have a particular role within the Christian community. If we understand what is entailed in this state of life, we can begin to see how this "contemplative" Gospel is also an "ecclesial" Gospel.

On the one hand, contemplation is inextricably intertwined with the sacramental and ascetical activities of the Church. Indeed, Aquinas associates the perfection of John's contemplation with "moral science"; one cannot know God without a comprehensive reshaping of the affections through the sacraments and ascesis.[12] In this regard, one might say that John's contemplation is "perfect" because it does not separate knowledge and love. On the other hand, the most perfect religious state is not that of the contemplative who knows and loves God but rather that of the teacher who seeks actively to share that knowledge with others. As Thomas says in the *Summa theologiae*, "Even as it is better to enlighten than merely to shine, so it is better to give to others the fruits of one's contemplation than merely to contemplate."[13] In the *Commentary on John*, Thomas harmonizes the story of Mary

11. *Super Io.* prologue 11.

12. *Super Io.* prologue 9; cf. *Summa theologiae* 2-2.180.2.

13. *Summa theologiae* 2-2.188.6.

of Bethany anointing Jesus in John 12:3 with Mark 14:3 and Matthew 26:7 to depict Mary (who traditionally represents the contemplative life) anointing both the head and the feet of Jesus. Commenting on this dual anointing, Thomas says, "One who honors Christ himself anoints the head of Christ; and one who serves his faithful anoints our Lord's feet."[14] For Thomas, John's purpose in writing his Gospel is identical with the purpose of any good Dominican's preaching: to share the fruits of contemplation. Thus, in Thomas's view, John cannot be described simply as a "contemplative" but as a particular kind of contemplative: a teacher of sacred doctrine—that is, one who initiates others into God's own self-knowing by initiating them into the evangelical language of the Christian community. As Thomas puts it, John's office was "to give testimony."[15]

Therefore, there is no problem with accepting Aquinas's portrayal of John as a contemplative and still maintaining that the overall purpose of both the Gospel and Thomas's *Commentary on John* is the formation of the community of Christian disciples. Certainly, part of what it means to be a disciple of Jesus is to seek always to fix him in one's vision so that one may ever more faithfully follow him. What makes the shared life of Christians possible is not superficial friendliness but rather the shared experience of prayer. In this sense, the vocation of the contemplative is absolutely central to the life of the Church; it is the contemplative vision that sees the temple not made with hands (see 2 Cor. 5:1; Heb. 9:11) after which the Church Militant is patterned.

It is not without purpose that Aquinas begins his *Commentary on John* with an exegesis of the opening verse of Isaiah's vision in the temple: "I saw the Lord seated on a high and lofty throne,

14. *Super Io.* 12.1.1599. This interpretation is not found in either Augustine or Chrysostom, the two chief sources Aquinas draws on in his commentary, nor can it be found in any of the other patristic sources collected in the *Catena Aurea*. What we seem to have here is a novel interpretation by Thomas that reflects his concern to commend the Dominican mode of life.

15. *Super Io.* 21.6.2654.

and the whole house was full of his majesty, and the things that were under him filled the temple."[16] He reads this as coming from the mouth of John the evangelist and attesting to the height, fullness, and perfection of John's contemplation.[17] What is perhaps of greater interest is this identification of John and Isaiah. Isaiah, whose vision of God's glory in the temple is the occasion for his call to bring the message of God's judgment and consolation to the people of Israel, is the typological prefiguring of John, whose encounter with God's glory in the Word made flesh is the foundation of his proclamation to the Church of the judgment passed by that incarnate glory. Isaiah speaks of the "latter days" when "the mountain of the house of the Lord shall be established as the highest of the mountains, and shall be raised above the hills; and all the nations shall flow to it" (Isa. 2:2). John speaks of the "hour" when Jesus was lifted up in his glorification on the cross, "raised above the hills," as it were, so as to draw all people to himself (see John 12:32). Isaiah looks to the future and John looks to the past, but both bear witness to the same thing: the day of Zion's lifting up and the gathering of the nations at the temple of true sacrifice.

What does it mean to speak of John and Isaiah "bearing witness" (see John 21:24)? While Aquinas does speak of John's apostolic office as one of "witness,"[18] more typically he speaks simply of "teaching." John, like Christ, is first and foremost a teacher. However, as in the case of what Thomas means by "contemplation," modern readers must be careful not to misunderstand what he means by "teaching": to modern ears, it has quite misleading, overly cognitive connotations. In particular, we cannot identify Thomas's use of "teaching" with the modern notion of a detached

16. Aquinas returns to this text (Isa. 6:1) in passing in the penultimate paragraph of the *Commentary on John* (*Super Io.* 21.6.2659).

17. Speaking specifically of the phrase "The things that were under him filled the temple," Aquinas says that these "things" are the sacraments of his humanity, which fill the faithful, "who are the temple of God" (*Super Io.* prologue 8).

18. For example, *Super Io.* 21.6.2654.

imparting of information in which the teacher is, or should be, separable from what is taught. When a nineteenth-century liberal such as Harnack presents Jesus as a teacher of the "higher righteousness," this is precisely in order to separate the *person* of Jesus from the *content* of his teaching. This is clearly not what Thomas means when he speaks of Jesus in the *Summa* as "the most excellent of teachers."[19] For, as he says in the *Commentary on John*, "the doctrine [i.e., teaching] of the Father is the Son himself."[20]

Teaching is always a self-involving activity. Particularly in the case of one who teaches a "way" of life, the greatness of a teacher is judged by how fully he or she embodies the teaching.[21] Indeed, Jesus is the best of all teachers precisely because he quite simply *is* the content of his teaching. Commenting on John 14:6, where Jesus says, "I am the way," Thomas writes, "Christ is the way to arrive at the knowledge of the truth, while still being the truth itself."[22] Similarly, the effectiveness of teaching is judged not so much by the quantity of information absorbed as it is by the degree to which the truth embodied in the teacher comes to be embodied in the pupil. If Christian teaching is instruction in a certain way, it cannot be said to be learned until one actually follows this way.[23] So to speak of Jesus or John or Aquinas him-

19. *Summa theologiae* 3.43.4.

20. *Super Io.* 7.2.1037. On *doctrina* as an activity rather than a "thing," see the comments of Jean-Pierre Torrell, *Le Christ en ses mystères: la vie et l'œuvre de Jésus selon saint Thomas d'Aquin* (Paris: Desclée, 1999), 1:242.

21. At one point, Thomas speaks of "two things which are necessary for preachers if they are to lead others to Christ. The first is clear, orderly speech. . . . The second is virtue, manifested in good actions" (*Super Io.* 12.4.1634). We ought to note, however, that the necessity of the teacher embodying the truth applies primarily when one is teaching a "way of life." It obviously is not true, for example, when teaching basic math concepts, precisely because we don't normally think of there being a "mathematical way of life."

22. *Super Io.* 14.2.1868.

23. Here, I am putting forward a version of what Bruce D. Marshall describes as a "weak pragmatic thesis." One's claim to have learned the Christian "way" can be disproved by a failure of practice, though successful practice is not itself sufficient proof that one has learned it. My claim is slightly different from the one Marshall himself examines, which has to do with the justification of Christian truth claims themselves. For a contrast between "strong" and "weak" versions of the pragmatic thesis, see *Trinity and Truth* (Cambridge: Cambridge University Press, 2000), 182–91. In terms of Thomas's own way of putting things, Christian teaching (i.e., *sacra*

self as a teacher is not to imply a disengaged communication of information. "Teaching" must always be placed within the martyrological context of bearing witness with one's life in order to form others to bear witness with their lives. Christian teaching is about the formation of disciples; it is about the "edification" or "building" of God's temple.[24]

***

If we wish to see what Aquinas has to say about the formation of disciples in the *Commentary on John*, we ought to look first at some of what he says about that "most excellent of teachers," Jesus. In his commentary, Thomas repeatedly stresses that Jesus's teaching is a comprehensive project of formation in which both his words and his actions are of crucial importance.[25] In the case of Jesus, teaching by example is particularly fitting since the union of humanity and divinity in Jesus means that the truth about God that Jesus wishes to teach is embodied in his human deeds and suffering. Referring to Jesus's saying, "I am the way, and the truth, and the life," Thomas notes, "[Christ] is the way by reason of his human nature, and the destination [i.e., truth and life] because of his divinity."[26] Christ is the way to arrive at the knowledge of the truth, while still being the truth itself.

One might describe the teaching that is Jesus's life as a "theandric" performance in which his divine person is both

doctrina) has as its ultimate aim the communication of "formed faith." This is not to say that faith without love is nothing, but it is not what Christian teaching aims at.

24. The Dominican ideal, articulated by Fra Humbert of Romans, general of the order during Thomas's lifetime, was *Docere verbo et exemplo*: "To teach by word and example." This meant that Dominicans saw their total deportment as part of their preaching, and consequently that their formation as Dominicans was as much, if not more, focused on bodily practices as it was on the conveying of information. For an example of this, see the discussion of how the iconography in the novices' cells at the convent of San Marco in Florence was key in this "bodily" formation in William Hood, *Fra Angelico at San Marco* (New Haven, CT: Yale University Press, 1993), 200–207.

25. For example, *Super Io.* 11.6.1555; 12.5.1652; 13.3.1781; 14.2.1870.

26. *Super Io.* 14.3.1868.

communicated and received in a pattern of human action and passion.[27] Commenting on Jesus's invitation to the two disciples of John the Baptist to "come and see" where he lives (John 1:39), Thomas notes that he issues this invitation "because the dwelling of God, whether of glory or grace, cannot be known except by experience: for it cannot be explained in words."[28] Regarding Jesus's words in John 14:4, "Where I am going you know, and the way you know," Thomas comments, "They knew the Father through Christ, and they knew Christ by living with him."[29] Not only does Jesus teach the truth of God by example, but also his disciples learn by imitating that example. Therefore, knowing the truth of God is not something in addition to the life of discipleship—as it were, a kind of reward for faithfulness. Rather, in the faithful following of Jesus through imitation of his example, the truth of God is embodied in the life of the disciple. Thomas quotes Augustine: "Walk like this human being and you will come to God."[30]

But how does one "walk like this human being"? Certainly, Aquinas is not suggesting that we can simply slap on our "What Would Jesus Do?" wristbands and step out into the life of discipleship. The imitation of Christ is central to Thomas's understanding of the Christian life and discipleship, but he also knows that we must discern *which* of Jesus's actions are exemplary in a given circumstance and *how* they are to be imitated. Key to this discernment is the practice of Christian teaching within a structured community of teachers and learners, all of whom seek to be disciples, taught by Jesus and the Spirit.

27. On Jesus's "theandric activity" see *Summa theologiae* 3.19.1 ad 1; on his "action and passion" (*acta et passa*), see the end of the prologue to the Third Part and the comments of Jean-Pierre Torrell, *Le Christ en ses mystères*, 1:15.

28. *Super Io.* 1.15.292.

29. *Super Io.* 14.2.1864.

30. *Super Io.* 14.2.1870. One ought also to note the role of the Spirit in this. Thomas writes, "Since the Holy Spirit is from the Truth [i.e., Christ], it is appropriate that the Spirit teach the truth, and make those he teaches like the one who sent him" (*Super Io.* 16.3.2102).

The communal life of discipleship is nonnegotiable as the context for Christian teaching and learning. Aquinas says that we ought to imitate the disciples who gathered in the upper room on the evening of Easter and on Pentecost, "for Christ came to them when they were united together, and the Holy Spirit descended on them when they were united together, because Christ and the Holy Spirit are present only to those who are united in charity."[31] If the teaching activity of the Church is to manifest the ongoing teaching of Christ and the Spirit, and not simply be our best guess about what Jesus would do, then it must occur within a community of disciples to whom Christ and the Spirit are present. Thomas writes that "all who are in the Church are taught, not by the apostles nor by the prophets, but by God himself."[32] We see here a certain circularity in which the fitting context for the teaching of Christ and the Spirit is the community that is itself established by that teaching. Just as Christ is both the "way" and the "destination" for Christians, the Church Militant is both the means and the goal of the edification of disciples.

Further, the Church is understood by Aquinas as a community united in love.[33] The language of "the Church Militant" may conjure for some today the image of crusaders cleaving the heads of infidels with cries of *Christus est Dominus*, but this is not what Thomas means.[34] He writes, "Anyone who wants to be in the army of Christ should be stamped with the emblem of charity," since "the special sign of a disciple of Christ is charity and mutual

31. *Super Io.* 20.4.2529.

32. *Super Io.* 6.5.944.

33. George Sabra writes, "If one were to study all of Thomas' ecclesiological statements in all of his writings with the intention of discovering which mark of the Church occupied him most, the result would be quite clear: unity" (*Thomas Aquinas' Vision of the Church*, 70).

34. The example of the crusader is obviously a reference to the now famous (or notorious) example given by George Lindbeck in his book *The Nature of Doctrine: Religion and Theology in a Postliberal Age* (Louisville, KY: Westminster John Knox, 1984), 64. For a subtle discussion of the issues regarding truth, meaning, and the justification of truth claims raised by the example, see Bruce D. Marshall, *Trinity and Truth*, 191–204.

love."[35] Thomas's injunction that preachers should "go forward in charity within the unity of the Church"[36] is less about guarding one's theological orthodoxy than it is about having one's teaching emerge from the context of unity in love that is a sign of the presence of Christ and the Spirit. Even more than this, the unity in love of the community of disciples is an icon of the love shared by Father, Son, and Holy Spirit. Thomas says, "Our unity resembles that of the divine nature, by which the Father and the Son are one. That is why we are invited to imitate divine love: 'Be imitators of God, as beloved children, and walk in love, as Christ loved us' [Eph. 5:1–2]."[37] The unity in love of the community of disciples is itself a preaching of God's nature as a community of love.

If the communal life of disciples as a unity in charity is to be a preaching of God's nature as love, then it must be an empirical reality, discernible through and fostered by concrete practices. Part of the point of a temple is to order and make holy the space around it through its visible presence. Though Aquinas will speak of Christ's Mystical Body as comprising "the predestined, the called, and the sanctified,"[38] this should not be confused with the view that the true Church of Christ is an invisible fellowship of believers. The Church is ultimately that friendship between human beings made possible through friendship with God, and, as Thomas notes, "it is of the very nature of friendship that it is not imperceptible; otherwise, it would not be friendship, but merely good will."[39] So if the friendship of disciples with each other in God is to be genuine, it must have some practices that are visible markers.

The key practices are sacramental ones, just as the chief activity of the temple on Mount Zion was the worship of Israel's God

35. *Super Io.* 13.7.1839.

36. *Super Io.* 21.1.2582.

37. *Super Io.* 17.5.2240; cf. 17.3.2214.

38. *Super Io.* 6.7.972.

39. *Super Io.* 13.7.1837.

through the offering of sacrifice. It is through the sacraments, as Thomas puts it (quoting 1 John 4:16), that the Church Militant "abides in God" and that the grace of Christ given through the Spirit "proliferates."[40] In particular, the Eucharist, which Thomas calls "the Church's meal"[41] and "the food of harmony,"[42] is "a food capable of making man divine and inebriating him with divinity," not only because it contains and signifies Christ but also because it signifies the unity in love of the Mystical Body.[43] Sacramental actions are irreplaceable precisely because they make clear that the mutual love that is the special sign of Christ's disciples is never a human achievement, something that the Church can make itself be, but is always fundamentally something received.[44] The sacraments, adapted as they are to our normal means of learning through the sensual apprehension of material objects,[45] also have a pedagogical function; they not only display but also engender the unity in love of Jesus's disciples. They are a means by which Christ and the Spirit make the community of disciples a visible reality. But as irreplaceable as sacramental actions are, they are not sufficient of themselves for the edification of the community of disciples. This can be seen in Thomas's own distinction between "sacramental eating" and "spiritual eating" in the Eucharist.[46] While Thomas in no way denies that anyone who receives the sacrament of the Eucharist truly receives the Body and Blood

40. *Super Io.* 20.4.2539; cf. 6.8.993.

41. *Super Io.* 21.2.2599.

42. *Super Io.* 6.7.966.

43. *Super Io.* 6.7.972.

44. Speaking of the "Church's meal," Aquinas says, "The ministers of the Church should also bring something to this meal; but whatever it is, it has come from God" (*Super Io.* 21.2.2599).

45. See *Super Io.* 3.1.443.

46. See, for example, *Super Io.* 6.7.972. It is striking how blessedly free Aquinas is from any compulsion to constantly assert his Catholic orthodoxy on the question of the *ex opere operato* nature of sacramental actions. Perhaps this is because he lived in a time after the controversy over Berengar's teachings on the Eucharist and prior to the sixteenth-century debates in which (apart from the Albigensians) this was not being seriously questioned, thus allowing Thomas to explore the "spiritual" dimension of the sacraments without worrying about compromising sacramental realism.

of Christ by way of "sacramental eating," he just as clearly maintains that this is something different from the "spiritual eating" of Christ. He writes, "That person eats the flesh of Christ and drinks his blood in a spiritual way who shares in the unity of the Church; and this is accomplished by the love of charity."[47] Aquinas goes so far as to say, "This sacrament has no effect on one who is insincere."[48]

Does this appeal to "sincerity" amount to a retreat from visible markers of discipleship into an indiscernible interiority? I think not. While we may have a cultural aversion to passing judgment on anyone's sincerity, such judgment clearly is possible, though of course not infallible. The way in which we normally judge someone's sincerity is not by means of some special ability to see inner attitudes but rather by observing the entire ensemble of his or her visible actions. In particular, we can observe the coherence or incoherence of a person's behavior in the diverse spheres of life. The prophets of Israel pointed out that if one shows devotion to God in a ritual context but abuses God's "little ones" in the context of economic transactions, then one shows oneself to be insincere. Similarly, Aquinas notes that, at the Last Supper, "Judas, along with the other disciples, ate bread with Christ, even consecrated bread,"[49] yet Judas's subsequent action of betrayal reveals the insincerity with which he eats that bread. Therefore, we can make the judgment that he eats Christ's Body sacramentally but not spiritually.[50]

The insincerity with which Judas eats Christ's sacramental Body is contrasted with Christ's total surrender of his life, displayed in the humility with which he washes his disciples' feet,

47. *Super Io.* 6.7.969.

48. *Super Io.* 6.7.976.

49. *Super Io.* 13.3.1790.

50. Of course, this is, like all the Church's judgments, a penultimate one (what Julian of Norwich called "the lower doom"), subject itself to the eschatological judgment of God (what Julian called "the higher doom").

even the feet of Judas.[51] This action of washing feet is, for Aquinas, a kind of summing up of the total practice of Jesus that we are called to imitate. Thomas, following Augustine, commends the literal practice of foot washing itself, "for when a person stoops down to the feet of his neighbor, humility is awakened in his heart, or if it is already there it is made stronger."[52] At the same time, the power of this example, since it is "the example of the Son of God, which cannot be in error and *is* adequate for all situations,"[53] extends beyond the specific action of washing feet to all of those practices that flow from the humility displayed and engendered by that action: "One who gives bread to the hungry washes his feet, as does one who practices hospitality, or gives food to one in need."[54] We might say that the Church Militant is called to a comprehensive imitation of Jesus's example in the upper room, obeying not only his command to receive him through sacramental eating but also his command to "wash each other's feet." Or, to put it in terms that are more familiar to us but that would probably puzzle Thomas himself (since for him worship is an act of justice), the visible markers of the community of disciples are not only ritual ones but also ethical ones.

***

The visibility of the Church Militant entails its concrete ordering as a community. This community is ordered *synchronically* according to various offices in the Church by which authority is exercised. While I think Thomas Gilby was correct in saying that

51. *Super Io.* 13.1.1741.

52. *Super Io.* 13.3.1779. Cf. Augustine, *Tractatus in Evangelium Iohannis* 58.4. There is something about that particular behavior, placed within the context of the story of Jesus, that has an almost sacramental power, even in cultures where it is not a normal custom. I suspect that, like many thirteenth-century mendicants, Thomas thought the greater danger lay not in following Jesus's example too literally but in not following it literally enough.

53. *Super Io.* 13.3.1781.

54. *Super Io.* 13.3.1779.

Aquinas was less "clericalist" than many in his day (particularly the canonists), it is also clear that he saw the Church as a structured community in which some are given the office of teacher and can therefore teach with authority.[55] Indeed, the diversity of ecclesiastical offices "is for the beauty and completion of the Church"[56] because they are the occasion for the decorous ordering of the community. In discussing the characteristics requisite for the pastoral office in the context of Peter's encounter with the risen Christ by the Sea of Tiberias, Thomas quotes Aristotle's *Politics* to the effect that "it is the natural order of things that the one who cares for and governs others should be better."[57] This applies in the Church Militant no less than in Aristotle's *polis.*

But we must also bear in mind that the Church is not the *polis.* What it means for Peter to be "better" is not for him to be Aristotle's magnanimous man but for him to love Jesus as Jesus wishes to be loved. What this means gets unfolded in a variety of ways, much of it associated with Peter's denial of Jesus and subsequent forgiveness. Because he himself has denied Christ and been forgiven, Peter can be compassionate toward sinners.[58] He has learned the depths of humility in not presuming even to know his own heart. Peter says to the risen Christ, "Lord, you know everything; you know I love you," and Thomas comments, "He is saying in effect: I do love you; at least I think I do. But you know all things, and perhaps you know something else that will happen."[59] It is this humbled Peter to whom Jesus gives the task of leadership in the Church Militant, precisely because in his humility he embodies what Christ taught by his example.

This community of disciples is ordered *diachronically* by the

55. Thomas Gilby, ed. and trans., *St. Thomas Aquinas: Theological Texts* (Oxford: Oxford University Press, 1955), 337n1.

56. *Super Io.* 6.5.938; cf. 1.4.119.

57. *Super Io.* 21.3.2619.

58. *Super Io.* 18.3.2309.

59. *Super Io.* 21.4.2627.

succession of apostolic office and by the normative status that the apostolic witness, as contained in Scripture, has in the process of communal discernment and teaching.[60] Aquinas scarcely mentions apostolic succession in the commentary, though he seems to presume it in discussing Jesus's command to Peter, "Feed my lambs."[61] He shows more interest in the normativity of apostolic witness. For Thomas, the Incarnation of the Word forms the hinge upon which history turns, the point of reference that makes it possible to understand both what comes before and what follows. Thomas writes, "Christ's actions are in a way midway between the events of the Old Testament and of the New Testament . . . Christ's actions are the rule and exemplar of the things that are done in the New Testament, and they were prefigured by the fathers of the Old Testament."[62] The event of the Word made flesh is to the Church as the Holy of Holies was to the temple: it is that around which the structure is organized; it contains the "law," by which the people of God are sanctified.[63] Whether one is a prophet like John the Baptist who comes before, or an Apostle like John the Evangelist who follows, the closer in time one is to this crucial event, the more authoritative one's witness.[64] What this means for the synchronic structure of the community of disciples is that those who lead the community in discernment by virtue of pastoral office must always seek to teach in accord with the apostolic witness and in the manner of the Apostles and prophets.

Part of what teaching in the manner of the Apostles means is attending to the narrative structure of the apostolic witness.[65]

60. *Super Io.* 21.6.2656; *Summa theologiae* 1.1.8 ad 2.

61. *Super Io.* 21.3.2623–25.

62. *Super Io.* 12.3.1626.

63. Note that Thomas says, "The Son himself is the commandment of the Father" (*Super Io.* 12.8.1725).

64. See *Summa theologiae* 2-2.174.6.

65. Bear in mind that even nonnarrative apostolic writings, such as the letters of Paul, all presume the story of Jesus (even if they were written before the actual Gospel narratives). See

Just as Jesus speaks and acts not simply as a way of imparting information about God but rather as a "theandric performance" of his divine personhood, so too John's Gospel is an "evangelical performance" in which God's self-donation in the Incarnation is re-presented to us—performed anew—in the Gospel narratives. It is striking that Aquinas says that in his prologue, John "insinuates [*insinuat*]" Christ's divinity, while in the remainder of the Gospel "he shows [*manifestat*] it by the things Christ did in the flesh."[66] Despite the prologue's clear declaration that "the Word was God," this remains an indirect stating, an insinuation of what can better be shown in the story of Jesus's action and passion. The narrative genre of the Gospel is uniquely suited to the proclamation of this theandric performance because it is in what is said and done by and to Jesus of Nazareth that the self-diffusive goodness of God is communicated to us.[67] At the end of his *Commentary on John*, Aquinas says, "To write about each and every word and deed of Christ is to reveal the power of every word and deed."[68] The Gospel narrative is a conduit of the divine power of the words and deeds of Jesus.[69]

Of course, one might well object to the attempt to claim that Aquinas has any interest in narrative at all, seeing this as simply an attempt to graft a once-trendy theological category onto an unwilling recipient. Is not Thomas's approach to theology much more conceptual than narrative? It certainly seems that Aquinas goes to great lengths in the *divisio* that opens each lecture to dismember any narrative continuity in John's Gospel so that

Stephen E. Fowl, *The Story of Christ in the Ethics of Paul: An Analysis of the Function of the Hymnic Material in the Pauline Corpus* (Sheffield, UK: JSOT, 1990), 198–202, especially 200n1.

66. *Super Io.* 1.1.23. Weisheipl and Larcher's translation reads "states" for *insinuat,* but Thomas's typical use of this term indicates an indirect form of assertion.

67. See *Summa theologiae* 3.1.1.

68. *Super Io.* 21.6.2660.

69. In his *Commentary on St. Paul's Letter to the Romans*, Thomas says that "the Gospel itself contains the power of God" (*Super Rom.* 1.6.98). Cf. *Super Rom.* 1.6.100, where he seems to ascribe healing power to the very material on which the Scriptures are written (though he also warns against *superstitiones characterum*—a kind of conjuring with texts).

the following *expositio* may treat the text as a series of conceptual points.[70] In fact, Thomas so dismembers the narrative that it is very difficult, when reading Thomas's *Commentary on John*, to keep track of the story.

In response to this objection, let me make clear that the claim that Thomas is cognizant of and concerned with the narrative character of the apostolic witness is simply to say, first, that for him the claims made about Jesus's person are inseparable from the scriptural stories of "the things Christ did in the flesh"[71] and, second, that the claims made by and for Jesus are unintelligible apart from the larger narrative structure of God's providence over creation.[72] It is not to claim that Thomas thinks that one can do theology simply by "telling stories" or that one does not need conceptual clarification. He is well aware that John's Gospel itself is not simply a chronicle of events; rather, it is a narrative that is structured in a particular way so as to convey a particular theological meaning. It is not simply an account of what Jesus said and did; it is an *interpreted* account that has a conceptual structure.[73] Thomas repeatedly shows us how John leads his readers through events so that they can avoid the conceptual (and moral) blind alleys and missteps that afflict Nicodemus, the Samaritan woman, Peter, and others in the story. As readers, we are not in the same position as the characters in the narrative because we have the benefit of John's interpretation of the events he recounts.

Likewise, in his *Commentary on John*, Thomas leads *his* students through John's narrative, helping them to avoid the missteps

70. See Wilhelmus G.B.M. Valkenberg, *Words of the Living God: Place and Function of Holy Scripture in the Theology of St. Thomas Aquinas* (Leuven: Peeters, 2000), 167.

71. *Super Io.* 1.1.23.

72. See Thomas S. Hibbs, *Dialectic and Narrative in Aquinas: An Interpretation of the "Summa Contra Gentiles"* (Notre Dame, IN: University of Notre Dame Press, 1995), especially 30–34.

73. Not only does Thomas see John as offering a more "contemplative" narrative than the other three evangelists, he also shows an awareness that John might have ordered events in a particular way in order to make a particular point. See, for example, *Super Io.* 21.1.2571, where Aquinas discusses John's reasons for telling the story of Jesus's appearance to the disciples beside the Sea of Tiberias after he seemed to have brought his Gospel to a conclusion.

and blind alleys that have afflicted earlier readers of John's Gospel, such as Arius or Nestorius. At the same time, just as John's interpretation must adhere to the events he recounts, so too Thomas's commentary must adhere to John's interpretation of those events. The *divisio* that opens each lecture is not a peeling off of the narrative husk so as to reveal the conceptual kernel; rather, it is more like sketching a road map of the country ahead so that we will not take a wrong turn or fail to attend to those parts of the landscape that previous pilgrims have considered most significant. Looking at the map is in no way a substitute for following on the journey itself. In other words, Thomas's commentary presumes readers who are already familiar with the narrative.

***

This process of commentary indicates that, while the apostolic witness of Scripture is normative, it continues to be interpreted by being reflectively lived out in the Church Militant, which is a community of both saints and sinners. Referring to the story of Jesus calling Philip, Aquinas says, "A disciple's vocation is to follow."[74] What John and Thomas are both trying to do is to teach us to be disciples of Jesus by faithfully "following" his story. The normative interpretive account of Jesus's example as contained in the Scriptures must be interpreted by the exemplary performance of the saints.[75] In the diverse ways that disciples have followed this story, new light has constantly been shed on *how* to follow it in shifting contexts. For example, Thomas is able to confidently extend the application of Jesus's example of washing feet to include the spiritual and corporal works of mercy—forgiving our enemies, praying for them, practicing hospitality, giving food to one in need—because this is how Jesus's example has

74. *Super Io.* 1.16.311.

75. *Super Io.* 18.4.2321.

been interpreted by the saints.[76] It is attention to the lives of the saints, which we might think of as reading the "narrative" of the Holy Spirit, that makes the imitation of Christ something more than just the mechanical repetition of Jesus's actions.

The activity of continually identifying exemplary lives of holiness is crucial for the Church Militant's ability to know what it means to "walk like this human being" in diverse contexts. Again, we have a kind of circularity: the holiness of the saint can be recognized only in the light of past examples, but at the same time, each new saint sheds light on what the imitation of Christ looks like in his or her particular time and place. Thérèse of Lisieux's holiness is recognizable because of such predecessors as Teresa of Avila, but she also reveals what it means to be crucified with Christ in the age of modern atheism when the world seems to obscure rather than reveal the presence of God. Maximilian Kolbe conforms in some ways to the pattern of the Christian martyr, while at the same time showing us what it means in the midst of the modern technologized genocide to love to the point of death.

But of course, the Church is not simply the Church of the saints; it is also the Church of sinners. Aquinas is startlingly blunt in his acknowledgment of the shortcomings of the Church. We find in him no attempt to distance an idealized Church from the flawed empirical Church.[77] In his allegorical interpretation of the storm that besets the disciples' ship (see John 6:17–18), Thomas, citing Augustine, says that such storms are "the trials and persecutions which would afflict the Church due to a lack of love."[78] Whereas Augustine interprets this story in an apocalyptic context, seeing it as a prefiguring of the winnowing tribulations at the end of time, Aquinas seems to see in it an allegory

76. *Super Io.* 13.3.1779.

77. The attempt to do this is a characteristic of what Nicholas Healy calls "blueprint ecclesiologies." See *Church, World and the Christian Life*, 37–38.

78. *Super Io.* 6.2.879. Cf. Augustine, *Tractatus in Evangelium Iohannis* 25.5–6.

of the *current*—dare one say *persistent*—lack of love that besets the Church. When Thomas says that true friendship must be "not imperceptible,"[79] his employment of the double negative shows an unblinking realism about life within the community of disciples (a realism perhaps born of his own experience in religious community), where human viciousness and vanity are sometimes held in check but never vanquished, where "affectionate" nicknames like "the dumb ox" are given. As Thomas says, the unity in love of the Church is not the perfected unity of the Church Triumphant but a "unity which is taking shape."[80]

But the failure to which the Church is subject reaches beyond mere lukewarmness in love; it reaches all the way to the betrayal of Christ. Regarding Jesus's saying, "Truly, truly, I say to you, one of you will betray me" (John 13:21), Aquinas notes, "He is careful to say, 'one of you,' i.e., one of those chosen for this holy society, so that we might understand that there would never be a society so holy that it would be without sinners and those who are evil."[81] While Thomas goes on to say that Jesus is reproving Judas and not the group as a whole, since "we should not think a group bad because one member is bad," he then adds, "Although if several are bad the group could be considered bad." Thomas makes no attempt to distinguish between the "objective" holiness of the Church and the "subjective" sinfulness of her members. While one bad member does not make the Church as a whole evil, neither does the Church as a whole appear immune from implication in the evil of her members. The Church Militant is, for Thomas, Christ's Bride, wedded to him in the womb of the Virgin Mary,[82] but it is also an instance of "human

79. *Super Io.* 13.7.1837.
80. *Super Io.* 17.5.2242.
81. *Super Io.* 13.4.1799.
82. *Super Io.* 2.1.338, 3.5.518.

society,"[83] subject to the same risks as other human societies.[84] Thomas believes, of course, in the holiness of the Church: that the Church lives by grace and that Jesus promises the gates of hell shall not prevail against her. But this is something different from the view, heard these days in certain ecclesiastical circles, that while *Christians* may sin, the *Church* cannot because she is objectively holy in her structures and sacraments.[85] As we saw in looking at Thomas's views on sacramental and spiritual communion, the sacraments of the New Covenant are, absent love, as capable as the sacrifices of Israel of spiritual emptiness.[86] The same could be said of the other structures of the Church.

Though Thomas does not work out the details, his comments indicate that one can maintain belief in the holiness of the Church without positing a "Church itself" that is somehow other than the saints and sinners who make up the Church Militant. And much is at stake in our ability to see the Church Militant exemplified in her sinners as well as in her saints. If the Church,

83. *Super Io.* 13.3.1791.

84. This is the theme explored at great length by Hans Urs von Balthasar in his 1948 essay "Casta Meretrix" (i.e., "the chaste whore") in *Explorations in Theology*, vol. 2, *The Spouse of the Word*, trans. John Saward (San Francisco: Ignatius, 1991), 193–288.

85. In his commentary on Matthew's Gospel, Thomas interprets the "gates of hell" verse (see Matt. 16:18) in what seems at first glance a rather triumphalist manner, using it as an occasion to claim that while the Church of Constantinople had at times fallen into heresy, the Church founded on Peter—not just Rome but the whole Western Church—had not. But two things should be pointed out. First, Thomas's focus in this verse is doctrinal orthodoxy, not sinfulness. Thomas's notion of unformed faith makes clear that one can believe and still sin. Second, when he comes to Matthew 16:23 ("Get behind me, Satan"), he emphasizes Peter's constant need of grace in order to know the truth of Christ. In other words, while Thomas believes that the Church founded on Peter shall not have the gates of hell prevail against it, this belief is not couched in terms of a distinction between "the Church itself" and her members. See *Super Mt.* 16.2.1385 and 16.3.1405. Of course, just because Aquinas did not hold this view does not mean it is wrong. After all, Thomas did not believe that Mary was conceived without sin either. The distinction between the holy Church and her sinful members may be a case of genuine doctrinal development. I don't think it is, largely based on the reasons sketched in the next paragraph, but it cannot be ruled out *a priori* as a possibility. At the same time, perhaps Aquinas is an indication that one can have a robust doctrine of the holiness of the Church without making such a distinction.

86. In this regard, Catholic Christians would do well to ponder what Paul means when he tells the Corinthian Christians, "When you meet together, it is not the Lord's supper that you eat" (1 Cor. 11:20). We ought not let our fear of being accused of Donatism keep us from taking Paul with all seriousness.

as Church, celebrates in the life and witness of Maximilian Kolbe the fruit of the tradition of the saints, ought it not also, *as Church*, repent of the life and witness of Christians who perpetrated the Holocaust as the fruit of the tradition of Christian anti-Jewish polemics?[87] Ought not the Church be able to see in such sinners not simply the failure of individual Christians but the failure of the community of disciples as a whole? If we cannot see this, then we have blinded ourselves to the paradoxical light cast by our shadows and have deprived the community of disciples of the edification of repentance.

***

The final thing that must be said is that, for Thomas, while the end of the Gospel is the upbuilding of the faithful as the temple of God, the Church Militant is not an end in itself. God's ultimate purpose is not the sanctification of the Church but the blessing of creation as a whole. The community of disciples teaches and learns not simply for its own edification but "so that the world might believe." If the world is to believe in the Gospel, then it must have some convincing reason to believe it to be true. Providing such a reason is the task of the Church.[88] Aquinas writes, "Nothing shows the truth of the gospel better than the charity of those who believe."[89] The unity in love of the community of disciples is not simply to provide them with a foretaste of heaven. It is to be a light to the nations that displays the truth of God and awakens in others the desire for communion with God and each other. So, we return to Isaiah's vision of the lifting up of Jerusalem and the pilgrimage of the nations. It is the fidelity of the people of

87. This question can be made even more pointed when one tries to account for the fact that Kolbe himself, while no Nazi or advocate of genocide, participated in anti-Jewish polemics prior to the war.

88. Of course, it is ultimately the task of the Spirit. The Church, however, is an instrumental cause.

89. *Super Io.* 17.5.2241.

God to the life of discipleship, a fidelity visibly displayed in their love for one another, that is the instrument by which the Gospel is made credible in the eyes of the world.

But while the Church has the task of showing the truth of the Gospel, it is of itself in no way adequate to this task. Aquinas is clear that the community of disciples is a thoroughly penultimate reality, possessed of a true but cloudy vision of the mystery it is called to embody. Thomas says, "We do see the kingdom of God and the mysteries of eternal salvation, but imperfectly."[90] On the day when there "shall come to pass the saying that is written: 'Death is swallowed up in victory'" (1 Cor. 15:54), we will see face to face, and there will be no more need for the enigmatic seeing through signs that characterizes the Church Militant.[91] And even prior to that day, the words of its stories are always exceeded by the Word of God; the boundaries of its identity are constantly being transgressed by God's will to save; its rituals and structures are but a pale image of the heavenly worship of the saints and angels who stand before the Lamb.

This should not be taken as a slight to the significance of the Church, which is, after all, the temple filled with the majesty of God. But it is an indication of what it means for it to be filled with the majesty of God. It means that it is like Isaiah, blessed and afflicted with a vision that shakes the doorposts of the temple and called by God to proclaim his word. It is like Peter, who stands in all his inadequacy before the risen Lord and receives his command: feed my sheep. It is like St. Thomas himself, reduced to the silence of learned ignorance in the face of the mystery of God. Finally, it is like John, blessed above all the other Apostles with a keen understanding, but in the end proclaiming only love. Thomas writes of John, "As an old man he was carried to the Church by his followers to teach the faithful. He taught only one

90. *Super Io.* 3.1.433.

91. *Summa theologiae* 3.61.4.

thing: 'Little children, love one another.' This is the perfection of the Christian life."[92] This, we might say, *is* the majesty of God.

92. *Super Io.* 21.5.2653.

13

"The Body of Christ Is Made from Bread"

Transubstantiation and the Grammar of Creation

The twentieth-century philosopher Josef Pieper, noting that what is most important in a thinker's work can go unnoticed by interpreters because it "goes without saying" for the author, goes on to say of Thomas Aquinas, "The notion of creation determines and characterizes the interior structure of *nearly all* the basic concepts in Thomas's philosophy of Being. And this fact is *not* evident; it is scarcely ever put forward explicitly; it belongs to the unexpressed in St. Thomas's doctrine of Being."[1] While demurring from Pieper's seeming restriction of this claim to the realm of Thomas's "philosophy of Being," I would want to affirm the importance of the idea of creation in all of Thomas's thought, as well as Pieper's observation that this can sometimes go unnoticed. We might say that the doctrine of creation displays with particular clarity the creator-creature relationship that constitutes the "grammar" of Thomas's theology, a grammar that is at work, although often unnoticed, throughout that theology. In what follows, I want to show the importance of the grammar of creation for Thomas by means of a single example. After first briefly sketching how Thomas understands creation, I will turn to Thomas's theology of

* Originally published as "'The Body of Christ is Made from Bread': Transubstantiation and the Grammar of Creation," *International Journal of Systematic Theology* 18, no. 1 (January 2016): 30–46.

1. Josef Pieper, *The Silence of St. Thomas: Three Essays*, trans. John Murray and Daniel O'Connor (South Bend, IN: St. Augustine's, 1999), 48.

Christ's Eucharistic presence and an important modern critique of that theology to show how the grammar of creation is at play in his thought, as well as how inquiry into an area like sacramental theology might help us gain insight into the grammar of creation.

CREATION: *RELATIO QUAEDAM AD DEUM CUM NOVITATE ESSENDI*

What does Thomas mean when he speaks of "creation"? He does not mean most fundamentally the six days of creation, though he offers in the *Summa theologiae* an account of the days of creation that is highly interesting and, alas, too often overlooked.[2] But because he always seeks to move beyond the simple repetition of sacred truths to a grasp of the fundamental principles involved—from knowing simply *what* is the case to a deeper grasp of *why* it is the case—Thomas wants to know what it means for something to be "created." To put it in a way that would not be alien to Thomas's medieval Scholastic idiom, he is not satisfied with a "material" account of creation that explores the biblical creation narrative but offers as well a "formal" account of creation that seeks to define what creation is. To put it in yet another way, Thomas seeks not simply to repeat statements about God's work of creation but to grasp the grammar of those statements. As David Burrell puts it, for Thomas, "the very structure of a well-formed sentence reflects the formal or constitutive features of the object spoken about."[3] The definition of createdness that Thomas works his way toward is, as he phrases it in his disputed questions *De potentia*, "a relation of something to God together with newness of existence" (*relatio quaedam ad Deum cum novitiate essendi*),[4] and this

2. See *Summa theologiae* 1.65–74.

3. David B. Burrell, *Exercises in Religious Understanding* (Notre Dame, IN: University of Notre Dame Press, 1974), 87.

4. *De potentia* 3.3; cf. *Summa theologiae* 1.45.3 ad 3.

definition can serve as an entry point for examining Aquinas's "formal" or grammatical account of creation.

So, first, Thomas thinks of creation in terms of a relation between creator and creature, specifically "the very dependence of created being [*esse creati*] on the ultimate source [*principium*] from which it comes."[5] To be a creature is simply to have an existence that depends on another; conversely, the ultimate source of creatures must have a nondependent existence. In other words, to be a creature is to be contingent with regard to existence and to be the creator is to have a necessary existence, where "necessity" means not simply that a thing does not pass into or out of existence but rather that a thing has existence through itself and not through another. Drawing upon the insights of Ibn Sina (Avicenna), Thomas conceives of the contingency of creation in terms of the distinction between essence (*essentia*)—what a thing is—and existence (*esse*)—the fact that a thing is. Thomas's argument for this distinction is, in brief, that one cannot fully understand what a thing is without knowing all of the essential parts of its definition (e.g., I can't understand what human beings are if I only know that they are animals without knowing that they are also rational). But I can know what something is apart from knowing whether or not it exists (e.g., I can grasp the definition of a unicorn whether or not unicorns exist). Therefore, the fact of something's existence is distinct from its essence, unless, he notes, there exists something the essence of which is existence itself.[6] What this means is that existence is not an essential property of things. Their existence depends upon something else—ultimately upon something in which essence and existence *are* identical. The ultimate dependence of things upon something outside themselves for their existence, their "existence through another," is the relation that Thomas calls "creation."

5. *Contra Gentiles* 2.18.2.

6. *De ente et essentia* 4.

Second, and following from this, creation has to do with the existence or "being" (*esse*) of things. Thomas notes, "God's first effect in things is existence itself."[7] What God creates are not abstract essences but substances, concretely existing things. Thomas thinks of the distinction of essence and existence in terms of the distinction between potentially being something and actually being something. That is, just as the bronze that is potentially a statue can become an actual statue, so too an essence, which can potentially exist, can come to actually exist.[8] So for Thomas, what it means for God to create is to bestow existence upon essences that are in themselves only potentially existing. Yet this existence is not an adventitious add-on to essences that somehow preexist; the essences are constituted as actual in the bestowal of existence. In this sense, creation is *ex nihilo*—not in the sense that there is a "nothing" that preexists creation but rather that creatures are, apart from the actualization of their existence by God, nothing.[9]

Third, as implied by this view on what it means for creation to be *ex nihilo*, Thomas thinks that the notion of creation itself does not necessarily imply a temporal beginning to the world. The issue of what is often called "the eternity of the world" was hotly contested in the Middle Ages, not least because the infinite temporal duration of the world was the nearly unanimous view of the Greek philosophical heritage, whether understood in terms of eternal matter to which God gives form (Plato) or eternally existing substances in motion (Aristotle). Some, including the Arabic philosophers Avicenna and Averroes, as

7. *Compendium theologiae* 1.68.

8. Of course, like all analogies, there is an element of dissimilarity here. That which actualizes a potential to be this or that sort of thing—i.e., the agent—need not have being this or that sort of thing as an essential characteristic. Thus, it is a sculptor who actualizes the potential of bronze to be a statue, not another statue (though the sculptor *does* have to possess the form of the statue in a nonessential way—i.e., as an idea in her mind). In other cases, as when dogs give birth to puppies rather than kittens and fire heats things rather than cooling them, the actualized potential *is* a constitutive feature of the agent. The case of existence is of the latter sort, such that the agent that actualizes the potential of essences to exist must itself have existence as its defining or essential nature since it must exist in order to be an agent.

9. *Summa theologiae* 1.45.1 ad 3.

well as their thirteenth-century followers who are referred to as "Latin Averroists," followed Aristotle in seeing the universe and its motion as being of infinite duration. Others, including Al-Ghazali in the Arabic-speaking world and Bonaventure among the thirteenth-century Scholastics, held that the eternity of the world and of motion not only contradicted divine revelation but was philosophically incoherent (implying things like an actual infinity of immortal souls), and also seemed to give creation a kind of necessity that rivaled God's. Thomas, along with Moses Maimonides, holds the position that, while we know from Scripture that the world is not infinite in temporal duration but rather is created "in the beginning," there is nothing in itself incoherent in the notion of a creation that exists eternally without a beginning or end in time, and therefore neither the eternity nor non-eternity of the world can be either proved or disproved. We might say that the grammar of creation does not necessarily include tense, being solely concerned with dependence upon God, which could conceivably be an eternal dependence.[10] In this way, the beginning of the world's duration in time belongs to the "material" account of creation rather than to the "formal" account.

Fourth, if "creation" does not necessarily imply temporal beginning, what then does Thomas mean when he includes *cum novitate essendi* ("with newness of existence") in his definition of existence? What is key for Thomas, and will become important in our discussion of his Eucharistic theology, is that creation is not simply a transformation of something that already exists—such as a calf growing into a cow or a cow being made into a hamburger—but rather the radical origin of things. The inclusion of "newness of existence" speaks not to temporal origin but to the fact that existence is imparted by God apart from any preexisting

10. For the various sides in this debate, see the introductions and the texts collected in St. Thomas, Siger de Brabant, and St. Bonaventure, *On the Eternity of the World*, ed. and trans. Cyril Vollert, Lottie H. Kendzierski, and Paul M. Byrne (Milwaukee, WI: Marquette University Press, 1964).

condition or potential. When we speak of creation as the actualization of potential to exist, we are speaking of "potential" in the sense of the non-impossibility that, for example, a triangle has the potential to be three-sided but not two- or four-sided, and not of the potential of a calf to grow into a cow or a cow to become a hamburger. These latter things are not instances of creation but rather of "change" (*mutatio*), which is the term Thomas uses to speak of giving new form to something that already exists.[11] "Creation from nothing" does not mean that nothingness begins to be something, but that creation involves simply "Making X to be" and not "Making X from Y." In creation, something exists solely from its relatedness to God, its source.

Fifth, the relation of radical dependence that constitutes creatures is uniquely a relationship to God. While creatures may cause various changes in other creatures, even to the point of making a new thing (as when a hamburger is newly made from a cow), only God makes things to be apart from any preexisting potential. At the same time, while creatures cannot cause things to be from nothing, they do possess a genuine causal efficacy. The nutrients in the grass really do cause the calf to become a cow and the agency of the butcher really does cause the cow to become hamburger.[12] For Thomas, this causal efficacy of creatures in no way detracts from God's power as the cause of existence; indeed, he thinks it is a testimony to God's power that he bestows the dignity of "secondary causality" on creatures.[13] As it is sometimes put, for Thomas, the relationship of God and creatures is "noncompetitive." There is no zero-sum relationship between God's creative activity and the creaturely activity of causing because they lie on different planes: God's activity of *creatio*—making things exist—and the creature's activity of *mutatio*—bringing about changes in things that exist. Those planes do sometimes intersect,

11. *Summa theologiae* 1.45.2 ad 2.

12. *Summa theologiae* 1.45.5.

13. *Summa theologiae* 1.22.3.

as in the case of miracles, but these do not figure into Aquinas's formal account of creation.[14] Still, there is an intimate connection between the two planes in all cases, since the creaturely capacity for *mutatio* is a participation in divine *creatio*.

These remarks, brief though they are, will have to serve as an account of Thomas's "formal" or grammatical account of creation, as we now turn to look at how the grammar of creation structures his account of Christ's presence in the Eucharist.

TRANSUBSTANTIATION ON TRIAL

Even though the term "transubstantiation" predates Thomas Aquinas by at least a century and is used by him only occasionally in his mature theology,[15] the doctrine of transubstantiation has often, rightly or wrongly (and I am inclined to think the latter), been taken to be his signal contribution of Catholic Eucharistic theology, employing Aristotle's philosophy to explain Christ's Eucharistic presence. Not everyone, of course, sees this contribution as a positive thing. Martin Luther opined that the church that had decreed the doctrine of transubstantiation was "the Thomistic—that is, the Aristotelian church." He saw it as an explanation that misused Aristotle, who himself was a dubious authority on matters of faith, such that Thomas was to be pitied for "building an unfortunate superstructure upon an unfortunate foundation."[16] Luther's objection gives voice to those who feel that Christ's Eucharistic presence should be left mysterious and not subjected to the torturous rigors of Scholastic logic and the

14. Indeed, in his material account of the six days of creation, Thomas, following Augustine, is very wary of describing any of what takes place in God's foundation of the world in terms of the category "miracle." See *Summa theologiae* 1.67.4 ad 3; 1.68.2 ad 1.

15. The word "transubstantiation" appears some sixty-one times in the early *Scriptum super libros Sententiarum*, not at all in the *Contra Gentiles*, and only five times in the *Summa theologiae*.

16. Martin Luther, *On the Babylonian Captivity of the Church*, in *Selected Writings of Martin Luther*, ed. Theodore G. Tappert, vol. 1, *1517–1520*, (Minneapolis, MN: Fortress, 2007), 381.

natural philosophy of Aristotle. Others have had an opposite, yet no less negative reaction, seeing transubstantiation as involving magical and irrational claims, as witnessed to by the term "hocus pocus," which the seventeenth-century Anglican divine Bishop Tillotson suggested was "a corruption of *Hoc est corpus*, by way of ridiculous imitation of the priests of the Church of *Rome* in their *trick* of *Transubstantiation*,"[17] a doctrine he thought riddled with "*monstrous absurdities*."[18] Engendering seemingly contradictory charges of hyperrationalism or magical irrationality, transubstantiation, and by extension Thomas, has been a principal piece of evidence in the case for the failings of medieval Catholic theology.

Of course, criticism of medieval Scholastic approaches to the sacraments is not solely the purview of Protestant theologians. The Catholic theologian and priest Louis-Marie Chauvet has developed a particularly sweeping and influential critique of Scholastic accounts of sacramental causality, a critique that does not spare Thomas Aquinas. While appreciative of what Thomas was attempting to achieve and judging him superior to many other Scholastics, Chauvet nonetheless sees his sacramental theology, including his theology of the Eucharist, as part of a tradition that is ultimately a dead end. His criticism of Aquinas is twofold. In broad terms, he includes Thomas in his rejection of the entire Scholastic tradition of speaking of sacraments as "causes," which he sees as "metaphysical" and "onto-theological." Second, he criticizes Aquinas's Eucharistic theology more specifically for the rupture it creates between the sacramental and ecclesial bodies of Christ. Both of these criticisms are indebted to Heidegger, whom Chauvet takes as the bellwether of our current postmodern situation.

Chauvet begins his masterwork, *Symbol and Sacrament*, by asking why it is that the Scholastics would make "cause" (along

17. John Tillotson, *A Discourse Against Transubstantiation* (London: Society for Promoting Christian Knowledge, 1833), 35, emphases in original.

18. Tillotson, 38, emphasis in original.

with "sign") a privileged category for understanding the sacraments. Why speak of sacraments as "causes of grace" when the term "cause" implies the production or augmentation of an object, and grace is "the paradigmatic case of something that is a *non*-object, a *non*-value"?[19] His answer is, in brief, that "the Scholastics were *unable to think otherwise*; they were prevented from doing so by the onto-theological presuppositions which structured their entire culture."[20] Chauvet takes Aquinas to be the most sophisticated representative of this tradition—one who avoids many of the most egregious excesses of onto-theology, while in the end being unable to escape its clutches.

Chauvet appreciates the primacy that Aquinas gives in the *Summa theologiae* to the category of "sign" over cause: sacraments are signs that have causal efficacy. This represents a shift from the theology of his *Sentences* commentary, in which sacraments are causes that signify.[21] Yet this "banishment" of causality is only temporary, for a few questions later (*Summa theologiae* 3.62), when Thomas inquires into the principal effect of the sacraments, which is grace, "causality returns in force"[22] as Thomas develops his mature view that sacraments are neither mere "occasions" of grace, nor simply "disposing causes" making human beings apt to receive grace, but rather are true instrumental efficient causes of grace. And with this, Thomas falls into the pit of what Chauvet calls "the productionist scheme of representation" in which being takes priority over becoming and grace is thereby reified as a "thing" that is produced rather than a gift that is given.[23] In the end, despite his valiant attempt to think sacraments as signs, Thomas cannot escape the onto-theological heritage in which

19. Louis-Marie Chauvet, *Symbol and Sacrament: A Sacramental Reinterpretation of Christian Existence*, trans. Patrick Madigan and Madeleine Beaumont (Collegeville, MN: Liturgical, 1995), 7.

20. Chauvet, 8.

21. Chauvet, 11.

22. Chauvet, 15.

23. Chauvet, 445.

being is "represented as the general and universal 'something' or 'stuff' that conceals itself beneath entities, which 'lies at the base' of each of them (*hypokeimenon*). A permanent 'subsistent being,' *substratum*, *sub-jectum*, and finally, as Descartes describes it, *sub-stantia*."[24]

Chauvet offers further criticisms of Aquinas's Eucharistic theology in particular. Again, he offers an appreciation of the subtlety and sophistication of Thomas's theological achievement and avoids simpleminded caricatures of transubstantiation. He recognizes that, by recourse to the language of "substance," which is "neither a 'this' or a 'that' nor anything which can be attained by sensible cognition," Thomas "*exorcises every spatial representation* of the Eucharistic presence."[25] Thus it is also "*outside any physicalism* and any more or less gross representation."[26] He further recognizes that transubstantiation is not reducible to Aristotelian metaphysics but, particularly in the claim that the accidents of bread and wine persist without inhering in a substance, calls for the "sacrificium intellectus" of faith.

Yet, as Chauvet sees it, a problem still remains in Aquinas's view that in the Eucharist, "its first effect (*res et sacramentum*) is *in ipsa materia* ('in the matter itself')."[27] Chauvet acknowledges that Thomas sees the "final purpose [*res tantum*]" of the Eucharist as the unity of the *totus Christus*—the Mystical Body, head and members—but believes that so long as the sacrament is seen as "perfected" in the consecration of the bread and wine, and not in the Eucharistic communion of the faithful, "the Church remains only the *extrinsic* end."[28] Thus, the culprit in all this, not surprisingly, is "the model of a metaphysical *substance*." As Chauvet puts it,

24. Chauvet, 26.

25. Chauvet, 385.

26. Chauvet, 386.

27. Chauvet, 388, citing *Summa theologiae* 3.73.1 ad 3.

28. Chauvet, 388.

> In the perspective of the Aristotelian "substance" as the expression of the *ultimate reality* of entities, one could express the integrality and radicalness of the real presence of Christ in the sacrament only by putting between parentheses, at least during the analysis of the "how" of Eucharistic conversion, its relation to the Church. This is exactly what happens with Thomas: if he strongly emphasizes the connection of the Eucharist to the Church both before and after his analysis of transubstantiation, he puts it *between parentheses* during this analysis.[29]

The language of "transubstantiation" implies that what the sacrament is really about is the production of the static "substance" of Christ's Body and Blood, which might be eaten or adored by the Christian faithful but that in its self-enclosed sufficiency can bear only an extrinsic relationship to the ecclesial Body of Christ. Chauvet's own view is that "the great *sacramentum* of Christ's presence is not the bread as such in its unbroken state. Or rather, it is indeed the bread, but *in its very essence*, bread-as-food, bread-as-meal, bread-for-sharing."[30] The presence of Christ is better described not as a substance that has been produced but as a gift that has been given.

Chauvet's critique is both subtle and sympathetic (the same cannot really be said of Frater Luther's or Bishop Tillotson's), yet to my mind, it is also quite wrong. To appreciate its wrongness, we need to attend to how the grammar of creation structures what Thomas says about Eucharistic presence. Fortunately, Thomas does this for us explicitly in his *Summa theologiae*, and I will proceed by looking in some detail at his discussion.

29. Chauvet, 389.

30. Chauvet, 406.

MAKING CHRIST'S BODY

Thomas concludes question 75 of the Third Part of the *Summa* with an article that begins, *Videtur quod haec sit falsa: "Ex pane fit corpus Christi"* ("It seems that this is false: 'The body of Christ is made from bread'").[31] The statement under scrutiny, of which Thomas will affirm the truth, would seem to be a prime example of what Chauvet calls the "productionist mentality" with regard to the sacraments. Before going on to examine whether or not this is the case, we should first appreciate the form of the question. It is in some ways reminiscent of the approach taken in question 16 of the Third Part of the *Summa*, in which Thomas inquires into such statements as "God is a human being" and "God was made a human being" and "Christ is a creature." In other words, Thomas proposes a particular piece of human speech and asks whether it can be affirmed as true. The question, then, is whether "The body of Christ is made from bread" is a well-formed sentence for speaking about the Eucharist and, if it is, what does it tell us about the formal or constitutive features of Christ's Eucharistic presence.

The four objections Thomas gives to the statement "The body of Christ is made from bread" lay out the basic issue at stake in this article: How is the Eucharistic conversion of bread into the Body of Christ located conceptually in relation to other ways in which particular substances come to be where they were not before—i.e., natural change and the divine act of creation? Put differently, in what ways do well-formed sentences about natural change provide a paradigm for well-formed sentences concerning Christ's Eucharistic presence, and in what ways do well-formed sentences about creation provide such a paradigm?

Objections 1, 2, and 4 see "The body of Christ is made from bread" as implying that Christ's Eucharistic presence involves some sort of change along the lines of the changes that we

31. *Summa theologiae* 3.75.8 arg.

encounter in nature, such that Eucharistic conversion is equivalent to a subject undergoing a change, whether this be a substance taking on an accident or a material substratum receiving a new substantial form. Each of these objections points to the absurdity of such an account of Eucharistic presence by showing the unacceptable further statements it would seem to authorize. Objection 1 reads "The body of Christ is made from bread" as treating "bread" like a subject that receives a new substantial or accidental form, authorizing us to say "Bread is made the body of Christ" in the same way that we might say "The calf becomes a cow" or "The cow becomes hamburger." Objection 2 sees it as treating the bread as the "stuff" from which Christ's Body is made, authorizing us to say "The bread is the body of Christ" in the same way that we might say "The cow flesh is hamburger." Objection 4 sees it as implying that there is a passive potential in bread to be Christ's Body, authorizing us to say "Bread can be the body of Christ" in the same way as we might say "A cow can be hamburger."

The third objection takes a slightly different tack: in the expression "The body of Christ is made from bread," the preposition "from" (*ex*) implies a conversion of one thing into another, and not simply the sort of conversion involved in natural change but the radical conversion of one whole substance into another whole substance. It is analogous to an individual cow becoming, not hamburger, but a different individual cow (Flossie becoming Bossie), in which the form "cow" is instantiated in different matter. This would seem to imply, the third objection goes on to state, that the Eucharistic conversion is "more miraculous" than God's act of creation, which we do not conceive of as a conversion of one entire thing into another entire thing but rather as a production presupposing nothing.[32] What is unstated in the objection, but made clear in Thomas's reply (ad 3), is that such a

32. See *Summa theologiae* 1.45.2.

conversion of one entire substance into another is more miraculous than creation because, as unimaginable as creation might be, it still conforms to the notion of causal production.[33]

Thus, the objections pose the difficulties with the proposition "The body of Christ is made out of bread." Objections 1, 2, and 4 see it as assimilating Eucharistic conversion to natural change; objection 3 argues that if it is *not* interpreted as implying natural change, then it implies a sort of divine activity exceeding the miracle of creation from nothing, which presumably cannot be exceeded since it is presupposed by all other miraculous activity. The *sed contra*, posing the difficulty with the position taken in the objections, notes that no less an authority than Ambrose had written, *Ubi accedit consecratio, de pane fit corpus Christi* ("When the consecration takes place, the Body of Christ is made of bread").[34] The question is, has Ambrose simply uttered an ill-formed sentence? If not, if we judge his sentence to be well-formed, what does this tell us about Eucharistic conversion?

As so often when confronted with a traditional formulation that seems in conflict with an established theological position, Thomas seeks to make key distinctions in order to save the traditional formulation. He recognizes that what we might call the "primary speech" of the Church—in this case, the mystagogical preaching of Ambrose, but also the language of Scripture and liturgy—does not always neatly conform to doctrinal rules, and that part of the task of *sacra doctrina* is to show how these primary utterances of faith can intelligibly fit together within the doctrinal grammar of the Church. Thus, he begins by saying that the "conversion of bread into the body of Christ in some respect

33. Thomas does not at this point apply the word "miracle" to the consecration itself, though elsewhere he seems to (e.g., *Summa theologiae* 3.77.5).

34. Ambrose, *De Sacramentis* 4.4.14. An even greater potential difficulty, not mentioned by Aquinas, is posed by the Roman Canon itself, which prays that the Eucharistic gifts *nobis corpus et sanguis fiat dilectissimi Filii tui, Domini nostri Iesu Christi*. Thomas avoids this difficulty by interpreting this part of the canon, on the basis of the *nobis*, as a prayer for the fruitfulness of the consecration rather than as a petition for the consecration of the elements to be fulfilled. See *Summa theologiae* 3.83.4.

fits [*convenit*] both with creation and with natural change, and in some respects differs from both."[35] This raises the question of the ways in which language akin to the language that we use to speak of natural change is a fitting way of signifying what takes place when bread and wine become Christ's Body and Blood, and in what ways such language is unfitting. Likewise, how is language akin to the language that we use in speaking of God's production of creatures from nothing a fitting way of signifying what takes place when bread and wine become Christ's Body and Blood, and how is such language unfitting? We might say that Aquinas is inquiring as to which grammar—the grammar of natural change or the grammar of creation—we ought to look to find our paradigm of a well-formed sentence regarding Eucharistic conversion.

Aquinas first notes that, in all three cases, our well-formed sentences have an "order of terms." Thomas means by this that our statements about creation, natural change, and transubstantiation all present two terms in such a way that one follows the other, and they do not present the two terms as existing simultaneously. Thus, we have nonexistence followed by creation, cow followed by hamburger, and bread followed by Christ's Body. In this way, whether we take natural change or creation as our paradigm for a well-formed sentence concerning the Eucharist, the statement "The body of Christ is made from bread" would seem to be a well-formed sentence. But while the linguistic ordering of the terms might be the same in both creation and in natural change, what it means for one thing to follow the other is quite different in the two cases. Which is to be preferred in speaking of the Eucharist?

Thomas notes that well-formed sentences about creation offer a uniquely fitting paradigm for speaking about the Eucharist inasmuch as in neither case ought we to speak as if there were

35. Note that Thomas, as he typically does when dealing with the mysteries of the Christian faith, casts the whole discussion in terms of "fittingness" [*convenientia*]. See chapters 10 and 11 above.

a subject underlying the terms of the statement. In the case of creation, it is clearly nonsensical to speak of there being a subject possessing the form of nonexistence that then undergoes a change such that it acquires the form of existence. Likewise, we ought not understand any statement regarding Eucharistic conversion (such as "The body of Christ is made from bread") as implying that there is a subject possessing the form of bread that undergoes a change such that it acquires the form of the Body of Christ. In this way, Eucharistic conversion conforms to the paradigm of creation: it is not *mutatio*, the kind of coming to be that we are familiar with from nature, in which a potential is realized in some subject; it is, rather, the beginning to be of an entire substance, matter and form, potential and actuality. It is, as we have seen, the divine gift of *esse*. If in this regard our statements about the Eucharist conform to the paradigm of natural change rather than to the paradigm of creation, they will be ill-formed, "unfitting" sentences.

But then Thomas goes on to say that there are two ways in which well-formed sentences about natural change *do* offer a fitting paradigm for speaking about the Eucharist. First, well-formed sentences in both cases will make clear that one term of the sentence "passes into" [*transit*] the other: just as we have a cow that becomes hamburger, so too we have bread that becomes the Body of Christ. As Stephen Brock has pointed out, one thing "passing into" another is a passage "from what is distinctive about one term to what is distinctive about another."[36] In creation, there is nothing "distinctive" about nonbeing, and thus there can be no passage from nonbeing to what is "distinctive" about being. Natural change and transubstantiation, on the other hand, *are* just such passages. Despite the radical difference in the two cases of what it means for one term to "pass into" the other—in the case

36. Stephen L. Brock, "St Thomas and the Eucharistic Conversion," *The Thomist* 65 , no. 4 (October 2001), 544n26. An example Thomas gives is a drop of water "passing into" a large quantity of wine (*Summa theologiae* 3.77.8).

of natural change involving the reception of successive forms by a subject (the flesh ceasing to be a cow and becoming hamburger) and in the case of Eucharistic conversion involving one entire substance beginning to be another (as if Flossie were to become Bossie)—both involve one distinct thing followed by another distinct thing, something clearly not the case in creation. Second, Thomas notes that in both natural change and transubstantiation there is "something that remains the same": in the case of natural change, this is the matter or subject that undergoes the change; in transubstantiation, this is the empirical reality (i.e., "accidents") of the bread and wine. This second similarity between natural change and Eucharistic conversion will, as we shall see, account for the possibility of misunderstanding certain statements contained within the primary speech of the Church.

Thomas then draws linguistic conclusions from this mapping of Eucharistic conversion in relation to natural change and creation. In all three cases, well-formed sentences cannot employ the present tense copula *est* to relate their terms—one cannot say that nonbeing is being, or that a cow is a hamburger, or that bread is the Body of Christ—but, because of the order of terms, one *can* employ the preposition *ex* to relate their terms—creation is properly spoken of as *ex nihilo*, hamburger comes *ex vaccam*, and the Body of Christ is *ex pane*. As Thomas explains in the reply to objection 1, the preposition "from" (*ex*) is used in sentences concerning creation and Eucharistic conversion in the same way that one says, "Out of morning comes day." There is no thing that is first morning and then becomes day.[37] Thus, it would seem that "from" is used analogously in statements about natural change, on the one hand, and creation and Eucharistic conversion, on the other.

In the cases of natural change and transubstantiation, but not

37. Unless (as he notes in his *Metaphysics* commentary 2.3.308) we are somehow conceiving of time as a "subject," which would not, of course, apply in the case of creation.

in the case of creation, one can employ the verb *conversionis*, since this implies the *transitus* of one subject "passing into" another, of one distinctiveness ending and another distinctiveness beginning from it. Yet the crucial difference between every natural change and the Eucharistic conversion is that in natural change, distinctiveness is a question of one form passing into another form, while in Eucharistic conversion, we have one entire substance passing into another entire substance, and this difference marks Eucharistic conversion with its own proper name: "transubstantiation."

The absence in transubstantiation of any perduring subject that undergoes the change leads to further linguistic consequences. We cannot speak of the bread having the potential to be the Body of Christ because something's potential to be something else depends upon the capacity of the perduring subject or matter to take on new forms. We might say that "a cow can be hamburger" or "the flesh of the hamburger is made of the flesh of the cow," since there is a common substrate of flesh in both the cow and the hamburger, but we ought not to say that "bread can be [*possit esse*] the Body of Christ" nor that "the Body of Christ is made of [*de*] bread," just as, in the case of creation, we ought not to say that "nonbeing can be being" or "being is made of nonbeing." In the cases of both creation and transubstantiation, the first term of the statement does not possess any potentiality to become the second term. Likewise, while we might say that "a cow will be a hamburger" or "a cow becomes a hamburger," we ought not to say that "bread will be [*erit*] the Body of Christ" or that "bread becomes [*fiat*] the Body of Christ," any more than we would say that "nonbeing will be being" or "nonbeing becomes being." While Eucharistic conversion is, like natural change, a *transitus*, it is so in a highly qualified sense—a sense that is qualified by its conformity to the grammar of creation as the coming to be of the whole substance.

Up to this point, Thomas seems to have offered us a fairly

clear set of linguistic rules, a tight grammar of Eucharistic speech. In statements in which the first term is "bread" and the second term is "the Body of Christ," we ought not to connect them by means of a word that implies their concurrent identity (such as "is" [*est*]), nor a word that posits a perduring subject with the potential both to be bread and to be the Body of Christ (such as "can be" [*potest*] or "is made of" [*de*] or "becomes" [*fit*] or "will be" [*erit*]). Words that we can use to join the two terms are those, such as *ex*, that signify only the order of terms, as well as those, such as *conversionis*, that signify one substance "passing into" another.

So far, so good. But then it all seems to fall apart, or at least the ligaments of the grammar loosen as it collides with the colloquialism of the primary speech of the Church. Thomas is forced to acknowledge that this primary speech sometimes does not conform to his criteria for well-formed sentences expressing the Eucharistic conversion. The example from Ambrose provided in the *sed contra* is a case in point: *Ubi accedit consecratio, de pane fit corpus Christi*. Here, we find both the preposition *de* and the verb *fit*, which Aquinas had earlier said implied a perduring subject.[38]

Thomas's way of accommodating these instances of primary Christian speech is to say that they may be allowed if understood in a certain sense (*secundum quandam similitudinem*); that is, they are allowable if the first term of the sentence, "bread," is taken to signify not the substance bread, but rather "that which is contained under the appearance of bread" (*hoc quod sub speciebus panis continetur*). In other words, in some statements, our use of the term "bread" is a kind of "pointing" that indicates the bread's dimensive quantity and the accidents inhering in it, which normally mediate the presence of the substance of bread but after the consecration mediate the presence of the substance

38. One can only imagine what Thomas would have thought of the offertory prayers of the reformed Rite of the Mass, which state that the bread and wine "will become" (*fiet*) the bread of life and spiritual drink.

of Christ's Body.[39] In this way, Ambrose ought to be understood as saying that when the consecration happens, that which appears under the appearance of bread ceases to be bread and begins to be the Body of Christ. We might say that the colloquial, primary speech of the Church quite naturally uses "bread" and "wine" as indeterminate "pointers" that can draw our attention first to the natural substances of bread and wine, and then to the Body and Blood of Christ.[40] Glossed in this way, not only the sentence posed in the original question, *ex pane fit corpus Christi*, but also Ambrose's sentence, *de pane fit corpus Christi*, can be understood as well-formed sentences.

TRANSUBSTANTIATION IN THE SPACE BETWEEN CREATION AND CHANGE

What might we draw from this somewhat torturously close analysis of an article from the *Summa theologiae*? In displaying this careful dissection of a single piece of Eucharistic language and suggesting that in the end even a statement like Ambrose's can be made to fit the parameters of doctrinal grammar, have I perhaps simply confirmed suspicions that transubstantiation hovers somewhere between a hyper-rational dissection of a mystery and sheer nonsensical magical assertion, that it is a conjuring trick with language that conveys a sense of logical rigor but can in fact accommodate almost anything? Moreover, does Thomas's justification of the language of "making" Christ's Body justify Chauvet's suspicion that he, too, falls prey to a "productionist"

39. For the language of the accidents as "mediating" see *Super Sent.* 4.10.1.1 ad 5; *Contra Gentiles* 4.64.4–5; *Summa theologiae* 3.76.5 and 3.76.7 ad 1.

40. Brock, "St Thomas and the Eucharistic Conversion," 559–61. A similar explanation is offered by Aquinas for Paul's words in 1 Corinthians 11:26: "For as often as you eat this bread," etc. See *Super I Cor.* 11.6.686.

account of sacramental causality? I hope to show that neither of these things is the case.

Perhaps what is most clear from the analysis that he offers in *Summa theologiae* 3.75.8 is that Thomas seeks to locate Eucharistic conversion in the logical space between natural change and creation by employing a kind of hybrid grammar, a creole. Sometimes statements about natural change provide a paradigm for well-formed sentences concerning Christ's Eucharistic presence, and sometimes statements about creation provide the appropriate paradigm. We might say that the proper conceptual location for Eucharistic conversion is an interstitial one, and this location is appropriately marked by the word "transubstantiation."[41] Why is this an appropriate location, and why is "transubstantiation" an appropriate marker for this location?

As to conceptual location: first, Eucharistic conversion is fittingly spoken of in the way that we speak of creation because both involve the production of an entire substance and not simply the educing of a new form in matter.[42] Of course, in speaking of substance, we are also speaking of being (*esse*), which is the proper act of a substance.[43] Thus Thomas writes in his commentary on First Corinthians, "The consecration does not occur by the consecrated matter merely receiving some spiritual power, but by the fact that it is transubstantiated according to its *esse* into

41. This is a point that Chauvet, for example, well recognizes. See his remarks in *Symbol and Sacrament*, 386.

42. This claim, involving as it does the word "substance," is a neuralgic point for some; there has been for several decades much handwringing among Catholic theologians over the presence of the word "substance" in the term "transubstantiation." After all, isn't "substance" (not to mention "accident") tied to an outmoded Aristotelian science? Don't we need newer, more up-to-date terms? Don't we need something less "onto-theological" or "metaphysical"? I think that at least in this case, such anxiety is radically misplaced. While Thomas's language of "substance" undoubtedly contains overtones of a view of the cosmos that most of us no longer hold, this is in no way a disqualifying debility. Particularly in the context of Eucharistic conversion, the way in which Aquinas uses "substance" sits so lightly to the details of Aristotle's account that one ought to understand it in its most bare-bones sense as *hoc aliquid*—"this something" (*In Physic.* 3.1.280).

43. *Contra Gentiles* 2.54.3.

the body of Christ."[44] What is ultimately at stake in speaking of the conversion of substance is precisely this claim that what we encounter in the Eucharist is the *esse substantiale* or, better, the *esse personale* of Christ. As Colman O'Neill emphasized, what is at stake in recognizing the substantial presence of Christ in the Eucharist is not the recognition of a kind of thing but of a unique person. He writes that if we "leave aside all but the most primitive of concepts and . . . concentrate on the utter purity of existential judgement which expresses our first, uncomplicated recognition of the other as other—perhaps when we say: 'Why, it is you'—then the authentic meaning of 'substance' is given because it has been instinctively recognized simply in recognition of the other."[45] Because what becomes present to us in the Eucharist is the act of existing that is the personal being of Jesus Christ, the Eucharistic conversion is spoken of in ways that conform to the production of substances *ex nihilo*, the beginning to be of *actus essendi* that we call "creation."[46] Indeed, while Aquinas locates transubstantiation between creation and natural change, the balance tilts rather decidedly toward creation and, therefore, the gift of *esse*.

And yet, Eucharistic conversion is also fittingly spoken of in the way that we speak of natural change. This is because Eucharistic conversion, like natural change, is an event that occurs in our world against the background of creation, whereas creation is not a change in our world but rather the reason why we have a world at all.[47] By virtue of the Resurrection and Ascension, Christ's body shares in God's own transcendence and impassibility, and any fitting account of his Eucharistic presence must take

44. *Super I Cor.* 11.5.670.

45. Colman E. O'Neill, *Sacramental Realism: A General Theory of the Sacraments* (Wilmington, DE: Michael Glazier, 1983), 155. See also Edward Schillebeeckx, *The Eucharist* (London: Burns and Oates, 2005), 63.

46. Of course, the bread beginning to be the Body of Christ is *un*like creation inasmuch as it is not a beginning to be *ex nihilo*, since the body of Christ already exists and, even more significantly, the person of Christ is eternal.

47. See chapter 4, above.

account of this. That is to say, Eucharistic conversion must be a change that occurs in *this* world, or it is no change at all. Stephen Brock notes, "This is the decisive point for Thomas: the body of Christ cannot begin to exist in the sacrament by any change in the body itself [Summa theologiae 3.75.2]. It must do so by a change undergone by something else."[48] The paradigm of natural change serves to point to the this-worldly character of the change that is transubstantiation. The tenseless grammar of creation is inadequate for indicating that there is a true process of becoming, a real *transitus*, involved: Christ becomes our food, not by becoming bread and wine, but by the this-worldly reality of bread and wine becoming Christ.

Thus, the balance tilts toward the language of creation, but not completely. And this is why Thomas says that Eucharistic conversion has "its own name," which is transubstantiation.[49] Neither creation nor natural change can in the end furnish us with the paradigm for well-formed sentences about Christ's Eucharistic presence. The uniqueness of the term "transubstantiation" is its combination of the *transitus* that we know from the immanent natural process of one substantial form "passing into" another with the transcendent beginning to be of substances that we call "creation."

Is it, then, the case that transubstantiation tends, as Chauvet claims, to a conceiving of the Eucharist as a process of production in which Christ's body becomes an object that is available in a fashion that is, as it were, indifferent to its reception by the faithful? Chauvet assumes that the language of efficient causality must imply the soulless production of inert objects, but this is not the case. Wouldn't we rather say that in creation *ex nihilo* God produces the world, yet not as an inert object but as the gift of existence? Bernhard Blankenhorn has suggested that Aquinas's

48. Brock, "St Thomas and the Eucharistic Conversion," 533. This is why, Brock notes, Thomas rejects the idea that the bread is annihilated (see Brock, 544).

49. *Summa theologiae* 3.75.4.

language of sacraments as instrumental efficient causes derives not from the onto-theological tradition but from the scriptural image of Wisdom as God's "artisan" (Wis. 7:22) through whom God creates the world out of love. As he notes, "Precisely when Scripture most explicitly connects the language of the Creator God to the notion of artistic production do we find the clearest teaching that creation is an act of divine love."[50] Likewise in the Eucharist. Located between creation from nothing and artisanal making, the language of transubstantiation seems almost designed to lead us *away* from a "productionist" model. Like creation, it is not a process of production because it is not a natural process at all but simply a supernatural gift. Yet, like natural change, it is a transformation that occurs in our world because it occurs for our sake. Christ is not present indifferently but personally, for us and for our salvation.

In Thomas, the term "transubstantiation" is the fruit of the modest, but ferociously difficult, endeavor to understand the primary speech of the Church about the Eucharistic mystery. It does not name a theory of Eucharistic conversion; it does not give us a list of ingredients (substance, accidents, dimensive quantity, etc.) nor describe the process of transformation by which Christ becomes present. Nor is it simply a fideistic affirmation of the magical presence of Christ behind the shadows of bread and wine. Rather, it gives us some glimpse of the Eucharistic mystery by locating the event of Christ's presence in an interstitial location, not between rationalism and magic, but between the grammars of creation and natural change. In response to the third objection in *Summa theologiae* 3.75.8, Aquinas grants the objector's point: speaking of the Eucharistic conversion of one entire substance into another entire substance *does* imply something more miraculous than creation. He simply does not think that this makes

50. Bernhard Blankenhorn, "The Instrumental Causality of the Sacraments: Thomas Aquinas and Louis-Marie Chauvet," *Nova et Vetera* 4, no. 2 (Spring 2006): 281.

transubstantiation false; rather, it situates it in a space of supreme wonder. Transubstantiation is more miraculous than creation, not because it requires more divine productive power, but because it shows forth more clearly the nature of that divine power by using the grammar of creation to speak of God's drawing near in redemption. For while creation might be ascribed to a deity who acts at a distance, the Eucharist shows forth a divine power that is transcendent precisely in being present to us as our pilgrim food.

Epilogue

Thomas Today

14

Augustine and Thomas in Modern Catholic Rhetoric

In Sint-Pieterskerk in Leuven, Belgium, there is a painting of Saint Augustine and Saint Thomas Aquinas by Pieter-Jozef Verhaghen (1728–1811), a late follower of Rubens, in which Augustine is pointing to a place in a book he is holding, possibly the Scriptures or one of Augustine's own works, and Thomas is peering intently at the place Augustine is indicating and writing diligently in the book he himself is holding. While hardly a masterpiece of Flemish painting, or even one of Verhaghen's own better works, it is interesting in the harmonious relationship it depicts between the two Doctors of the Church, as well as Augustine's tutelage of Thomas, which indicates not only Thomas's debt to Augustine but even a certain subservience: it is clear who is the teacher and who is the student. The relationship depicted is particularly striking because in modern, post–Vatican II Catholic theology, Augustine and Thomas have come to serve as rhetorical "tropes"—symbolic stand-ins—for distinct and even opposed styles of theological reflection.[1] Specifically, "Thomas" serves as a marker for an attitude of optimistic openness to the modern world while "Augustine" stands for all who are pessimistically disposed to that same modern world.

* Originally published as "Augustine and Aquinas," in *The T&T Clark Companion to Augustine and Modern Theology*, ed. Chad Pecknold and Tarmo Toom (Edinburgh: T&T Clark, 2013), 113–30.

1. For this particular use of the term "trope," see Hayden White, *Tropics of Discourse: Essays in Cultural Criticism* (Baltimore, MD: Johns Hopkins University Press, 1978).

As will probably come as no surprise, this rhetorical use of the names "Augustine" and "Thomas" does scant justice to the complexity of the actual theology of these two writers and the debt that Thomas owes to Augustine. Moreover, if one compares recent uses of these names as tropes to earlier ones, one sees that they have not always functioned as metonyms for pessimism and optimism, and that confusing earlier rhetorical deployments of Augustine and Thomas with later ones can lead to misleading ways of mapping the territory of contemporary Catholic theology. Moreover, the terms themselves are something less than value-neutral descriptions and as such seem to me ultimately neither helpful in understanding the current theological terrain nor for imagining how Augustine and Thomas might serve as useful resources for theologians today.

THOMAS THE AUGUSTINIAN

No Western Christian theologian escapes the influence of Augustine, and the depth of Thomas's debt to Augustine is widely recognized among historical theologians.[2] Servais Pinckaers notes that in the Second Part of the *Summa theologiae*, for example, Thomas cites Augustine 1,630 times, slightly more often than he cites Aristotle (1,546) and far more often than he cites Gregory the Great, who comes in a distant third (439).[3] In Thomas's commentary on the Gospel of John, we find an almost continual stream of citations from Augustine's own *Tractates* on John. But Thomas's Augustinianism goes beyond what can be quantified by totaling up citations.

Some of Augustine's influence on Thomas might be

2. See the essays collected in *Aquinas the Augustinian*, ed. Michael Dauphinais, Barry David, and Matthew Levering (Washington, DC: The Catholic University of America Press, 2007), especially the introduction.

3. Servais-Théodore Pinckaers, "The Sources of the Ethics of St. Thomas Aquinas," in *The Ethics of Aquinas*, ed. Stephen J. Pope (Washington, DC: Georgetown University Press, 2002), 17.

characterized as "philosophical." Though interpreters of Thomas disagree on how best to understand the Neoplatonic elements in his thought—whether as grace notes in an essentially Aristotelian worldview or as the key to a distinctive synthesis of Platonism and Aristotle—what is clear is that Augustine, along with Dionysius the Areopagite, is a significant source of those elements.[4] Notions such as divine ideas and the blending of Aristotelian causality with Platonic participation are part of Thomas's inheritance from Augustine. At the same time, because Thomas must deal with the flood of Aristotelian and quasi-Aristotelian texts that entered the West in the twelfth century, he in many ways lives in a vastly different philosophical world than Augustine—not least because it is a world in which a distinction between "philosophy" and "theology" is beginning (but only beginning) to be comprehensible.

On many doctrinal points, Thomas uses Augustine in ways that are unsurprising for a medieval Catholic theologian. For example, in his treatment of the Trinity, he follows virtually all Western theologians in using Augustine's "psychological analogy" of human memory, understanding, and will.[5] However, Thomas uses Aristotle's understanding of "immanent operations" to enrich and refine Augustine, arguing that, just as reasoning produces an idea that is itself not "outside" the mind, so too the Word proceeds from the Father without being "outside" of what it is to be God, thus making the analogy arguably more dynamic than it is in Augustine.[6] At the same time, Thomas modifies Aristotle—for whom an immanent operation is in no sense productive of anything—in an Augustinian direction by arguing that, at least in a

4. Wayne Hankey, however, argues that the Proclian Neoplatonism of Dionysius is a more significant influence on Thomas than the Plotinian Neoplatonism of Augustine. See *God in Himself: Aquinas' Doctrine of God as expounded in the "Summa Theologiae"* (Oxford: Oxford University Press, 1987).

5. See Augustine, *De Trinitate* 10.

6. See *Summa theologiae* 1.27.

Trinitarian context, the immanent operation of the Father issues in the divine Word, who is a distinct person within God.[7]

Perhaps even more indicative of Thomas's debt to Augustine than his adoption of and engagement with Augustinian commonplaces are the theological points at which he takes a distinctively Augustinian position over and against the prevailing Western medieval consensus.

One example is Thomas's account of the sacraments, in which he continues the rehabilitation, begun by Peter Lombard, of Augustine's theology of sacraments as belonging to the category of "sign." This view of sacraments, which can be found in various places in Augustine's writings,[8] fell under something of a cloud in the High Middle Ages, in part because of the use to which it was put by Berengar of Tours in his Eucharistic theology. Berengar's view was that if the Eucharist is, as Augustine said, a sign of Christ's body, then it could not be the reality of Christ's body, since a sign (*signum*) is by definition distinct from the thing (*res*) to which it refers.[9] Lombard sought to retrieve the Augustinian theology of sacraments as signs of grace by supplementing it with the notion of sacraments as causes of grace: in addition to being signs, sacraments were also causes.[10] This supplementation presumably would banish the specter of Berengar from sacramental theology. Thomas's insight was that the Augustinian theology of sacramental signs did not need supplementation by a theology of sacramental causality but rather simply the clarification that it is by virtue of their signification that sacraments are causes: *sacramenta significando causant.*[11] Sacraments are not two kinds of things—signs and causes—but rather a particular *kind*

7. See Gilles Emery, *The Trinitarian Theology of Saint Thomas Aquinas*, trans. Francesca Aran Murphy (Oxford: Oxford University Press, 2007), 58–59.

8. See, e.g., Augustine, *De civitate Dei* 10.5; *De catechizandis rudibus* 26.50.

9. This was at least what Berengar was understood by his opponents to be saying. See Lanfranc of Canterbury, *De corpore et sanguine Domini adversus Berengarium* 20.

10. Peter Lombard, *Sententiae* 4.1.4.

11. *De veritate* 28.2 ad 12.

of sign: one that brings about an effect and not simply a pointer to something else. Thus, Thomas can affirm, even more strongly than Lombard, the sign-character of sacraments without compromising their causal efficacy.

An even clearer example of Augustine's influence on Thomas is the way in which his views on grace developed over the course of his life. In his earlier writings, Thomas follows the prevailing theological view of his day that one can dispose oneself to the reception of God's grace by doing what is within one's capacity to do, and to such a one, God will not deny grace.[12] It was through reading Augustine's later writings on grace that Thomas came to see that such a view was inadequate, leading him to modify his views such that even one's preparation to receive sanctifying grace must itself be a work of God's grace.[13] Just as Thomas uses Aristotle's notion of immanent operations to enrich Augustinian Trinitarian theology, here Thomas affirmed this Augustinian position on grace by means of the Aristotelian understanding of the need for matter to be properly disposed to receive a form, thus using Aristotle to help him articulate a *more* Augustinian position than he had held previously.

These two examples must suffice to bolster the claim that, while Thomas did not feel compelled to follow him in all matters, Augustine remained a determinative influence upon Thomas, so much so that Thomas is fruitfully understood as representing one strand of the medieval Augustinian heritage, as much as Bonaventure or Henry of Ghent.[14] This claim also seems to run against the grain of modern Catholic tropes that divide the theological world up into Augustinians and Thomists. But what if the division between Augustine and Thomas is not a material one between specific

12. See *Super Sent.* 2.5.2.1; cf. 2.28.4.1.

13. *Summa theologiae* 1-2.109.6.

14. On the difficulties inherent in using a term like "the medieval Augustinian heritage," see Eric Leland Saak, *Creating Augustine: Interpreting Augustine and Augustinianism in the Later Middle Ages* (Oxford: Oxford University Press, 2012), 1–22.

theological conclusions but rather a "formal" one, a difference in fundamental attitude? This would seem to be the implicit claim of those who invoke Augustine and Thomas as rhetorical tropes. If we look at the way one set of early-twentieth-century Catholic thinkers used the terms "Augustinian" and "Thomist," it may help us to critically evaluate more recent uses of those tropes.

THE RESTLESS HEART AND THE SCIENTIFIC MIND

The term "Augustinian" is not a medieval term; it first appears in the seventeenth century as an adjective associated with the Order of Saint Augustine. The first use in English of "Augustinianism" to identify a theological position was in 1830 when it was used to describe, interestingly enough, the theology of grace in Thomas Aquinas.[15] The fact that the term arrives so late upon the scene, and was at times used to characterize Thomas's position over and against others, indicates that even when the terms "Augustinian" and "Thomist" have been used, they have not always been used in the same way.

In the first part of the twentieth century, one way of figuring the Augustine-Thomas distinction was as a distinction between a theology flowing directly from religious experience and a theology that had been rationally structured so as to attain a "scientific" status. Given the great authority of both Augustine and Thomas, there was little interest in pitting them against each other.[16] Rather, the difference was seen as a complementary one in which the Augustinian focus on experience needed Thomas's scientific methodology in order for theology to be a rational discipline, while Thomistic theological science needed the existential

15. Saak, 3.

16. An exception seems to be Lucien Laberthonnière (1860–1932), who early on identified himself as an "Augustinian" and later in his life apparently harangued the young Étienne Gilson, while riding together on a trolley, concerning the evils wrought by Thomas Aquinas in Catholic thought. See Marvin R. O'Connell, *Critics on Trial: An Introduction to the Catholic Modernist Crisis* (Washington, DC: The Catholic University of America Press, 1994), 367.

fervor of Augustine in order not to degenerate into mere rationalism. There were, however, different emphases with regard to which was the more pressing need.

These different emphases can be seen in a collection of essays published in 1930 to commemorate the fifteen-hundredth anniversary of Augustine's death. Contributors included some of the most illustrious Catholic public intellectuals of the early twentieth century, including Jacques Maritain (1882–1973), Maurice Blondel (1861–1949), and Étienne Gilson (1884–1978). Maritain and Gilson can rather uncontroversially be described as "Thomists," while Blondel is sometimes described as "Augustinian," though it was only late in his life that he turned to an actual study of Augustine.[17] All three posit a fundamental harmony between Augustine and Thomas while recognizing real differences between them and parsing those differences in distinct ways.

Maritain describes the difference between Augustine and Thomas by quoting with approval a remark by Pascal: "The heart has its order, and so has the mind."[18] For Maritain, Augustine's favored philosophical framework, Neoplatonism, is "incontestably deficient,"[19] but this in no way harms his theology because it is rooted not in acquired human reason but in infused divine wisdom.[20] One can speak only equivocally of the "metaphysics" of Augustine, if we mean by this a rational human discourse on being;[21] what he in fact offers is a rich metaphysical intuition rooted in religious experience.[22] Augustine's thought is best conceived of as something like the raw material upon which Thomistic science

17. See Oliva Blanchette, *Maurice Blondel: A Philosophical Life* (Grand Rapids, MI: Eerdmans, 2010), 360.

18. Jacques Maritain, "St. Augustine and St. Thomas Aquinas," in *St. Augustine: His Age, Life, and Thought* (New York: Meridian Books, 1957), 199, citing Pascal, *Pensées*, §283.

19. Maritain, 203.

20. Maritain, 206.

21. Maritain, 209.

22. Maritain, 210.

operates, giving it order and the rationally compelling power of the deductive syllogism. Maritain writes,

> How foolish to oppose Thomism and Augustinianism as two systems (I mean the Augustinianism of St. Augustine himself)! The first is a system, the second is not. Thomism is the scientific state of Christian wisdom; in the case of the Fathers and St. Augustine, Christian wisdom is still a mere spring.[23]

The wisdom flowing from this spring has passed entirely into Thomism, where it has been transformed into Christian philosophy.[24] This Christian philosophy must "live and spiritualize itself in contact with the living faith and experiences of the Christian soul" while at the same time it "is rigorously independent of the subject's own dispositions, and wishes to be regulated by objective necessities and intelligible constraints."[25] It is Augustine who recalls for us the former truth, and Thomas who reminds us of the latter, and in this division of labor we find their complementarity.[26]

Gilson, perhaps thinking of philosophers like Maritain, notes the "disfavor of which St. Augustine, *qua* philosopher, has been the butt in the minds of many Catholic thinkers."[27] Augustinianism is, Gilson says, "structurally quite different" from Thomism, particularly in its "incompleteness" and the "intuitive rather than systematic genius" with which Augustine Christianized Platonism.[28] These features leave it open to the kinds of misunderstanding and

23. Maritain, 219.

24. Maritain, 218.

25. Maritain, 223.

26. There seems to be at least a formal similarity between the relationship of Augustinian religious experience to Thomist theological science, on the one hand, and Maritain's understanding of the relationship of "eidetic visualization" (i.e., the intuition of being) and metaphysics proper on the other. For the latter, see the description of Maritain's metaphysics in Helen James John, *The Thomist Spectrum* (New York: Fordham University Press, 1966), 17–24.

27. Étienne Gilson, "The Future of Augustinian Metaphysics," in *St. Augustine: His Age, Life, and Thought*, 291.

28. Gilson, 291–92.

distortions we find in Cartesianism and Ontologism. These can be overcome, however, by a return to Augustine himself and a recognition of the role of grace in his thought.[29] Without grace, Augustinianism is "a strange metaphysical monster," for it is grace that "turns knowledge into wisdom and moral effort into virtue."[30] The very notion of a metaphysics in which grace plays an essential role already indicates Gilson's distance from Maritain. Like Maritain, Gilson sees Thomas's thought as proceeding along a path quite distinct from Augustine, but he sees this as the difference between two different philosophies rather than between what is philosophy and what is something else. By comparison with Augustine's philosophy, Thomas's is oriented less toward the soul and more toward the cosmos—a cosmos that operates according to the laws intrinsic to created natures.[31] With their philosophical differences, Augustine and Thomas "can meet again in the same conclusions, but the roads leading to them, though constantly crossing, never follow at any point the same direction."[32]

For Maritain, there is a single philosophy, Thomism, which alone can raise theology to the status of a true science. For Gilson, there are multiple philosophies that can be employed by theologians, and Augustine and Thomas provide two of these, one more subjectively focused and the other more objective. Despite his philosophical pluralism, however, Gilson shows a clear preference for Thomism, which has in his eyes already shown its ability to incorporate the insights flowing from Augustine's focus on the human soul; it remains to be seen for Gilson whether Augustinianism can similarly incorporate the insights that flow from Thomas's cosmological focus.

Like Gilson, Blondel finds in Augustine a philosophy worthy of the name. Unlike Gilson, however, he sees this philosophy as

29. Gilson, 300–301.

30. Gilson, 307–8.

31. Gilson, 310.

32. Gilson, 311.

in no need of having to prove itself vis-à-vis Thomism. Rather, because it presumes "a unity of thought and life," it is "a novel and superior kind of philosophy in close relation to the aspirations and needs of many contemporary minds."[33] It combines, to a supreme degree, "a generally successful effort to achieve such intelligibility as might satisfy a mind possessed of the highest degree of acuteness and perspicacity" with "an impetuosity which masters every detail and seems to transport the whole soul far beyond the regions where dialectic, however vivid and swift, seems a mere bloodless and desiccated assortment of bones."[34] In common with Maritain and Gilson, he rejects all attempts to pit Augustine and Thomas against each other. However, he rejects Maritain's approach, in which Augustine and Thomas were seen as pursuing quite distinct ends by quite distinct means; he likewise rejects Gilson's approach, in which Augustine and Thomas follow distinct paths to a common end.[35] Blondel, rather, seems to interpret Thomas in light of Augustine. He agrees in a sense with Maritain that there is no *separable* philosophy in St. Augustine but says that the same is true of Thomas himself. Both Augustine and Thomas affirm that "there is in the nature of a spiritual being a desire to see God, an aspiration toward beatitude . . . a desire which sets our mind and will in motion toward a goal inaccessible in the order of nature."[36] In other words, Blondel interprets Thomas's account of the mind's dynamic orientation toward knowledge of causes in light of Augustine's account of the restless heart that can find rest only in God.

In Blondel's reading of Thomas in light of Augustine, we see sketched what would become a key issue in mid-twentieth-century Catholic theology: the question of the

33. Maurice Blondel, "The Latent Resources in St. Augustine's Thought," in *St. Augustine: His Age, Life, and Thought*, 319.

34. Blondel, 320.

35. Blondel, 325.

36. Blondel, 330–31.

natural desire for the supernatural vision of God and the implications of this for how one understands the relationship between nature and grace.[37] This is not unrelated to how one conceives of the "scientific" status of theology: Is theology, as many Thomists would have it, a deductive process employing natural human reason to draw conclusions from revealed premises, or is it the quest of the soul, stirred by grace, to seek an understanding adequate to that experience of grace? Blondel saw the thought of Augustine as needed to "stimulate a science of inner dynamism" that can overcome the tendency of neo-Scholastic Thomism to see grace as an extrinsic gift "subsequently imposed on a nature in full possession of itself and capable of ensuring its self-sufficiency."[38] Augustine's account of the restless heart is a necessary reminder that while theology may be a science, it is a science that seeks to conform thought to the exigencies of the spiritual life, and without such a reminder, Thomist science becomes mere rationalism. "The revival of Thomism makes the revival of Augustinianism still more desirable."[39]

If we think of "Augustine" and "Thomas" as rhetorical figures or tropes, then Maritain, Gilson, and Blondel agree in letting Augustine stand for a way of thinking oriented to the human subject and the dynamic of the spiritual life, and in letting Thomas stand for a style of thought more oriented toward a rational grasp of the order of the cosmos. "Augustine" means existential engagement, and "Thomas" means objectivity and abstraction. For Maritain, this means that only Thomas offers a true philosophy and the possibility of a genuinely scientific theology. For Gilson, the Augustinian and Thomist approaches present two different philosophical possibilities, the latter of which has proved its usefulness for theology and the former of which must still be developed. For Blondel, it is Augustine who has proved himself capable of

37. See chapters 1 and 3 above.

38. Blondel, 340–41.

39. Blondel, 342.

uniting thought and life, and it is Thomism (if not Thomas himself) that must be transformed by contact with the philosophical insights of Augustine so as to become capable of articulating the truth that can satisfy the heart's restless yearning for God.

It is Blondel's position that would prove to be influential among many mid-twentieth-century Catholic theologians. As Jürgen Mettepenningen says, "Known for his *theologia affectiva*, Augustine was employed as a sort of crowbar, as it were, to help break through the monopoly of neo-scholasticism."[40] Not least among the theologians who saw Augustine in this way was Joseph Ratzinger, who, in recalling his early theological formation in the immediate aftermath of the Second World War, comments that his encounter with the personalist philosophy of Martin Buber "was for me a spiritual experience that left an essential mark, especially since I spontaneously associated such personalism with the thought of St. Augustine, who in his *Confessions* had struck me with the power of all his human passion and depth." He continues, "By contrast, I had difficulties penetrating the thought of Thomas Aquinas, whose crystal-clear logic seemed to me to be too closed in on itself, too impersonal and ready-made." Ratzinger does go on to acknowledge that at least part of his difficulty was the "rigid, neoscholastic" form of Thomism that he was taught,[41] and later in life he would describe Thomas's thought not as "impersonal" but as "precise, lucid and pertinent."[42] We might say that the Thomas that Ratzinger comes to appreciate is not the Thomas of Thomistic science but the Thomas who is read, in the manner of Blondel, as an heir to the Augustinian project of seeking a knowing adequate to the yearnings of the restless heart. Interestingly, this is not how many modern interpreters of the

40. Jürgen Mettepenningen, *Nouvelle Théologie—New Theology: Inheritor of Modernism, Precursor of Vatican II* (London: T&T Clark, 2010), 145.

41. Joseph Ratzinger, *Milestones: Memoirs: 1927–1977*, trans. Erasmo Leiva-Merikakis (San Francisco: Ignatius, 1998), 44.

42. Benedict XVI, "St. Thomas Aquinas (3)," general audience, June 23, 2010, vatican.va.

post-conciliar theological scene understand the Augustinianism of Ratzinger and how it differs from Thomism.

CHURCH AND WORLD: PESSIMISM AND OPTIMISM

Various theologians seeking to map the world of Catholic theology after the Second Vatican Council have employed "Augustine" and "Thomas" as tropes in ways quite different from the way they are employed by Maritain, Gilson, and Blondel. Here, the relevant distinction is not between subjectivity and objectivity or between the heart and the mind but between pessimism and optimism, particularly with regard to the modern world. Thus, Ratzinger's early attraction to Augustine and rejection of Thomism is seen as an incipient manifestation of a pessimistic theology.[43] Such an interpretation is given a degree of plausibility to the degree that one accepts a particular use of "Augustine" and "Thomas" as rhetorical tropes for pessimism and optimism and ignores earlier uses, such as we find in Maritain, Gilson, and Blondel.

To choose one example among many of such uses, Dominic Doyle, in discussing the "Augustinian" character of Pope Benedict's encyclical *Spe Salvi*, notes that he will use the terms "Augustinian" and "Thomist" as "imprecise generalizations that attempt to name differing emphases in theologians who take their lead from Augustine or Thomas respectively." He goes on to say that "an 'Augustinian' sensibility would insist on a sharp contrast between eschatological and secular hope, the deep and ineradicable nature of sin, and thus the limits—even tragic flaws—of all human projects." A Thomist sensibility, in contrast, would follow Thomas in his defense of "'true yet imperfect virtues' that intend temporal goods, such as 'the welfare of the state.'"[44] In

43. See, for example, Massimo Faggioli, *Vatican II: The Battle for Meaning* (New York: Paulist, 2012), 72.

44. Dominic Doyle, "*Spe Salvi* on Eschatological and Secular Hope: A Thomistic Critique of an Augustinian Encyclical," *Theological Studies* 71, no. 2 (May 2010): 350–79, at 351n3.

other words, an Augustinian casts a wary eye at the modern world and its projects for human progress, seeing them as irrevocably marked by human pride, whereas a Thomist embraces, albeit not uncritically, the genuine goods that the modern world has to offer, seeing human historical progress as contributing in some way to the growth in history of God's kingdom.

This distinction is often used, without Doyle's caveat concerning "imprecise generalizations," to describe the way in which those who at the Second Vatican Council were united in their opposition to neo-Scholasticism split in the aftermath of the council into opposed camps. Massimo Faggioli identifies not only Ratzinger but also Henri de Lubac, Jean Daniélou, Hans Urs von Balthasar, and Louis Bouyer as "neo-Augustinians" and Yves Congar, Marie-Dominique Chenu, Edward Schillebeeckx, Karl Rahner, and Bernard Lonergan as examples of "reinterpreted Thomism" (presumably to distinguish their views from preconciliar neo-Thomism).[45] Prior to the council, one sometimes finds "Augustine" and "Thomas" used, particularly by those who identify as "Thomist," as tropes for pessimism and optimism—world-denial and world-affirmation—but it is with the debate over "Schema 13," which became the Pastoral Constitution on the Church in the Modern World, *Gaudium et Spes*, that divisions within the preconciliar "progressives" begin to become apparent.[46] So let us look at a representative figure that Faggioli identifies with each of these two camps to see the sense in which they are "Thomist" and "Augustinian."

Perhaps no one was as resolute in identifying an optimistic affirmation of the world as "Thomist" against a purported "Augustinian" pessimism than the Dominican Marie-Dominique Chenu (1895–1990). Writing prior to the council, he contrasted

45. Faggioli, *Vatican II*, 69, 75–76.

46. See Joseph A. Komonchak, "Augustine, Aquinas or the Gospel *sine glossa*? Divisions over *Gaudium et Spes*," in *Unfinished Journey: The Church 40 Years After Vatican II: Essays for John Wilkins*, ed. Austen Ivereigh (London: Continuum, 2003), 102–18.

Augustine's view that the workings of grace in history appear to us only as incomprehensible "haphazard events" with Thomas's "ontological optimism" that the order of the world is graspable by the human mind.[47] In a collection of essays published a few years after the council, Chenu speaks of Thomas's recognition of the value of corporeality as the foundation of "his optimistic vision of man and of the world."[48] This optimistic vision is that "it is the human and divine truth of man that his spirit should penetrate the corporeal world, including his own body, for man is the demiurge of that world and responsible for it before his Creator."[49] This provides the foundation for engagement with the world, for secular history is the theater in which the world's salvation is played out. Chenu describes Augustine, on the other hand, as "a temporary victim of Manicheism" whose "whole life was colored by an unusually sad experience of uncontrolled passion."[50] Whereas Blondel had seen Augustine's thought as close to the aspirations of modern people, Chenu argues that "it is only by accepting this [Thomist] view of creation and in accepting this Christian meaning of man that the Christian can take his place in our new scientific and technological civilization."[51] Just as Thomas embraced the new Aristotelian science of his day and put it to an evangelical purpose, so modern-day Christians should embrace the insights and aspirations of their day—even those coming from modern-day "pagans"—and place them in service of the Gospel.

One frequently named "Augustinian" is Jean Daniélou (1905–1974), who early in his career made remarks critical of neo-Scholastic Thomism and proposed the Fathers of the early

47. Marie-Dominique Chenu, *Aquinas and His Role in Theology* [1959], trans. Paul Philibert (Collegeville, MN: Liturgical, 2002), 88.

48. Marie-Dominique Chenu, *Faith and Theology*, trans. Denis Hickey (New York: MacMillan, 1968), 136.

49. Chenu, 134.

50. Chenu, 108.

51. Chenu, 111.

Church as the way forward for theology. Further, Daniélou writes that in comparison to optimistic views of history, "pessimistic doctrines . . . seem far more sensible" and that "those who have seen furthest into human nature are all pessimists, like Augustine, Pascal, and Kierkegaard."[52] He speaks with approval of Augustine's spiritual interpretation of the season of Lent as representing life in this world, "through which we make our way under the constant attractions and repulsions of the march of time, the instability and mutability of human affairs, the irresistible flow of change."[53] Our modern period is, Daniélou asserts, "heathen . . . and divided, and ruinous."[54] Here the charge of an Augustinian pessimism seems to be borne out. However, despite his mention of Augustine, Daniélou never identifies his own position as an "Augustinian" one. In fact, while the author of *The City of God* would seem to necessarily play a significant role in any Western theologian's account of history, Daniélou has a greater affinity for the Greek Fathers.[55] And when he comes to discuss hope, which he sees as the true Christian attitude toward history rather than pessimism, Daniélou invokes Thomas (*Summa theologiae* 2-2.17.3) to make the point that, because of the bonds of charity, the object of hope is never simply the individual but "the final destiny of the world and of the whole human race."[56] In the end, hope trumps both pessimism and optimism.

When we compare Chenu and Daniélou, we can see the curious asymmetry in the assigning of the labels "Augustinian" and "Thomist" in the postconciliar theological world. That is, it seems to be primarily those who assign the label "Thomist" to themselves who are also the ones who assign the label "Augustinian"

52. Jean Daniélou, *The Lord of History: Reflections on the Inner Meaning of History*, trans. Nigel Abercrombie (London: Longmans, Green, 1958), 342.

53. Augustine, *Sermon* 252 (PL 38:1177–78), quoted in Daniélou, *Lord of History*, 266.

54. Daniélou, *Lord of History*, 346.

55. He was also appreciative of the thought of Teilhard de Chardin, who is rarely accused of pessimism.

56. Daniélou, *Lord of History*, 353.

to others. While one can certainly find theologians who, like Daniélou, write sympathetically of Augustine's views on a range of issues, one has a bit more trouble finding those who identify *themselves* as "Augustinian" *rather than* "Thomist." It is perhaps a measure of the esteem accorded to Thomas after the encyclical *Aeterni Patris* that everyone felt that they needed to be Thomist in some sense, and that the theological high ground could be seized by identifying oneself as "Thomist," even if, as sometimes happens, a closer inspection of the actual theological views of the one claiming the Thomist mantle proved to be quite different from those of Thomas himself. Massimo Faggioli speaks of the recognition by "progressive" neo-Thomists of the need "to adopt Thomas's approach rather than his conclusions."[57] This is an interesting contrast with the view of Gilson noted earlier, in which Augustine and Thomas, while their philosophical approaches differed, were compatible inasmuch as their theological conclusions concurred. For Faggioli, Thomas's actual conclusions seem somewhat beside the point; it is his approach of openness to the world, so different from Augustinian pessimism, that is to be valued today. One cannot help but suspect that in such cases, Thomas is being invoked more as an ornament than as an expert.[58] It is certainly to the advantage of theologians to be able to claim the authority of Thomas for their own position, particularly in the postconciliar context when so much seems up for grabs. It is reassuring to have the "common doctor" endorse one's policy of openness to the modern world.

This focus on Thomas's general approach rather than his specific conclusions also helps in separating "Augustinians" and "Thomists" into distinct camps. As we have seen, Thomas agrees

57. Faggioli, *Vatican II*, 79.

58. The terms "expert" and "ornament" are taken from Carlo Leget, who gives a nuanced taxonomy of the different ways the authority of Thomas can be invoked in various realms of argumentation. See "Authority and Plausibility: Aquinas on Suicide," in *Aquinas as Authority*, ed. Paul van Geest, Harm Goris, and Carlo Leget (Leuven: Peeters, 2002), 277–93, esp. 286–87.

with Augustine in many of his theological positions. But if one relativizes the importance of those positions in favor of claiming kinship with his "approach," then it becomes easier to map the theological territory of contemporary Catholicism. Thus Augustine, who in the early twentieth century served as a crowbar to break through the stranglehold of neo-Scholasticism on Catholic theology, can become a metonym for reactionary pessimism.

THOMAS THE AUGUSTINIAN REDUX: *PEREGRINI* AND *VIATORES*

The shifting significance of Augustine makes us question how helpful it is to speak, as Faggioli does, of Augustinian or Thomist "schools." Both Augustine and Thomas were thinkers whose written output is vast in scope and variegated in character. Any "school" that we might identify as Augustinian or Thomist will surely be characterized by only a small subset of the positions held by the historical figure from which it draws its name. If we are concerned that the terms "Augustinian" and "Thomist" be actually meaningful, then it is incumbent upon us to specify exactly what we mean by the terms. If we speak of someone's position as "Augustinian," do we mean that she holds to some form of knowledge via divine illumination rather than abstraction from sense experience, or do we mean that she holds to a theology whose form of rationality is not some version of Aristotelian science, or do we mean that she sees the virtues of non-Christians as "splendid vices" rather than real but imperfect human virtues, or do we mean that she holds that there is a plurality of substantial forms that make up the human person rather than the rational soul being the single substantial form of the human being? All of these and more have been used at various points in history to identify an "Augustinian" view over and against a "Thomist" one. It is not only dubious that these positions were all held by the historical figure Aurelius Augustinus Hipponensis, but it is also not clear that these various positions necessarily hold together in such a way as to form a school of thought.

Even if one specifies that one means by "Augustinian" not specific theological conclusions but an attitude of pessimistic suspicion toward the world, and by "Thomist" an attitude of optimistic openness to what the modern world has to offer, problems remain. Chenu made as good an effort as anyone to show how Thomas's metaphysics, ethics, and theology all hung together in a way that allowed a joyful embrace of the world, an embrace that should characterize Christians in their approach to the world today. But in the end, his picture of Thomas remains somewhat unconvincing. Even if we prescind from specific theological positions, Thomas remained by disposition as "otherworldly" as Augustine—indeed, perhaps more so. Augustine was not only a fierce combatant in the theological controversies of his day, he was also involved in very mundane aspects of life in Hippo by virtue of his role as bishop, ranging from providing pastoral care to settling property disputes.[59] In the case of Thomas, there is more than simply hagiography at work in the story of the student who, admiring the city of Paris from a distance, said to him, "What a beautiful city Paris is," to which Thomas replied, "I would rather have the homilies of Chrysostom on the Gospel of blessed Matthew."[60] We misread Thomas if we forget that he was a thirteenth-century mendicant friar who lived a highly ascetic lifestyle that was single-mindedly devoted to the preaching of the Gospel for the edification of the Church and the intellectual defeat of her enemies. Even his meticulous commentaries on Aristotle were ordered to that end. Moreover, it is good to remember that the Thomas who wrote that "grace perfects and does not

59. See F. van der Meer, *Augustine the Bishop: The Life and Work of a Father of the Church*, trans. Brian Battershaw and G.R. Lamb (London: Sheed & Ward, 1961), 255–70.

60. Guillame de Tocco, *Ystoria sancti Thome de Aquino*, ed. Claire le Brun-Gouanvic (Toronto: Pontifical Institute of Mediaeval Studies, 1996), ch. 42.

destroy nature"[61] also wrote, "The more things we do or suffer for God's sake that are contrary to our will, the more the will is found ready for divine love."[62] Thomas, no less than Augustine, recognizes the damage that sin has done to nature and the need for ascetical practices, cooperating with divine grace, to reorient our nature. Commenting on Romans 12:2, Thomas writes,

> Just as a person with a diseased palate does not have right judgment concerning the taste of foods but sometimes recoils from what is sweet and desires what is disgusting, whereas a person with a healthy palate has right judgment concerning tastes, so too a person whose affections are corrupted by conformity to worldly things does not have right judgment concerning the good, whereas a person who has upright and sound affections, because his sense has been renewed by grace, has right judgment concerning the good.[63]

Rather than an undifferentiated, optimistic embrace of the world, Thomas offers criteria by which we can discern between the world as God's good creation and the worldliness that leaves us with a diseased palate, unable to distinguish between the sweetness of divine love and the bitterness of worldly concupiscence.

Likewise, Augustine cannot be characterized simply as a pessimist. We forget at our peril that Augustine and Thomas were alike in rejecting dualist forms of religion—for Augustine the Manichees and for Thomas the Cathars—and affirming the fundamental goodness of creation. In the final book of the *City of God*, Augustine memorably catalogs at great length the miseries of this life: oppressive laws, tedious labor, lies and fraud, extremes of heat and cold, floods and earthquakes, rabid dogs, and famines so severe that mothers eat their children. Such things, Augustine

61. *Summa theologiae* 1.1.8.

62. *De perfectione* 12.

63. *Super Rom.* 12.1.967.

says, teach us "to bewail the calamities of this life and to desire the felicity of the life to come" and remind us that "from this hell upon earth there is no escape, save through the grace of the Savior Christ, our God and Lord."[64] What is less often recalled, however, is the catalog of the blessings in this life that follows this: our very existence and the human capacity for reproduction, the powers of reason and understanding and the arts and sciences that flow from them, human language and culinary arts, mathematics and astronomy, the functioning of our bodily organs and senses, the beauty and utility of our embodied existence, heavenly bodies and earthly creatures, ants and whales, and the subtle variety of all the shades of green that adorn the world.[65] Even amid the devastation wrought by original sin, Augustine can discern the fundamental goodness of creation, not simply the goodness of the natural world, but also and especially the goods of human culture, human scientific ingenuity, and human love. If even in our misery God bestows such a gift on us, what shall be the reward of the blessed?

Without denying the real differences between Augustine and Thomas with regard to how Christians should relate to the world, they share a keen sense of Christians as *peregrini* or *viatores*—those who are on a journey to their heavenly *patria* or homeland. For Thomas, the wayfarer "is threatened by many dangers both from within and without,"[66] the object of her hope is veiled,[67] and yet this hope has a kind of certainty born of faith.[68] For both Augustine and Thomas, the wayfarer's life is characterized by a restless desire to know the God who is the source of her being, a desire to advance toward the God in whom she will find rest. Of course, the form the pilgrim's life took in Augustine's day was

64. Augustine, *De civitate Dei* 22.22.

65. *De civitate Dei* 22.24.

66. *Summa theologiae* 1.113.4.

67. *Summa theologiae* 2-2.17.2 ad 1.

68. *Summa theologiae* 2-2.18.4.

quite different from the form it took in Thomas's, reflecting the quite different situation of Augustine's Church and Thomas's—the difference between a Church that still lived to a large degree alongside a pagan culture, albeit one in the beginning of its death-throes, and a Church that had for centuries been the conserver and conveyor of the culture of antiquity. Yet there remains substantial continuity between Augustine's *peregrini* and Thomas's *viatores*.

Thomas quotes with approval Augustine's statement that the wayfarer advances toward God "not by steps of the body but by affections of the soul," particularly the virtue of love.[69] For Augustine and Thomas, with regard to whether one embraces or rejects the world, pessimism and optimism are somewhat beside the point. What matters is the pilgrim's journey through this world, which is undertaken by means of love—love of God and love of neighbor. The wayfarer's attitude toward the world is neither simple acceptance nor rejection but a discerning love of neighbor for the sake of God. In this sense, there is for both Augustine and Thomas an openness to the world, but it is an openness that takes seriously the possibility that the world will hate and persecute the followers of Jesus, and that recognizes that even the good things of this world must be subordinated to the supreme good of the vision of God in the world to come. In this regard, Augustine and Thomas share not simply certain theological conclusions but also a common theological approach.

69. *Summa theologiae* 2-2.24.4, quoting Augustine, *Tractates on the Gospel of John* 32.

AUGUSTINE AND THOMAS IN THE MODERN THEOLOGICAL TROPICS

How then ought we assess the use of "Augustine" and "Thomas" in postconciliar Catholic theology as tropes for pessimism and optimism with regard to the modern world?

First, we ought not to think that such tropes tell us anything useful about Augustine or Thomas as historical figures. To state the obvious, neither Augustine nor Thomas had any knowledge of our modern world and were neither pessimistic nor optimistic regarding it. Perhaps less obviously, to characterize Augustine as a pessimist and Thomas as an optimist with regard to the world outside the Church in their own times ignores both the complexity of each thinker's views and the historical differences between how the Church was situated vis-à-vis the world in the fourth century and how it was situated in the thirteenth century. Thomas's *viator* is the direct descendent of Augustine's *peregrinus*, though how this pilgrim status was lived out was quite different for a thirteenth-century friar than it was for a fourth-century bishop. To distill these complexities into a simple attitude of pessimism or optimism with regard to the world outside of the Church or to human culture is to miss both the similarities and the differences between Augustine and Thomas.

Further, even prescinding from historical claims about Augustine or Thomas, the use of these tropes to map the postconciliar theological landscape is not particularly illuminating of the situation of Catholic theology. For example, theologians who are typically grouped together as "Augustinian" or "Thomist" often reveal, upon closer examination, their own complexities. For example, Chenu's Thomist optimism grows, at least in part, from Blondel's Augustinian view of the relationship of theology to the experience of grace. That is to say, according to the way these terms were used in the 1930s, Chenu is more "Augustinian" than "Thomist" because he sees theology as "a spirituality that has found rational instruments adequate to its religious experience."[70] Similarly, one might see the Augustinian pessimism of Daniélou, which sharply distinguishes historical progress from the growth of the kingdom of God, as observing a properly Thomist distinction between nature and grace. The differences between theologians of the depth and subtlety of Chenu and Daniélou calls for a deeper analysis than applying the labels "Augustinian" and "Thomist" allows, even if, as in the case of Chenu, they sometimes themselves resort to these tropes.

Finally, while rhetorical tropes might help us satisfy the "blessed rage for order" that seeks to identify the species of everything it encounters, they do not carve the theological world at the joints. We should not fool ourselves into thinking that categories like "Augustinian" or "Thomist" describe natural kinds nor that they are innocent terms, particularly given the status of Thomas in Catholic theology and the persistent suspicion that there is something vaguely Protestant or Jansenist in excessive enthusiasm for Augustine. For that matter, why should we think that terms like "optimism" and "pessimism," or "acceptance" and "rejection," are adequate to characterizing the Christian's relationship to the world? How convincing is it really to think that there are only two fundamental attitudes toward the modern world among postconciliar theologians? As Tom Robbins notes in his novel *Still Life with Woodpecker*, "There are two kinds of people in this world: those who believe there are two kinds of people in this world and those who are smart enough to know better."[71] If one's first move is to map the terrain in terms of Augustinian

70. Marie-Dominique Chenu et al., *Une école de théologie: le Saulchoir* (Paris: Cerf, 1985), 148–49.

71. Tom Robbins, *Still Life with Woodpecker: A Sort of Love Story* (New York: Bantam Books, 1980), 82. One of the strengths of Joseph Komonchak's essay "Augustine, Aquinas or the Gospel *sine glossa*?" is that, in addition to the Augustinian Ratzinger and the Thomist Chenu, he also discusses Giuseppe Dossetti, who seems to offer an alternative that is more radically evangelical than either "Augustinianism" or "Thomism."

pessimism and Thomist optimism, one risks forgetting that the map is not the territory.

In Verhaghen's painting of Augustine and Thomas, a baroque cherub stands in the foreground holding up a heart that burns with the flame of charity, the source of light by which Thomas reads the passage indicated to him by Augustine and by which he writes in his own book. The danger of using "Augustine" and "Thomas" as rhetorical tropes for different tendencies in modern theology is that it can lead us to overlook that, for all their differences, it is the common light of charity in which they read and write their texts that unites Augustine and Thomas in a shared theological project. If we read their texts, and write our own, by the light of that same charity, then both Augustine and Thomas can offer us a way to engage the modern world, its joys and hopes, its sorrows and fears, in a way that is neither pessimistic nor optimistic, offering neither blanket acceptance nor rejection, but is rooted in the discerning faith, hope, and love that are God's gifts to his people.

Coda
A Homily for the Feast of Saint Thomas Aquinas

Wisdom 7:7–10, 15–16
1 Corinthians 2:1–10a
Matthew 23:8–12

The ancient Greek philosopher Aristotle
wrote that "all people by nature desire to know."
Aristotle thought that what it meant to be human
was to be the kind of animal whose greatest desire
was to answer the question "Why?"
Why does fire make things hot
and ice make things cool?
Why do crabs move the upper part of their claws
and not the lower part?
Why do we judge some actions
to be worthy of praise
and others to be worthy of condemnation?
Because this constant asking of "Why?"
is built into our nature,
it appears in us
pretty much as soon as we learn to speak,
as any parent of a toddler can tell you.

St. Thomas,
who referred to Aristotle
simply as *the* Philosopher,
agreed with him on this,

* Preached at St. Thomas Aquinas Church, Baltimore, MD, January 28, 2024.

as he did on many things.
He, too, thought that what makes us different
from all the other animals in the world
is that we ask questions,
and we ask them because we want to know things,
and we want to know things because, ultimately,
we want to understand ourselves
and our place in the world.
We human beings desire wisdom
because wisdom leads to happiness.

But Thomas did not need Aristotle
to tell him this.
He already had King Solomon,
who in today's first reading
compares wisdom to a beautiful woman,
and says, "I preferred her to scepter and throne,
and deemed riches nothing in comparison with her . . .
I chose to have her rather than the light,
because the splendor of her never yields to sleep."
Both Solomon and Thomas recognized
that we humans will never understand
ourselves and our place in our world,
until we know the whys
and the wherefores of things,
and not just of this or that thing,
but of *every*thing;
not just the why of heating and cooling
and the claws of crabs
and human praise,
but why there is anything at all—
why there is something
rather than nothing.

And to know the why
and the wherefore of everything
is to know God,
for he is our Creator and,
as Solomon tells us,
"both we and our words
are in his hand."

So Thomas Aquinas devoted his life to asking "Why?"
and to teaching other people how to ask "Why?"
until they arrived at the end of "Why?"
and there found God.
He sought wisdom everywhere:
in ancient pagan philosophers
like Aristotle,
in Jewish and Muslim thinkers
like Maimonides and Avicenna,
in Christian theologians
like Augustine and Gregory the Great,
but above all in the pages of Sacred Scripture,
where he found Jesus Christ,
the way and the truth and the life,
God's wisdom in human flesh.

The story is told of a time
near the end of Thomas's life
when he was praying in front of a crucifix
and Christ spoke to him from the cross:
"You have written well of me, Thomas.
What reward would you receive
from me for your labor?"
Thomas responded to the image of the crucified:
Non nisi te, Domine—"Nothing but you, Lord."

For all his great learning,
for all his scholarly accomplishments,
Thomas, like Paul in our second reading,
in the end "resolved to know nothing . . .
except Jesus Christ, and him crucified."
Nothing but you, Lord.

Nothing but you,
not because I no longer desire
to know the whys and wherefores of things,
not because I no longer yearn
to understand myself
and my place in the world,
not because I have fallen out of love
with the beautiful Lady Wisdom,
but because I am more deeply in love with her
than ever before,
and have come to see that God's wisdom
is not the wisdom of the rulers of this age
but is a wisdom mysterious and hidden,
a wisdom wrapped within your cross, O Jesus,
a wisdom that seems like foolishness to the world
because it says that the greatest among us
must become the servant of all,
that "whoever exalts himself will be humbled;
but whoever humbles himself will be exalted."

All people by nature desire to know,
and what St. Thomas desired to know
was the wisdom of the cross.
All our knowing amounts to nothing
if we do not take for our teacher
Jesus Christ and him crucified;

for he is the why
and the wherefore of everything.
St. Thomas says in one of his sermons
that whoever wishes
to live a fully human life
must reject what Christ rejected on the cross
and embrace what he embraced:
we must reject the false wisdom of the world
and embrace a wisdom
that might look like foolishness,
a wisdom that rejects pride and embraces humility,
a wisdom that rejects the desire to dominate and control
and embraces faith in the power of God.
For to embrace the wisdom of the cross
is to know the God who can sustain us
at the lowest points in our lives:
when it seems that hope is lost
and darkness has eclipsed the light.
To embrace the wisdom of the cross
is to know also the resurrection
and the power of God to save;
it is to know the light
whose splendor never yields to sleep.

All people by nature desire to know.
As we seek to grasp
the why and wherefore of all things,
let us learn from St. Thomas,
not because he knew
how to draw subtle philosophical distinctions,
not because he knew the writings
of Aristotle and Avicenna and Augustine,
not even because of his superb knowledge

of God's revelation in Sacred Scripture;
let us learn from him
because he knew the wisdom of the cross.
Let us learn from him how to say to Jesus,
Non nisi te, Domine—"Nothing but you, Lord."
Let us learn to live in the light
whose splendor never yields to sleep.

Citation of Thomas Aquinas

Listed below are the titles by which Thomas's works are cited in the notes, followed by the full Latin title (where these differ), generally taken from the Catalog found in Jean-Pierre Torrell, OP, *Saint Thomas Aquinas,* vol. 1, *The Person and His Work,* trans. Robert Royal (Washington, DC: The Catholic University of America Press, 1996). The Latin texts used are those at https://www.corpusthomisticum.org. Unless otherwise noted, translations are my own, but for each work I have supplied an English translation where available. This is followed by an explanation of how I have cited texts within each work.

Catena aurea = *Glossa continua super Evangelia (Catena aurea)*	*Catena Aurea: Commentary on the Four Gospels Collected Out of the Works of the Fathers*, vol. 4, *St. John* [1841], trans. John Henry Newman (London: Saint Austin, 1997). Cited by chapter.lecture.
Compendium theologiae = *Compendium theologiae seu brevis compilation theologiae ad fratrem Raynaldum*	*Compendium of Theology*, trans. Richard J. Regan (Oxford: Oxford University Press, 2009). Cited by book.chapter.
Contra Gentiles = *Summa contra Gentiles*	*Summa Contra Gentiles*, trans. Anton Pegis et al., 5 vols. (Notre Dame, IN: University of Notre Dame Press, 1975–76). Cited by book.chapter.paragraph.

De decem praeceptis = Collationes in decem praecepta	Partial translation in "How Christians Should Live: The Commandments," trans. Joseph B. Collins, in *The Aquinas Catechism* (Nashua, NH: Sophia Institute, 2000). Cited by article as found in the Turin edition.
De ente et essentia	*Aquinas on Being and Essence: A Translation and Interpretation,* ed. and trans. Joseph Bobik (Notre Dame, IN: University of Notre Dame Press, 1988). Cited by chapter.
De malo = Quaestiones disputatae De malo	*On Evil,* trans. John A. Oesterle and Jean T. Oesterle (Notre Dame, IN: University of Notre Dame Press, 1995). Cited by question. article. Unless found in the body of the article, texts are further cited by objection (arg.) or response (ad).
De perfectione = De perfectione spiritualis vitae	"On the Perfection of the Spiritual Life," in *Thomas Aquinas and the Mendicant Controversies: Three Translations*, trans. John Proctor, ed. Mark Johnson (Merrimack, NH: Thomas More College Press, 2007). Cited by chapter.
De potentia = Quaestiones disputatae De potentia	*On the Power of God*, trans. Laurence Shapcote (Westminster, MD: Newman, 1952). Cited by question.article. Unless found in the body of the article, texts are further cited by objection (arg.) or response (ad).

De rationibus fidei = *De rationibus fidei ad Cantorem Antiochenum*	*Aquinas: On Reasons for Our Faith Against the Muslims, Greeks and Armenians*, trans. Peter Damian M. Fehlner, ed. James Likoudis (New Bedford, MA: Franciscans of the Immaculate, 2002). Cited by chapter.
De unitate intellectus = *De unitate intellectus contra Averroistas*	*On the Unity of the Intellect Against the Averroists*, trans. Beatrice H. Zedler (Milwaukee, WI: Marquette University Press, 1968). Cited by chapter.
De veritate = *Quaestiones disputatae De veritate*	*Truth*, trans. Robert W. Mulligan et al., 3 vols. (Chicago: Henry Regnery, 1952–54). Cited by question.article. Unless found in the body of the article, texts are further cited by objection (arg.) or response (ad).
De virtutibus = *Quaestiones disputatae De virtutibus*	*Disputed Questions on the Virtues*, trans. E.M. Atkins, ed. E.M. Atkins and Thomas Williams (Cambridge: Cambridge University Press, 2005). Cited by question.article. Unless found in the body of the article, texts are further cited by objection (arg.) or response (ad).
Expositio Posteriorum = *Expositio Libri Posteriorum*	*Commentary on Aristotle's "Posterior Analytics,"* trans. Richard Berquist (South Bend, IN: Dumb Ox Books, 2008). Cited by book.lecture.paragraph.
In Physic. = *Sententia super Physicam*	*Commentary on Aristotle's "Physics,"* trans. Richard J. Blackwell, Richard J. Spath, and W. Edmund Thirkel (South Bend, IN: Dumb Ox Books, 1999). Cited by book.lecture.paragraph.

In Symbolum Apostolorum = Collationes in Symbolum Apostolorum	*The Sermon-Conferences of St. Thomas Aquinas on the Apostles' Creed,* trans. Nicholas Ayo (Notre Dame, IN: University of Notre Dame Press, 1988). Cited by article.
Q. d. de anima = Quaestio Disputata De Anima	*Questions on the Soul,* trans. James H. Robb (Milwaukee, WI: Marquette University Press, 2005). Cited by question. Unless found in the body of the article, texts are further cited by objection (arg.) or response (ad).
Quodlibet = Quaestiones de quodlibet I-XII	*Thomas Aquinas's Quodlibetal Questions,* trans. Turner Nevitt and Brian Davies (Oxford: Oxford University Press, 2020). Cited by quodlibet.question. article. Unless found in the body of the article, texts are further cited by objection (arg.) or response (ad).
Sententia De anima = Sentencia libri De anima	*Commentary on Aristotle's "De Anima,"* trans. Kenelm Foster and Silvester Humphries (South Bend, IN: Dumb Ox Books, 1994). Cited by book.lecture. paragraph.
Sententia De sensu = Sentencia libri De sensu et sensato	*Commentaries on Aristotle's "On Sense and What Is Sensed" and "On Memory and Recollection,"* trans. Kevin White and Edward M. Macierowski (Washington, DC: The Catholic University of America Press, 2005). Cited by tractate.chapter. Note that the second tractate is sometimes treated as a separate commentary, entitled *Sententia De memoria et reminiscentia.*

Sententia Ethic. = *Sententia libri Ethicorum*	*Commentary on Aristotle's "Nicomachean Ethics,"* trans. C.I. Litzinger (South Bend, IN: Dumb Ox Books, 1993). Cited by book.lecture.paragraph.
Sententia Metaphysicae = *Sententia super Metaphysicam*	*Commentary on Aristotle's "Metaphysics,"* trans. John P. Rowan (South Bend, IN: Dumb Ox Books, 1995). Cited by book.lecture.paragraph.
Serm. =*Sermones*	*The Academic Sermons*, trans. Mark-Robin Hoogland (Washington, DC: The Catholic University of America Press, 2010). Cited by the number of the sermon as found in the Leonine Edition, followed by the Latin title of the sermon.
Summa theologiae	*Summa theologiae* ("Blackfriars edition"), various trans., 60 vols. (London: Eyre & Spottiswoode, 1964–1976). An older translation, by Laurence Shapcote, is widely available online (e.g., https://www.newadvent.org/summa/). Cited by part.question.article. Unless found in the body of the article, texts are further cited by objection (arg.) or response (ad).
Super Col. = *Super Epistolam B. Pauli ad Colossenses lectura*	*Commentary on Colossians*, trans. Fabian Larcher (Naples, FL: Sapientia, 2006). Cited by chapter.lecture.paragraph.
Super I Cor. = *Super I Epistolam B. Pauli ad Corinthios lectura* *Super II Cor.* = *Super II Epistolam B. Pauli ad Corinthios lectura*	*Commentary on the Letters of Saint Paul to the Corinthians*, trans. Fabian Larcher, Daniel Keating, and Beth Mortensen (Lander, WY: Aquinas Institute, 2012). Cited by chapter.lecture.paragraph.

Super De divinis nominibus = *Super librum Dionysii De divinis nominibus*	*An Exposition of "The Divine Names," the Book of Blessed Dionysius*, trans. and ed. Michael Augros (Nashua, NH: Thomas More College Press, 2021). Cited by chapter.lecture.paragraph.
Super De Trinitate = *Super Boetium De Trinitate*	*Faith, Reason and Theology* (qq. 1–4) and *The Division and Methods of the Sciences* (qq. 5–6), trans. Armand Maurer (Toronto: Pontifical Institute of Mediaeval Studies, 1986–1987). Cited by question.article. Unless found in the body of the article, texts are further cited by objection (arg.) or response (ad).
Super Eph. = *Super Epistolam B. Pauli ad Ephesios lectura*	*Commentary on Saint Paul's Epistle to the Ephesians*, trans. Matthew L. Lamb (Albany, NY: Magi Books, 1966). Cited by chapter.lecture.paragraph.
Super Heb. = *Super Epistolam B. Pauli ad Hebraeos lectura*	*Commentary on the Epistle to the Hebrews*, trans. Chrysostom Baer (South Bend, IN: St. Augustine's, 2006). Cited by chapter.lecture.paragraph.
Super Io. = *Lectura super Ioannem*	*Commentary on the Gospel of John*, trans. Fabian Larcher and James A. Weisheipl, 3 vols. (Washington, DC: The Catholic University of America Press, 2010). Cited by chapter.lecture.paragraph.
Super Is. = *Expositio super Isaiam ad litteram*	*Commentary on Isaiah,* trans. Louis St. Hilaire (Lander, WY: Aquinas Institute, 2021). Cited by chapter.lecture.paragraph.

Super Mt. = *Lectura super Matthaeum*	*Commentary on the Gospel of Matthew*, trans. Jeremy Holmes and Beth Mortensen, 2 vols. (Lander, WY: Aquinas Institute, 2013). Cited by chapter.lecture.paragraph.
Super Rom. = *Super Epistolam B. Pauli ad Romanos lectura*	*Commentary on the Letter of St. Paul to the Romans,* trans. Fabian Larcher (Lander, WY: Aquinas Institute, 2012). Cited by chapter.lecture.paragraph.
Super Sent. = *Scriptum super libros Sententiarum*	*Commentary on the Sentences*, trans. Chris Decaen, Beth Mortensen, and Dylan Schrader, 10 vols. (Lander, WY: Aquinas Institute, 2018–2024). Cited by book.distinction.question.article, adding, if needed, a reference to sub-questions.
Super I Thes. = *Super I Epistolam B. Pauli ad Thessalonicenses lectura*	"First Letter to the Thessalonians," trans. Michael J. Duffy, in *Commentary on St. Paul's First Letter to the Thessalonians and the Letter to the Philippians* (Albany, NY: Magi Books, 1969). Cited by chapter.lecture.paragraph.
Super I Tim. = *Super I Epistolam B. Pauli ad Timotheum lectura*	"The Commentary of St. Thomas Aquinas on the First Epistle of St. Paul to Timothy," in *Commentaries on St. Paul's Epistles to Timothy, Titus, and Philemon*, trans. and ed. Chrysostom Baer (South Bend, IN: St. Augustine's, 2007). Cited by chapter.lecture.paragraph.

Works Cited

Abelard, Peter. *Commentary on the Epistle to the Romans*. Translated by Steven R. Cartwright. Washington, DC: The Catholic University of America Press, 2011.

———. *Ethical Writings: "Ethics" and "Dialogue Between a Philosopher, a Jew and a Christian"*. Translated by Paul Vincent Spade. Indianapolis: Hackett, 1995.

Alan of Lille. *De incarnatione Christi rhythmus perelegans*. In *Patrologia Latina*, edited by J.-P. Migne, 210:577–80. Paris, 1855.

Ambrose. *De Sacramentis*. In *St. Ambrose on the Sacraments and on the Mysteries*, edited with introduction and notes by J.H. Styrawley, translated by T. Thompson, 75–140. London: S.P.C.K., 1950.

Anatolios, Khaled. *Deification Through the Cross: An Eastern Christian Theology of Salvation*. Grand Rapids, MI: Eerdmans, 2020.

Anscombe, G.E.M. "Modern Moral Philosophy." In *Human Life, Action and Ethics: Essays by G.E.M. Anscombe*. Edited by Mary Geach and Luke Gormally, 169–94. Exeter, UK: Imprint Academic, 2005.

———. and Peter T. Geach. *Three Philosophers: Aristotle, Aquinas, Frege*. Oxford: Basil Blackwell and Mott, 1961.

Anselm. *De conceptu virginali*. In *Anselm: Basic Writings*, edited and translated by Thomas Williams, 327–60. Indianapolis: Hackett, 2007

Aristotle. *Poetics*. In *The Complete Works of Aristotle*, edited by Jonathan Barnes, 2316–40. Princeton, NJ: Princeton University Press, 1984.

Auerbach, Erich. *Mimesis: The Representation of Reality in Western Literature*. Translated by Willard R. Trask. Princeton, NJ: Princeton University Press, 1953.

Augustine. *De catechizandis rudibus*. ET: *The First Catechetical Instruction*. Translated by Joseph P. Christopher. Ancient Christian Writers 2. Westminster, MD: Newman, 1962.

———. *De civitate Dei*. ET: *The City of God*. Translated by Henry Bettenson. London: Penguin Books, 1972.

———. *De Trinitate*. ET: *Saint Augustine: The Trinity*. Translated by Stephen McKenna. The Fathers of the Church 45. Washington DC: The Catholic University of America Press, 1963.

———. *On the Spirit and the Letter*. In *The Works of Saint Augustine: A Translation for the 21st Century*, pt. 1, vol. 23: *Answer to the Pelagians I*, translated by Roland J. Teske, edited by John Rotelle, 144–94. Hyde Park, NY: New City, 1997.

———. *Retractiones*. ET: *The Retractions*. Translated by Mary Inez Bogen. The Fathers of the Church 60. Washington, DC: The Catholic University of America Press, 1968.

———. *Sermones A. Mai*. In *Miscellanea Agostiniana*, 1:285–386. Rome: Tipografia Poliglotta Vaticana, 1930–31.

———. *Tractatus in Evangelium Iohannis*. ET: *Tractates on the Gospel of John*. 5 vols. Translated by John W. Rettig. The Fathers of the Church. Washington, DC: The Catholic University of America Press, 1988–95.

Bacon, Francis. *The Advancement of Learning*. London: MacMillan, 1876.

Balthasar, Hans Urs von. *Explorations in Theology*. Vol. 2, *The Spouse of the Word*, translated by John Saward. San Francisco: Ignatius, 1991.

Barthes, Roland. *Image—Music—Text*. Edited and translated by Stephen Heath. London: Fontana, 1977.

Bejczy, István P. "The Cardinal Virtues in Medieval Commentaries on the *Nicomachean Ethics*, 1250–1350." In *Virtue Ethics in the Middle Ages: Commentaries on Aristotle's "Nicomachean Ethics," 1200–1500*, edited by István P. Bejczy, 199–221. Leiden, NL: Brill, 2008.

Benedict XVI. *Caritas in Veritate.* Encyclical letter, June 29, 2009. vatican.va.

———. "St. Thomas Aquinas (3)." General audience, June 23, 2010. vatican.va.

Berkel, Klaas van, and Arie Johan Vanderjagt, eds. *The Book of Nature in Early Modern and Modern History.* Leuven: Peeters, 2006.

Blanchette, Oliva. *Maurice Blondel: A Philosophical Life.* Grand Rapids, MI: Eerdmans, 2010.

Blankenhorn, Bernhard. "The Instrumental Causality of the Sacraments: Thomas Aquinas and Louis-Marie Chauvet." *Nova et Vetera* 4, no. 2 (Spring 2006): 255–94.

Blondel, Maurice. "The Latent Resources in St. Augustine's Thought." In *St. Augustine: His Age, Life, and Thought*, 317–54. New York: Meridian Books, 1957.

Bonaventure. *Collationes in Hexameron.* ET: *Collations on the Six Days.* Translated by José de Vinck. The Works of St. Bonaventure 5. Patterson, NJ: St. Anthony Guild, 1970.

———. *Itinerarium Mentis in Deum.* ET: *The Journey of the Mind to God.* Edited by Stephen F. Brown. Translated by Philotheus Boehner. Indianapolis: Hackett, 1993.

Bonino, Serge-Thomas. "Charisms, Forms, and States of Life." Translated by Mary Thomas Noble. In *The Ethics of Aquinas*, edited by Stephen J. Pope, 340–52. Washington, DC: Georgetown University Press, 2002.

———. "Le rôle de l'image dans la connaissance prophétique d'après saint Thomas d'Aquin." *Revue thomiste* 89, no. 4 (1989): 533–68.

Bonnefoy, Jean-François. *Christ and the Cosmos*. Edited and translated by Michael D. Meilach. Paterson, NJ: St. Anthony Guild, 1965.

Boyle, Leonard. *The Setting of the "Summa Theologiae" of Saint Thomas*. Toronto: Pontifical Institute of Mediaeval Studies, 1982.

Brock, Stephen L. "St Thomas and the Eucharistic Conversion." *The Thomist* 65, no. 4 (October 2001): 529–65.

Burke, Kevin F. *The Ground Beneath the Cross: The Theology of Ignacio Ellacuría*. Washington, DC: Georgetown University Press, 2000.

Burrell, David B. *Exercises in Religious Understanding*. Notre Dame, IN: University of Notre Dame Press, 1974.

Bushlack, Thomas J. *Politics for a Pilgrim Church: A Thomistic Theory of Civic Virtue*. Grand Rapids, MI: Eerdmans, 2015.

Calvin, John. *Institutes of the Christian Religion*. Edited by John T. McNeill. Translated by Ford Lewis Battles. 2 vols. Louisville, KY: Westminster John Knox, 1960.

Carruthers, Mary. *The Book of Memory: A Study of Memory in Medieval Culture*. Cambridge: Cambridge University Press, 2008.

Castillo, Daniel P. "Reconfiguring Ignacio Ellacuría's Symbolic Conception of 'the Crucified People': Jesus, the Suffering Servant, and Abel." *Theological Studies* 84, no. 1 (March 2023): 8–29.

Catherine of Siena. *The Dialogue*. Translated by Suzanne Noffke. New York: Paulist, 1980.

Cessario, Romanus. *The Godly Image: Christ and Salvation in Catholic Thought from Anselm to Aquinas*. Petersham, MA: St. Bede's, 1990.

Chauvet, Louis-Marie. *Symbol and Sacrament: A Sacramental Reinterpretation of Christian Existence.* Translated by Patrick Madigan and Madeleine Beaumont. Collegeville, MN: Liturgical, 1995.

Chenu, Marie-Dominique. *Aquinas and His Role in Theology.* Translated by Paul Philibert. Collegeville, MN: Liturgical, 2002.

———. *Faith and Theology.* Translated by Denis Hickey. New York: MacMillan, 1968.

———. *Toward Understanding St. Thomas.* Translated by A.M. Landry and D. Hughes. Chicago: Henry Regnery, 1964.

Chenu, Marie-Dominique, et al. *Une école de théologie: le Saulchoir.* Paris: Cerf, 1985.

Coleridge, Samuel Taylor. *Biographia Literaria.* Edited by John T. Shawcross. Vol. 1. Oxford: Clarendon, 1907.

Colish, Marcia L. *Faith, Fiction and Force in Medieval Baptismal Debates.* Washington, DC: The Catholic University of America Press, 2014.

Cross, Richard. *Duns Scotus.* Oxford: Oxford University Press, 1999.

Daniélou, Jean. *The Lord of History: Reflections on the Inner Meaning of History.* Translated by Nigel Abercrombie. London: Longmans, Green, 1958.

Dante Alighieri. *Paradiso.* Translated by Mark Musa. In *The Portable Dante*, edited by Mark Musa, 389–586. New York: Penguin Books, 1995.

Dauphinais, Michael, Barry David, and Matthew Levering, eds. *Aquinas the Augustinian.* Washington, DC: The Catholic University of America Press, 2007.

Davidson, Donald. *The Essential Davidson.* Oxford: Oxford University Press, 2006.

Davies, Brian. *The Thought of Thomas Aquinas.* Oxford: Clarendon, 1992.

Decosimo, David. *Ethics as a Work of Charity: Thomas Aquinas and Pagan Virtue*. Stanford, CA: University of Stanford Press, 2014.

Delio, Ilia. "Revisiting the Franciscan Doctrine of Christ." *Theological Studies* 64, no. 1 (February 2003): 3–23.

Doyle, Dominic. "*Spe Salvi* on Eschatological and Secular Hope: A Thomistic Critique of an Augustinian Encyclical." *Theological Studies* 71, no. 2 (May 2010): 350–79.

Eklund, Rebekah. *The Beatitudes through the Ages*. Grand Rapids, MI: Eerdmans, 2021.

Elie, Paul. *The Life You Save May Be Your Own: An American Pilgrimage*. New York: Farrar, Straus and Giroux, 2003.

Ellacuría, Ignacio. *Freedom Made Flesh: The Mission of Christ and His Church*. Translated by John Drury. Maryknoll, NY: Orbis Books, 1976.

———. *Ignacio Ellacuría: Essays on History, Liberation, and Society*. Edited by Michael E. Lee. Maryknoll, NY: Orbis Books, 2013.

Emery, Gilles. *The Trinitarian Theology of Saint Thomas Aquinas*. Translated by Francesca Aran Murphy. Oxford: Oxford University Press, 2007.

———. *Trinity in Aquinas*. Translated by Matthew Levering et al. Ave Maria, FL: Sapientia, 2003.

Ernst, Cornelius. *Multiple Echo: Explorations in Theology*. Edited by Fergus Kerr and Timothy Radcliffe. London: Darton, Longman and Todd, 1979.

Evagrius Ponticus. *Praktikos*. In *The Prakticos and Chapters on Prayer*, translated by John Eudes Bamberger, 12–42. Kalamazoo, MI: Cistercian, 1981.

Faggioli, Massimo. *Vatican II: The Battle for Meaning*. New York: Paulist, 2012.

Fakhry, Majid. *A History of Islamic Philosophy*. 2nd ed. New York: Columbia University Press, 1983.

Farkasfalvy, Denis. *Inspiration and Interpretation: A Theological Introduction to Sacred Scripture.* Washington, DC: The Catholic University of America Press, 2010.

Farrell, Walter. *A Companion to the Summa.* Vol. 1, *The Architect of the Universe.* New York: Sheed & Ward, 1941.

Finnis, John. *Aquinas: Moral, Political, and Legal Theory.* Oxford: Oxford University Press, 1998.

Flores, Angel. "Magical Realism in Spanish American Fiction." *Hispania* 38, no. 2 (May 1955): 187–92.

Florovsky, Georges. *Collected Works of George Florovsky.* Vol. 3, *Creation and Redemption.* Belmont, MA: Nordland, 1976.

Foucault, Michel. *Discipline and Punish: The Birth of the Prison.* Translated by Alan Sheridan. New York: Vintage Books, 1979.

———. *Language, Counter-Memory, Practice: Selected Essays and Interviews.* Edited by Donald F. Bouchard. Translated by Donald F. Bouchard and Sherry Simon. Ithaca, NY: Cornell University Press, 1980.

Fowl, Stephen E. *The Story of Christ in the Ethics of Paul: An Analysis of the Function of the Hymnic Material in the Pauline Corpus.* Sheffield, UK: JSOT, 1990.

Francis. *Laudato si'.* Encyclical letter, May 24, 2015. vatican.va.

Freccero, John. "Dante's Pilgrim in a Gyre." *PMLA* 76, no. 3 (June 1961): 168–81.

Frei, Hans. *The Eclipse of Biblical Narrative: A Study in Eighteenth and Nineteenth Century Hermeneutics.* New Haven, CT: Yale University Press, 1974.

Gallagher, Edmon L. "Deuterocanonical Books in Latin Tradition." In *The Oxford Handbook of the Latin Bible,* edited by H.A.G. Houghton, 91–105. Oxford: Oxford University Press, 2023.

Galot, Jean. *Jesus, Our Liberator: A Theology of Redemption.* Rome: Gregorian University Press, 1982.

Galvin, John P. "Jesus Christ." In *Systematic Theology: Roman Catholic Perspectives*, vol. 1, edited by Francis Schüssler Fiorenza and John P. Galvin, 251–324. Minneapolis, MN: Fortress, 1991.

Getz, Lorine M. *Flannery O'Connor: Her Life, Library and Book Reviews*. Lewiston, NY: Edwin Mellen, 1980.

Gilby, Thomas, ed. and trans. *St. Thomas Aquinas: Theological Texts*. Oxford: Oxford University Press, 1955.

Gilson, Étienne. "The Future of Augustinian Metaphysics." In *St. Augustine: His Age, Life, and Thought*, 287–316. New York: Meridian Books, 1957.

Girard, René. *I See Satan Fall Like Lightning*. Translated by James G. Williams. Maryknoll, NY: Orbis Books, 2001.

Gregory the Great. *Forty Gospel Homilies*. Translated by David Hurst. Kalamazoo, MI: Cistercian, 1990.

———. *Moralia in Job*. ET: *Moral Reflections on Job*. 6 vols. Translated by Brian Kerns. Athens, OH: Cistercian, 2014–22.

Griffiths, Alan, trans. *We Give You Thanks and Praise: The Ambrosian Eucharistic Prefaces*. Franklin, WI: Sheed & Ward, 2000.

Guerric of Saint-Quentin. *Quaestiones de quolibet*. Edited by Walter H. Principe. Revised by Jonathan Black. Toronto: Pontifical Institute of Mediaeval Studies, 2002.

Gui, Bernard. "The Life of St. Thomas Aquinas." In *The Life of St. Thomas Aquinas: Biographical Documents*, edited and translated by Kenelm Foster, 25–81. London: Longmans, Green, 1959.

Gutiérrez, Gustavo. *Las Casas: In Search of the Poor of Jesus Christ*. Translated by Robert R. Barr. New York: Orbis Books, 1993.

Haas, John M. "The Relationship of Nature and Grace in Saint Thomas." In *The Ever-Illuminating Wisdom of St. Thomas Aquinas: Papers Presented at a Conference Sponsored by the Wethersfield Institute*. San Francisco: Ignatius, 1999.

Hankey, Wayne. *God in Himself: Aquinas' Doctrine of God as expounded in the "Summa Theologiae."* Oxford: Oxford University Press, 1987.

Harnack, Adolf von. *History of Dogma*. Translated by Neil Buchanan. Vol. 6. New York: Dover, 1961.

Hauerwas, Stanley. *Character and the Christian Life: A Study in Theological Ethics*. Notre Dame, IN: University of Notre Dame Press, 1994.

———. *A Community of Character: Toward a Constructive Christian Social Ethic*. Notre Dame, IN: University of Notre Dame Press, 1991.

———. *Sanctify Them in the Truth: Holiness Exemplified*. Nashville, TN: Abingdon, 1998.

———. *Vision and Virtue: Essays in Christian Ethical Reflection*. Notre Dame, IN: University of Notre Dame Press, 1981.

———. *With the Grain of the Universe: The Church's Witness and Natural Theology*. Grand Rapids, MI: Brazos, 2002.

Hauerwas, Stanley, and Charles Pinches. *Christians Among the Virtues: Theological Conversations with Ancient and Modern Ethics*. Notre Dame, IN: University of Notre Dame Press, 1997.

Healy, Nicholas M. *Church, World and the Christian Life: Practical-Prophetic Ecclesiology*. Cambridge: Cambridge University Press, 2000.

———. *Thomas Aquinas: Theologian of the Christian Life*. Aldershot, UK: Ashgate, 2003.

Healy, Nicholas M. "Three Theological Appropriations of Analytic-Philosophical Readings of Thomas Aquinas." In *Analytical Thomism: Traditions in Dialogue*, edited by Craig Paterson and Matthew S. Pugh, 37–58. Aldershot, UK: Ashgate, 2006.

Hedley, Douglas. *Living Forms of the Imagination*. London: T&T Clark, 2008.

Hess, Peter J. "'God's Two Books': Revelation, Theology and Natural Science in the Christian West." In *Interdisciplinary Perspectives on Cosmology & Biological Evolution*, edited by Hilary D. Regan and Mark Worthing, 19–49. Adelaide, AU: ATF, 2002.

Hibbs, Thomas S. *Dialectic and Narrative in Aquinas: An Interpretation of the "Summa Contra Gentiles."* Notre Dame, IN: University of Notre Dame Press, 1995.

———. "Interpretations of Aquinas's Ethics Since Vatican II." In *The Ethics of Aquinas*, edited by Stephen J. Pope, 412–25. Washington, DC: Georgetown University Press, 2002.

Himes, Michael J., and Kenneth R. Himes. *Fullness of Faith: The Public Significance of Theology*. New York: Paulist, 1993.

Holmes, Jeremy. "Aquinas' *Lectura in Matthaeum*." In *Aquinas on Scripture: An Introduction to His Biblical Commentaries*, edited by Thomas G. Weinandy, Daniel A. Keating, and John P. Yocum, 73–97. London: T&T Clark, 2005.

Hood, William. *Fra Angelico at San Marco*. New Haven, CT: Yale University Press, 1993.

Hugh of St. Victor. *De Sacramentis*. ET: *On the Sacraments of the Christian Faith*. Translated by Roy J. Deferrari. Cambridge, MA: Medieval Academy of America, 1951.

Hunter, Justus H. *If Adam Had Not Sinned: The Reason for the Incarnation from Anselm to Scotus*. Washington, DC: The Catholic University of America Press, 2020.

Inglis, John. "Aquinas's Replication of the Acquired Moral Virtues: Rethinking the Standard Philosophical Interpretation of Moral Virtue in Aquinas." *The Journal of Religious Ethics* 27, no. 1 (Spring 1999): 3–27.

Jenkins, John I. *Knowledge and Faith in Thomas Aquinas.* Cambridge: Cambridge University Press, 1997.

Jenson, Robert. "For Us He Was Made Man." In *Nicene Christianity: The Future for a New Ecumenism*, edited by Christopher R. Seitz, 75–86. Grand Rapids, MI: Brazos, 2001.

John of Salisbury. *The Metalogicon of John of Salisbury: A Twelfth-Century Defense of the Verbal and Logical Arts of the Trivium.* Translated by Daniel D. McGarry. Berkeley: University of California Press, 1955.

John Paul II. "All Creation Will Be 'Recapitulated' in Christ." General audience, February 14, 2001. vatican.va.

———. *Crossing the Threshold of Hope.* Translated by Jenny McPhee and Martha McPhee. New York: Alfred A. Knopf, 1994.

———. *Dives in Misericordia.* Encyclical letter, November 30, 1980. vatican.va.

———. *Fides et Ratio.* Encyclical letter, September 14, 1998. vatican.va.

———. "Address of John Paul II to the Members of the Scotus Commission." February 16, 2002. vatican.va.

———. "Only Christ Can Fulfill Man's Hopes." General audience, November 8, 1995. ewtn.com.

———. "Program for Year 2000 Must Help Us Discover Glory of God Revealed in Christ." Homily, November 30, 1996. ewtn.com.

———. *Redemptor Hominis.* Encyclical letter, March 4, 1979. vatican.va.

John Paul II. "Second Coming of Christ at the End of Time." General audience, April 22, 1998. vatican.va.

John, Helen James. *The Thomist Spectrum*. New York: Fordham University Press, 1966.

Johnson, Mark. "Augustine and Aquinas on Original Sin: Doctrine, Authority, and Pedagogy." In *Aquinas the Augustinian*, edited by Michael Dauphinais, Barry David, and Matthew Levering, 145–58. Washington, DC: The Catholic University of America Press, 2007.

Jordan, Mark D. *Rewritten Theology: Aquinas after His Readers*. Oxford: Blackwell, 2006.

Julian of Toledo. *Commentarius in Nahum Prophetam*. In *Patrologia Latina*, edited by J.-P. Migne, 96:706–58. Paris: 1862.

Kenny, Anthony. *Aquinas*. Oxford: Oxford University Press, 1980.

———. *Aquinas on Mind*. London: Routledge, 1993.

———. "Intellect and Imagination in Aquinas." In *Aquinas: A Collection of Critical Essays*, edited by Anthony Kenny, 273–96. Notre Dame, IN: University of Notre Dame Press, 1969.

Kerr, Fergus. *After Aquinas: Versions of Thomism*. Malden, MA: Blackwell, 2002.

King, Martin Luther, Jr. "Letter from Birmingham Jail." In *Why We Can't Wait*. New York: Harper and Row, 1964.

King, Peter. "Aquinas on the Passions." In *Thomas Aquinas: Contemporary Philosophical Perspectives*, edited by Brian Davies, 353–84. Oxford: Oxford University Press, 2002.

Komonchak, Joseph A. "Augustine, Aquinas or the Gospel *sine glossa*? Divisions over *Gaudium et Spes*." In *Unfinished Journey: The Church 40 Years After Vatican II: Essays for John Wilkins*, edited by Austen Ivereigh, 102–18. London: Continuum, 2003.

Ladner, Gerhart. "*Homo Viator*: Mediæval Ideas on Alienation and Order." *Speculum* 42, no. 2 (April 1967): 233–59.

Lanfranc of Canterbury. *De corpore et sanguine Domini adversus Berengarium*. In *Lanfranc of Canterbury: On the Body and Blood of the Lord & Guitmund of Aversa: On the Truth of the Body and Blood of Christ in the Eucharist*, translated by Mark G. Vaillancourt. The Fathers of the Church, Medieval Continuation 10:29–90. Washington, DC: The Catholic University of America Press, 2009.

Laporte, Jean-Marc. "Christ in Aquinas' *Summa Theologiae*: Peripheral or Pervasive?" *The Thomist* 67, no. 2 (April 2003): 221–48.

Lassalle-Klein, Robert. *Blood and Ink: Ignacio Ellacuría, Jon Sobrino, and the Jesuit Martyrs of the University of Central America*. Maryknoll, NY: Orbis Books, 2014.

Lear, Jonathan. *Aristotle: The Desire to Understand*. Cambridge: Cambridge University Press, 1988.

Lee, Michael E. *Bearing the Weight of Salvation: The Soteriology of Ignacio Ellacuría*. New York: Crossroad, 2009.

Leget, Carlo. "Authority and Plausibility: Aquinas on Suicide." In *Aquinas as Authority*, edited by Paul van Geest, Harm Goris, and Carlo Leget, 277–93. Leuven: Peeters, 2002.

Lewis, Charlton T., and Charles Short, eds. *A Latin Dictionary, Founded on Andrews' edition of Freund's Latin dictionary*. Oxford: Clarendon, 1879.

Lindbeck, George. *The Nature of Doctrine: Religion and Theology in a Postliberal Age*. Louisville, KY: Westminster John Knox, 1984.

Luther, Martin. *On the Babylonian Captivity of the Church*. In *Selected Writings of Martin Luther*, edited by Theodore G. Tappert, vol. 1, *1517–1520*. Minneapolis, MN: Fortress, 2007.

MacIntyre, Alasdair. *After Virtue: A Study in Moral Theory*. 2nd ed. Notre Dame, IN: University of Notre Dame Press, 1984.

———. *Three Rival Versions of Moral Enquiry: Encyclopaedia, Genealogy, and Tradition*. Notre Dame, IN: University of Notre Dame Press, 1991.

———. *Whose Justice? Which Rationality?* Notre Dame, IN: University of Notre Dame Press, 1988.

Mahoney, Edward P. "Sense, Intellect, and Imagination in Albert, Thomas, and Siger." In *The Cambridge History of Later Medieval Philosophy*, edited by Norman Kretzmann, Anthony Kenny, Jan Pinborg, and Eleanore Stump, 602–22. Cambridge: Cambridge University Press, 1982.

Maier, Martin. "Karl Rahner: The Teacher of Ignacio Ellacuría." In *Love That Produces Hope: The Thought of Ignacio Ellacuría*, edited by Kevin F. Burke and Robert Lassalle-Klein, 128–43. Collegeville, MN: Liturgical, 2006.

Maloney, George A. *The Cosmic Christ: From Paul to Teilhard*. New York: Sheed & Ward, 1968.

Maritain, Jacques. "St. Augustine and St. Thomas Aquinas." In *St. Augustine: His Age, Life, and Thought*, 197–224. New York: Meridian Books, 1957.

Marshall, Bruce D. *Trinity and Truth*. Cambridge: Cambridge University Press, 2000.

McCabe, Herbert. "Appendix 3: 'Signifying Imperfectly.'" In Thomas Aquinas, *Summa theologiae*, edited and translated by Herbert McCabe, vol. 3, *Knowing and Naming God*. New York: McGraw-Hill, 1964.

———. *Faith Within Reason*. Edited by Brian Davies. London: Continuum, 2007.

———. *On Aquinas*. Edited by Brian Davies. London: Burns and Oates, 2008.

McDermott, Timothy. *How to Read Aquinas*. London: Granta Books, 2007.

McEvoy, J. "The Absolute Predestination of Christ in the Theology of Robert Grosseteste." In *Sapientiae doctrina*, edited by H. Bascour et al., 212–30. Leuven: Peeters, 1980.

McGrath, Alister E. *Scientific Theology*. Vol. 1, *Nature*. Grand Rapids, MI: Eerdmans, 2001.

McInerny, Ralph. *Studies in Analogy*. The Hague: Martinus Nijhoff, 1968.

Meer, F. van der. *Augustine the Bishop: The Life and Work of a Father of the Church*. Translated by Brian Battershaw and G.R. Lamb. London: Sheed & Ward, 1961.

Mettepenningen, Jürgen. *Nouvelle Théologie—New Theology: Inheritor of Modernism, Precursor of Vatican II*. London: T&T Clark, 2010.

Muis, Jan. "The truth of metaphorical God-talk." *Scottish Journal of Theology* 63, no. 2 (May 2010): 146–62.

Mulchahey, M. Michèle. *"First the Bow Is Bent in Study": Dominican Education before 1350*. Toronto: Pontifical Institute of Mediaeval Studies, 1998.

Müller, Gerhard Ludwig. "Incarnation." In *Handbook of Catholic Theology*, edited by Wolfgang Beinert and Francis Schüssler Fiorenza, 377–80. New York: Crossroad, 1995.

Murdoch, Iris. *The Sovereignty of Good*. 2nd ed. London: Routledge, 2001.

Murray, John Courtney. *The Problem of God: Yesterday and Today*. New Haven, CT: Yale University Press, 1964.

———. *We Hold These Truths: Catholic Reflections on the American Proposition*. New York: Sheed & Ward, 1960.

Narcisse, Gilbert. *Les raisons de Dieu: Arguments de convenance et esthétique théologique selon saint Thomas d'Aquin et Hans Urs von Balthasar*. Fribourg, CH: Éditions Universitaires de Fribourg, 1997.

Nietzsche, Friedrich. *The Portable Nietzsche*. Edited and translated by Walter Kaufmann. New York: Penguin Books, 1954.

O'Connell, Marvin R. *Critics on Trial: An Introduction to the Catholic Modernist Crisis*. Washington, DC: The Catholic University of America Press, 1994.

O'Connor, Flannery. *Flannery O'Connor: Collected Works*. Edited by Sally Fitzgerald. New York: Library of America, 1988.

———. *The Habit of Being: Letters of Flannery O'Connor*. Edited by Sally Fitzgerald. New York: Vintage Books, 1980.

———. *Mystery and Manners*. Edited by Sally and Robert Fitzgerald. New York: Farrar, Straus and Giroux, 1969.

O'Meara, Thomas Franklin. *Thomas Aquinas: Theologian*. Notre Dame, IN: Notre Dame University Press, 1997.

O'Neill, Colman E. *Sacramental Realism: A General Theory of the Sacraments*. Wilmington, DE: Michael Glazier, 1983.

Origen. *Philocalia*. ET: *The Philocalia of Origen: A Compilation of Selected Passages from Origen's Works Made by St. Gregory of Nazianzus and St. Basil of Caesarea*. Translated by George Lewis. Edinburgh: T&T Clark, 1911.

Ott, Ludwig. *Fundamentals of Catholic Dogma*. Edited by James Canon Bastible. Translated by Patrick Lynch. Cork: Mercier, 1958.

Partner, Nancy F. "Medieval Histories and Modern Realism: Yet Another Origin of the Novel." *MLN* 114, no. 4 (1999): 857–73.

Payer, Pierre J. *Bridling of Desire: Views of Sex in the Later Middle Ages*. Toronto: University of Toronto Press, 1993.

Peter Lombard. *Sententiae*. ET: *The Sentences*. 4 vols. Translated by Giulio Silano. Toronto: Pontifical Institute of Medieval Studies, 2007–10.

Pieper, Josef. *The Silence of St. Thomas: Three Essays*. Translated by John Murray and Daniel O'Connor. South Bend, IN: St. Augustine's, 1999.

Pinckaers, Servais. *The Sources of Christian Ethics*. Translated by Mary Thomas Noble. Washington, DC: The Catholic University of America Press, 1995.

———. "The Sources of the Ethics of St. Thomas Aquinas." Translated by Mary Thomas Noble. In *The Ethics of Aquinas*, edited by Stephen J. Pope, 17–29. Washington, DC: Georgetown University Press, 2002.

Pope, Stephen J. "Overview of the Ethics of Thomas Aquinas." In *The Ethics of Aquinas*, edited by Stephen J. Pope, 30–53. Washington, DC: Georgetown University Press, 2002.

Porter, Jean. *The Recovery of Virtue: The Relevance of Aquinas for Christian Ethics*. Louisville, KY: Westminster John Knox, 1990.

Pouivet, Roger. *After Wittgenstein, St. Thomas*. Translated by Michael Sherwin. South Bend, IN: St. Augustine's, 2006.

Rahner, Karl. *Theological Investigations*. Vol. 4, *More Recent Writings*. Translated by Kevin Smyth. New York: Crossroad, 1982.

———. *Theological Investigations*. Vol. 5, *Later Writings*. Translated by Karl-H. Kruger. New York: Crossroad, 1983.

———. *The Trinity*. Translated by Joseph Donceel. New York: Crossroad Herder, 1997.

Ratzinger, Joseph. *Milestones: Memoirs: 1927–1977*. Translated by Erasmo Leiva-Merikakis. San Francisco: Ignatius, 1998.

Rikhof, Herwi. "Aquinas' Authority in the Contemporary Theology of the Trinity." In *Aquinas as Authority*, edited by Paul van Geest, Harm Goris, and Carlo Leget, 213–34. Leuven: Peeters, 2002.

Robbins, Tom. *Still Life with Woodpecker: A Sort of Love Story*. New York: Bantam Books, 1980.

Romero, Óscar. "A Torch Raised on High." Homily, June 19, 1977. The Archbishop Romero Trust. http://www.romerotrust.org.uk/sites/default/files/homilies/ART_Homilies_Vol1_16_TorchRaisedOnHigh.pdf.

Saak, Eric Leland. *Creating Augustine: Interpreting Augustine and Augustinianism in the Later Middle Ages*. Oxford: Oxford University Press, 2012.

Sabra, George. *Thomas Aquinas' Vision of the Church: Fundamentals of an Ecumenical Ecclesiology*. Mainz, DE: Matthias-Grünewald, 1987.

Schillebeeckx, Edward. *The Eucharist*. London: Burns and Oates, 2005.

Schlitzer, Albert. *Redemptive Incarnation: Sources and Their Theological Development in the Study of Christ*. Notre Dame, IN: University of Notre Dame Press, 1956.

Scotus, John Duns. *Ordinatio*. In *Opera Omnia*, vols. 1–14. Vatican City: Typis Polyglottis Vaticanis, 1950–2013.

Sertillanges, A.-D. *St. Thomas Aquinas and His Work*. Translated by Godfrey Anstruther. London: Burns, Oates and Washbourne, 1932.

Simpkins, Scott. "Magical Strategies: The Supplement of Realism." *Twentieth Century Literature* 34, no. 2 (Summer 1988): 140–54.

Smalley, Beryl. *The Study of the Bible in the Middle* Ages. Notre Dame, IN: University of Notre Dame Press, 1964.

Sobrino, Jon. *The Principle of Mercy: Taking the Crucified People from the Cross*. Maryknoll, NY: Orbis Books, 1992.

Svensson, Manfred. "A Defensible Conception of Tolerance in Aquinas?" *The Thomist* 75, no. 2 (April 2011): 291–308.

Tanquerey, Adolphe. *A Manual of Dogmatic Theology*. Vol. 2. Translated by John J. Byrnes. New York: Desclée, 1959.

Thomas Aquinas. *Somme Théologique: La prophétie, 2a-2ae, Questions 171–178*. 2nd ed. Edited and translated by Paul Synave and Pierre Benoit. 2nd ed. fully updated by Jean-Pierre Torrell. Paris: Cerf, 2005.

———. *Summa Theologiae*. Vol. 24, *The Gifts of the Spirit*, edited by Edward D. O'Connor. London: Eyre and Spottiswoode, 1973.

———. Siger de Brabant, and Bonaventure. *On the Eternity of the World*. Edited and translated by Cyrill Vollert, Lottie H. Kendzierski, and Paul M. Byrne. Milwaukee, WI: Marquette University Press, 1964.

Tillotson, John. *A Discourse Against Transubstantiation*. London: Society for Promoting Christian Knowledge, 1833.

Tocco, Guillaume de. *Ystoria sancti Thome de Aquino*. Edited by Claire le Brun-Gouanvic. Toronto: Pontifical Institute of Mediaeval Studies, 1996.

Torrell, Jean-Pierre. *Le Christ en ses mystères: la vie et l'œuvre de Jésus selon saint Thomas d'Aquin*. Vol. 1. Paris: Desclée, 1999.

Valkenberg, Wilhelmus G.B.M. *Words of the Living God: Place and Function of Holy Scripture in the Theology of St. Thomas Aquinas*. Leuven: Peeters, 2000.

Vatican Council II. *Gaudium et Spes*. In *Decrees of the Ecumenical Councils*, vol. 2, edited by Norman P. Tanner, 1069–1135. London: Sheed & Ward, 1990.

Watt, Ian. *The Rise of the Novel: Studies in Defoe, Richardson and Fielding*. London: Chatto and Windus, 1957.

White, Hayden. *Tropics of Discourse: Essays in Cultural Criticism*. Baltimore, MD: Johns Hopkins University Press, 1978.

Wilson, Adrian. "Foucault on the 'Question of the Author': A Critical Exegesis." *The Modern Language Review* 99, no. 2 (April 2004): 339–63.

Wissink, Jozef. *Thomas van Aquino: De actuele betekenis van zijn theologie*. Zoetermeer, NL: Meinema, 1998.

Wittgenstein, Ludwig. *Philosophical Investigations*. 4th ed. Translated by G.E.M. Anscombe. Hoboken, NJ: Wiley-Blackwell, 1998.

Wolfson, Harry Austryn. "The Internal Senses in Latin, Arabic, and Hebrew Philosophic Texts." *Harvard Theological Review* 28, no. 2 (1935): 69–133.

Zubiri, Xavier. *The Fundamental Problems of Western Metaphysics*. Translated by Joaquín Redondo. Revised by Thomas Fowler. Lanham, MD: University Press of America, 2009.

Index